Cultural Geographies

second edition

EDITED BY

kay **anderson**

fay **gale**

LONGMAN

First published 1992
Second edition 1999

Cover design by Lisa Formby
Printed in Malaysia

National Library of Australia Cataloguing-in-Publication data

Cultural geographies.
2nd ed.
Includes index.
ISBN 0582 81086 8.
1. Human geography. I. Anderson, Kay, 1958– . II. Gale, Fay, 1932– .

304.2

The publisher's policy is to use **paper manufactured from sustainable forests**

Contents

CONSTRUCTING GEOGRAPHIES: IDENTITIES OF INCLUSION

Notes on contributors

John Agnew is Professor and Chair of Geography at UCLA, Los Angeles, USA. His most recent publications are *Geopolitics: Re-Visioning World Politics* (Routledge, 1998) and *Political Geography: A Reader* (Arnold, 1997). His current research concerns the interpretation of political change in Italy and the geography of the Italian Northern League.

Kay Anderson is Associate Professor of Geography at University College, University of New South Wales. Her recent research has centred on the nexus of race/culture/nature with publications on geographies of civility and wildness in *Progress in Human Geography*, 'the savage' in *Ecumene* and animality discourses in *Society and Space* (forthcoming). These interests form the basis for the forthcoming *Domesticating the Wild: Rethinking the Colonial Encounter in Australia* with Oxford University Press.

Jacquelin Burgess is Professor of Geography at University College London. She is particularly interested in the different ways in which people attribute meaning and value to nature. She enjoys working across disciplinary boundaries and in a policy-relevant context. Recent projects have included a cross-cultural study of public understanding of environmental change and qualitative research to challenge the dominance of environmental economists' ways of valuing the natural world.

Mona Domosh is Associate Professor of Geography at Florida Atlantic University. Her current research focuses on gender and urban form in nineteenth-century America. She is the author of *Invented Cities: The Creation of Landscape in 19th-Century New York and Boston* (Yale University, 1996) and a recent *Annals, of the Association of American Geographers* article about 'polite politics and public space'.

James Duncan is a cultural geographer and Lecturer at Cambridge University. His recent books include *Writes of Passage: Travel Writing, Place and Ambiguity* (jointly edited with Derek Gregory, Routledge, 1997) and forthcoming with Nancy Duncan, *Suburban Pre-texts* (John Hopkins University Press). He is founding editor of *Ecumene* and in 1996 received an award from the Institute of British Geographers and Royal Geographical Society for contributions to cultural geography.

Kevin Dunn is a Lecturer in Geography at the University of New South Wales, Australia, where he teaches cultural and social geography and qualitative research methods. His main research areas include the geography of migrant settlement, local government responses to cultural difference, the construction of place identity, resident activism and the politics of heritage and memorial landscapes.

Kevin Frawley is Senior Environmental Policy Planner with the National Capital Authority in Canberra. He has a long-standing interest in Australian forest and land management, forest history, natural area planning and conservation ideas.

Fay Gale is President of the Australian Academy of the Social Sciences in Australia, former Vice-Chancellor of the University of Western Australia and former President of the Australian Vice-Chancellors Committee. She is an Officer of the Order of Australia, a Fellow of the Academy of Social Sciences and an Honorary Life Member of the Australian Institute of Geographers. She is a cultural geographer who has worked extensively at the interface of Aboriginal and European relations in Australia. She has published many books in various areas of cultural geography, in addition to numerous book chapters and journal articles.

Jon Goss is Associate Professor in the Department of Geography at the University of Hawaii. His main research interests are in urban geography and Southeast Asia, but he enjoys writing on popular culture and tourism. He has recently published articles on forms of land allocation in Metro Manila (*Philippine Sociological Review*) and has an article forthcoming on the Mall of America (*Annals of the Association of American Geographers*).

Peter Jackson is Professor of Human Geography at the University of Sheffield. He is the author of *Maps of Meaning* (Routledge, 1992) and co-author of *Shopping, Place and Identity* (Routledge, 1998). Previous work has focused on the social construction of 'race' and the geography of racism. Current research focuses on questions of culture and identity including a study of men's lifestyle magazines (funded by the Economic and Social Research Council) and an oral history of Ukrainians in Bradford (funded by the Leverhulme Trust).

Jane M. Jacobs is a Senior Lecturer in Geography at the University of Melbourne, Australia. Since gaining her PhD from University College London, Dr Jacobs has published widely in the area of cultural geography. Her specific interests include racialised identity politics, urban studies and postcolonialism. She is the author of *Edge of Empire: Postcolonialism and the City* (Routledge, 1996), co-author, with Dr Ken Gelder, of *Uncanny Australia: Sacredness and Identity in a Postcolonial Nation* (Melbourne University Press, 1988) and co-editor, with Prof. Ruth Fincher, of *Cities of Difference* (Guilford, 1998).

David Ley is Professor of Geography at the University of British Columbia, Vancouver, and Co-Director of the Vancouver Centre of Excellence for Immigration Studies. His research covers a range of social and cultural issues in the city, including landscapes of consumption, gentrification, and, currently, the social geographies of immigration in large Canadian cities. His most recent book is *The New Middle Class and the Remaking of the Central City* (Oxford University Press, 1997).

Janice Monk is Executive Director of the Southwest Institute for Research on Women and Adjunct Professor of Geography at the University of Arizona. She has written numerous articles and chapters in feminist geography and co-authored and co-edited several books, among them *The Desert is No Lady: Southwestern Landscapes in Women's Writing and Art* (co-edited with Vera Norwood), *Full Circles: Geographies of Women over the Life Course* (with Cindi Katz) and *Women of the European Union: The Politics of Work and Daily Life* (with Maria Dolors Garcia-Ramon). She is also Executive Producer of the film *The Desert is No Lady.*

Kris Olds is Lecturer in Geography at the National University of Singapore. He is a geographer and urban planner with a PhD from the University of Bristol. His current research focuses on issues related to globalisation and urban change in the Asia-Pacific region. He is the co-editor of *Globalisation and the Asia-Pacific: Contested Territories* (Routledge 1999) and author of *Globalisation and Urban Change: Capital, Culture and Pacific Rim Mega-Projects* (Oxford University Press, forthcoming).

Eric Pawson is Associate Professor of Geography at the University of Canterbury, New Zealand. He is the co-editor of the two *Changing Places* volumes (1992, 1996) that analyse the wide-ranging economic and cultural restructurings of New Zealand in the 1980s and 1990s. He is contributing editor of the *New Zealand Historical Atlas* (1997) and chaired its advisory committee for the seven years that the project was in preparation.

David Sibley teaches social and cultural geography at the University of Hull, England. In addition to his long-standing interest in nomadic cultures, his research interests include the geographies of childhood, relations between people and animals in cities and the production of knowledge in the social sciences. Recent publications include *Geographies of Exclusion* (Routledge, 1995), 'Constructing geographies of difference', in *Human Geography Today* (eds D. Massey and J. Allen, Polity Press, 1998) and 'The racialization of space in Britain', *Soundings*, 1998.

Hilary P.M. Winchester teaches social and cultural geography at the University of Newcastle, Australia, and is also currently President of Academic Senate. She undertook undergraduate and postgraduate training at the University of Oxford, UK. She is author of *Contemporary France* and has worked recently on marginalised groups, gender issues in geography and the social construction of place.

Elspeth Young is Reader and Director of Studies, Graduate Studies in Environmental Management and Development, at the National Centre for Development Studies, the Australian National University. Over the last two decades she has studied the socio-economic transformation of rural indigenous communities, principally in Australia but also in Canada and Botswana. Her current research focuses primarily on indigenous land management and sustainable development planning. Her recent publications include *Third World in the First: Development and Indigenous Peoples* (Routledge, 1995) and a number of articles and book chapters on indigenous sustainable development issues.

Preface

This book, when first published as *Inventing Places* in 1992, was the outcome of both enthusiasm and frustration on our part as teachers, students and researchers of cultural geography. The task of assembling reading lists for undergraduate cultural geography courses had left us both weary and unsatisfied. We harboured a nagging concern that the intellectual rewards of the field were being denied to students as long as practising cultural geographers wrote only to, and for, each other. If cultural geography were to join the mainstream of undergraduate course offerings in university departments across the globe, as we believed it should, a gap in the market seemed in need of a plug.

At the time of publication of this revised second edition, the challenges persist. The sheer vitality of the field has enlarged such a market despite the welcome addition of a number of other works that have appeared to fill the gap. *Cultural Geographies* joins them in offering to undergraduates an updated (and in some cases, substantially revised) version of the essays that appeared in the 1992 volume.

Our first debt of gratitude, therefore, goes to the many authors who attempted to write for their undergraduate audience. We have learnt this is no simple task. We would also like to thank the many authors who took the time to update their chapters. Our special thanks go to Julie Kesby of the School of Geography and Oceanography at University College, who formatted the revised chapters and generally helped administer the project.

Our primary acknowledgement, however, goes to our cultural roots, the Department of Geography at the University of Adelaide, which in Aboriginal terms was 'the land that grew us up'. Of different generations, nevertheless we are both graduates of the cultural geography that emanated from that department. It was an early offshoot of the Sauer Berkeley School, adapted and metamorphosed to interpret the Australian landscape. The theme developed from the cultural imprint on the land through cultural imperialism to an appreciation of the dynamics and politics of place making.

By today, cultures of the 'self' and 'nation' are being critically rethought in this 'southern space'. As Australia is being unmade from within and restructured from without, concepts of hybridity and transnationality have entered cultural geography's agenda. By definition they are themes common to places across the globe and ones that we hope will be read by students through the lens of both their global and local imaginations.

Kay Anderson
Fay Gale
Canberra and Adelaide
March 1999

Acknowledgments

We are grateful to the following for permission to reproduce material in this book.

Austral International: Figure 9.1 (p. 184).
Cermak, Anton/The Fairfax Photo Library: Figure 13.6 (p. 285).
Egan, Jeannie: Figure 15.2a (p. 330).
Henderson, Reddie: Figure 10.3 (p. 214).
Ley. D. and Olds, K. 'Landscape as spectacle: World's Fairs and the culture of heroic consumption' from *Environment and Planning D: Society and Space*, vol. 6, 1998, Pion, London, pp. 191–212: Chapter 11 (pp. 221–40).
MacCormac, Richard: Figure 12.4 (p. 253).
Murray, Derek: Figure 11.2 (p. 232).
National Library of Australia: Figure 13.5 (p. 280).
New York Historical Society Collection: Figures 5.1 (p. 102) and 5.2 (p. 104).
Phyllis Walters Ltd., London: Figure 7.1 (p. 138).
Romford Recorder: Figures 14.2 (p. 300), 14.3 (p. 301) and 14.4 (p. 305).
Smithsonian National Museum of Natural History: Figures 6.1 (p. 119), 6.2 (p. 122), 6.3 (p. 123), 6.4 (p. 124), 6.5 (p. 125) and 6.6 (p. 129).
The Movie Show SBS Television: p. 189.
Urban Land Institute: Figure 10.2 (p. 208).
Wilborn and Associates: Figure 10.1 (p. 201).

Every effort has been made to trace and acknowledge copyright. However, should any infringement have occurred, the publishers tender their apologies and invite copyright owners to contact them.

1

Introduction

Kay Anderson

The variety of social domains described in the language of 'culture' in recent commentaries suggest that the term 'culture' has grown significantly in scope and application in the last few decades. Human scientists, journalists and policy-makers alike have seen fit to ascribe a coherence of meaning to arenas once glossed over as mere ripples in our (supposedly) homogeneous metropolitan societies. Corporate cultures, popular cultures, retail cultures, service cultures, strategic cultures and so on are just a few of the networks of everyday meaning and action that are attracting fresh anthropological notice.

Not long ago, 'culture' was regarded by most human scientists as the preserve of just two domains: first, of those non-western people and nations whose artefacts, customs, rituals and landscapes had apparently escaped the trajectory of 'progress' in whose image the cosmopolitan west had been made. Second, the term was applied to that category of westerners removed by privilege from ordinary people, who have a peculiar penchant for opera, literature and art. 'High' culture was their artistic and intellectual creation and its possession rendered them 'cultured'. In both usages of the term, culture was the 'thing' or sphere occupied by the exotic. Now, however, there is a range of local worlds in both western and non-western contexts whose modes of understanding, speaking and behaving are the subject matter of the topical field called 'cultural geography'.

This volume grows out of the freshly recovered interest by geographers in the commonsense subjectivities of people at 'home' and 'abroad'. It seeks to devote the kind of quizzical attention usually reserved for the distant—both the non-western 'other' and local classes of elites—to advanced capitalist societies like Australia, New Zealand, the United States, the United Kingdom and Canada. The 'ways of seeing' (Berger 1972) of those two groups can now be enjoined to a range of groups that cohere around situated visions, languages and codes of practice. Such 'textual communities', in the words of Stock (1983), are the focus of the recently invigorated field of cultural geography to which this collection contributes.

To what tendencies does the recently expanded use of the word 'culture' refer? What processes does the term's currency reflect? A range of answers to this question is possible. First, culture's currency might signal the proliferation of reference groups that have emerged during the recent phase of economic and social restructuring in the west when old lines of class division are being fractured around new sources of identity and political mobilisation (see Calhoun 1994; Castells 1997). Environmental lobbies, for example, are forging new ways of seeing and relating to nature that are rallying people of all political persuasions and class affiliations. Other oppositional cultures of disabled groups, racialised minorities and peace activists, to name just a few, are combining—often on a local basis—around visions of alternative futures.

A second explanation for the enlarged usage of the term 'culture' is possible. It has been argued by some geographers that ever-more flexible regimes of capital accumulation are structuring western economies and that increasingly specialised economic complexes are taking (and requiring for their maintenance) a corresponding diversity of ideological forms (Harvey 1989; Watson and Gibson 1995). Cases in point are our increasingly differentiated consumer and retail culture, including the niche occupied by the heritage industry; also the appearance of downtown festival marketplaces (like Darling Harbour in Sydney and Covent Garden in London) that attract thousands of pleasure-seekers and transform declining sites into profitable theme parks (Zukin 1995). These visible testimonies to the 'postmodernity' of the contemporary urban condition—in which signs and symbols are torn free of their original referents and recycled in different contexts—are for some interpreters the 'cultural clothing' of late capitalism.

Finally, it might be suggested that the new expansiveness of the term 'culture' reflects shifts in academic fashion. The twin critiques of post-structuralism and feminism have prompted social scientists to renounce totalising explanatory models and confront the relativity of all forms of knowledge, both popular and scientific. For geographers who have grown up in a cultural climate of positivism, the call to dispense with modernist holds on absolute truth has not been easy or without challenge. Outside geography, the loss of the sense of an absoluteness of western accounts of history (see Said 1978; Young 1990) has precipitated a self-consciousness about European culture's own historical relativity. In anthropology, claims to universal (ungendered, ethnocentric) truths have mostly been abandoned (Marcus and Fisher 1986; James, Hockey and Dawson 1997). In geography, this has heralded a challenge and research agenda, one that seeks to show how people's frames of mind and action are situated within the cultural worlds they inhabit. It is an 'anthro-geography' that is now well under way for the west, with its multiplicity of cultures, both urban and rural, and which is increasingly also recasting the geographic study of non-western contexts (see as examples

Agnew, Mercer and Sopher 1984; Barnes and Duncan 1992; Cloke et al. 1994; Crang 1998; Cosgrove and Daniels 1988; Duncan and Ley 1993; Holdsworth and Mitchell 1998; Jackson 1989; Kong 1997; Shurmer-Smith and Hannam 1994; also the journal *Ecumene: International Journal of Culture, Environment and Meaning*).

PEOPLE WITHIN CULTURAL WORLDS

Whatever the complex origins of the cultural worlds that characterise all societies, it is important that their myriad forms and impacts be made the subject of closer investigation. This undergraduate collection of readings is devoted to precisely such an exposition, describing select ways of being and seeing that resonate in the everyday experience of all of us. We all, as humans, rely on meanings and vocabularies to help us interpret our relationship to others and the world at large, our experience and social change. Often without being aware of it, each of us imposes a 'plot' on our daily existence, picking and choosing and arranging detail to make sense of it and prepare each day for the next one. This is the creative act of living, and while elements of our narrative plot belong to us as individuals, we make meanings within and across cultural worlds. Moreover, increasingly in western societies our meanings are constituted at the interface of local and global influences (Massey and Jess 1995).

To be sure, much of people's 'sense-making' is so ordinary as to be unworthy of geographers' notice. The taken-for-granted minutiae of dress conventions, traffic rules, table manners, codes of humour, funeral rituals, subtleties of fashion shifts and definitions of personal beauty are probably beyond the purview of geographers. Other imaginative leaps, however—other creative acts that symbolically 'translate' the raw materials of history, geography, biology, politics, environment, memory and desire—command the critical attention of geographers. Think, for example, of the markers of human skin colour and the anatomical features distinctive to each sex. The beliefs among Europeans (and others) that 'races' exist naturally and that gender roles and statuses likewise owe their origin to identities we can simply take for granted, have made the cues of skin colour and sexual difference far more culturally significant than their mere physical reality. Many westerners also accept that the ensemble of life forms including animals and called 'nature' exist at a lower point on the 'chain of being' than humans; that commodities hold some inherent 'magic' that (if purchased) will give them status and identity; that the artefacts of the past possess some intrinsic 'character'; that the (green and pleasant) English countryside is the universal ideal of 'landscape'; that saucepans belong to 'culture' while boomerangs are part of 'nature' and so on. These 'inventions' (Hobsbawm and Ranger 1983) require analysis because, far from being definitive and irresistible truths, they are the cultural stuff out of which moral and material systems are changed and transformed (Philo 1991). They are 'maps of meaning' (Clarke et al. 1976; Jackson 1989), that whether 'right' or 'wrong' are taken up in diverse ways for diverse purposes by people, groups and institutions. They are acted upon, reproduced, hardened into seeming 'fact' (and potentially 'unmade') in a process that constructs both social structure and real world topographies. If culture can be defined at all, then it refers to these shared codes of understanding, communication and practice that set one of many contexts for human thought and action.

Such a definition departs in significant ways from that used in earlier traditions of cultural geography. Carl Sauer, a dominant figure in the Berkeley School, worked with a view of culture as a 'way of life' and inspired some forty years of study into the differences from region to region in the symbolic and practical activities of human communities. The focus was mainly on rural landscapes which were 'read' by Sauer and his students for cues of (sequent) human occupancy. Wagner and Mikesell's (1962) collection called *Readings in Cultural Geography* was one important text to be influenced by the Berkeley School. The editors conceived of cultures as assemblages of 'verifiable common characteristics' that provide 'a means of classifying areas according to the character of the human groups that occupy them' (Wagner and Mikesell 1962, p. 2). In a similar vein, world regional geography of the 1950s and 1960s classified the globe's populations into 'culture worlds', as if cultures and regions were homogeneous and easily bounded entities. These 'worlds', including the Oriental and Arab regions, were conceived by world regional geographers of the time such as Russell and Kniffen (1951) as 'unified subdivisions' whose 'traits' and 'similar ways of changing landscapes' made their occupants 'alien to the inhabitants of other culture worlds'.

Since the mid-1970s, a number of geographers have distanced themselves from the tradition of Berkeley cultural geography, dismissed by some critics as the 'geography of artefacts' (Goss 1988). I do not wish to rehearse the difficulties with this tradition of cultural geography, nor to overstate the magnitude of recent shifts away from it. For the purposes of the perspective illustrated in this book, however, I recall two major points of the Berkeley School critique, one relating to culture and agency, the other to the theorisation of landscape (see also Cosgrove and Jackson 1987).

First, the authors in this book share the view that culture is a *process* in which people are actively engaged. The contributors see culture as a dynamic mix of symbols, beliefs, languages and practices that people create, not a fixed thing or entity governing humans. It is not some evolutionary inheritance, as culture was for Sauer (Duncan 1980; Anderson 1997). Back in the 1920s, Sauer had suggested that culture was an independent force moulding people and landscapes in its image. Others since Sauer's time have rightly argued, however, that the decisive agents in constructing social life and landscape are not inherited baggages of customs, but rather people. People grasp, interpret and *re-present* their worlds with the use of symbols and vocabularies through which they construct cultures and geographies. 'We are all intellectuals', Horne (1986) writes, and people often without knowing it, impose bias on the ordering of experience. While the forms of such bias might support the Sauerian label of 'customs', to do so risks eclipsing some important points about social life. First, it carries the danger of depicting people as passive recipients of thoughts and behaviours ineluctably handed down to subsequent generations. While it is true that people live with and through the 'realities' they inherit, it is also the case that people re-present those realities according to their own motivations and always possess the capacity to question and criticise, and so create fresh hypotheses about existence. Second, the term 'customs' conjures up images of characteristics that are uniformly imbibed across whole societies, whereas societies are complexly differentiated by class, ethnicity, gender, age and so on. It is therefore more appropriate to speak in terms of multiple rather than unitary (ethnic or national) cultures. Third, the terminology of 'customs' carries images of traditional and rural settings, when the dominant culture in western societies is overwhelmingly metropolitan, increasingly informed by globalising and diasporic elements. Finally, the language of customs has a conservative inflection, potentially directing attention to the continuity of cultural systems and obscuring their vulnerability to manipulation, criticism and change.

The cultural process by which people construct their understandings of the world is an inherently geographic concern. In the course of generating new meanings and decoding existing ones, people construct spaces, places, landscapes, regions and environments. In short, they construct geographies. By the term 'geographies' I refer to the spaces and places through which social life is constituted, structured and changed. Some of these geographies—such as the ceremonial spaces of migrant worship, or in the case of Australia's Aboriginal population, their sacred sites—embody frames of thought and action that seem unambiguously 'cultural'. Other geographies, such as the building of suburban estates or the mining of uranium, emerge out of impulses that are less conspicuously 'cultural'. They are not deliberate acts of cultural construction but nonetheless, when excavated for their meaning, bear the stamp of culturally distinctive beliefs. In the case of outlying suburban estates, we can find within their constitution sets of assumptions about the cultural separation of 'home' and 'work' and the respective gender roles and statuses that attach to each activity. Likewise, the mining of the earth for elements such as uranium relies on mythologies about the separation of humans from nature and on resource appraisals that are thoroughly culturally-bound.

In constructing cultures, therefore, people construct geographies. They arrange spaces in distinctive ways; they fashion certain types of landscape, townscape and streetscape; they erect monuments and destroy others; they evaluate spaces and places and transform them accordingly; they organise the relations between territories at a range of scales from local to global. In direct and indirect ways, both wilful and unintentional, people construct environments, regions and places. In that sense, geographies do not just exist 'out there' as inert reflections of cultures, a point which brings us to the second element of the Berkeley School critique.

In 1925 Sauer wrote 'Culture is the agent, the natural area is the medium, the cultural landscape is the result' (p. 46), a view which led cultural geographers of Sauer's time to conceive of landscapes as inert imprints of culture. A more dynamic model is possible, however. For just as cultures are constitutive of geographies, so are geographies *inherent* to the culture-building process. Space itself is no inert or absolute 'thing' other than a social artefact constituted by the interplay of people, institutions and structures. Landscapes are under continuous transformation by agents whose habits of mind are themselves recreated (and revised) through geographic arrangements. In short, cultures and their geographies reciprocally inform each other, in process and in time.

The chapters in this book illuminate both sides of this dialectical relationship between culture and geography. In colonial and postcolonial settings such as New Zealand, the divergence in, and hierarchising of, Maori and pakeha cultures has had far-reaching implications for the character of that society—its land use, economy and politics. Chapter 2, in illustrating the profound conflict over contrasting ways of seeing and using land, introduces the volume. Three chapters then examine the making of identities and geographies surrounding class status, localism and corporate status. Chapter 3 examines elite group status and landscape character in a Canadian city over a hundred-year period; Chapter 4 assesses the role of place identifications in the electoral geography of post-war Italy, demonstrating that places can be cultural resources and not just 'outcomes' of politics; while Chapter 5 addresses the networks that link corporate identity, business and architectural form in New York City. Each of the authors demonstrates that places, landscapes and buildings are social fields in which ingroup identifications (inclusive identities) are constructed and communicated, with bearings on wider regimes of class and politics.

Group identities have multiple sources and can be ascribed by non-group members as well as negotiated among like-minded people. Four chapters pursue the theme of identity ascription, examining the ideologies out of which exclusionary identities have been conferred and spaces assigned to categories of people who are deemed 'different'. People's beliefs relating to race are the focus of Chapters 6 and 7. Chapter 6 examines the distorted representations of North American Indians and their landscapes as rendered by image-makers such as photographers; while Chapter 7 addresses concepts of Gypsy people in England and their translation into spatial practices of marginalisation. Chapters 8 and 9 then examine the ideologies and popular mediums (including film) through which sexual difference has been interpreted and hierarchised in cross-cultural and Australian settings. In combination, the four chapters demonstrate that in the service of Eurocentric and patriarchal world views, distinctive geographies mark cultural boundaries of privilege and marginality between an ingroup of 'us' and an outgroup of 'them'.

Increasingly ascendant in western culture and economy are images surrounding people's pursuit of commodities (Chapter 10) and entertainment experiences (Chapter 11). Many inner-city environments bear the stamp of consumption aesthetics and activities, to which these two chapters are useful in bringing different explanatory emphases. An equally popular feature of contemporary western culture and economy is the idealisation of the past. The break with modernist aesthetics has been made in many cities, including London, where groups (with opposed stakes and purposes) attach 'heritage value' to settings and buildings once deemed to be defunct (Chapter 12). As that chapter demonstrates, 'the past' is not pre-given; it is *produced* and packaged.

Other contributors develop their analyses from the side of the culture/space dialectic occupied by 'nature' and environment. If our urban spaces have been adapted in the image of people's belief systems, so also do our physical landscapes provide a window on cultural constructs. The evolution of Australian environmental attitudes over the last century is discussed in Chapter 13, while Chapter 14 examines the diverse stakes in environmental decision-making over a section of London's marshland designated for redevelopment. Chapter 15 then concludes (and, along with Chapter 2, frames) the book by highlighting once again the fundamental relativity of the lenses through which worlds are seen and made. It underlines that point by contrasting the land and resource 'maps' of European and indigenous populations in remote parts of North America and Central Australia. The terrain covered by the contributors ranges widely indeed, but the chapters are united conceptually by a respect for the habitual practices out of which geographies are made and unmade. In so doing they lay bare the socio-cultural basis of geographies that has often been concealed in dominant ways of theorising space and place.

INSTITUTIONS AS CULTURAL DOMAINS

Most of the chapters in this book have as their aim something more ambitious than a description of distinctive world views. Unveiling such understandings constitutes an essential, but preliminary, step in contemporary cultural analysis. Many authors are also concerned with the sources of cultural knowledge, the penetration of such knowledge into wider moral and material fields and the functions that cultural understandings perform. Central to these concerns is the role that institutions (as structured forms of agency) potentially play in processes of cultural construction.

Just as people frame their actions in terms of shared definitions of situations, so do organisations and institutions operate as cultural domains. They too rely on shared (if unspoken) understandings of their roles and functions. Universities, banks, the military, the levels of state, the law, the church, corporations, schools, the media and even families impose some narrative plot onto their activities, binding members to the unit and justifying their existence to themselves and society at large. For example, of all the things that families might say about themselves they often specify the priority of 'blood ties' as their defining characteristic; the military invokes 'defence of nation' as its rationale; politicians claim to have the 'public interest' as their raison d'etre; immigration departments often proclaim their mission is to 'protect the fabric of the nation', as do environmentalist groups for the whole earth. Finally, sectors of the media purport to be 'objective informers of the public', as if the 'facts' of news somehow speak for themselves.

One might legitimately counter that such pronouncements are themselves 'factual'; moreover that they are morally defensible. I wish to suggest that the important point, however, is not the 'truth' or otherwise of such positions—as if such definitive things as absolute facts and iron-clad moralities exist in social life—but rather their partiality and historical specificity. Discourses about the 'public interest', 'family', the 'nation' and even high-sounding rhetoric about global environmental commitment can serve partisan interests, promote elitist goals and perform ignoble functions. The western cultural ideal of 'home'—typically conceived to be contiguous with a nuclear unit of man, woman and children—is often surrounded by rhetoric (e.g. 'home is where the heart is') that eclipses the gender and generational conflicts embodied (literally) within domestic space (McDowell 1997). Heterosexist discourse also tends to marginalise the practice and imagining of alternative domestic arrangements. Newspaper publishers and editors, for another example, make strategic judgements about what their readers (buyers) wish to hear when selecting from an infinity of events the things that seem newsworthy. So, for example, the complexity of 'Ethiopia' becomes reduced in readers' minds to the cycles of war, flood and famine that plague helpless black people. In the case of the courts, judges 'manufacture' decisions out of discursive contests (Clark 1985). In such examples of the language surrounding home and the so-called 'facts' of law and the news, specific conceits are 'naturalised' (Duncan and Duncan 1988) through institutions that give them legitimacy.

The discourses that organisations articulate to interpret themselves to each other and the world at large can clearly uphold unequal relations between people and places. Powerful institutions (including nations) can work to ensure that what are partial, culturally-bound interpretations of reality are accepted as 'natural' and 'correct' by the public at large. Think, for example, of the widely held view that freeways facilitate the flow of traffic and goods. Few people would dispute the truth of such a view. However, implicit within such a 'truth' has been an ethos, a world view governed by the language of efficiency (rather than, for example, environmental impact or equity) which has tended to marginalise alternative versions of 'trips' and different proposals for urban transportation (see Law forthcoming). Such has been the cultural strength of economists, engineers, and oil magnates in urban planning circles that many democratically-elected politicians have been persuaded to accept efficiency arguments that, when implemented, empower certain groups and spaces over others (and possibly endanger us all). Social life is replete with struggles for imaginative dominance of precisely this kind, and one of the goals of cultural critique is to unveil them from the geographies they inhabit.

CULTURE AND POWER

If frames of mind are sources of cultural understanding and identity for people and institutions, they are also sources of control, conflict and contest. While all of us participate in symbolising the world, people do not enjoy equal access to the conditions for creating those shared meanings. Struggles for imaginative supremacy are perhaps as endemic as those that course, both overtly and latently, between economic classes in advanced capitalist societies. Inspired by Michel Foucault's conceptualisation of power as something more pervasive and differentiated than either class capacity or formal politics, cultural geographers have been moved to examine what has been called the 'power of definition'. Indeed, human geographers of diverse leanings have increasingly been exploring those regimes of 'difference' which are designated as 'other' to the social norm and which, for example, surround race, gender, nation, sexuality, age, disability and mental illness (see, for example, Anderson 1991; Jackson and Penrose 1993; Rose 1993; Johnson 1995; Bell and Valentine 1995; Laws 1994; Gleeson 1998; Philo 1997).

It will be clear from the above comments that structures of domination and oppression are potentially implicated in the concepts that groups and institutions use to interpret the world. The meaning surrounding the label 'Australian' is a case in point. It often conjures up in popular and official imaginations, associations and spaces of masculinised wilderness—myths that, for all their appeal, mask significant and enduring lines of social division in Australian society. Women have marginalised status in this version of an 'Australian', as do settlers of non-white European background, and, remarkably also, city-dwellers. Distinctive forms of masculinity (e.g. 'lovable larrikins') are also privileged (see special issue of *Journal of Australian Studies* 1998). Yet this version of nation is immensely powerful and still forms the discursive material from which landscape iconographies of the country are made and sold (Waitt 1997). More seriously, it has long informed public and private sector practices in relation to the life chances of excluded groups. Australian women continue to experience wage discrimination and racialised minorities, most obviously Aboriginal people, do not by any means enjoy equality with 'white' Australians in the rewards of citizenship. This is not simply a matter of cultural attitudes, vilifying or otherwise. Rather, such disenfranchisement underwrites the operation of gendered and racialised systems of power and entitlement.

The example highlights the general point that cultural inventions (in this case the space that came to bear the name of 'Australia') penetrate far beyond the gestalt field of people's minds and hearts into tangible institutional spheres such as the workplace, public policy and the corporate world where people's material circumstances are determined. Cultural norms are located in the practices of their institutionalisation. In the process cultural meanings move across scales and well beyond the local and domestic. Meanings surrounding nation-states can even help configure geopolitical alliances and rivalries at a world regional scale (Agnew and Corbridge 1995). Culture does not occupy an autonomous sphere, therefore, and cultural geographers need continually to confront the connections between culture, economies, technologies and the workings of power. This is especially so if we are to avoid a style of self-congratulatory discourse analysis where the researcher is consumed by the task of deconstructing knowledges to the neglect of their political functions.

CULTURE AND RESISTANCE

The process by which cultural understandings become constructed and reproduced through time and space is complexly negotiated. It involves not just the efforts of powerful groups to secure conceptual and instrumental control, but also the struggles of weaker groups to resist definitions that marginalise them. Consider, for example, the challenges made by poor, inner-city dwellers in advanced capitalist societies during the 1960s to the dominant definition of their neighbourhoods as 'slums' (or, in the words of civic bureaucracies of the time, 'revenue sinks' in need of 'rationalisation'). The struggle of such residents continues into the present when upwardly mobile professionals have reclassified the same old homes and districts as 'places of character' fit for gentrification (Ley 1997; Mills 1988).

There have also been myriad resistances on the part of Aboriginal Australians and their indigenous counterparts in New Zealand, the United States and Canada to the racialised ascriptions and practices that accompanied their typically violent dispossession under colonialism (see Chapter 2). Likewise, a range of groups in western societies contest essentialist assumptions about gender and sexual difference that justify male privilege, female subordination and non-heterosexual relations (see, for example, Valentine 1993). By way of another example, unruly behaviours can and often do disrupt those disciplined 'play spaces' of the postmodern Disney theme park (Yaeger 1996). Space and place afford a base from which to construct a radical politics, or at least 'heretical geographies' in the case of graffiti artists and peace protesters (Cresswell 1996). There are potential cracks in dominant cultures, therefore, and we have evidence from many societies that they are often prised open by voices typically submerged in the discourses of power (see, for example, Pile and Keith 1993).

I noted above that dominant groups and institutions have the power to 'make over' the world in the image of select interests by defining for all groups what is considered 'natural'. A number of chapters make this clear, while at the same time being alert to people's capacity to subvert the labels and spaces they occupy. People can decode messages in ways not intended by their producers. Transgression is not necessarily, however, a self-consciously oppositional process on the part of aggrieved groups any more than the exertion of control by powerful groups is a deliberate act of engineering of the public imagination. Cultural relations are infinitely more complex and subtle than that, showing evidence of both compliance and resistance, accommodation and conflict, retrieval (of lost practices) and reappropriation. Moreover, cultural process is always a *situated* set of practices. The contingencies introduced by particular settings deny researchers anything as easy, satisfying, formulaic, or for that matter possible, as generalisable models of cultural life.

This book demonstrates that geographies are valuable documents of the power plays out of which social life is constructed. The struggles on the part of differentially empowered groups are the focus of chapters on the cultural politics of land and resource use, consumption, heritage designations, hallmark events, electoral outcomes, race, gender, and sexualised codings and the making of elite and corporate streetscapes. The authors bring evidence to show how the hegemonic projects of colonialism, modernity, patriarchy, racism and redevelopment are realised in and through distinctive geographies. Some authors also explore the linkages between cultural and economic determinants of these geographies (for example, retail complexes, corporate landscapes, heritage settings and European inscriptions on 'New World' land). In this sense, 'ways of seeing' combine with 'ways of being' to an extent that renders false any separation of the material and symbolic domains. Nor, as mentioned above, is the dominance of powerful groups a unidirectional event. As Chapters 11 and 14 demonstrate, potentially profitable projects (such as urban redevelopments and World's Fairs) are open to various interpretations by people who lack the power of definition.

CULTURAL GEOGRAPHY'S PLACE WITHIN HUMAN GEOGRAPHY

This is not the place to rehearse the lively history of philosophical shifts in the diverse strands of work that constitute human geography (see Cloke and Philo 1991; Gregory 1994). Nor is it the place to chronicle the history of the traffic of influences between the 'parent' discipline of human geography and the branch that bears the title of cultural geography. Some highly condensed comments to situate the foregoing discussion in disciplinary context thus follow.

We are by now well acquainted with the weaknesses of the research field called 'behavioural geography' that gave us 'mental maps' in the 1970s (see, for example, Jackson and Smith 1984). Like the tradition of subcultural studies in sociology in the 1950s and 1960s (see, for example, Whyte 1943; Suttles 1968), perception studies failed to situate the workings of human cognition in the broader contexts that informed it. While helpfully showing that the 'facts' of situations (say, of the absolute distance between places) are less decisive in influencing behaviour than people's construction of the facts (cognitive distance), behavioural geography failed to investigate the preconditions for, and functions of, human perceptions. It reminded us that people see and evaluate the same things differently, but ignored the issue of why certain interpretations come to prevail over others in the struggle between groups for dominance. For that matter, it ignored groups and institutions, focusing almost exclusively on individuals. All these limitations left it open to the charge of idealism, and silent to the power plays and conflicts that reside within ideological fields.

For some years, from the mid-1970s through the 1980s, Marxist scholars seized the explanatory ground in human geography by situating people's versions of reality in the sphere of what was called 'ideology'. According to those geographers, capitalism moulded people's consciousness in the image of its needs for capital accumulation. There was little interest in examining the diverse forms of people's sense-making, not because Marxist geographers were insensitive to them, but because they were deemed to be only distorted reflections of more decisive economic pressures. The radical critique of both behavioural and spatial science geographies certainly expanded the scope of human geographers' substantive concerns and explanatory frameworks. Behavioural and humanistic geographers of the late 1970s who studied place essences, for example, were forced to confront the limits of not only their answers about human subjectivity, but also their questions. The challenge precipitated the lively engagement of human geography with social theory that ensued and which persists to today.

The rise of postmodernism, feminism and post-structuralism saw a maturing of cultural geography's theoretical apparatus. Post-structuralism was perhaps the most influential body of thought in philosophically bolstering cultural geography's long-standing sensitivity to 'difference'. To the extent that it questioned the coherence and fixity in categories (of, for example, identity, class, the state, citizenry, the market, the west, the spheres of public and private), it created a hunger for what has been called 'problematising'; for situating within narrative context that which is assumed to rest on a bedrock of truth. And yet while cultural geographers choose to emphasise the specificity of people's languages about the world, they do not claim that signifying systems belong to a free-floating realm of 'discourse' any more than those with an economistic leaning argue that culture is mere 'icing' on the economic base of capitalism. Efforts in the 1980s to transcend the dualism of 'the ideological' and 'the material' (see, for example, Kobayashi and Mackenzie 1989) have mutated in the 1990s to ones that bring together 'the economic' and 'the cultural' in geographic analysis (see, for example, Fincher and Jacobs 1998). The way has thus been cleared for productive conversation across and between theoretical traditions—political economy, feminist, post-structuralist and (more recently) psycho-analytic among them.

In these exciting moves towards conceptual intersection there should be no ambiguity, however, about the distinctive contribution of 'cultural' analysis in geography. Cultural geographers continue to insist upon the need to take people's signifying systems seriously, especially those which are constitutive of broader moral and material systems. The everyday knowledge of ordinary and elevated people—however distorted, contradictory, partial and biased—makes its *own* contribution to macro social and spatial structures, economic and political arrangements, technological developments, environmental quality and other conditions. Indeed, precisely because people's cultural knowledge forms a building block out of which social formations are made and transformed, we dedicate a book to the exposition of some of its more influential forms. By listening to the 'micro-order' of people's sense-making, we can, as Knorr-Cetina and Cicourel argued some time ago, 'hear the macro-order tick' (1981, p. 42).

METHODOLOGICAL MATTERS

Retrieving data about people's cultural constructs from the contexts that shape them is a difficult task, and one persistently undervalued by geographers trained in seemingly more rigorous paradigms. Struggles for imaginative dominance as to what constitutes 'good' geography, and indeed 'geography' itself, exist between schools of geographers. One of the credibility problems that cultural geographers face is in the types of data sets they use and generate. It is often alleged by critics that sample populations are too small, that conclusions cannot be 'disproven' and that the findings do not propel us towards 'models' of geographical reality. These and other charges have recurred in different guises in the authenticity debates between positivists and non-positivists which have raged for decades inside geography departments and journals.

Yet it is precisely because cultural geographers are so conscious of the inconclusive nature of such methodological debates and the philosophical issues on which the debates turn that they take care in the way they use and combine a range of techniques. Cultural geographers see no need to argue the merits of qualitative methods over the quantitative, non-digital over digital data, since both have a contribution to make to the task of uncovering people's constructions of the world and their socio-spatial articulation (see special issue of *Environment and Planning A* 1998). It should not be presumed that interest in mythologies breeds whimsical accounts without rigour or a lack of concern for what happens 'in reality'. The necessity for empirical work has been emphasised since Carl Sauer first led the revival in cultural geography in the 1920s. The Berkeley School was deeply committed to observation (though not usually its extension into experimentation) and, equally, contemporary cultural geographers are careful to document the empirically specifiable impacts of ways of seeing the world on social patterns and policy.

As will be evident in this book, the research procedures of cultural geographers range across a wide spectrum of techniques including observation, the use of interview schedules and questionnaires often favoured by sociologists, participant observation approaches common to anthropologists, the integration of quantitative data, as well as a close reading of texts such as photographs, maps, speeches, films, council minutes and newspaper accounts. 'Deconstruction' has been the name given to the technique for analysing such texts, and in geography it has been adapted to the task of 'reading the landscape' for the inscriptions encoded within it (see Meinig 1979; Cosgrove and Jackson 1987; Barnes and Duncan 1992). The survey maps and place names that enshrined the gaze of colonial powers have been particularly fertile texts for these critical excavations (Harley 1992). While few of the contributors to this book undertake 'deconstructionism' in the strict sense of its post-structuralist founder Derrida (1967), many adopt a version of it. This can be found in Chapters 3, 6, 9 and 12 which, in different ways, unpack popular knowledges and their geographies and nest them within their surrounding contexts. Other contributions (see, for example, Chapter 13) are intellectual histories of a more conventional, but no less useful kind.

For the cultural geographer, then, a range of techniques is appropriate, and often several may be used in concert to unveil the connections between subjective worlds and objective cartographies. The task requires an equally diverse range of skills: a sensitivity to people's subjectivity; a willingness to 'learn to learn' (Spivak 1996) that requires engagement with subjects (and not only subaltern ones) in their 'field'; a keen eye to the topographies that people fashion; a conscientious and creative contextualising of the connections between people and place, agency and structure; a sense of the politics inherent in even the most mundane and habitual geographies; a commitment to rigorous documentation and plausible argumentation; and an honest confrontation with the relativity of our own interpretations. As the challenges of cultural geography are considerable, so too are its rewards, which this book hopes to communicate.

CULTURAL GEOGRAPHY AT THE MILLENNIUM

In the years since *Inventing Places* was published, the so-called 'new' cultural geography has matured and differentiated into a loose fellowship of endeavours. Not only has the 'cultural turn' had a lasting impact on human geography, it has also attracted the interest of allied social sciences to whom geographers have always looked for theoretical direction. The concepts of space and place, margin and centre, local and global now figure prominently (if sometimes anaemically) in the disciplines of anthropology, literary studies, history and sociology (see, for example, Bird et al. 1993; Chaney 1994; Yaeger 1996). Needless to say there is no single 'new cultural geography', but rather an array of approaches that share a 'critical' focus. The conclusion to this chapter is not the appropriate place to review all such pursuits, but a broad (though by no means exhaustive) canvas of directions the subject has taken over the 1990s will be helpful to new students.

Important among the conceptual developments that will be considered in more detail below are the following: the emergence of concepts of hybridity and transnationality; of embodiment and performance; and the spaces (networks) of 'flow' through which global/local exchanges articulate. New avenues for research have also been opened up in the substantive areas of, to name a few: cultural industries including music, sport, the performing and visual arts, film and television (see, for example, Pratt 1997; Schwartz and Ryan 1998); non-visual geographies, including sound and music (see, for example, Smith 1997; Kong 1996); cultures of nature (see, for example, Whatmore and Boucher 1993; Anderson 1995); geographies of consumption (see, for example, Bell and Valentine 1997; Jackson and Thrift 1995; Wrigley and Lowe 1996; and special issue *Urban Studies* 1998); topographies of publicity and privacy (see, for example, Anderson and Jacobs, 1999; Mitchell 1997a); and mapping of emotion and other 'anti-knowledges' (see, for example, Nash 1998; forthcoming issue of *Space and Culture*). Regarding this latter field, geographies of emotion, there would seem to be scope for research into the more discordant aspects of everyday life—of love, avarice, envy, loss, hope, grief, conscience, cruelty and other expressive impulses which have effectively been put to sleep by rationalist science and practice. Indeed, governing systems, as well as human scientists, might yet have to configure human feeling as something that is central to politics and not an excessive *outside* to 'real' concerns. Also noteworthy in recent phases of cultural geography's development have been the efforts from 'southern spaces' of the globe to specify distinctive regional characters within a subject that has had a predominantly 'northern' (Anglo-American) lineage (see special issues of *Australian Geographical*

Studies 1997 and *New Zealand Geographer* 1997). Such 'emplaced' cultural geographies do themselves speak to the possibility of new models of unity that are invited by the very recognition of site-specific knowledges.

The 1990s has seen a lively extension of the theme of the politics of difference. From race to religion, music to madness, sacredness to sexuality, the domestic to the diasporic, interest in the 'cultural politics' entailed in the meaning and making of 'difference' has intensified. Perhaps most usefully, given the persistent concerns about cultural geography's descent into discourse, such explorations have, in grounding difference in the conditions that make it possible, helped underline the inherent materiality of cultural life. In this sense, and despite claims that the field risks 'evacuating the social' (Gregson 1995), cultural geography remains alert to lived experience and the 'hard' materiality of the inequalities that structure difference. After all, difference is a matter of both cultural recognition and material oppression (Butler 1998). Some differences flourish while others are repressed, inviting attention also to the spatialities of identity's production (Massey 1996). It follows that the apparently more 'robust' business of politics, justice, equity, poverty, health and redistribution will continue to require critical cultural inflection (see Kearns and Gesler 1998; Philo 1995; Yapa 1998).

Empirical work on 'difference' has also sought to address the concern that the very attempt to deconstruct the power of categories (of, for example race and gender) reinscribes their force in dominant discursive systems. Breaks with the binary fix of self and other have come in a number of ways. First, there have been the efforts to complicate the social field; to show how it is transected by classed, gendered and other identities that cross-cut each other often in contradictory ways (see, for example, the essays in Duncan 1995; also Gibson-Graham 1996). The trend has been to chart the *dis*-organised faces of oppression and its unruly faces. The unveiling of 'hybrid' senses of self among transnationals (such as refugees and business migrants) has further undercut premises of pure and unified subjectivities. Others still, drawing on postcolonial theory, are unsettling the narrative force of the all-too-familiar coordinates of 'us' and 'them' by mapping the struggles of indigenous people who inhabit and divide the so-called centre (see, for example, Jacobs 1996). The self/other model of identity has also been pressed into more critical service by geographers who, after Freud, wish to explore the repressions (of, for example, desire and violence) that lie at the heart of the self's *social* production (see, for example, Sibley 1995; Pile 1996).

The foregoing comments might seem to suggest that the reach of contemporary cultural geography is exhausted by the study of identity, multivalent and mobile. Yet the themes of the field are considerably more diverse. For that matter we can speak of an influential move 'beyond identity' that insists that the 'subjects' of geographical research are not only 'constructed' and inscribed with signifiers of identity in an ideational sense, but are 'embodied'. This realisation has led to work on the embodied practices through which human subjectivity is made (Pile and Thrift 1995; Nast and Pile 1998). Research is flourishing on the constitutive relationship between bodies and spaces, and the 'performances' that enact their connections (see as examples McDowell 1995; Johnston 1997). Indeed, among the more interesting developments in the field have been the efforts to theorise social life in more corporeal and relational ways. These efforts take in the 'rhizomatic' philosophies of Deleuze and Gattari, Donna Haraway's 'cyborg' ontologies, actor-network theory after Latour and Serres, and others dubbed by Thrift (1996, p. 1) as 'non-representational theories'. Each of these perspectives invokes vocabularies of fluidity, flight, travel and flow that further undo identity essences and linear narratives of time/space.

The international flows of commodities, information, people and money that constitute the processes called 'globalisation' and 'transnationalism' have attracted no small measure of interest from geographers. It is work that brings together cultural, economic, and political geography in some fertile exchanges. The uncoupling of people and place has, for example, given rise to interest in the literal and metaphorical 'border-crossings' entailed in people-movements, the fluid geopolitics of money and the state's role in containing or facilitating flows of capital and people (see the overview by Mitchell 1997b). Deterritorialisation (the unmoorings of nations and peoples, of real times and real spaces) has also enforced the need for new ways of talking about space (Thrift 1996). In this vein, attention has also turned to the 'virtual spaces' that people produce and access through information technologies (Adams and Warf 1997). So too has the production of 'natures' (of, for example, endangered species) been positioned within circuits of commerce and power that traverse the globe. Not that 'globalisation' is a universalising force that is somehow taking over the world. Places, in all their particularity, disrupt such imaginings and pretensions, and will continue to be the focus of cultural geographies into the next millennium.

Efforts to unsettle and enlarge the coordinates of the 'social field' have come from further sources still in recent years. These efforts return us to issues of power and identity and the question of the 'human' in human geography. The so-called 'animal turn' in human geography has not only opened up useful substantive forays into human–animal relations, in connection for example with pet-keeping, meat eating, angling and hunting, speciesism and ever-more elaborate breeding experiments (see special issue *Environment and Planning D: Society and Space* 1995). There have also been important conceptual advances in the configuring of the category 'human'. These efforts have sought to disturb the boundaries which have for so long segregated humanity and animality in western thought and practice (see, for example, Wolch and Emel 1998). Such efforts connect with recent moves within cultural geography to confound that cherished divide, marked out by science, and according to which 'culture' and 'nature' occupy separate realms (see, for example, Anderson 1998; Light 1997; Willems-Braun 1997). By today, we have come to see such categories in thoroughly relational ways and to seek to show their co-construction under specific material conditions. Cultural geographies of nature thus no longer involve studies of the human use of passive nonhuman subjects whether animal, vegetable or mineral (Matless 1997). In that 'borderland' zone of culture/nature, all variety of earthlings meet in a politics of their making and unmaking.

REFERENCES

Adams, P. & Warf, B. 1997, 'Introduction: cyberspace and geographical space', *The Geographical Review,* vol. 87, no. 2, pp. 139–145.

Agnew, J. & Corbridge, S. 1995, *Mastering Space: Hegemony, Territory and International Economy*, Routledge, London.

Agnew, J., Mercer, J. & Sopher, D. 1984, *The City in Cultural Context*, Allen & Unwin, Boston.

Anderson, K. 1991, *Vancouver's Chinatown: Racial Discourse in Canada,* McGill Queens University Press, Kingston.

Anderson, K. 1995, 'Culture and nature at the Adelaide Zoo: at the frontiers of "human" geography', *Transactions of the Institute of British Geographers*, vol. 20, no. 3, pp. 275–94.

Anderson, K. 1997, 'A walk on the wild side: a critical geography of domestication', *Progress in Human Geography*, vol. 21, no. 4, pp. 463–85.

Anderson, K. 1998, 'Science and the Savage: The Linnean Society of New South Wales, 1874–1900', *Ecumene*, vol. 5, no. 2, pp. 125–143.

Anderson, K. & Jacobs, J.M. 1999, 'Geographies of publicity and privacy: residential activism in Sydney in the 1970s', *Environment and Planning A,* vol. 31.

Australian Geographical Studies special issue 1997, vol. 35, no. 1., March/April. (devoted to the sub-discipline of cultural geography).

Barnes, T. & Duncan, J. 1992, *Writing Worlds: Discourse, Text and Metaphor in the Representation of Landscape*, Routledge, London.

Bell, D. & Valentine, G. 1997, *Consuming Geographies: We Are Where We Eat*, Routledge, London.

Bell, D. & Valentine, G. (eds) 1995, *Mapping Desire*, Routledge, London.

Berger, J. 1972, *Ways of Seeing the World*, Penguin, Harmondsworth.

Bird, J., Curtis, B., Putman, T., Robertson, G. & Tickner, L. (eds) 1993, *Mapping the Futures: Local Cultures Global Change*, Routledge, London & New York.

Butler, J. 1998, 'Merely cultural', *New Left Review*, vol. 227, pp. 33–44.

Calhoun, C. (ed.) 1994, *Social Theory and the Politics of Identity*, Blackwell, Oxford.

Castells, M. 1997, *The Information Age: Economy, Society and Culture,* Blackwells, Oxford.

Chaney, D. 1994, *The Cultural Turn*, Routledge, London.

Clark, G. 1985, *Judges and the Cities*, University of Chicago Press, Chicago.

Clarke, J., Hall, S., Jefferson, T. & Roberts, B. 1976, 'Subcultures, cultures and class: a theoretical overview', in *Resistance Through Rituals*, eds S. Hall & J. Henderson, Hutchinson/Centre for Contemporary Cultural Studies, London, pp. 9–74.

Cloke, P., Philo, C. & Sadler, D. 1991, *Approaching Human Geography*, Paul Chapman, London.

Cloke, P., Doel, M., Matless, D., Phillis, M. & Thrift, N. 1994, *Writing the Rural: Five Cultural Geographies*, Paul Chapman, London.

Cosgrove, D. & Jackson, P. 1987, 'New directions in cultural geography', *Area*, vol. 19, pp. 95–101.

Cosgrove, D. & Daniels, S. (eds) 1988, *The Iconography of Landscape*, Cambridge University Press, Cambridge.

Crang, M. 1998, *Cultural Geography,* Routledge, London.

Cresswell, T. 1996, *In Place/Out of Place: Geography, Ideology and Transgression,* University of Minnesota Press, Minneapolis.

Derrida, J. 1967, *De la Grammatologie, Les Editions de Minuit, Paris* (translated as J. Derrida 1974, *Of Grammatology,* John Hopkins University Press, Baltimore).

Duncan, J. 1980, 'The superorganic in American cultural geography', *Annals, Association of American Geographers*, vol. 70, no. 2, pp. 181–98.

Duncan, J. & Duncan, N. 1988, '(Re)reading the landscape', *Environment and Planning D: Society and Space,* vol. 6, no. 2, pp. 117–26.

Duncan, J. & Ley, D. (eds) 1993, *Place/Culture/Representation*, Routledge, London & New York.

Duncan, N. (ed.) 1995, *Bodyspace: Destabilizing Geographies of Gender and Sexuality*, Routledge, London.

Ecumene: International Journal of Culture, Environment and Meaning, Edward Arnold, London.

Environment and Planning A 1998, special issue, 'Reconsidering quantitative geography', vol. 30, no. 2.

Environment and Planning D: Society and Space 1995, special issue, 'Bringing the animals back in', vol. 13, no. 6, pp. 632–781.

Fincher, R. & Jacobs, J. (eds) 1998, *Cities of Difference*, The Guilford Press, New York.

Gibson-Graham, J.K. 1996, *The End of Capitalism (as we know it): a Feminist Critique of Political Economy*, Blackwell, Oxford.

Gleeson, B. (1998) *Geographies of Disability*, Routledge, London.

Goss, J. 1988, 'The built environment and social theory: towards an architectural geography', *Professional Geographer,* vol. 40, no. 4, pp. 392–403.

Gregory, D. 1994, *Geographical Imaginations*, Blackwell, Oxford.

Gregson, N. 1995, 'And now it is all consumption?', *Progress in Human Geography*, vol. 19, no. 1, pp. 135–41.

Harley, B. 1992, 'Deconstructing the map', in *Writing Worlds: Discourse, Text and Metaphor in the Representation of Landscape*, eds T. Barnes & J. Duncan, Routledge, London, pp. 229–45.

Harvey, D. 1989, *The Condition of Postmodernity: An Enquiry into the Origins of Cultural Change*, Blackwell, Oxford.

Hobsbawm, E. & Ranger, T. 1983, *The Invention of Tradition,* Cambridge University Press, Cambridge.

Holdsworth, D. & Mitchell, D. 1998, *Cultural Geography: A Reader*, Arnold, London.

Horne, D. 1986, *The Public Culture: The Triumph of Industrialism,* Pluto Press, Sydney.

Jackson, P. 1989, *Maps of Meaning,* Unwin Hyman, London.

Jackson, P. & Penrose, J. (eds) 1993, *Constructions of Race, Place and Nation*, University College Press, London.

Jackson, P. & Smith, S. 1984, *Exploring Social Geography,* George Allen & Unwin, London.

Jackson, P. & Thrift, N. 1995, 'Geographies of consumption', in *Acknowledging Consumption: A Review of New Studies,* ed. D. Miller, Routledge, London, pp. 204–36.

Jacobs, J. 1996, *Edge of Empire: Postcolonialism and the City*, Routledge, London & New York.

James, A., Hockey, J. & Dawson, A. (eds) 1997, *After Writing Culture: Epistemology and Praxis in Contemporary Anthropology,* Routledge, London & New York.

Johnson, N. 1995, 'Cast in stone: monuments, geography and nationalism', *Environment and Planning D: Society and Space*, vol. 13, no. 1, pp. 51–65.

Johnston, L. 1997, 'Queen(s') street or Ponsonby poofters? Embodied HERO Parade sites', *New Zealand Geographer*, vol. 53, no. 2, pp. 29–33.

Journal of Australian Studies 1998, special issue, 'Australian masculinities', no. 56, pp. 1–179.

Kearns, R. & Gesler, W. 1998, *Putting Health into Place: Landscape, Identity and Wellbeing*, Syracuse University Press, Syracuse.

Knorr-Cetina, K. & Cicourel, A. (eds) 1981, *Advances in Social Theory and Methodology: Toward an Integration of Micro- and Macro-Sociologies*, Routledge & Kegan Paul, Boston.

Kobayashi, A. & Mackenzie, S. (eds) 1989, *Remaking Human Geography*, Unwin Hyman, London.

Kong, L. 1997, 'A new cultural geography?', *Scottish Geographical Magazine*, vol. 113, no. 3, pp. 177–85.

Kong, L. 1996, 'Popular music in Singapore: local cultures, global resources and regional identities', *Environment and Planning D: Society and Space*, vol. 14, no. 3, pp. 273–92.

Law, R. forthcoming, 'Gender and transport', *Progress in Human Geography*.

Laws, G. 1994, 'Aging, contested meanings and the built environment', *Environment and Planning A*, vol. 26, no. 11, pp. 1787–802.

Ley, D. 1997, *The New Middle Class and the Remaking of the Central City*, Oxford University Press, Oxford.

Ley, D. 1983, *A Social Geography of the City*, Harper & Row, New York.

Longhurst, R. 1997, '(Dis)embodied geographies', *Progress in Human Geography*, vol. 21, no. 4, pp. 486–501.

Light, J. 1997, 'The changing nature of nature', *Ecumene*, vol. 4, no. 2, pp. 181–95.

Marcus, G. & Fisher, M. 1986, *Anthropology as Cultural Critique: An Experimental Moment in the Human Sciences*, University of Chicago Press, Chicago.

Massey, D. 1996, 'Space/power. Identity/difference: tensions in the city', in *The Urbanisation of Injustice*, eds A. Merrifield & E. Swyngedouw, Lawrence & Wishart, London, pp. 100–16.

Massey, D. & Jess, P. 1995, *A Place in the World? Places, Cultures and Globalisation*, Open University, Milton Keynes.

Matless, D. 1997, 'The geographical self, the nature of the social, and geoaesthetics: work in social and cultural geography', *Progress in Human Geography*, vol. 21, no. 3, pp. 393–405.

McDowell, L. 1995, 'Bodywork: heterosexual gender performances in city work places', in *Mapping Desire: Geographies of Sexuality*, eds D. Bell & G. Valentine, Routledge, London.

McDowell, L. (ed.) 1997, *Undoing Place?: A Geographical Reader*, Arnold, John Wiley & Sons, London, New York.

Meinig, D. (ed.) 1979, *The Interpretation of Ordinary Landscapes*, Oxford University Press, New York.

Mills, C. 1988, '"Life on the upslope:" the postmodern landscape of gentrification', *Environment and Planning D: Society and Space*, vol. 6, pp. 169–89.

Mitchell, K. 1997a, 'Conflicting geographies of democracy and the public sphere in Vancouver BC', *Transactions, Institute of British Geographers*, vol. 22, pp.162–79.

Mitchell, K. 1997b, 'Transnational discourse: Bringing geography back in', *Antipode*, vol. 29, no. 2, pp. 101–14.

Nash, C. 1998, 'Mapping emotion', *Environment and Planning D: Society and Space*, vol. 16, no. 1, pp. 1–9.

Nast, H. & Pile, S. (eds) 1998, *Places Through the Body*, Routledge, London & New York.

New Zealand Geographer 1997, special issue, '(Re)Formations: Cultural geographies of Aotearoa/New Zealand', eds L. Berg & R. Kearns, vol. 53, no. 2.

Philo, C. 1997, 'The chaotic spaces of medieval madness: thoughts on the English and Welsh experience', in *Nature and Society in Historical Context,* eds M. Teich, R. Porter & B. Gustafsson, Cambridge University Press, Cambridge, pp. 51–90.

Philo, C. 1991, 'Delimiting human geography: new social and cultural perspectives', in *New Words, New Worlds: Reconceptualising Social and Cultural Geography,* C. Philo (compiler), proceedings of a conference, Aberystwyth, pp. 14–27.

Pile, S. & Keith, M. (eds) 1993, *Place and the Politics of Identity,* Routledge, London & New York.

Pile, S. 1996, *The Body and the City: Psychoanalysis, Space and Subjectivity,* Routledge, London.

Pile, S. & Thrift, N. (eds) 1995, *Mapping the Subject: Geographies of Cultural Transformation,* Routledge, London & New York.

Pratt, A. 1997, 'Guest editorial: Production values: from cultural industries to the governance of culture', *Environment and Planning A,* vol. 29, no. 11, pp. 1911–17.

Rose, G. 1993, *Feminism and Geography: The Limits to Geographical Knowledges,* Polity Press, Cambridge.

Russell, B. & Kniffen, D. 1951, *Culture Worlds,* Harper & Row, New York.

Said, E. 1978, *Orientalism,* Pantheon Books, New York.

Sauer, C. 1925, *The Morphology of Landscape,* University of California Publications in Geography, vol. 2, pp. 19–53.

Schwartz, J.M. & Ryan, J. (eds) 1998, *Picturing Place: Photography and the Geographical Imagination,* John Wiley & Sons Ltd, London.

Shields, R. 1991, *Places on the Margin: Alternative Geographies of Modernity,* Routledge, London.

Shurmer-Smith, P. & Hannam, K. 1994, *Worlds of Desire, Realms of Power: A Cultural Geography,* Edward Arnold, London.

Sibley, D. 1995, *Geographies of Exclusion: Society and Difference in the West,* Routledge, London & New York.

Smith, S. 1997, 'Beyond geography's visible worlds: a cultural politics of music', *Progress in Human Geography,* vol. 21, no. 4, pp. 502–30.

Spivak, G. 1996, 'Subaltern talk', in *The Spivak Reader,* eds D. Landry & G. Maclean, Routledge, London, pp. 287–308.

Stock, B. 1983, *The Implications of Literacy,* Princeton University Press, Princeton.

Suttles, G. 1968, *The Social Order of the Slum,* University of Chicago Press, Chicago.

Thrift, N. 1996, *Spatial Formations,* Sage, London.

Urban Studies 1998, 'Review issue: Urban consumption', vol. 35, no. 5/6, pp. 815–1001.

Valentine, G. 1993, '(Hetero)sexing space: lesbian perceptions and experiences of everyday spaces', *Environment and Planning D: Society and Space,* vol. 11, no. 4, pp. 395–413.

Wagner, P. & Mikesell, M. 1962, *Readings in Cultural Geography,* University of Chicago Press, Chicago.

Waitt, G. 1997, 'Selling paradise and adventure: representations of landscape in tourist advertising', *Australian Geographical Studies,* vol. 35, no. 1, pp. 47–60.

Watson, S. & Gibson, K. (eds) 1995, *Postmodern Cities and Spaces,* Blackwell, Oxford.

Whatmore, S. & Boucher, S. 1993, 'Bargaining with nature: the discourse and practice of "environmental planning gain"', *Transactions, Institute of British Geographers,* vol. 18, no. 2, pp. 166–79.

Whyte, W. 1943, *Street Corner Society,* (2nd edn 1955), University of Chicago Press, Chicago.

Willems-Braun, B. 1997, 'Buried epistemologies: the politics of nature in (post)colonial British Columbia', *Annals, Association of American Geographers,* vol. 87, no. 1, pp. 3–31.

Wolch, J. & Emel, J. (eds) 1998, *Animal Geographies: Place, Politics and Identity in the Nature-Culture Borderlands*, Verso, New York.

Wrigley, N. & Lowe, M. 1996, *Retailing Consumption and Capital: Towards the New Retail Geography*, Longmans, London.

Yaeger, P. 1996, 'The strange effects of ordinary space', in *The Geography of Identity*, ed. P. Yaeger, The University of Michigan Press, Ann Arbor, pp. 1–39.

Yapa, L. 1998, 'The poverty discourse and the poor in Sri Lanka', *Transactions, Institute of British Geographers*, vol. 23, no. 1, pp. 95–115.

Young, R. 1990, *White Mythologies: Writing History and the West*, Routledge, London & New York.

Zukin, S. 1995, *The Culture of Cities*, Blackwell, Oxford.

The land in cultural context

2

Postcolonial New Zealand?

Eric Pawson

INTRODUCTION

At the beginning of 1990, the fourteenth Commonwealth Games were held in Auckland. They had been brought to New Zealand's largest city to initiate celebrations marking the 150th anniversary of the signing of the Treaty of Waitangi between Maori chiefs and the British Crown. The opening ceremony was a lavish spectacle portraying a bicultural national history. In a massive choreographed display, thousands of brightly outfitted people carpeted the arena and, with minimal props, enacted a Maori story of creation and occupation of the land and the subsequent arrival of Pakeha (the Maori designation for Europeans), culminating in the signing of the treaty in 1840. The show was witnessed by national teams of athletes from the Commonwealth, each previously escorted into the stadium by Maori warriors in traditional dress.

The underlying message of the occasion was clear. Here, hosting representatives of a fraternity of nations, was a country that wanted to be seen as a model of cultural fraternity, in which the descendants of European colonists co-existed easily with an indigenous people, the Maori. The message was designed to confirm to a global television audience New Zealand's widely assumed place as a harmonious society and also to reinforce to New Zealanders themselves that this was indeed the case. As a spectacle it worked. Even the most critical local onlooker could not help but be moved by a sense of pride.

Yet the critic must ask questions. Has New Zealand been an unusual example of a cooperative, bicultural venture in an intensely competitive world? In other words, was the spectacle realistic? Or did it mask the history of cultural relations that it sought to represent? To explore such questions is an exercise in cultural geography. It must uncover the meanings of experience to the very different peoples involved—Maori and Pakeha—in order to chart the main contours of the relationships between them and the lands that they have occupied. It is therefore also an exercise in reading the past, as without this, the circumstances of the present cannot be understood. '[T]hinking historically is no luxury; on the contrary, it is an essential part of doing human geography' (Driver 1988, p. 504).

There is, however, more than one way of thinking historically. Histories are shaped by the memories of the people who make them. And memories are constructed in very different ways, depending on whose they are. What is remembered and emphasised by some people may be erased by or obscured to others (Samuel 1994). This type of approach is central to what has been called the 'postcolonial critical project' (Jacobs 1996, p. 29). Such a project seeks to expose the ways in which the expression of dominant cultural perspectives through colonial occupation has marginalised, or normalised within narrow limits, those who are different or have been rendered less powerful. It is concerned with both the hegemonic discourse and material operations of colonisation, and how these have been ongoing and persistent, constantly reinscribed and renegotiated but always underwritten by relations of unequal power (Moore-Gilbert 1997; cf. Berg and Kearns 1996). The 'post' in 'postcolonial' in other words does not mean 'after', but refers to a continuous engagement with the lasting effects of colonialism (Spoonley 1995).

The first purpose of this chapter is to highlight the greater depth of understanding of cultural relations in New Zealand generated by postcolonial scholarship in order to unsettle the frames of reference constructed through colonialism and carried unconsciously forward therefrom. To facilitate this it will examine the very different cultural contexts and practices that Maori and Pakeha brought together. It will then discuss the manner in which Pakeha subsequently sought cultural dominance and suppression of Maori memories. Consideration of how this history has been retrieved in recent years leads to the second purpose of the chapter, which is to indicate something of the ways that cultural identities are being destabilised in the decade since 1990, as political, jurisprudential and popular debates[1] have become less masked. In fact the wider use amongst non-Maori of 'Pakeha', although a contested term that is itself a product of the oppositional categories of colonisation, is indicative of some degree of acceptance amongst them of postcolonial formations.

CULTURAL CONTEXTS AND PRACTICES

Written histories long regarded the signing of the Treaty of Waitangi as marking the formal annexation into the British Empire of the territories called New Zealand. A Pakeha historian has suggested that 1840 has been over-privileged and that a more useful perspective would focus on the question 'why, how and when was British rule imposed on the Maori?' (Belich 1996, p. 181). This process, he argues, was much more spasmodic and drawn out than the use of a single date would imply.

Certainly, there had been contact for over half a century before 1840, with the coastal peripheries of the North and South Islands being part of the 'informal empire' visited by, and with temporary settlements of, European sealers, whalers and traders. These activities had been tolerated, even welcomed, by coastal Maori peoples as opportunities for trade and acquisition of European goods, but on Maori terms. However, due to distance, expense and limited Crown resources, the question of annexation had not been favoured earlier. Indeed, a number of British parliamentary acts from 1817 onwards had recognised the New Zealanders, that is, the Maori, as independent peoples (Orange 1987).

Changing conditions in Europe meant that this situation could not long persist. Victorian Britain was the leading impulse in a rapidly developing European crucible of capitalism, a country seeking ever-widening horizons for trade, capital export and emigration. The European world was in ferment and Britain in particular was becoming industrialised, urbanised and class-divided. Between 1815 and 1914 as many as ten million Britons (Baines 1985) moved overseas. Most went to North America, with much smaller numbers to South America, southern Africa, the tropical colonies and Australasia. New Zealand was one of the last significant links in a worldwide chain. However, it caught the eye of a prominent theorist of colonisation, Edward Gibbon Wakefield, whose New Zealand Company was ready to plant settlements there by the late 1830s. It was a desire to control these settlements and the Europeans moving in from New South Wales, as well as to extend some protection to the Maori, that the Treaty of Waitangi was drawn up by the British Crown (Adams 1977; Orange 1987).

In this regard, the British were maintaining a long tradition of usually acting as if to secure the consent of indigenous peoples through treaties as a condition of the constitutionality of their imperium (Williams 1989). Indeed, the recognition of Maori property and non-property rights in the treaty and in the Crown's instructions to the first Governor was 'greatly in advance' of what had happened in the Americas or in Australia (Ward 1997a, p. 43). In Australia there had been no treaty at all: it having been declared 'terra nullius', the Aboriginal peoples considered not to possess even 'the rudest forms of civil polity' (cited in McHugh 1989, p. 57). But in New Zealand there was a treaty, which for Pakeha thereafter was taken to mark the founding of New Zealand as a modern state.

The Treaty of Waitangi exemplifies, however, the ways in which texts can be invested with widely differing meanings (Orange 1987; Kawharu 1989; Walker 1990). Some interpretation of this text is required in order to gain insight into the memories that stem from it. To do this it is necessary to explore the very different cultural contexts and understandings of the treaty signatories. This is no simple task, as the ways in which people represent cultural tradition changes. In postcolonial situations identities can be re-imagined to focus upon particular cultural elements, in order to construct shared subjectivities in opposition to other identities (Keesing 1989; Wall 1997). Care must therefore be taken in 'reading off' cultural characteristics from available sources to pre-colonial situations. However, people everywhere are social beings with the manner of that sociality being culturally determined. In the broadest terms, sometimes competitive themes are emphasised and sometimes more cooperative ones. To a greater or lesser extent in every culture, these themes characterise the manner of relationships between people and between people and nature. They not only describe such relationships as practised, but are also employed in cultural mythologies to represent and proscribe experience.

In general, since neither theme is by any means absent in the other, it can be said that the guiding motif of nineteenth-century British life was that of competition, whereas Maori life was organised on more cooperative lines. This is not to suggest that either way was somehow morally superior, although Pakeha certainly assumed theirs to be so. Nor is it to romanticise a pre-colonial Maori past, as is sometimes a tendency amongst both Maori and Pakeha today (Wall 1997). It is to point out that, in terms of their own cultural evolution, Maori peoples had found their interests to be better served by co-operative strategies (cf. Ridley 1996). The Pakeha colonisation of New Zealand thus brought together peoples whose underlying cultural assumptions and practices were very different.

At the time, populations in northern Europe were growing rapidly. From this fact, inescapable in the evidence of early censuses and expanding cities, Wakefield drew his conclusions concerning the necessity of emigration to accommodate 'surplus' people. Malthus, however, used it to derive his infamous 'natural law' of the inevitability of strife, famine and war as populations outstripped their means of subsistence. It was this portrayal of competitive struggle that Darwin appropriated in his own theory of evolution as the mechanism to explain processes of adaptation to environment by those species fittest to survive (Young 1985). Although Darwin himself was often reluctant to draw moral conclusions from nature, others showed no such hesitation. The theory of evolution was in turn used to explain and celebrate the apparent cultural and material progress of Europe, as well as to justify the intense dog-eat-dog laissez-faire capitalism on which it was based (Peet 1985). Hence a prominent Darwinist could write that '... so long as ... man [*sic*] increases and multiplies without restraint, so long will peace and industry not only permit, but they will necessitate, a struggle for existence as sharp as any that ever went on under the regime of war' (Huxley 1894, p. 209).

Thus competition between individuals, families, classes and companies in an increasingly atomistic society was legitimated by recourse to a seemingly natural—and hence powerful—analogy. Wealth among people who had long lived by the rules of the marketplace was measured in ownership of commodities and control of the means of production. The drive to colonise was little more than the desire to commodify the rest of the world: as Marx was to observe, to bring what to Europeans were territories of the global periphery into an international division of labour as producers of food and raw materials (in Feagin and Smith 1987, p. 4). For Britain, the process extended access to an ever-widening stock of resources in order to cement its position in the struggle between states. Access to land for these purposes was of course critical.

Inevitably this drive brought Pakeha into conflict with indigenous peoples who measured wealth very differently and did not regard land as a tradeable commodity. The material operations of colonisation were underwritten by a racialised and gendered 'discourse of colonisation' (Gibbons 1991, p. 28; cf. Berg and Kearns 1996) that deemed indigenes not to be using land in ways that the new colonisers considered productive, hence adoption of the term 'wastelands' to describe that which was not cultivated (Pawson and Cant 1992; Brooking 1996). From a Pakeha evolutionary standpoint, such peoples were a negative 'other', inhabitants of a 'wilderness', whose portrayal as different lent legitimacy to the colonising project. Using the metaphor of a 'chain of being', the 'other' were assigned a lowly place as 'lesser races' (Figure 2.1a). The position of the Maori in this chain, or ladder, was however more 'advanced' than that of many other indigenes because the British respected their military prowess, concept of chieftainship, cultural artefacts and willingness to embrace the habits of trade and literacy.

The colonial stereotyping of Maori within this frame of reference was, however, flexible (Belich 1996, pp. 19–22; Wall 1997). Hence, as Pakeha

PAKEHA COLONIAL REPRESENTATIONS

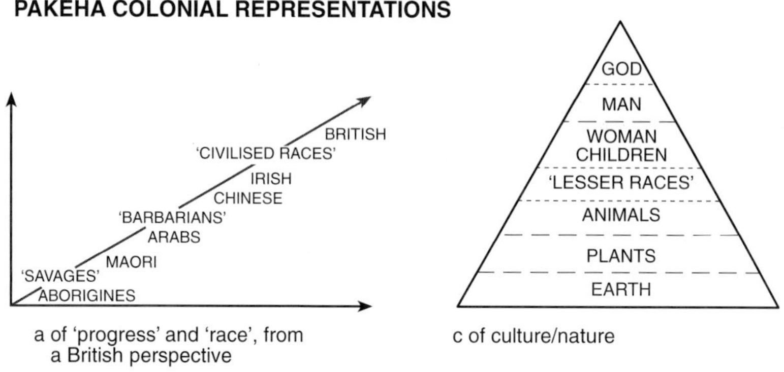

MAORI REPRESENTATION

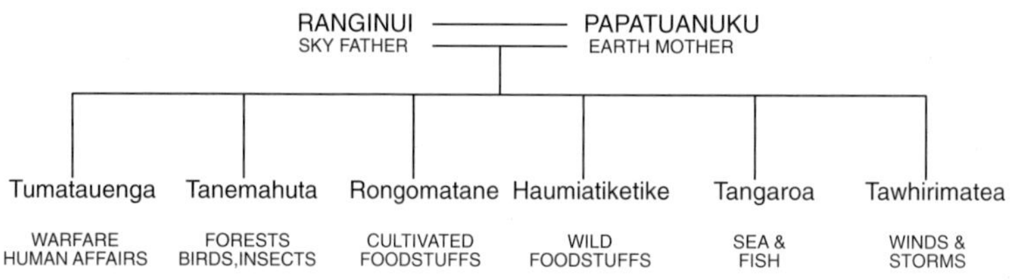

b of the 'environmental family'

FIGURE 2.1 Cultural representations.
Sources: (a) and (c) constructed by the author from various sources, including Thomas (1984) and Brooking (1996); (b) redrawn from Roberts et al. (1995, 11).

numbers grew, and as demands for land became more insistent, Maori were re-imagined as a threat to the colonial project (cf. Moore-Gilbert 1997, pp. 50–1). They were condemned for the 'beastly communism' of social orders built on affiliation to whanau (the extended family) and hapu (groupings of families) and allied by kin relations into iwi (tribes). Traditionally they had not had an ethic of capital accumulation. Although rivalry and competitive combat between hapu and iwi were commonplace, within and often between them social esteem depended on what was given and the interests of the individual were subordinate to those of the group. This contrasted sharply with Pakeha ways, in which social esteem was a product of what was acquired and group interests were often subordinate to those of the individual.

Nonetheless, an understanding of cooperative relations was not absent from European traditions and re-emerged strongly in nineteenth-century socialism. Marx, whilst recognising in Darwin's model 'the basis in natural history for our own view' (in Young 1985, p. 20), that is, the progressive theory of historical materialism, nonetheless saw in humans a potential for sociality which he sometimes expressed in the term 'species-being'. An element of this has been described as 'a capacity unique to members of the human species for empathising and co-operating with fellow members of the species' (Conway 1987, p. 33). Kropotkin, reacting strongly against Huxley and other social Darwinists, developed a natural analogy of 'mutual aid' derived from myriad examples of co-operation between members of the same species. He asked who were the fittest to survive, the answer being that 'we at once see that those animals which acquire habits of mutual aid are undoubtedly the fittest' (Kropotkin 1914, p. 6; cf. Ridley 1996, pp. 2–5). As a renowned geographer-anarchist, he urged respect for other peoples of the world (Kropotkin 1885), a message that was too inconvenient for most Pakeha to hear because of the colonising desire for land.

Maori relations to land had much in common with those of other indigenous peoples, although there was no single Maori perspective on this subject, or any other (Roberts et al. 1995). They exercised a complex regime of rights over land and water bodies (or 'aboriginal title', the nature of which varied between tribal territories). Each hapu controlled a defined stretch of territory, with families and their kin being allocated rights of occupation and use over specific resources (Stokes 1996; Bennion 1997). However, the mana of the land, broadly translated as its integrity and creative power, was vested in the chief, and only the chief with the consent of the group could alienate land. Territory was maintained by the ability of hapu to defend it and the precedence of social over individual interests was summarised by the aphorism 'a house that stands alone will be consumed by fire' (Walker 1982, p. 70). Maori had a strong sense of place and attachment to land which they verbalised in the form of 'motto-maxims', identifying their mountain, river and iwi on formal occasions (Yoon 1986).

Maori cultural practices were thus focused upon nature, given the immediacy of their material reliance upon it. But the features of land and water bodies were also woven through with spiritual meaning and Maori creation myths, which explain the descent of all living things from the children of

Ranginui (the sky father) and Papatuanuku (the earth mother), portray all of nature, including people, as linked together using the metaphor of a family (Figure 2.1b). This mythology established a primacy of people in nature and validated their right to use its resources. People, however, were not regarded as above nature and had to observe well-established rules of propitiation and conservation that had been developed in order to increase the odds of social survival. Maori saw themselves as not owning the land, but belonging to it. For them there was a strong element of the sacred in nature (Yoon 1986; Roberts et al. 1995).

It was certainly not sacred to Pakeha. Although there has been much debate about White's (1967, p. 1207) characterisation of the 'orthodox Christian arrogance toward nature' (see Pepper 1996), it is clear that Christian Europe assigned spiritual significance only to the relationship between people and God. Europeans saw themselves as above nature, a belief legitimated in their own creation story in Genesis when Adam was given dominion over the animals. Theirs was a combative relationship with the natural world, for having erred in the Garden of Eden, people were made to sweat for their livelihoods thereafter. Hence their hierarchical view of creation, ordered from God to man, woman and then the 'lesser races', down to the beasts and plants (Figure 2.1c): a scheme reflecting the gender and class relations of their own societies (Thomas 1984; Brooking 1996). Lacking spiritual significance, nature was to be used for material benefit and land commodified for individual use and gain.

These were the very different cultural contexts that the parties to the Treaty of Waitangi brought to the signing of the document in 1840. It is a brief statement, comprising a preamble and three articles. It was drawn up in both Maori and English written versions, although in all probability the oral agreements negotiated at treaty signings were as or more important to the chiefs at the time (Belich 1996). There are certainly crucial differences between the English and Maori texts, reflecting in part the problems of translating concepts central in meaning to one culture into the language of another (Biggs 1989). Overall, however, the Maori text portrays a sharing of power and authority. The English text 'is about a transfer of power' (Williams 1989, p. 79): it is part of the discourse of colonisation.

Almost all the chiefs who signed did so on the Maori version. It confirmed to them 'te tino rangatiratanga', 'the unqualified exercise of their chieftainship over their lands over their villages and over their treasures' (Kawharu 1989, pp. 319–20). It gave to the Crown 'kawatanga' or governorship. The English versions ceded 'sovereignty' but guaranteed Maori 'possession' of their lands, fisheries and other properties until such time as they wished to alienate them. Both versions extend to Maori the Crown's protection and the rights of citizenship. Hence 1840 is a critical marker in Maori memory for the guarantees the treaty appeared to give. For the Crown, it dates the formal establishment of British sovereignty. In another sense, 1840 is much less significant, being but part of a drawn out process of cultural interactions. This process rapidly became increasingly aggressive, turning into contests in power over the rights to land, and how this was to be used and regulated.

CONTESTS AND APPROPRIATIONS

By the late nineteenth century, the territories of New Zealand were overwhelmingly in Pakeha hands (Figure 2.2). The Pakeha population had grown at a rate unforeseen by Maori in 1840: from a few thousand then, to 60 000 in 1860 and 770 000 by 1900. As the strength of the Pakeha position relative to that of the Maori increased, the intent of the obligations spelled out in the treaty diminished. That this was not yet so in the late 1840s, when Crown authority had been threatened in the far north, was recognised by a former British Prime Minister, Sir Robert Peel. In a private letter in 1848 he wrote: 'If the obligations of good faith vary with the military skill and prowess of the parties to a Treaty, the New Zealanders [i.e. the Maori] have put in a claim to be respected which it has become prudent on our part to recognize' (cited in Adams 1977, p. 245).

With the transfer of authority from direct British rule to local settler government from 1853, 'respect' and 'prudence' ceased to be on the agenda. The question that arises, however, is how Maori lost so much land, and hence material and social well-being when, initially at least, the treaty seemed to guarantee rights to all that they wished to keep. Recent research suggests that this was because even in the treaty process the cards were stacked against them. The courts might have respected aboriginal title in the 1840s, but its exchange value in Pakeha eyes was never high. London's instructions to the new Governor in 1839 stated that 'the price to be paid to the natives … will bear an exceedingly small proportion to the price for which the same lands will be re-sold by the government to the settlers' (cited in Ward 1997a, pp. 43–4).

This was not at the time considered unjust to Maori as they were supposed to gain from the increased values of their remaining lands as colonisation proceeded. It was enforced through the Crown's treaty right of pre-emptive purchase. This right was intended to give the Crown the means to direct settlement where it wished, and simultaneously to provide a revenue to finance the far distant colony. But the Crown also interpreted the right of pre-emption as forbidding the direct leasing of land to settlers by Maori or its sale. Maori were thus unable to realise value from land, except at the Crown's very low prices (Bennion 1997; Ward 1997a; Waitangi Tribunal 1991). But why would they sell land at all?

Individualised use rights were well established among Maori, but individual land ownership was not. Initially, it is likely that Pakeha offers of guns, goods and money were interpreted as providing only for rights of occupancy. The granting of such rights had been commonplace as gestures of mutual aid to allies and kinsfolk made destitute in times of war (Ward 1974). To Maori, contracts were not about transferring property but about defining relationships between people. Hence in contractual terms, the *quid pro quo* for allowing Pakeha to use land would have been the benefits to hapu and iwi of trade (Waitangi Tribunal 1997a, p. 4). Maori were not slow to appreciate the nature of Pakeha trade. In contrast to the assumptions of Eurocentric historiography that indigenous peoples the world over were essentially

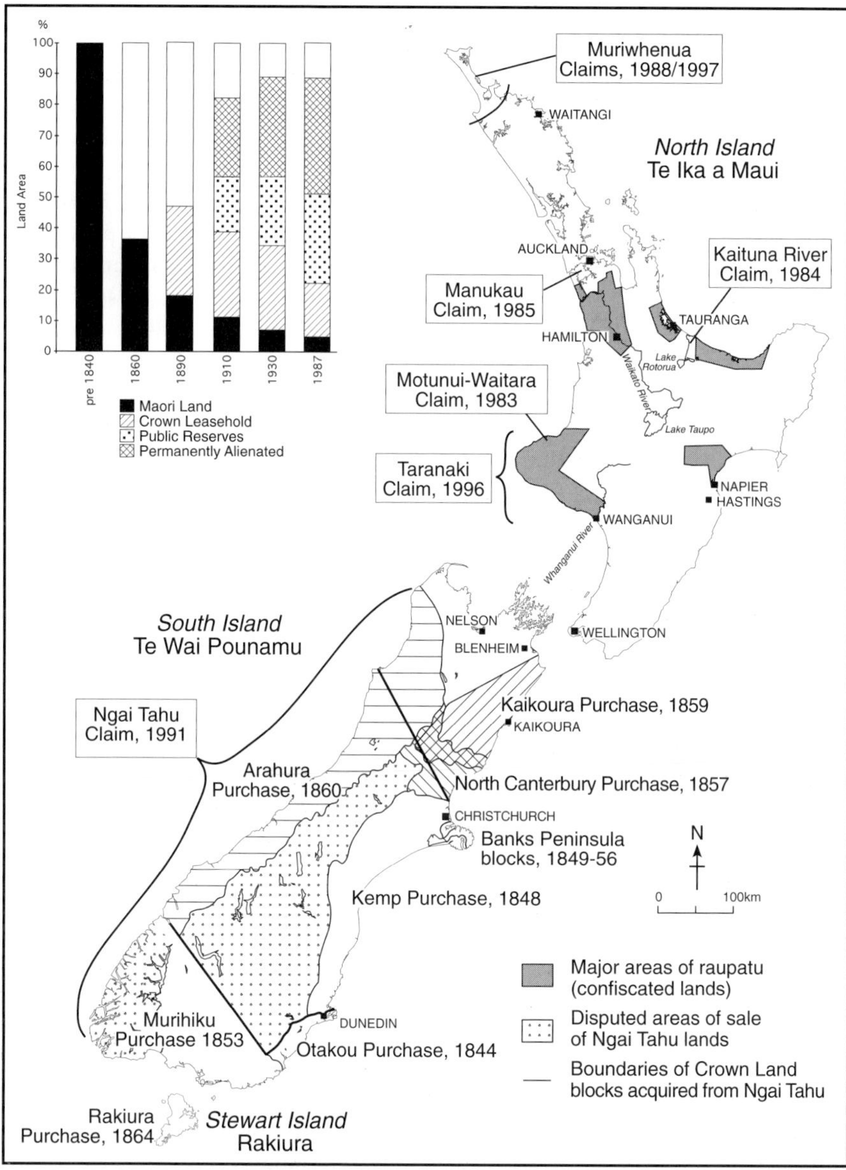

FIGURE 2.2 Location map for places, claims, confiscations and South Island land purchases discussed in the text. The graph highlights changes in land status categories since the 1830s.
Sources: map based on Waitangi Tribunal 1991, pp. 6–7 and Stokes (1992, 185). Graph drawn from data in *New Zealand Official 1990 Yearbook*, Department of Statistics, Wellington, p. 417, supplemented by Maori land information for 1860 and 1890, calculated from data derived from Ward (1997b).

culturally static, the Maori millennium in New Zealand had been one of constant adaptations to shifting circumstances.

This was so in terms of both changing traditions and material living. Upon arrival in New Zealand, Maori migrants had discovered that most of their Pacific islands' staple foods would not grow, so that it was necessary to shift to a diet rich in birdmeat and fish. As these resources became increasingly scarce, they not only adopted environmental rules to conserve them, but also developed horticultures using vegetables such as taro and kumara (Davidson 1984; McGlone et al. 1994). European crops and animals such as pigs were readily incorporated from stocks left by early Pakeha sailors. It was thus a short step to the exchange of surplus food with Pakeha for trade goods. So successful were Maori cooperative economies in this regard that, in the 1840s and early 1850s, they supplied the bulk of the food consumed in the new Pakeha settlements of Wellington and Auckland (Asher and Naulls 1987; Belich 1996).

Land given in exchange for money, cattle and other items of trade, however, did not come back. There is no doubt that this was quickly understood, although faster in some places than in others (Waitangi Tribunal 1997a). But if the demand for Pakeha goods, or the imposition of Pakeha taxes, outstripped Maori capacity to earn, selling land was the only option. In some other cases, chiefs took advantage of old rivalries to deal with the Crown in selling places that did not belong to them, as happened with much of the land of north Canterbury and Kaikoura in the South Island, sold in the Wairau Deed of 1847 by Ngati Toa, despite these being Ngai Tahu territories. When the latter's interests were recognised with Crown purchases in 1857 and 1859 (Figure 2.2), their bargaining position had been seriously weakened as much of the land had already been occupied by Pakeha. As Crown agents moved to purchase more and more areas for a growing Pakeha population, Maori began to lose control of the situation.

The vast Kemp (20 million acres) and Murihiku (seven million) blocks (Figure 2.2) were bought by the Crown for the paltry sums of £2000 and £2600. Not only were the boundaries of what was agreed in the sales long disputed, but hapu wishes to retain their cultivations and food gathering districts were in many cases ignored. Due to the Crown's assumption of sovereignty, English land law was presumed to apply to the whole of these blocks, with the proviso that lands reserved for Ngai Tahu should be 'handed back' to be held under Crown title. According to the guarantees in the treaty, they should never have been taken; very little was handed back—only 6359 and 4875 acres respectively (O'Regan 1989; Waitangi Tribunal 1991; Ward 1997b, p. 266).

Crown methods of land acquisition in the North Island, where the Maori population was far more numerous, generated fierce resistance. Not until recently have the lengths to which indigenous peoples everywhere contested the loss of their lands been recognised by historical writers (Pawson and Cant 1992). Enmeshed in the settled binaries of the discourse of colonisation (Moore-Gilbert 1997, pp. 37–8), they long assumed that peoples of the global 'periphery' were too weak and 'uncivilised' to compete militarily, and hence neither sought nor saw evidence to the contrary. The extent of such resistance in New Zealand's North Island has, however, been extensively documented by James Belich.

Some Maori, because it was advantageous to do so (e.g. to protect trade or to settle old scores), sided with the Crown, but there was widespread iwi cooperation designed to curb land alienation. In response to this, the state precipitated a series of armed conflicts in the 1860s that were 'more akin to classic wars of conquest than we would like to believe' (Belich 1986, p. 80). Governor Grey, an astute politician, elicited an imperial commitment of 12 000 professional soldiers at the height of these wars, more than were available for the defence of England at the time. Maximum Maori strength was closer to 2–3000 (Belich 1996, p. 236), and they regularly defeated forces several times larger than their own. The numerical norms of imperial warfare were completely reversed and awareness of the conflicts was suppressed in Pakeha memory, unlike the heroics of British campaigns in Africa or Asia. Integral to the discourse of colonisation was the expectation of victory: failure to secure it was accounted for in ways that credited Maori with courage but not with military ability; defeat was attributed to the terrain or to failed leaders or failed troops (Belich 1986).

The success of Maori military resistance was in fact due to better strategy and tactics, based in part on more intimate knowledge of the landscape. It also owed much to effective means of mutual aid. Pakeha troops were frequently drawn away from homeland areas into dense bush and left to attack fortifications that had often been deliberately emptied. These fortifications were essentially trench systems designed to protect Maori from superior enemy firepower—the victory at Gate Pa at Tauranga in 1864 was won when assaulting British troops were massacred from deeply hidden protective positions, having advanced after an artillery bombardment roughly twenty times as intense as that later used in the initial Allied assault on the Somme in the First World War. Maori had perfected trench warfare decades before Europeans did so (Belich 1986, pp. 295–7). In order to resist incursions effectively, warriors were often drawn from wide geographical areas, with a constant turnover of man for man to enable hapu to maintain food production. In such ways, tribal organisation resisted a standing army, foreshadowing the success of later guerilla campaigns in other wars elsewhere in the world.

Substantive sovereignty was eventually enforced over much of the North Island by the expedients of land confiscation (raupatu) and individualisation of title. The Crown declared over five million acres of prime iwi lands, over which it had won some authority, to be confiscated (Figure 2.2). About half was returned as belonging to Maori who could demonstrate that they had not resisted or engaged Crown aggression; however often not as customary land, but after conversion into individual interests (Waitangi Tribunal 1996; Ward 1997a, pp. 60–7). The Native Land Court was established in 1865 to carry this process of individualisation through all Maori lands, with pressure to sell being applied further through the ending of the Crown's right of pre-emption. The Court required a limited number of Maori claimants to their own lands to register title in person, failure to do so resulting in its loss. Communal relations were undermined, just as intended, by conflict between those who wished to retain their titles and those who did not, the latter often forced to sell to recoup the cost of the court proceedings (Sorrenson 1981; Bennion 1997).

Pakeha justification for effacing the treaty in these ways was simple and reflected the increasingly racialised stereotyping of Maori as threatening (Wall 1997). The New Zealand Settlements Act, which gave authority for the confiscations, deemed many Maori to be 'in open rebellion'; hence discussing the bill in Parliament, the Premier had asserted that 'the Natives', not the Crown, had 'violated the Treaty of Waitangi' (NZPD 1863, p. 869). His predecessor had considered that 'the want of [force] has been the one great cause of failure of all the attempts ... to raise and civilise the Natives' (AJHR 1863, A8a, p. 11). In a later discussion on the Native Land Court, the Minister of Justice said '... [we sought] the detribalization of the Natives,—to destroy ... [their] principle of communism which ... stood as a barrier in the way of all attempts to amalgamate the Native Race into our own social and political system' (NZPD 1870, IX, p. 361). Debate echoed Wakefield's earlier forecast that the only choice for the Maori lay between 'amalgamation and extermination' (cited in Miller 1974, p. 97). They were expected, in other words, to conform to a Pakeha model of society, to make do with a minimal amount of land, or to die.

In such ways were the precepts of capitalist colonisation used to break the authority of Maori cultural practices. Landscapes, once secured, were re-made according to 'the social and material forms of the metropolitan world' (Gibbons 1991, p. 53). The speed of this process was remarkable: one geographer has observed that what took twenty centuries in Europe, and four in North America, was brought about in only one in New Zealand (Cumberland 1941). Only now can its extent be readily comprehended with the availability of the comprehensive plates in the *New Zealand Historical Atlas* (McKinnon 1997). The intricate pre-colonial geographies of the Maori were often seemingly erased and the land symbolically claimed for Pakeha in a process that has been described as 'naming as norming' (Berg and Kearns 1996). Male military associations were often recalled, as in the towns of Wellington, Napier, Hastings, Blenheim and Nelson (Figure 2.2). Only smaller settlements in regions retaining predominantly Maori populations kept or adopted Maori names (Yoon 1980).

Landscapes were redesigned according to the simplified requirements of the surveyor and farmer. They were normalised by destroying what was 'alien', that is, native bush, swamps and grasslands, and substituting the imported species of flora and fauna upon which the new capitalist economy depended. Crosby (1986) has referred to the introduction of such species as part of a process of 'ecological imperialism', its agents of course being Pakeha settlers, although the new plants and animals were often credited with superior competitive qualities in a 'battle' with native species. A local botanist considered the 'defeat' of the latter to be 'almost certain' (Travers 1869, p. 312), echoing the view of a renowned authority, Joseph Hooker, that 'many of the small local genera of Australia, New Zealand and South Africa, will ultimately disappear' (in Crosby 1986, p. 165). Another element of ecological imperialism was introduced diseases against which Maori had limited immunity. As had happened in the Americas and Australia, epidemics of acute infectious, diarrhoeal, respiratory and sexually transmitted diseases took a heavy toll. A population of about 100 000 in the early 1800s had fallen to about 60 000 by 1858. The nadir of 42 000 was reached at the turn of the century (Pool 1991).

As early as 1837 a colonist remarked that '... the natives are perfectly sensible of this decrease ... they conclude that the God of the English is removing the aboriginal inhabitants to make room for [Pakeha]' (in Crosby 1986, p. 250). Later interpretations were overtly Darwinian. Darwin himself, using examples from New Zealand, Tasmania and Hawaii in 1871, concluded that 'when civilised nations come into contact with barbarians the struggle is short' (Darwin 1901, p. 283). Another stereotype gained in prominence, romanticising the vanishing 'race', echoing an earlier Pakeha tradition, that of the noble savage (Wall 1997). A striking icon in the re-made landscape was subsequently erected on a hill above Auckland, close to the site of the Commonwealth Games stadium. It is an obelisk, a monument to the Maori people, flanked by a lone imported pine in place of earlier native totara trees.

PAKEHA AND MAORI MEMORIES

If thinking historically in this way reveals such a stark picture of cultural contests and appropriations, why did Pakeha New Zealand long foster a reputation for benevolent race relations (see Sinclair 1971; Berg and Kearns 1996)? Much Pakeha memory of the nineteenth century has been framed heroically in terms of the growing identity, or belonging, derived from 'reclaiming the wilderness'. The claims of the inhabitants who were displaced by this reclamation were silenced. This is partly a result of historical amnesia—Maori no longer being envisioned by Pakeha as threatening—but it also stems from the long relative isolation of the two cultures from each other. After the wars of the 1860s, the only iwi to flourish were those in the centre and on the northern and eastern fringes of the North Island. They had held on to land remote from the main towns, much of it of marginal quality to Pakeha eyes. Hence as late as the 1940s three-quarters of the Maori population lived in rural districts still substantially characterised by their own values. 'This segregation—geographical, social, cultural—was the artificial basis for New Zealand's reputation for sound race relations' (King 1985, p. 189).

In fact, expressions of unequal power continued to be to the fore in colonial discourse. It was still considered that Maori could be 'civilised' according to the norms of the now dominant culture. Pearson (1990) characterises such attitudes as ethnocentric and assimilationist. But they stand in contrast to the racist and exclusionary stance Pakeha often adopted towards another group of outsiders: the few Chinese and Indians in the country. In common with other British settler colonies, the New Zealand parliament passed a stream of legislation between 1870 and 1920 designed to keep out or limit numbers of Asian peoples. All Maori men, however, were given the vote as early as 1867. This move was integral to 'amalgamation' and was designed to weaken Maori allegiance to the consensual forums of the hapu and iwi. Democracy ensured that as a minority, the Maori vote could always be overridden by that of the majority, a factor reinforced by that vote long being restricted to only four specially created parliamentary seats.

This was one means by which the agencies of the state were used to normalise Pakeha values and marginalise those of the Maori. Discourse operates through all social structures and institutions, however; hence the courts moved from having confirmed treaty rights in the 1840s (at least from the English version (Bennion 1997)) to later denying their validity. Throughout the British Empire, as the substantive power of the coloniser over the colonised grew, politicians and judges moved to dismiss indigenous rights claimed in reliance on treaties (Williams 1989). In 1877 the Chief Justice declared the Treaty of Waitangi 'a simple nullity', a position widely accepted in New Zealand until the 1970s (Sorrenson 1989). Schools were used as a means of cultural reproduction, inculcating the individualised ethics and language of the coloniser (Walker 1990). Furthermore, the process of geographical colonisation was greatly extended in the 1890s. The Liberal government undertook a huge land buying programme in order to encourage more Pakeha farmers onto the land. As part of this process it acquired 2.7 million acres of Maori land in six years at an average of four shillings an acre; simultaneously individualisation of title through the Native Land Court was accelerated until it was all but complete (Brooking 1996).

This further substantial acquisition of Maori land has been completely overshadowed in Pakeha memory by the Liberals' moves to break up big Pakeha estates for closer settlement, even though in policy terms the latter was far less successful than the former. The average per acre price (over £4) paid for the big estates was about twenty times that given for Maori estates (Brooking 1996). This was at a time when the extension of state activities into other arenas was earning New Zealand the sobriquet of 'social laboratory of the world'. These renegotiated colonial structures brought some benefit to Maori in new primary health measures focusing on environmental sanitation, personal hygiene and improved maternal and child health. Coupled with growing immunity to infections, the result was an expansion of the Maori population, which—far from dying out—reached 64 000 in 1926 and 167 000 by 1961 (Pool 1991).

Maori memories of these years are quite different. The treaty guarantees made in 1840 were not forgotten, as the evidence of continual petitions to parliament and direct to the British Crown indicate (Orange 1987; Walker 1990). Memories were strengthened by new pieces of legislation introduced up until the 1960s which were designed to facilitate further alienation of Maori land (Bennion 1997), as was the taking of land for public works purposes. The ongoing effects of fragmentation, due to division through inheritance of individualised shares, contributed further to land loss and to problems of raising capital for development. A major government report published in 1961 reasserted a hegemonic colonialism, portraying Maori ways as inappropriate for contemporary living. It proposed 'integration' in place of amalgamation, although this seemed to amount to the same thing. 'Integration ... implies some continuation of Maori culture. Much of it, though, has already departed and only the fittest elements ... have survived the onset of civilisation. Language, arts and crafts, and the institutions of the marae are the chief relics. Only the Maoris themselves can decide whether these features of their ancient life are, in fact, to be kept alive ...' (Hunn 1961, p. 15).

The urbanisation of the Maori population was then proceeding rapidly, openly encouraged by the state in order to provide a cheap labour force for industrialisation. By the 1970s, three-quarters lived in towns and cities. Such trends might be taken as endorsement of the official view. But paradoxically a climate was being created that was more favourable to the mobilisation and expression of difference. Urban proximity to Pakeha made levels of deprivation amongst Maori very visible to members of both cultures. Some young Maori began to urge the adoption of Pakeha methods of direct action to draw attention to their memories. The advent of television and its broadcasting of civil rights and independence movements elsewhere reshaped the context within which Maori voices could be heard (Pawson and Cant 1992). Protest became more vigorous, culminating in a well-supported land rights march through the length of the North Island to parliament in Wellington in 1975. The same year, the third Labour government, whose party had been allied with Maori political forces since the 1930s, moved to give statutory recognition to both Maori and English texts of the Treaty of Waitangi (Williams 1989, p. 77).

RETRIEVING TE TIRITI

The *Treaty of Waitangi Act 1975* established the Waitangi Tribunal as a roving commission of enquiry to 'make recommendations on claims relating to the practical application of the Treaty and to determine whether certain matters are inconsistent with the principles of the Treaty'. In establishing what these principles are, the tribunal has authority 'to determine the meaning and effect of the Treaty of Waitangi as embodied in the English and Maori texts, and to decide upon issues raised by the differences between them' (Waitangi Tribunal 1997b, v, p. 3). Its mandate was not initially retrospective, however, and it could make recommendations only about claims from Maori with respect to treaty breaches arising from Crown policies or practices then or thereafter in force. 'The Crown' now signifies the government of New Zealand, although constitutionally its authority is still derived from the monarch via an appointed Governor General.

By the mid-1980s the tribunal, with both Maori and Pakeha members, was proving to be an increasingly credible forum amongst both Maori and Pakeha publics. It conducted much of its business on the marae (traditional meeting place), observing Maori protocol and using Maori as well as English as its language (Temm 1990). It won a reputation for establishing a vigorous but non-adversarial arena of debate informed by extensive historically-based research, and for carefully constructed reports which urged politically attainable resolutions (Figure 2.3). It emphasised the importance of the Maori text of te Tiriti as it would have been understood by the signatories (Kingsbury 1989). Its reports on the Motunui-Waitara, Kaituna and Manukau claims (Figure 2.2), which all involved the pollution of water bodies relied upon by hapu for food, were hailed as part of a 'radical reinterpretation of New Zealand [written] history' (Sorrenson 1989). Furthermore, it is a history that is alert to 'spatial sensibility' in the past and the ways in which this is registered in the present (cf. Jacobs 1996, p. 22).

FIGURE 2.3 One version of the motif used by Waitangi Tribunal on the cover of its reports. In its own description, this motif invokes 'the signing of the Treaty of Waitangi and the consequent development of Maori-Pakeha history interwoven in [New Zealand], in a pattern not yet completely known, still unfolding'. Reproduced courtesy of the Waitangi Tribunal.

The three claims mentioned above were each from Maori who had lost most of their lands during the confiscations of the 1860s; the reports also exposed fundamental environmental differences between Maori and Pakeha. Water bodies have often been used by Pakeha as convenient sewers; for Maori water is endowed with spiritual qualities that must be fostered in order to sustain stocks of seafood. The Motunui report highlighted the foolishness of using marine outfalls to dispose of human, animal and industrial waste that can then be carried back to shore by prevailing winds (James and Pawson 1995). The Kaituna report showed that attempting to resolve the sewage disposal problems of the tourist centre of Rotorua by transferring the effluent from the lake, which is one of the town's main assets, to its river outflow, would be merely to recreate the issue further along the same ecosystem. The Manukau report indicated how tribal fisheries had been destroyed over a long period by use of the harbour as if it were Auckland's back passage (Cant 1995).

That these claims focused on issues of environmental as well as cultural significance enhanced the tribunal's growing credibility with many Pakeha, as these were things with which they could identify as well. The claims raised the expectations of many Maori. In exploring the meaning of 'the principles of the treaty', the tribunal drew on a new generation of constitutional lawyers (Kawharu 1989). As a result, the view of the treaty as a 'simple nullity' was declared 'as a matter of international law ... clearly untenable' (Kingsbury 1989, p. 121). Instead the treaty started to be seen as 'the foundation for a developing social contract' (in Sorrenson 1989, p. 162), not merely a historical document. Thus when the fourth Labour government came to office in 1984, it took the inevitable next step and amended the Treaty of Waitangi Act a year later to enable the tribunal to hear Maori claims resulting from treaty violations right back to 1840.

This measure opened the floodgates to claims, about 650 of which had been lodged by 1997 (Ward 1997a), although many are relatively minor, or can or have been grouped for concurrent enquiry. Appointments to the tribunal were increased to enable it to consider several claims simultaneously. To explore 'the commonality of the issues', research was commissioned to provide 'a series of district overviews of historical grievances and injuries and a series of studies of themes of national relevance' (in Ward 1997a, p. xiii). The claims process itself has been outlined by Stokes (1992, 1996), an academic geographer who is also a member of the tribunal. Major claims heard, or resolved, have concerned fisheries, confiscated lands (especially those of Taranaki and Waikato-Tainui—although the latter was negotiated directly between the claimants and the Crown without involvement of the tribunal) and problematic land sales, notably the Ngai Tahu claim concerning transactions over much of the South Island and the Muriwhenua claim of the tribes of Northland (Figure 2.2).

In 1988 the tribunal issued an important report on the fisheries component of the Muriwhenua claim, spurred by a government move to privatise access to all of New Zealand's offshore fisheries. It not only established the considerable extent to which the peoples of Northland harvested the fisheries before 1840, but it also observed that the Crown had never purchased any fisheries rights from Maori, despite these rights having being specifically guaranteed in the treaty. Its recommendation that the two treaty partners negotiate a solution was used by government to seek means of resolving all iwi fishing claims. As a result 10 per cent of commercial fish quota was allocated to Maori, increased to about 25 per cent in 1992 when the Sealord company was bought in order to give access to more quota (Price 1996; Sharp 1997). But in a striking demonstration of the vigour of contemporary identity politics, the Treaty of Waitangi Fisheries Commission, the body set up to allocate this quota (at that time by far the most valuable claim redress to have been made), was still seeking agreed ways of doing so five years later.

The Ngai Tahu claim was based on breach of contract, given that the Crown did not make sufficient reserves, nor protect and maintain access to *mahinga kai* (traditional food sources) even though these measures were agreed at the time of the original purchases. Earlier official investigations had admitted the validity of much of the claim. The tribunal did not find in favour of the claimants with respect to the disputed boundaries of the Kemp and Murihiku blocks (Figure 2.2), but it did conclude that 'the predominant theme that constantly arises in [our] findings ... and indeed almost as constantly conceded by the Crown, is the failure of the Crown to ensure Ngai Tahu were left with ample land for their present and future needs' (Waitangi Tribunal 1991, p. 174). The subsequent matter of the realistic extent and types of compensation took Ngai Tahu and the Crown six years to resolve. The final settlement included, apart from financial resources, return of title to some significant food gathering areas and seasonal camping rights at others, as well as some co-management arrangements for Crown resources and, significantly, official recognition of many Maori names for places in the South Island (Cant 1998).

Legally, only Crown assets, or those acquired by it, can be used to settle treaty claims. In a celebrated case in 1987, the Court of Appeal found in favour of the national Maori Council in its desire to restrain the potential privatisation of Crown assets involved in claims before the tribunal. In its findings, the Court spelled out its interpretation of the treaty's principles. It described the treaty as a 'partnership' between Crown and Maori, one which the judges felt the Crown had an active responsibility to promote (Temm 1990; Ward 1997a). It is this decision that Ranganui Walker, a prominent Maori writer and activist, hailed as 'pitch[ing] New Zealand firmly into the postcolonial era' (1990, p. 265).

IDENTITIES AND ARTICULATIONS

To explore some of the implications of Walker's claim, it is necessary to recall that colonial politics demonised Maori as the 'other', an uncivilised 'race' organised according to principles unacceptable to the coloniser, principles which had to be eradicated using policies of 'amalgamation' or 'integration'. This positioning was reproduced through a hegemonic discourse of colonisation, sedimenting it in Pakeha memory. In contrast, a postcolonial politics seeks to validate alternative memories. It is based on an unmasking of histories of appropriation and suppression, exposing the 'pliancy and persistence' (Wall 1997, p. 41) of cultural stereotypes derived from colonial oppositional forms (e.g. civilised-tribal; cultivated-wasteland) that have been empowered to legitimate dominance and inequality. It recognises the extents to which the categories of 'Pakeha' and 'Maori' can be destabilised through an enlarged perspective that both are differentiated and positioned in more complex ways (cf. Anderson 1998).

Recent censuses suggest that more New Zealanders are choosing to identify themselves as Maori; census forms are also now structured to allow for this. Until the 1986 census, a biological definition was used: only people of half or more Maori origin were deemed to be part of the Maori population for its purposes. In the 1986 census, self identification was legitimised; in and since the 1991 census all Maori have also been able to declare iwi affiliations. At the 1996 census, 15 per cent of the New Zealand population (523 000 people) was classified as being in the 'Maori ethnic group', about half identifying themselves as 'Maori' and half as identifying with Maori ethnicity and at least one other ethnicity. This was a 20 per cent increase on 1991.

How are the subjectivities of such Maori identities articulated in everyday life? The concept of 'articulation' can take a variety of forms. It can mean 'to express in words'; it can describe the process of 'linking together'; and it can denote the ways in which something is 'projected' into a wider world. The first of these senses is exemplified by more Maori choosing to name themselves as such, especially through the use of iwi affiliation. This has grown as the treaty claims process has developed, given that that process emphasises the role of iwi and hapu. Belonging to these groups was the manner by which the indigenous peoples identified themselves before colonial contact; identities expressed in this way do not rely on a shared subjectivity constructed in opposition to 'Pakeha'. Rather, iwi and hapu affiliation articulates a tie to a specific group or groups which links people to their ancestry and to the territory of the ancestors. These relations are shown very clearly in the iwi plates of the *New Zealand Historical Atlas* (McKinnon 1997). Hence it is becoming apparent to Pakeha, and to many Maori, that pre-colonial geographies are not forgotten and exist, to those that can read them, in parallel to re-made landscapes (James and Pawson 1995).

Over a quarter of Maori, however, do not declare any iwi affiliation in the census. These people are mostly urban dwellers who may not know their whakapapa (genealogy), or choose not to identify with it. This is one cause of the prolonged search by the Treaty of Waitangi Fisheries Commission for ways of allocating quota amongst Maori. Another has been the debate regarding whether the quota should be determined using methods based on iwi coastline length (in which case the South Island's Ngai Tahu would be a major beneficiary), according to population (in which case the Muriwhenua tribes for example would be) or some combination of the two. The Commission has argued that the treaty right to fish belongs only to traditionally recognised iwi hence, controversially, it has not been clear whether, or how, urban Maori would benefit (Price 1996; Sharp 1997). It has been suggested, however, that a contestable trust fund could be established for this purpose. This situation further warns against any uncritical notion of a singular Maori identity, as have ongoing vigorous discussions over the exercise and regulation of customary fishing rights.

An aspect of the second meaning of articulation, that of linking together, is the construct of 'partnership' that the Court of Appeal found to be at the heart of the treaty. This is a good example of Moore-Gilbert's warning (1997, p. 116) that 'the identities and positionings of coloniser and colonised [do not always] exist in stable and unitary terms which are absolutely distinct from, and necessarily in conflict with, each other'. Nonetheless, 'partnership' is an ambivalent term, potentially destabilising yet simultaneously reinforcing the binary codes of colonisation. Hence the Court found, following the tribunal, that the Crown had an active duty of protection towards Maori (Stokes 1992), but that 'the principles of the Treaty do not authorise unreasonable restrictions on the right of a duly elected government to follow its chosen policy' (in Ward 1997a, p. 2). This qualifier is of some moment given the adherence of New Zealand governments to neo-liberal frameworks of economic competitiveness since the mid-1980s. Nonetheless, the 'duty of protection' strongly implies that space must be created for the exercise of rangatiratanga, which Ward describes as 'legitimate scope for autonomous Maori action'. This, he considers, requires resources to 'underpin autonomy and self-determination at the individual and tribal level' and the 'establishment or re-establishment of mechanisms of consultation and empowerment' to give Maori a voice in 'the decision making institutions that affect their lives and their resources' (Ward 1997a, p. 34). In treaty terms, these are appropriate forms of redress, but inevitably will only be granted within limits acceptable to the Crown.

A measure of the extent to which such limits had broadened politically was the passage of *Te Ture Whenua Maori Act 1993*, which was described in parliament by the Minister of Maori Affairs as representing 'a significant departure from the agenda of dispossession, alienation and fragmentation that has characterised the trend of Maori land law in this country' (NZPD 1993, p. 13656). It strongly emphasises the retention of Maori land for Maori use (Bennion 1997). Nonetheless, the Crown's avowed goal of 'resolving of all major claims by the year 2000' (Waitangi Tribunal 1997b, p. 21) was set within a cap of one billion dollars, a policy—widely resented amongst Maori—known as the 'fiscal envelope' (Stokes 1996). Also, by 1995 very little land had been returned as a result of treaty negotiations. After that some significant movement did occur, particularly with the signing of the Waikato-Tainui settlement in 1995, and that with Ngai Tahu in 1997.

A third meaning of 'articulation', that of something projected into the wider world, is reflected in the postcolonial manner in which the Waikato-Tainui and Ngai Tahu settlements were made. Both involved comprehensive apologies from the Crown, in Maori and English, detailing its breaches of the treaty (as in the

Waikato Raupatu Claims Settlement Act 1995). This acknowledgment of grievances has been recognised as a key to moving away from preoccupations with the past towards a focus on projecting strategies to tackle the long-term consequences of marginalisation (Waitangi Tribunal 1997b, p. 6). Both settlements are being used as platforms for development. In the case of Ngai Tahu, an iwi corporate structure has been established with one arm to manage commercial activities which, in turn, supports a development arm to contribute to the educational, cultural, health and welfare needs of its people.

The tribunal recognises that the land and resources given in treaty settlements 'can help form an economic base and address some of the negative statistics pertaining to Maori' (Waitangi Tribunal 1997b, p. 6). It accedes to the view that a degree of aboriginal autonomy (Durie 1996) is a model for Maori development in the future, rather than the earlier colonially derived policies of amalgamation or integration. The guarantees of citizenship in the treaty have not, by any measure, produced a similar profile of educational, health or social outcomes for Maori as for Pakeha (Te Puni Kokiri 1996). Thus an alternative approach that allows Maori some self-determination in the resolution of such matters seems consistent with developing practices in international law and with 'partnership', given that the treaty's cession of sovereignty to the Crown was qualified by Maori retention of te tino rangatiratanga (Sharp 1997).

MULTIPLE IDENTITIES?

A postcolonial approach to understanding cultural relations in New Zealand seeks to unmask the nature of processes of domination, established historically but constantly reinscribed, and to examine the ways in which these have moulded memories and identities. In the last two decades New Zealand politics and jurisprudence have reflected the impact of formal decolonisation in the Third World, as well as settlements with First Nations in North America. Hence a new validity has been accorded to claims for aboriginal autonomy or at least to recognition of a greater range of possibilities for being Maori. The mechanisms developed (such as the Waitangi Tribunal) have greatly aided the insight that there are ways of reading the past other than that of the hegemonic discourse of colonisation, as well as revealing something of the complexities of coloniser/colonised relations and the manner in which these have been constantly renegotiated and reproduced.

Nonetheless, it would be foolish to imagine that processes of colonial power do not persist in postcolonial New Zealand just as they do elsewhere. The treaty claims policy has proceeded at the same time as a radical commitment by recent New Zealand governments to neo-liberal policies of economic and social reform. Following Giddens (1981), the state can therefore be both a force for emancipation as well as a defender of the interests of the powerful. A consequence of the neo-liberal policy regime and its resurrection of metaphors of competition has been sharply increased levels of unemployment with the dismantling of protection for industry and the reorganisation, and often sale, of state enterprises. As these were the very employment areas into which Maori were brought during the urbanisation of the 1950s and 1960s, job loss has hit them disproportionately hard (Pearson 1990; Britton et al. 1992). Therefore, just as Maori identities are being articulated in new ways, pre-existing levels of disadvantage are being reinforced (Te Puni Kokiri 1996; Sharp 1997). In turn, these changing material circumstances have led some Pakeha to reinvest in the stereotyping of Maori as unsuited to contemporary capitalistic ways of life.

Hence in New Zealand, as Jacobs suggests for Australia, 'the historical moment in which … neo-colonialism [is] superseded is elusive' (1996, p. 24). The colonial categories of 'Maori' and 'Pakeha' have not been decentred (Spoonley 1995). If anything, the treaty claims process has reinvigorated them. But this is occurring in ways that are destabilising both the categories and the nature of relations between them. There is a clear sense of Maori reinventing themselves as a strategy of decolonisation with, for example, the declaration of ancestrally-derived multiple subjectivities as well as new identities of autonomy. Increasingly Pakeha are prepared to identify themselves using that Maori term, that is, in a manner which is indigenous to New Zealand, rather than being refracted from an externally-sourced history of coloniser/colonised relations. Nonetheless, the term remains strongly contested by many other Pakeha (Spoonley 1995), for whom treaty claims may signify a threat to the 'othering' of Maori. There are, therefore, not just two New Zealands, but multiple New Zealands, with different memories, identities and places. Debate is opening up as to how to specify the complexities of the relations between them (Berg and Kearns 1996, 1997; Stokes 1996). This chapter concludes with just two examples of contemporary Maori/Pakeha relations, both portraying events less masked than the spectacle of the Commonwealth Games with which it opened.

In November 1997, representatives of Ngai Tahu and the Crown met in Kaikoura on the South Island's east coast to ratify the tribe's treaty settlement. Media coverage was muted and the politics of place went unexplained. The gathering, however, was at Takahanga marae, which had been completely recrafted by Maori seeking work skills after the local fishing industry had collapsed and railways employment had been cut in the late 1980s. Today Kaikoura is the site of Ngai Tahu's most conspicuous enterprise, a whale watching business started following completion of the marae refurbishment. Whale Watch Kaikoura has since won international awards and is responsible for turning what was essentially an unknown town into one visited by two hundred thousand tourists annually.

At the end of February 1995 large numbers of Whanganui Maori moved into Moutoa Gardens in the North Island city of Wanganui, a garrison town during the wars of the 1860s. The occupation lasted until mid May but ended without attaining its overt goal, which was the return of the gardens to iwi ownership (Moon 1996). It was fuelled, however, by anger at the government's fiscal envelope policy and the Waitangi Tribunal's slow progress with the Whanganui river claim. Media coverage was extensive and nationwide (Wall 1997), but rarely sought to contextualise the action and ignored the dramatic iconography of the site. The gardens are full of colonial symbols: one of these, a statue, was beheaded and later smashed. This statue was a depiction of John Ballance, the first Prime Minister in the Liberal government that undertook the extensive Maori land purchase programme of the 1890s.

ACKNOWLEDGMENTS

I am grateful to Garth Cant, Michele Slatter and Ben McBride for their comments on and discussions of earlier drafts, to Tim Nolan for drawing Figures 2.1 and 2.2 and to Kay Anderson for her encouragement in the re-invention of this essay for the new edition.

NOTE

1 As a guide to these debates, internet resources are invaluable. Waitangi Tribunal reports and the full summary of its national overview project (Ward 1997a, 1997b) are available at www.knowledge-basket.co.nz/waitangi/welcome.html. The website for Te Puni Kokiri (the Ministry of Maori Development) is at www.tpk.govt.nz/ For newspaper editorials and correspondence, see www.press.co.nz/

REFERENCES

Adams, P. 1977, *Fatal Necessity. British Intervention in New Zealand, 1830–1847*, Auckland University Press, Auckland.

AJHR 1863, 'Memorandum on Roads and Military Settlements in the Northern Island of New Zealand', A–8A, *Appendix to the Journals of the House of Representatives*, The Printing Office, Auckland.

Anderson, K. 1998, 'Sites of difference: beyond a cultural politics of race polarity', in *Cities of Difference*, eds R. Fincher & J. Jacobs, Guilford, New York, pp. 201–25.

Asher, G. & Naulls, D. 1987, *Maori Land*, New Zealand Planning Council, Planning Paper No. 29, Wellington.

Baines, D. 1985, *Migration in a Mature Economy. Emigration and Internal Migration in England and Wales, 1861–1900*, Cambridge University Press, Cambridge.

Belich, J. 1986, *The New Zealand Wars and the Victorian Interpretation of Racial Conflict*, Auckland University Press, Auckland.

Belich, J. 1996, *Making Peoples. A History of the New Zealanders, From Polynesian Settlement to the End of the Nineteenth Century*, Allen Lane, The Penguin Press, Auckland.

Bennion, T. 1997, 'Maori land', in *Guide to New Zealand Land Law*, A. Alston, T. Bennion, M. Slatter, R. Thomas & E. Toomey, Brooker's Ltd, Wellington, pp. 196–223.

Berg, L.D. & Kearns, R.A. 1996, 'Naming as norming: "race", gender, and the identity politics of naming places in Aotearoa/New Zealand', *Environment and Planning D: Society and Space*, vol. 14, no. 1, pp. 99–122.

Berg, L.D. & Kearns, R.A. (eds) 1997, '(Re)formations: cultural geographies of Aotearoa/New Zealand', special issue, *New Zealand Geographer*, vol. 53, no. 2.
Britton, S., Le Heron, R. & Pawson, E. (eds) 1992, *Changing Places in New Zealand. A Geography of Restructuring*, New Zealand Geographical Society, Christchurch.
Biggs, B. 1989, 'Humpty-Dumpty and the Treaty of Waitangi', in *Waitangi. Maori and Pakeha Perspectives of the Treaty of Waitangi*, ed. I.H. Kawharu, Oxford University Press, Auckland, pp. 300–12.
Brooking, T. 1996, *Lands for the People? The Highland Clearances and the Colonisation of New Zealand. A Biography of John McKenzie*, University of Otago Press, Dunedin.
Cant, G. 1995, 'Reclaiming land, reclaiming guardianship: the role of the Treaty of Waitangi in Aotearoa New Zealand', *Aboriginal History*, vol. 19, no. 1, pp. 79–108.
Cant, G. 1998, 'Memory recovered and a basket of remedies negotiated: a Pakeha perspective on the Ngai Tahu claim', *New Zealand Journal of Geography*, vol. 105, pp. 8–16.
Conway, D. 1987, *A Farewell to Marx. An Outline and Appraisal of his Theories*, Penguin, Harmondsworth.
Crosby, A.W. 1986, *Ecological Imperialism. The Biological Expansion of Europe, 900–1900*, Cambridge University Press, Cambridge.
Cumberland, K.B. 1941, 'A century's change: natural to cultural vegetation in New Zealand', *Geographical Review*, vol. 31, no. 4, pp. 529–54.
Darwin, C. 1901, *The Descent of Man and Selection in Relation to Sex* (2nd ed), John Murray, London.
Davidson, J.M. 1984, *The Prehistory of New Zealand*, Longman Paul, Auckland.
Driver, F. 1988, 'The historicity of human geography', *Progress in Human Geography*, vol. 12, no. 4, pp. 497–506.
Durie, E. 1996, 'Tribunal chairperson advocates "aboriginal autonomy"', *Te Manutukutuku*, no. 36, p. 3.
Feagin, J.R. & Smith, M.P. 1987, 'Cities and the new international division of labour: an overview', in *The Capitalist City. Global Restructuring and Community Politics*, eds M.P. Smith & J.R. Feagin, Blackwell, Oxford, pp. 3–34.
Gibbons, P. 1991, 'Non-fiction', in *The Oxford History of New Zealand Literature in English*, ed. T. Sturm, Oxford University Press, Auckland, pp. 25–104.
Giddens, A. 1981, *A Contemporary Critique of Historical Materialism*, Macmillan, London.
Hunn, J.K. 1961, *Report on Department of Maori Affairs*, Government Printer, Wellington.
Huxley, T.H. 1894, *Evolution and Ethics and Other Essays*, Macmillan, London.
Jacobs, J.M. 1996, *Edge of Empire. Postcolonialism and the City*, Routledge, London.
James, P. & Pawson, E. 1995, 'Contested places: the significance of the Motunui-Waitara claim to the Waitangi Tribunal', *Aboriginal History*, vol. 19, no. 2, pp. 111–25.
Kawharu, I.H. 1989, 'Introduction', 'Appendix' in *Waitangi. Maori and Pakeha Perspectives of the Treaty of Waitangi*, ed. I.H. Kawharu, Oxford University Press, Auckland, pp. x–xxiii, 316–21.
Keesing, R.M. 1989, 'Creating the past: custom and identity in the contemporary Pacific', *The Contemporary Pacific*, vol. 1, nos 1 & 2, pp. 19–42.
King, M. 1985, *Being Pakeha. An Encounter with New Zealand and the Maori Renaissance*, Hodder & Stoughton, Auckland.
Kingsbury, B. 1989, 'The Treaty of Waitangi: some international law aspects', in *Waitangi. Maori and Pakeha Perspectives of the Treaty of Waitangi*, ed. I.H. Kawharu, Oxford University Press, Auckland, pp. 121–57.
Kropotkin, P. 1885, 'What geography ought to be', *The Nineteenth Century*, vol. 18, pp. 940–56.

Kropotkin, P. 1914, *Mutual Aid. A Factor of Evolution*, Extending Horizons Books, Boston.

McGlone, M.S., Anderson, A.J. & Holdaway, R.N. 1994, 'An ecological approach to the Polynesian settlement of New Zealand', in *The Origins of the First New Zealanders*, ed. D.G. Sutton, Auckland University Press, Auckland, pp. 136–63.

McHugh, P. 1989, 'Constitutional theory and Maori claims', in *Waitangi. Maori and Pakeha Perspectives of the Treaty of Waitangi*, ed. I.H. Kawharu, Oxford University Press, Auckland, pp. 25–63.

McKinnon, M. (ed.) 1997, *New Zealand Historical Atlas*, David Bateman Ltd, Auckland in association with Historical Branch, Department of Internal Affairs, Wellington.

Miller, J. 1974, *Early Victorian New Zealand. A Study of Racial Tension and Social Attitudes 1839–1852*, Oxford University Press, Wellington.

Moon, P. 1996, *The Occupation of the Moutoa Gardens*, Auckland Institute of Technology, Auckland.

Moore-Gilbert, B. 1997, *Postcolonial Theory. Contexts, Practices, Politics*, Verso, London.

NZPD various dates, *New Zealand Parliamentary Debates*, Government Printer, Wellington.

Orange, C. 1987, *The Treaty of Waitangi*, Allen & Unwin/Port Nicholson Press, Wellington.

O'Regan, T. 1989, 'The Ngai Tahu Claim', in *Waitangi. Maori and Pakeha Perspectives of the Treaty of Waitangi*, ed. I.H. Kawharu, Oxford University Press, Auckland, pp. 234–62.

Pawson, E. & Cant, G. 1992, 'Land rights in historical and contemporary context', *Applied Geography*, vol. 12, no. 2, pp. 95–108.

Pearson, D. 1990, *A Dream Deferred. The Origins of Ethnic Conflict in New Zealand*, Allen & Unwin/Port Nicholson Press, Wellington.

Peet, R. 1985, 'The social origins of environmental determinism', *Annals of the Association of American Geographers*, vol. 75, no. 3, pp. 309–33.

Pepper, D. 1996, *Modern Environmentalism. An Introduction*, Routledge, London.

Pool, I. 1991, *Te Iwi Maori. A New Zealand Population, Past, Present & Projected*, Auckland University Press, Auckland.

Price, R.T. 1996, *Assessing Modern Treaty Settlements: New Zealand's 1992 Treaty of Waitangi (Fisheries Claims) Settlement and its Aftermath*, Macmillan Brown Working Paper Series, No. 3, Macmillan Brown Centre for Pacific Studies, University of Canterbury, Christchurch.

Ridley, M. 1996, *The Origins of Virtue*, Viking, London.

Roberts, M., Norman, W., Minhinnick, N., Wihongi, D. & Kirkwood, C. 1995, 'Kaitiakitanga: Maori perspectives on conservation', *Pacific Conservation Biology*, vol. 2, pp. 7–20.

Samuel, R. 1994, *Theatres of Memory, Vol 1: Past and Present in Contemporary Culture*, Verso, London.

Sharp, A. 1997, *Justice and the Maori. The Philosophy and Practice of Maori Claims in New Zealand since the 1970s*, 2nd edition, Oxford University Press, Auckland.

Sinclair, K. 1971, 'Why are race relations in New Zealand better than in South Africa, South Australia, or South Dakota?', *New Zealand Journal of History*, vol. 5, no. 2, pp. 121–7.

Sorrenson, M.P.K. 1981, 'Maori and Pakeha', in *The Oxford History of New Zealand*, ed. W.H. Oliver, Oxford University Press, Wellington, pp. 168–93.

Sorrenson, M.P.K. 1989, 'Towards a radical reinterpretation of New Zealand history: the role of the Waitangi Tribunal', in *Waitangi. Maori and Pakeha Perspectives of the Treaty of Waitangi*, ed. I.H. Kawharu, Oxford University Press, Auckland, pp. 158–78.

Spoonley, P. 1995, 'Constructing ourselves: the post-colonial politics of Pakeha' in *Justice and Identity. Antipodean Practices*, eds M. Wilson & A. Yeatman, Bridget Williams Books Ltd, Wellington, pp. 96–115.

Stokes, E. 1992, 'The Treaty of Waitangi and the Waitangi Tribunal: Maori claims in New Zealand', *Applied Geography*, vol. 12, no. 2, pp. 176–91.

Stokes, E. 1996, 'Maori identities' in *Changing Places. New Zealand in the Nineties*, eds R. Le Heron & E. Pawson, Longman Paul, Auckland, pp. 360–72.

Te Puni Kokiri, 1996, *Post Election Brief 1996: Brief to the Incoming Minister of Maori Affairs*, (www.tpk.govt.nz/).

Temm, P. 1990, *The Waitangi Tribunal. The Conscience of the Nation*, Random Century, Auckland.

Thomas, K. 1984, *Man and the Natural World. Changing Attitudes in England 1500–1800*, Penguin, Harmondsworth.

Travers, W.T.L. 1869, 'On the changes effected in the natural features of a new country by the introduction of civilised races', part I, *Transactions of the New Zealand Institute*, vol. 2, pp. 299–313.

Waitangi Tribunal, 1991, *The Ngai Tahu Report 1991, Volume 1*, Brooker and Friend Ltd, Wellington.

Waitangi Tribunal, 1996, *The Taranaki Report. Kaupapa Tuatahi*, GP Publications, Wellington.

Waitangi Tribunal, 1997a, *Muriwhenua Land Report*, GP Publications, Wellington.

Waitangi Tribunal, 1997b, *Business Strategy 1997. For the Provision of Services to the Waitangi Tribunal*, Department for Courts, Wellington.

Walker, R. 1982, 'Development from below: institutional transformation in a plural society', in *Development Tracks. The Theory and Practice of Community Development*, ed. I. Shirley, Dunmore Press, Palmerston North, pp. 69–89.

Walker, R. 1990, *Ka Whawhai Tonu Matou. Struggle Without End*, Penguin, Auckland.

Wall, M. 1997, 'Stereotypical constructions of the Maori "race" in the media', *New Zealand Geographer*, vol. 53, no. 2, pp. 40–5.

Ward, A. 1974, *A Show of Justice: Racial Amalgamation in Nineteenth Century New Zealand*, Australian National University Press, Canberra.

Ward, A. 1997a, *National Overview, Volume 1*, Waitangi Tribunal Rangahaua Whanui Series, GP Publications, Wellington.

Ward, A. 1997b, *National Overview, Volume 3*, Waitangi Tribunal Rangahaua Whanui Series, GP Publications, Wellington.

White, L. 1967, 'The historical roots of our ecologic crisis', *Science*, vol. 155, pp. 1203–7.

Williams, D. 1989, 'Te Tiriti o Waitangi—unique relationship between Crown and tangata whenua?', in *Waitangi. Maori and Pakeha Perspectives of the Treaty of Waitangi*, ed. I.H. Kawharu, Oxford University Press, Auckland, pp. 64–91.

Yoon, H-K. 1980, 'An analysis of place names for cultural features in New Zealand', *New Zealand Geographer*, vol. 36, no. 1, pp. 30–4.

Yoon, H-K. 1986, *Maori Mind, Maori Land. Essays on the Cultural Geography of the Maori People from an Outsider's Perspective*, Peter Lang, Berne.

Young, R.M. 1985, *Darwin's Metaphor: Nature's Place in Victorian Culture*, Cambridge University Press, Cambridge.

Constructing geographies

identities of inclusion

3

Elite landscapes as cultural (re)productions

the case of Shaughnessy Heights

James Duncan

INTRODUCTION

This chapter examines the way in which a particular elite landscape, Shaughnessy Heights in Vancouver, Canada, has been produced. Shaughnessy Heights is not simply a cultural production in the sense that it is the product of a particular group of people at a particular time and place. It is also, as will be argued below, a cultural (re)production in the double sense that it not only reproduces a cultural landscape model from another place and time (nineteenth-century England), but also reproduces a particular class distinctiveness and model of elite consumption within contemporary Canadian society. By tracing the history of Shaughnessy Heights from its founding by the railroad as a speculator suburb in the early twentieth century until the early 1980s when it was defined as a historic resource, the chapter will show how cultural production is enmeshed within a whole sociopolitical complex of development companies, zoning boards, city planning departments, and city council and heritage committees. Particular attention will be paid to the period of the late 1970s and early 1980s when the Shaughnessy Heights Property Owners' Association successfully steered a new and highly restrictive zoning code and neighbourhood design guidelines through the City Planning Department and City Council, effectively institutionalising an elite landscape model.[1] The final section of this chapter explores some working-class responses to the institutionalisation of this elite landscape model.

CULTURAL (RE)PRODUCTION

The term 'culture' is used in a variety of ways in the English language. One is to refer to 'high' culture or what is at times termed 'civilisation', a body of elite knowledge or canon encompassing what is thought to be most valuable in art, literature and social mores. Such knowledge is transmitted by an intellectual elite both within universities (in Western Civilisation courses, for example) and outside such formal institutions in the form of books, films and lectures on literary and art criticism for an educated public. A second notion of culture, the one that concerns us in this chapter, is a more democratic notion. In this second usage, which is drawn from twentieth-century anthropology, culture is not the exclusive preserve of elites within a society, but something in which all members of a society participate equally. It is the way of life of a people. In this usage, for example, a night out at the pub is every bit as much a part of English culture as the plays of Shakespeare or the paintings of Constable. Although this chapter subscribes to this more democratic view of culture, it is important to qualify in a small but important way the manner in which we think about it. Most people consider culture something that we simply 'have' because we are all born into a particular culture (and social class, for that matter) that existed before we came into the world and will continue long after we die. It is precisely this collective quality of culture that makes it appear to be something external to us as individuals. It can be argued, however, that it is analytically more useful to think of culture as something that we actively (re)produce rather than something external to us.

What are the implications of people (re)producing rather than simply having culture? The major one is that it allows us to deal with the question of agency; that is, people are not portrayed by social science as passive carriers of culture, rather their culture is something that they not only learn, but also sustain, defend, resist and even create or reject. When viewed in this way, we can see that culture as a system of ideas is inextricable from the social structuration of a society and from political process. For example, we can see the interlinkage between cultural ideas of race and gender on the one hand and political practice on the other in current debates in the United States over the role of women or African Americans within the society. Similarly, we can see cultural definitions of home and neighbourhood being worked out politically and economically in city councils, zoning board meetings and lawsuits between property owners.

This chapter explores the (re)production of culture by examining the behaviour of an elite group in Vancouver, Canada. While all groups engage in such (re)production, the production process is more clearly discernible at some times than at others. For example, during times of conflict, when a group feels threatened, cultural production processes which are normally submerged from view and operate at a deep level can rise closer to the surface. At such times people highlight cultural assumptions in order to frame arguments against their adversaries. During such periods of 'foregrounding' or, to use Giddens' (1979, p. 5) terms, during the shift from practical to discursive knowledge, cultural assumptions are open to review and contest both within the group that holds the views and from others. While cultural assumptions rise closer to the surface during such times of conflict, they nevertheless remain partially submerged, as people tend to develop an awareness of the strategic effect of their arguments on others and thus selectively highlight or mask their beliefs in order to forward their cause. This can be illustrated by considering the attempt by the board members of the Shaughnessy Heights Property Owners' Association to convince a largely sympathetic City Planning Department and a rather less sympathetic City Council to support their plan to rezone the neighbourhood and institute design guidelines on all future development. Until the members of the board of the Property Owners' Association met with planning officials, they operated with a largely unarticulated understanding of their own cultural assumptions about what their neighbourhood should look like and how best to institute changes. The meetings with city officials forced them to articulate their assumptions and then refine them in light of how they thought city officials would react to them. In meetings between board members and city officials, there was an initial foregrounding of cultural assumptions by board members, but also a subsequent repackaging of these ideas in order to make them acceptable to both planners and city councillors who did not necessarily share all of these assumptions. The result of this process was a cultural production, a neighbourhood that conformed to a particular elite style which is termed 'Anglophile'. This style will be examined in more detail later.

If the notion of 'having' culture seems too passive to capture the contested nature of cultural process, how might we conceptualise it more effectively? For our purposes perhaps the most satisfactory conception of culture has been put forward by Raymond Williams (1982). He (p. 13) defines culture as 'the signifying system through which necessarily (though among other means) a social order is communicated, reproduced, experienced and explored'. He argues that cultural practice and cultural production are not 'simply derived from an otherwise constituted social order but are themselves major elements in its constitution' (1982, pp. 12–13). Williams distinguishes cultural production from other kinds of social organisation such as the political or economic systems and from more specific systems of signs while emphasising that, as a signifying system, culture is embedded in other systems as a constitutive component. Williams cites dwellings as an example of this interpenetration. While dwellings primarily satisfy the need for shelter, they also signify a particular kinship or family system and further signify internal social differentiations (1982, p. 211). In certain cases, especially among elites, the signifying factor overrides the normally primary factor of shelter. There are several advantages to Williams' definition of culture. One is that cultural systems, although analytically distinct from social and political systems, are conceptualised as dialectically related to the latter. Another is that such a definition emphasises both the systematic quality of culture (as a structured system of signs) and its processual quality as something which is temporal, dynamic, contested and reaffirmed.

ANGLOPHILIA AS A CULTURAL SYSTEM

We will now elaborate upon the rather abstract notion of culture as a signifying system. In the case of the Shaughnessy elite, the system of signs is adopted from a nineteenth-century English upper-class cultural model. This system of signs is expressed in different media: in language, in dress, in demeanour, in institutions such as social clubs and private schools, and in the residential landscape.

This chapter will focus upon the landscape, not only because it is an essential part of geography, but because it is one of the central (and for an individual and the city government the costliest) elements in a cultural system. Landscapes are ordered assemblages of objects which act as a signifying system through which a social system is communicated, reproduced, experienced and explored. By acting as a signifying system a landscape does more than simply fulfil obvious, mundane, functional requirements. For example, residential dwellings do more than provide shelter from the elements. Rather, by encoding within a landscape various conventional signs of such things as group membership and social status, individuals are able to tell morally charged 'stories' about themselves and the social structure of the society in which they live. A number of authors, including Firey (1945), Lowenthal and Prince (1965), Duncan (1973), Duncan and Duncan (1980, 1984), Pratt (1981), Hugill (1986) and Wyckoff (1990) have argued that landscapes are a major repository of symbols of social status.

The importance of the residential landscape as a symbol of individual or group identity varies cross-culturally (Duncan 1981, 1985; Rapoport 1981). In highly individualistic capitalist societies such as Australia, Canada and the United States, where status is largely achieved rather than being ascribed by membership in a caste or kin group, such as in South Asia, a major means of communicating social identity is through the private 'conspicuous' consumption of objects. The dwelling, together with the status level of the neighbourhood, is one of the principal symbols of social status. The creation and preservation of residential landscapes serve as part of the vehicle through which the integrity of a social group is maintained. Landscapes and the other elements of a culture are used to define membership in a social group through reaffirmation of members' values, and exclusion of non-members. The process not only involves conscious sociopolitical action, but also the unintended consequences of collective action based on unarticulated, 'taken-for-granted' values. A residential landscape helps in the reproduction of a class or status group because it is an important repository of symbols of social class and ethnic heritage. Increasingly subtle variations allow it to continue to serve this function for a particular social group.

Having reviewed the role played by the landscape in a cultural system, let us now outline a particular cultural model (the Anglophile), then examine the manner in which the Shaughnessy elite of Vancouver have made use of this signifying system and the way the economic and political systems of the city have interpenetrated it. At the heart of this landscape system stands the English country house and garden. Of course the real English country house and garden as a cultural system are not simply mortar, stone, wooden beams and overgrown perennial beds, but a complex web of social and place relations which could not be exactly reproduced outside England. What can be created, however, is a simulation, a sign system which stands for an emulated system of relations. However, it is actually more complicated than this. There is no simple relation between the simulated and the authentic, as the nineteenth- and early twentieth-century English version which serves as an original for the twentieth-century Vancouver version is itself a simulation of an earlier version with its own somewhat different symbolic code.

In the late eighteenth century, the urban English upper and upper middle classes adopted an increasingly romantic view of the countryside and country pursuits. These attitudes became formalised in the nineteenth century in the form of idealised country residences situated on the peripheries of English cities (Lowenthal and Prince 1965, pp. 189–90). The effect sought was the picturesque, a landscape that evoked a mood of nostalgia for the rural past. Within an urban context, the picturesque had the qualities of closeness, variety and intimacy and the ever-recurring contrasts of tall and low, large and small, wide and narrow, straight and crooked, closes and retreats and odd leafy corners (Pevsner 1957, p. 105).

Architects and landscape architects sought to make the new look like the old and blend unobtrusively into a 'naturalised' setting (Girouard 1981, p. 228). During the latter half of the nineteenth century, nostalgia for the life of the gentry was signified within English cities by 'Old English' style houses. By the early twentieth century this nostalgia was manifested in the rage for 'Tudor' style houses and diffused from urban elites to the more modest structures of the middle classes (Wiener 1981, p. 66). Coupled with this Tudor revival was a dramatic increase of interest in the preservation of old buildings. The result of these two trends was 'a generalised historicity and rusticity—the purpose of which was to convey a feeling of old rural England, rather than to adhere to any particular and consistent style' (Wiener 1981, p. 650). According to Raymond Williams (1973, p. 248), this yearning for an idealised past on the part of generations of upper- and middle-class English people was deeply ironic because in the late nineteenth and twentieth centuries in England 'there was almost an inverse proportion … between the relative importance of the working rural economy and the cultural importance of rural ideas'.

When the country house style was transferred to England's colonies and former colonies it became doubly coded, signifying not only the status of gentry which it did in England, but also an abstract concept of Englishness which was seen by Anglophile elites as the most prestigious ethnic identity. Such a landscape model is to be found in such geographically diverse locations as hill stations in India (Kenny 1995) and Sri Lanka (Duncan 1989), the suburb of Toorak in Melbourne, Australia (Ley 1993), many major cities around the United States (Hugill 1986; Wyckoff 1990) and most of the large cities of Canada (Ley 1993).

SHAUGHNESSY HEIGHTS AS A CULTURAL (RE)PRODUCTION 1907–83

Shaughnessy Heights serves as a fine example of how Anglophilia as a cultural system is fundamentally interconnected with the economic and political systems of a society. For example, the English cultural model was initially used in Vancouver to achieve a particular end, the sale of land by the Canadian Pacific Railroad (CPR) to an elite. Increasingly, however, this link between a particular Anglophile cultural model and the economic goals (profits for CPR from the sale of land) which that cultural model was designed to support could only be sustained by enmeshing it within a political framework both at the provincial and municipal levels. CPR sought to protect the value of its undeveloped land in the area by restricting the free market in land through zoning regulations. By the 1970s, however, the relationship between this cultural model, economic goals and the local political framework had been redefined. The Anglophile houses in Shaughnessy were no longer a way for the railway to make money. Rather, they were seen as part of the heritage of the city of Vancouver and therefore something to be protected through legislative action from an economic rationality that argued that a greater profit was often to be made by subdividing large lots and tearing down early twentieth-century mansions.

In 1884 CPR was granted 2428 ha (6000 acres) of land in Vancouver in exchange for extending the transcontinental railroad to that fledgling port city. In 1907 CPR began clearing 140 ha (345 acres) immediately to the south of

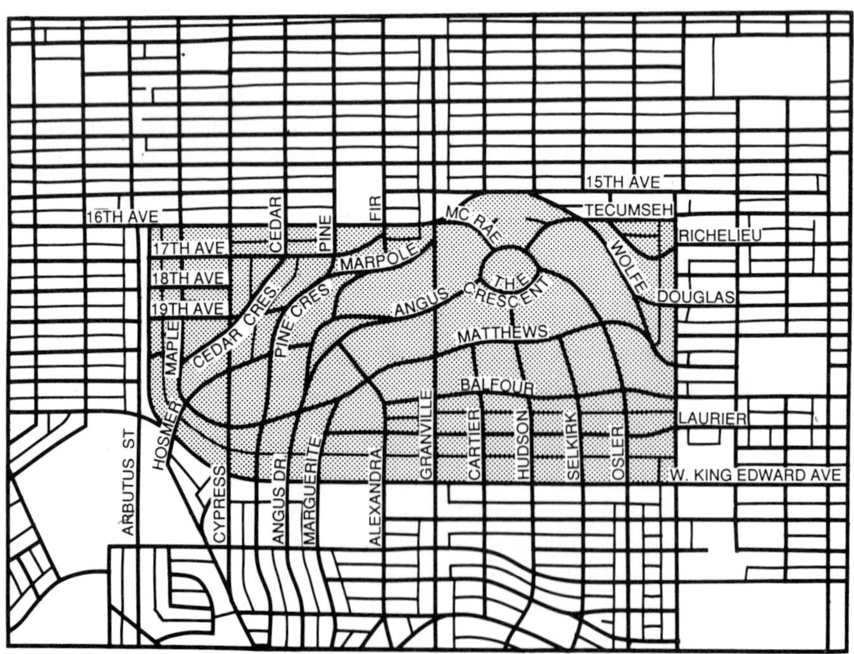

FIGURE 3.1 Map of Shaughnessy Heights (the shaded area represents Shaughnessy Heights).

the central business district which it hoped to convert into the most prestigious residential suburb in the city. The suburb was to be named Shaughnessy Heights after the current president of CPR, Lord Thomas Shaughnessy. The railroad then retained the services of Frederick Todd, a landscape architect from Montreal who was greatly influenced by the work of Frederick Law Olmsted, the American landscape architect whose romantic English-inspired 'country in the city' designs were the rage during the latter part of the nineteenth century. Taking advantage of the hilly topography of the subdivision, streets were laid out in a sinuous fashion to follow contours, and sewer and water lines were built. The lots ranged in size from 810 m^2 (one-fifth of an acre) to 6000 m^2 (1.5 acres) and the area was transected by several handsome boulevards and a 2 ha (5 acre) park (Figure 3.1). It is estimated that before a single house was built $1 million were spent on developing the land. CPR planned, however, to recover this sum many times over through the sale of lots to the wealthy citizens of this rapidly growing city. The railway threw the full weight of its prestige behind the development of Shaughnessy Heights in order to make it the kind of high status Anglophile environment that would appeal to businesspeople and professionals. Streets were named after four of its directors, prominent local figures and two Prime Ministers—one Canadian and one British. In 1909, to show his confidence in the project, Richard Marpole, the local head of CPR, built the first house in the area.

Land was sold in the subdivision for $25 000 per hectare ($10 000 per acre), a large sum of money for undeveloped land in those days. Only single-family dwellings were permitted, with a minimum price of $6000. In order to entice investors to build in Shaughnessy Heights, CPR loaned buyers 90 per cent of the price of the land (at 6 per cent for eight years) and 66 per cent of the price of the building (up to a maximum of $5000). Altogether the company set aside the huge sum of $5 million for loans on homes. Such loans were, however, only available if the plans for the building met the standards set by CPR. Building plans were carefully checked, not only to ensure that they adhered to the price guidelines, but also for their overall appearance including positioning on the lot, house style and quality of building materials. Thus, from the beginning there were design controls on housing which would ensure that the house and lot would conform to the English country house style. The only zoning restrictions at this time, however, were that the area remain single-family residential. The result was a residential area of very large lots with Victorian and Tudor style mansions, many of which had gate houses and stables (Figure 3.2). The average lot size was nearly 1500 m^2 (16 000 ft^2), compared to 370 m^2 (4000 ft^2) for single-family detached housing in middle-class sections of the city. Approximately half of the Shaughnessy Heights houses are still over 370 m^2 (4000 ft^2) in area. In other words, these houses exceed the average lot size of nearby middle-class areas.

By 1914, 243 houses had been completed, approximately 40 per cent of the present stock. The company sought to protect its investment by safeguarding the exclusive nature of the development and its control over the area's appearance. To achieve this, in 1914 it paid for a group of Shaughnessy

FIGURE 3.2 A Shaughnessy mansion.

residents to travel to Victoria in order to convince the provincial government to allow Shaughnessy Heights to break away from the municipality of Point Grey (then an independent suburb of Vancouver) and become a separate municipality. Point Grey also sent a delegation to oppose the secession. Although the provincial legislature rejected the proposal for secession, it created the Shaughnessy Heights Settlement Act which allowed the area to become a separate ward of Point Grey with the important proviso that taxes collected in the area were to be used solely for its benefit. These funds were not only spent on schools, but also on maintaining highly manicured parks and streetscapes (Figure 3.3).

Although in 1922 Point Grey became the first municipality in Canada to pass zoning regulations, these controls were not seen as restrictive enough by CPR. The railway, therefore, once again turned to the provincial government which in December 1922 passed the Shaughnessy Heights Building Restriction Act, removing zoning control from Point Grey and creating a special provincial zoning prohibiting subdivision. The Act further stipulated that any resident was entitled to take out an injunction against a zoning violator. It was correctly assumed that the threat of legal action by CPR or affluent residents would dissuade any would-be violators. To further safeguard the Anglophile single-family character of the area, which was seen as crucial to maintaining high property values, CPR placed restrictive covenants on Shaughnessy deeds forbidding multiple-family occupancy of homes. All these controls were apparently secured with the approval of residents, who saw a convergence of their interests with those of CPR. By the end of the 1920s CPR had created a housing development which was not only a financial success but which was increasingly seen by its residents as an important part of their status as the elite of this growing western Canadian city. As such, the

FIGURE 3.3 A Shaughnessy streetscape.

Anglophile landscape created to make money for CPR simultaneously became a part of the cultural reproduction of the Vancouver elite.

The Depression, however, brought to an end both the period of growth and the era of harmony between the interests of CPR and property owners. As a result of the financial crisis, many prominent residents were forced to file for bankruptcy and sell their mansions. Although property values declined to a fraction of their earlier market value, taxes remained at their previous levels, contributing to the financial crisis. Residents began to take in boarders illegally and many single-family homes were converted to rooming houses. In 1938 the Shaughnessy Heights Property Owners' Association (SHPOA) was formed, with the primary goal of combating the conversion of mansions to multiple-occupancy units. The leaders of SHPOA were successful businessmen and professionals who, unlike some of their neighbours who had fallen on hard times, were financially secure and committed to the area as a place to live. One of SHPOA's first acts was to file a petition in 1939 with the provincial government to extend the Building Restriction Act to 1970. The provincial government not only accepted this proposal, but granted SHPOA the right to register complaints against and prosecute violators of the act.

The advent of the Second World War, however, further undermined SHPOA's goal of maintaining a financially stable single-family area of large houses. Because of the housing shortage in Canada during the war years, in 1942 the federal government permitted the establishment of multi-family dwellings in all areas previously zoned as single-family. This law accelerated what the Depression had started—the wholesale conversion of single-family houses into rooming houses. Furthermore, there were subdivisions of large properties. After the war SHPOA appealed to the provincial government to ban all existing rooming houses, but the government compromised and banned all conversions after 1955. Any single-family houses converted before that date could remain as legal non-conforming uses. A survey conducted in 1957 showed that 30 per cent of the houses in the area were multiple-occupancy. As these represented a disproportionate number of the largest mansions, SHPOA was concerned that this severely compromised the elite nature of the area and thus the claims of the residents to high status.

During the post-war economic recovery, Shaughnessy regained a good deal of its prestige and popularity with executives. The area was convenient to the city business area and house prices, which had still not recovered from the effects of the Depression, were also affordable. Existing houses and undeveloped building lots sold quickly. Most of the houses that were built during these decades, though large by city standards, were smaller than the mansions built forty years earlier. Many of these large bungalows were built on smaller one-fifth of an acre lots, creating a discernible shift in landscape aesthetics away from the English country house look and towards a new Californian model which was more middle-class. With the return of prosperity, rooming houses were slowly reconverted to single-family housing. Although members of SHPOA were delighted by these recovered mansions, they were dismayed by the increase in smaller houses which in their opinion undermined the 'exclusive' character of the area. Once again, SHPOA discovered its limits. As long as minimum lot size was adhered to there was little the Association could do to prevent the appearance of bungalows or Spanish colonials. For the Anglophile elite, different models of housing undermined the image that they wished to foster in the area. However, SHPOA members could exercise vigilance in detecting violations of the zoning code. Members actually patrolled the neighbourhood looking for any signs of building activity or code violations. Any suspected violators were reported to SHPOA's legal committee or directly to the provincial government.

In 1970 the Building Restriction Act expired and the City of Vancouver assumed responsibility for Shaughnessy's zoning. The City established a new zoning category for Shaughnessy, setting the minimum lot size at 882 m^2 (9500 ft^2) and the minimum frontage at 26 m (85 ft). It was hoped both by SHPOA and the City Planning Department that this would provide greater protection against subdivision than had previously existed. However, as the average lot size in the heart of Shaughnessy was 3950 m^2 (42 500 ft^2) and the average frontage 47.5 m (156 ft), there still remained the possibility of subdivision. As an added safeguard, therefore, the City's Director of Planning was given some discretion over subdivision. Since SHPOA felt that the City in the past had been insufficiently vigorous in prosecuting zoning violators, it convinced the City to change its charter to allow SHPOA itself to prosecute violators. As it turned out, even these extraordinary provisions were not sufficient to preserve all of the houses and large lots.

Although the pace of demolition and subdivision was slowed, the activities could not be halted and after six years of working within the context of the 1970 zoning category, SHPOA decided that a new zoning law would better conserve what remained of the Anglophile landscape. To this end, in 1976 a private firm was commissioned by SHPOA to propose a new plan for Shaughnessy that would reflect the members' Anglophile landscape taste and desire to retain the district's elite Anglophile character. A modified version of this plan was sent to the City Planning Department in 1978. The Planning Department, which favoured neighbourhood self-determination and heritage preservation, was broadly supportive of the proposal and recommended that a Working Committee be formed to assist the Planning Department in drawing up a new Shaughnessy Plan. This Working Committee was composed of ten members of SHPOA, three owners of rooming houses, two tenants, a member of the Vancouver Heritage Advisory Committee and a representative of the City Planning Department. The composition of the committee, which had the approval of the City Planning Department, was a clear acknowledgment of the pre-eminence of SHPOA in Shaughnessy. Its members numerically dominated the committee, thereby ensuring that the final results would reflect their views. Of the three owners of boarding houses, only one, a rather timid person who was treated with benign condescension by the members of SHPOA, attended regularly. The tenants on the committee had been recruited by SHPOA and did not appear to represent the true interest of tenants in the area, which normally would be the retention of affordable rental accommodation.

Before discussing the workings of the committee it is important to establish the sociopolitical context of these deliberations. The immediate political context during the early to mid-1970s was a City Council dominated by The Electors' Action Movement (TEAM), a liberal political party whose platform was the 'liveable city'. It included a concern both on the part of the City Council and the TEAM-appointed Director of Planning for the issues of quality of life, landscape aesthetics and neighbourhood protection. The 'Goals for Vancouver' survey of 5000 people in 1979 sampled attitudes in order to help set the goals for city planning in the 1980s. The responses to this survey placed great emphasis upon aesthetics, preserving green spaces, supporting the individual character and identity of neighbourhoods, and preserving 'heritage and character' areas. The Planning Department and the City Council adopted these goals, which well-suited the arguments about Shaughnessy that SHPOA had put forward during the previous forty years. The Association could argue that its desire for heritage preservation and green space was not merely in its own interest, but was endorsed by the city as a whole. Seventy years earlier, when the first house was built by CPR in what was clearly a development suburb, the cultural model of Anglophilia had been a marketing strategy designed to sell land. By 1979 the relationship between cultural and economic forces in Shaughnessy Heights had shifted so that the development of imitation English houses had become an important part of Vancouver's heritage to be preserved for the citizenry at large. An aesthetic value that had been pressed into service for economic motives had entered the realm of high culture and was to be protected from the economic sphere (developers who wished to make a profit from subdivision and the demolition of large mansions). It was only by tightly enmeshing this culture model of Anglophilia into a political framework of zoning laws, heritage committees and design guidelines that it could be saved from what were portrayed as unrestrained economic forces. Of course, economic forces were still very much implicated in this cultural model. Large mansions in Shaughnessy cost millions of dollars and zoning controls provided a kind of hidden subsidy to the residents of the area, many of whom could not have afforded to be surrounded by such a landscape had there existed an unrestricted market in land.

If liveability was on Vancouver's political agenda in the late 1970s, there was also the countervailing reality of a housing shortage of near crisis proportions. A rental vacancy rate consistently below 1 per cent and a shortage of land for building were raising housing costs to unprecedented levels. Shaughnessy was characterised by low housing densities on land near the heart of the city. It was uncertain whether arguments over green space, heritage and neighbourhood protection would prevail over arguments for more plentiful and affordable housing.

The very general goals of the Shaughnessy Planning Committee were to try to preserve the 'English country house in the city' appearance of the area and maintain its single-family residential status. This overall goal implied several subgoals: first, to halt subdivision of large lots; second, to provide financial incentives to owners of the largest mansions so that they would not demolish them; third, to encourage owners of rooming houses to convert them either to single-family structures or to 'strata title' tenure so that houses would remain owner-occupied and the outside appearance of the house would remain unchanged; and fourth, to create a set of guidelines so that all new building in the area would conform to SHPOA's English country house ideal.

Since the appearance of the landscape was of crucial importance to the SHPOA committee members, their attention focused on the content of the proposed design guidelines and its implementation. The guidelines controlled everything from house style and siting on the lot to types of windows and planting. The issue of responsibility for ensuring the guidelines were followed was the subject of intense debate. In the end it was decided that SHPOA members were to compose the majority of a design committee, thereby guaranteeing that the English country house ideal would be reflected in all new development in the area.

Much of the discussion in the planning meetings revealed the 'old money' values of SHPOA members, set against newcomers whom they considered to be nouveaux riches bringing new housing tastes to Shaughnessy and thereby threatening the status of the old elite. One of the committee members described the type of landscape she wanted to maintain in Shaughnessy: 'We are striving for tasteful seclusion, privacy, trees, [and] setbacks. We hate tacky bungalows with their open lots. They look functional, like they are for living and nothing else. We love old Tudors, Victorians, things which are authentic.' However, for political reasons in the official minutes of their meetings and in the final draft of the plan to be presented to the City Council, the committee members tried their best to downplay the image of the area as a haven of the upper class and portray it as a park-like, 'heritage' landscape for all Vancouver citizens to enjoy. As one member put it: 'We should decrease in emphasis the "well to do exclusiveness" of the area [which appeared in an early draft of the plan]. Is this good public relations? Does it add to our claim of historic preservation? We must present Shaughnessy as an area of historical significance to people in Burnaby [an outer suburb], etc. Perhaps the mention of rich people will turn them off.' A second member of SHPOA agreed: 'Yes, remove the reference to helping people maintain large properties. The press will pick this up as a preoccupation of ours. Do you want to see this printed in the press?' A planner for the city who attended some of the committee meetings made a welcome suggestion that showed his empathy for the SHPOA point of view: 'If you have an 8000 square foot house, you don't want one 5000 square feet of the same height behind it. Probably you want a smaller house beside it that would look like a coach house. This then wouldn't spoil the character of the 8000 foot house.' The committee was impressed and members began to espouse the idea. At a later meeting one said: 'We want coach houses next to large houses to make it appear like an estate.'

This argument, when combined with the Planning Department and City Council's strong belief in neighbourhood self-determination, made it difficult for even a left of centre Council to reject the Shaughnessy plan. The result was that in 1982 the City Council met and approved the Shaughnessy plan which, in the face of a citywide housing crisis, increased the minimum lot size in the area and displaced several hundred lower-income renters.

The upper-class members of SHPOA did not invent the ideologies of the liveable city, green space, architectural heritage, neighbourhood protection and local control. These had been espoused primarily by middle-class liberal academics, bureaucrats and politicians with an eye to improving the quality of life in middle- and working-class districts. SHPOA skilfully employed this ideology and its sometimes contradictory social consequences because it genuinely believed in the importance of green space, heritage and the right to self-determination. SHPOA members found the ideology of the liveable city congenial not simply because it was expedient for them, but because they recognised in it old English upper-class ideas about the importance of aesthetics, locality and history. In other words, the ideology of the liveable city had made traditional upper-class landscape tastes and ideals acceptable to the political left, centre and right alike. The exclusionary class interest of SHPOA had been intentionally masked by a rhetoric of the general interest, incidentally ensuring that the liveable city would continue to be more liveable for some than for others.[2]

SHAUGHNESSY HEIGHTS: THE VIEW FROM THE WORKING CLASS

It is highly tempting, based upon the Shaughnessy story, to conclude that a group of upper-class residents manipulated liberal planners and politicians and that the big losers, despite the rhetoric of the general good, were the working-class people who were spoken for by these groups but who were not heard from directly. The voices of the working class reveal another side of the (re)production of elite landscape that in some respects is infinitely-more disturbing than the (at times) rather cynical manipulation of middle-class ideologies of green space, heritage and participation by an elite.

When fifty working-class residents of the predominantly low-income east side of the city were asked whether they felt that it was in the interest of the city as a whole to preserve and enhance the character of Shaughnessy, an astonishing 79 per cent said it was. Why, in the face of a housing crisis, would so many working-class people want to preserve something that did not appear to be in their material interests? The answer is complex. The residents who favoured the preservation of the character of Shaughnessy were able to articulate very little specifically about the history or even the components of Anglophile landscape taste, but they nevertheless recognised it as a general elite model and thought it was beautiful and worth preserving. In a similar fashion, although they knew little of the details of the lifestyle of the Shaughnessy elite, they supported the idea of reproducing that elite culture. Landscape symbolism, it can be argued, helps us to understand these working-class attitudes towards the elite. For these members of the working class, Shaughnessy was not simply a material thing, a neighbourhood of mansions on one and a half acre lots. The landscape symbolically performed several functions. First, it provided a focus for working-class pride in the beauty of Vancouver. Although they infrequently passed through the neighbourhood, as residents of the city they could vicariously share in the Shaughnessy image, thus underpinning the official Planning Department view that Shaughnessy is part of every resident's heritage irrespective of social class. Second, it mediated between the reality of their working-class lives and the optimistic ideology of individualism so dominant in North America today. Shaughnessy did not raise issues of class conflict or a sense of social injustice as it might in some societies, but evoked individualistic feelings about aspirations, opportunities and personal worthiness. An important part of the ideology of western society is that anyone, no matter how humble his or her origins, can become wealthy. Informants expressed these sentiments when asked about preserving Shaughnessy. Some felt that it should be retained for its symbolic value. As one person said, 'Shaughnessy serves as an example to others.' The landscape conveys the promise of social mobility. A number discussed this theme in terms of a dream. One said, 'Shaughnessy is the last of the dream areas', suggesting that although it is not available to them in reality, it is in fantasy. Yet the notion of a 'dream world' has a double meaning—part fantasy and part guide to what the future might hold. Some seemed to argue that it was a right of working-class people such as themselves that such places exist. 'People are entitled to their dream', one person said, while another said 'It would be awful to take away the dream of thousands of people'.

A second theme is the belief that the class structure of society is natural and just. Some even see it as based upon the differential worthiness of individuals. 'Of course there are class differences', one woman said, 'that's the way it has to be'. Another said, '... people must accept that some will have a higher standard of living'. There is a belief that the class system is just and people get what they deserve. 'Rich people worked hard for what they got and shouldn't have it taken away from them', another person said. The explanations were highly individualistic rather than social. Nothing was seen other than personal failings. As one person said, 'If people really wanted to get into Shaughnessy, they could'. Another impugned the motives of those whom she believed to be opposed to preserving the area by saying, 'People who don't want to preserve the area are simply envious of the rich'. Another argued against change by saying 'Increasing the density, especially with town houses, would mean lower income people would come in and that would take away from its niceness'.

The above statements bear a strong similarity to what Sennett and Cobb (1973) found when they interviewed poor people in the United States about success. The authors argued that the psychological impact on the poor of an ideology of individual responsibility for position in the class system was very great. In a society where it is believed that anyone can succeed if he or she has the personal qualities, those who remained at the lower end of the class system perceived themselves as personally responsible for their failure. They believed that failure stemmed not from a system of institutionalised inequality and differential access to opportunity but from individually generated inequality. Sennett and Cobb discuss the feelings of unworthiness associated with a lack of success in America. They call this the 'hidden injuries of class'. The other side of this coin is what might be termed the 'hidden benefits of class' as derived by a Shaughnessy elite who can gain the support of liberal planners and city politicians for their Anglophile landscape tastes because such tastes have been incorporated into the discourse of liberal planning under the guise of heritage preservation and green space. As such, public officials intervene on behalf of the residents to preserve a landscape and thereby reproduce an elite. The working class are also implicated in this process of reproducing an elite. By supporting the idea that Shaughnessy is part of the heritage of all of the residents of the city and by preserving it as a fantasy of upward mobility, they help ensure its preservation as a reality.

CONCLUSION

This chapter has traced the history of a particular cultural production, an elite neighbourhood in Vancouver, Canada. In doing so we have seen that people do not simply possess culture, but must struggle over it, and that this is true even for the dominant classes. Shaughnessy Heights is not simply a cultural production (a material landscape) interpenetrated by political and economic structures; it is also a cultural (re)production in that it reproduces the meaning of belonging to an Anglophile elite in a western Canadian city. Finally, as shown by bringing in the voices of the working class, Shaughnessy as a class production also serves to reproduce class distinctions within Canadian society and also to mystify the nature of class relations in a capitalist society.

NOTES

1 This case study is primarily based on two years of participant observation (1979–81) at meetings between the First Shaughnessy Citizens' Working Committee and the Vancouver City Planning Department.
2 Editors note: For an account of the extension of Shaughnessy's contested character into the 1990s, see Mitchell (1997).

ACKNOWLEDGMENTS

I am indebted to the editors of this volume and to Nancy Duncan and Joanne Sharp for comments on earlier drafts of this chapter.

REFERENCES

Duncan, J.S. 1973, 'Landscape taste as a symbol of group identity: a Westchester County Village', *Geographical Review*, vol. 63, pp. 334–55.

Duncan, J.S. 1981, 'From container of women to status symbol: the impact of social structure on the meaning of the house', in *Housing and Identity: Cross-Cultural Perspectives,* ed. J.S. Duncan, Croom Helm, London, pp. 36–59.

Duncan, J.S. 1985, 'The house as symbol of social structure: notes on the language of objects among collectivistic groups', in *Home Environments. Human Behaviour and Environment: Advances in Theory and Research*, eds I. Altman & C.M. Werner, vol. 8, Plenum New York, pp. 133–52.

Duncan, J.S. 1989, 'The power of place in Kandy, Sri Lanka: 1780–1980', in *The Power of Place: Bringing Together Geographical and Sociological Imaginations,* eds J. Agnew & J.S. Duncan, Unwin-Hyman, Boston, pp. 185–201.

Duncan, J.S. & Duncan, N.G. 1980, 'Residential landscapes and social worlds: a case study in Hyderabad, Andhra Pradesh', in *An Exploration of India: Geographical Perspectives in Society and Culture*, ed. D.E. Sopher, Cornell University Press, Ithaca, pp. 271–86.

Duncan, J.S. & Duncan, N.G. 1984, 'A cultural analysis of urban residential landscapes in North America: the case of the anglophile elite', in *The City in Cultural Context*, eds J. Agnew, J. Mercer & D. Sopher, Allen & Unwin, Boston, pp. 255–76.

Firey, W. 1945, 'Sentiment and symbolism as ecological variables', *American Sociological Review*, vol. 10, pp. 140–8.

Giddens, A. 1979, *Central Problems in Social Theory*, University of California Press, Berkeley.

Girouard, M. 1981, *Life in the English Country House*, Penguin, Harmondsworth.

Hugill, P. 1986, 'English landscape tastes in the United States', *Geographical Review*, vol. 76, pp. 408–23.

Kenny, J. 1995, 'Climate, race and imperial authority: The symbolic landscape of the

British Hill Station in India', *Annals of the Association of American Geographers*, vol. 85, no. 4, pp. 694–714.

Ley, D. 1993, 'Past elites and present gentry: neighbourhoods of privilege in Canadian Cities', in *The Changing Social Geography of Canadian Cities*, eds L. Bourne & D. Ley, McGill-Queens University Press, Montreal.

Lowenthal, D. & Prince, H. 1965, 'English landscape tastes', *Geographical Review*, vol. 55, pp. 186–222.

Mitchell, K. 1997, 'Conflicting geographies of democracy and the public sphere in Vancouver, B.C.', *Transactions, Institute of British Geographers*, vol. 22, no. 2, pp. 162–79.

Pevsner, N. 1957, *London Volume 1: The Cities of London and Westminster*, Penguin, Harmondsworth.

Pratt, G. 1981, 'The house as an expression of social worlds', in *Housing and Identity: Cross-Cultural Perspectives*, ed. J.S. Duncan, Croom-Helm, London.

Rapoport, A. 1981, 'Identity and environment: a cross-cultural perspective', in *Housing and Identity: Cross-Cultural Perspectives*, ed. J.S. Duncan, Croom-Helm, London pp. 6–35.

Sennett, R. & Cobb, J. 1973, *The Hidden Injuries of Class*, Vintage, New York.

Wiener, M.J. 1981, *English Culture and the Decline of the Industrial Spirit*, Cambridge University Press, Cambridge.

Williams, R. 1973, *The Country and the City*, Chatto & Windus, London.

Williams, R. 1982, *The Sociology of Culture*, Schocken Books, New York.

Wyckoff, W.K. 1990, 'Landscapes of private power and wealth', in *The Making of the American Landscape*, ed. M.P. Conzen, Unwin-Hyman, London, pp. 335–54.

4

Place and politics in post-war Italy

a cultural geography of local identity in the provinces of Lucca and Pistoia

John Agnew

INTRODUCTION

Intense loyalty to local football (soccer) clubs has become an important feature of everyday life for people, especially young men, all over Europe. Nowhere is this more the case than in Italy, where fanatical adherence to 'the team' recalls older forms of identification with locality generally referred to in Italian as *campanilismo*. Italy is a relatively 'new' state, only unified under one national government in the 1860s, and local identities are still very strong. In the region of Tuscany (Toscana) in central Italy, the Florence team, Fiorentina, has the largest mass following relative to other major Italian football teams, reflecting the prominent position that the city of Florence has occupied historically within the region. However, in the province of Lucca, to the west of Florence between the Apennine mountains and the Tyrrhenian Sea, Juventus of Turin, the arch-enemy of Fiorentina in contemporary Italian football, has thirteen supporters' clubs to the five of Fiorentina, a figure roughly three times greater than any other Tuscan province. This is because the population of Lucca, a separate republic independent of Tuscany until 1847, has an identity distinct from the other Tuscan provinces. Even when there is no local team capable of challenging that of Florence, many *lucchesi* throw in their lot with a successful team in distant Turin rather than convert to support for Fiorentina.

The phenomenon of local identity is not unique to Italy. Regionally and locally-based political cultures characterise the United States, Canada and many European countries. Political geography, especially the geography of elections, has been relatively silent about this, probably because of that field's lack of attention to the concept of culture. In the Italian case this silence is difficult to fathom. It can be plausibly argued that if today 'localism' is in the ascendancy again in Italy, as shown by the electoral success of essentially local and regional political movements (such as the *Lega Nord*, or Northern League), Italy had never been strongly homogenised by an Italian national culture in the first place (Forgacs 1990). Why, then, should social science in general and political geography in particular have had difficulty seeing local identity and the cultural contexts from which it springs as essential for understanding political action?

In modern social science local identity has been viewed as either residual, something fading under the onslaught of modernisation and its political twin national identity, or primordial, related to a cultural drive in which culture is viewed as a fixed bundle of traits and beliefs formed in the distant past and reproduced unwittingly by local populations. In studies of Italian politics these have been the dominant perspectives. The 'residualists', the majority group among students of Italian politics, have stressed the slow emergence of the modern 'individual' engaged in opinion voting, with a decline in political action based on group identity or clientelism (see, for example, Parisi and Pasquino 1980). The 'primordialists' have emphasised the impact on political activities and voting behaviour of relatively fixed 'regional cultures' or subcultures, especially the Catholic subculture of north-east Italy, the socialist subculture of central Italy and the clientelistic subculture of the south and Sicily (see, for example, Putnam 1993).

In this chapter, after a review of these positions, an alternative perspective will be proposed. This sees local identity (or sense of place) as one dimension of a concept of place in which 'culture' is a dynamic phenomenon, a set of practices, interests and ideas subject to collective revision, changing or persisting as places and their populations change or persist in response to locally and externally generated challenges. Attention then turns to interpreting Italian electoral politics since the Second World War, firstly at the level of the country as a whole and secondly with respect to two Tuscan provinces, Lucca and its neighbour towards Florence, Pistoia. These two provinces have been chosen to illustrate the central theme of this chapter: what is possible politically is defined by the evolving cultures of specific places.

LOCAL IDENTITY AS RESIDUAL OR PRIMORDIAL

A widely-accepted premise of modern political science is that political outlooks and alignments are increasingly organised around national social cleavages to produce national patterns of political mobilisation. Increasingly, political differences are seen as 'nationalised', as membership in national census categories displaces geographical location as the primary predictor of political behaviour. In Italy this point of view became popular among political scientists in the late 1960s. A major study of Italian political behaviour conducted between 1963 and 1965 argued that a 'nationalisation' of Italian politics had occurred between 1946 and 1963 (Galli and Prandi 1970). The pattern of an electorate divided into two parts, left and right, and spread throughout the country—as in other 'representative democracies'—had come to Italy (see Table 4.1). From this point of view, individual opinion voting had replaced identification with social group or locality as the main source of political identity (Parisi and Pasquino 1980). 'Modern' voting behaviour is seen as an expression of personal choice constrained by access to information and by particular socio-demographic characteristics, such as class, age, education, etc.

Certainly, national and province-level election results in the period 1963–76 can be used to support this perspective. There was a tendency towards homogenisation of support for the main Italian political parties of the time: the Christian Democrats (DC), the Communists (PCI) and the Socialists (PSI) (Agnew 1998). This could be explained partly in terms of the 'saturation' of support for parties in some areas and partly in terms of common national processes of political mobilisation (Bartolini 1976; Parisi and Pasquino 1980). There was also a sense of greater electoral instability as voters became more volatile in their political affiliations (Barbagli et al. 1979). Neither homogenisation nor electoral volatility in themselves, however, can be taken as signals of a permanent shift from a geographically fragmented to a nationally homogeneous process of political mobilisation (Agnew 1988). As the huge literature on neighbourhood effects in voting suggests, opinion voting is not an isolated individual act but is subject to local social influences (Agnew 1987; Johnston 1986). Moreover, homogenisation and volatility have been insufficient in recent Italian electoral history to justify total abandonment of older models of political behaviour involving recourse to concepts of local identity and subculture. Even proponents of the trend towards nationalisation based on opinion voting stress the important 'residual' role of identity and clientelistic (vote-favour exchange) voting as expressive of local histories and interests (for example, Parisi and Pasquino 1980).

Considerable empirical evidence now suggests that nationalisation of voting patterns was a feature of the period 1963–76 rather than a permanent trend (Pavsiv 1985; Agnew 1988). This has led to a revival of 'geographical' models of political behaviour which emphasise regional subculture and the persistence of regional 'types' of voting. Such models identify historical-cultural rather than socio-economic factors as the primary determinants of political cleavages. The 'rootedness' of parties in particular areas through their organisation and institutional strength is given special weight as a factor producing socialisation into different political traditions. Key periods in the past—medieval communal organisation, the years after unification, the period of labour organising early in the twentieth century, and the period after the collapse of fascism, 1943–46—are viewed as critical in the establishment of regional political traditions. The Catholic subculture of north-east Italy, the socialist subculture of the centre and the clientelistic subculture of the south and Sicily are regarded as the major traditions that have resulted.

There are perhaps three specific models that rely on fixed subculture-regional conceptions of political action: first, regional taxonomies of cultural traditions; second, historical studies of local political cultures; and third,

Party[a]	1946	1948	1953	1958	1963	1968	1972	1976	1979	1983	1987
DC	35.1 (207)	48.5 (305)	40.1 (263)	42.4 (273)	38.3 (260)	39.1 (266)	38.8 (267)	38.7 (292)	38.3 (262)	32.9 (225)	34.3 (234)
PCI	18.9 (104)	31 (183)[b]	22.6 (143)	22.7 (140)	25.3 (166)	26.9 (177)	27.2 (179)	34.4 (228)	30.4 (201)	29.9 (198)	26.6 (198)
PSI	20.7 (115)	—	12.8 (75)	14.2 (84)	13.8 (87)	14.5 (91)[b]	9.6 (61)	9.6 (57)	9.8 (62)	11.4 (73)	14.3 (94)
PSDI	—	7.1 (33)	4.5 (19)	4.5 (22)	6.1 (33)	—	5.1 (29)	3.4 (15)	3.8 (20)	4.1 (23)	3.4 (17)
PRI	4.4 (23)	2.5 (9)	1.6 (5)	1.4 (6)	1.4 (6)	2 (9)	2.9 (14)	3.1 (14)	3 (16)	5.1 (29)	3.7 (21)
PLI	6.8 (41)	3.8 (19)	3 (13)	3.5 (17)	7 (39)	5.8 (31)	3.9 (21)	1.3 (5)	1.9 (9)	2.9 (16)	2.1 (11)
PR	—	—	—	—	—	—	—	1.1 (4)	3.5 (18)	2.2 (11)	2.6 (13)
DP	—	—	—	—	—	—	—	1.5 (6)	0.8 (—)	1.5 (7)	1.7 (8)
PdUP	—	—	—	—	—	—	—	—	1.4(6)	—[c]	—
MSI	—	2 (6)	5.8 (29)	4.8 (24)	5.1 (27)	4.4 (24)	8.7 (56)	6.1 (35)	5.3 (30)	6.8 (42)	5.9 (35)
Monarchists	2.8 (16)	2.8 (14)	6.9 (40)	4.8 (25)	1.7 (8)	1.3 (6)	—	—	—	—	—
Others[d]	9.5 (50)	2.5 (5)	2.7 (3)	1.7 (5)	1.3 (4)	6.0 (26)	4.0 (4)	0.8 (4)	2.7 (6)	3.2 (6)	5.8 (10)

Party[a]	1992		1994[e]	1996
DC	29.7 (206)	FI	21.0 (99)	20.6 (123)
PDS	16.1 (107)	PDS	20.4 (109)	21.1 (171)
RC	5.6 (35)	RC	6.0 (14)	8.6 (35)
PSI	13.6 (92)	Lega	8.4 (117)	10.1 (59)
PSDI	2.7 (16)	AN	13.5 (109)	15.2 (93)
PRI	4.4 (27)	PPI	11.1 (33)	6.8 (71)
PLI	2.9 (17)	Others	19.6 (139)	17.1 (78)
MSI	5.4 (34)			
Lega	8.6 (55)			
Others[d]	10.8 (41)			

Source: Instituto Centrale di Statistica (ISTAT)

[a] DC (Democrazia Cristiana), PCI (Partito Comunista Italiano), PSI (Partito Socialista Italiano), PSDI (Partito Socialista Democratico Italiano), PRI (Partito Repubblicano Italiano), PLI (Partito Liberale Italiano), PR (Partito Radicale), DP (Democrazia Proletaria), PdUP (Partito di Unita Proletaria per il Communismo), MSI (Movimento Sociale Italiano), PDS (Partito Democratico della Sinistra), RC (Rifondazione Comunista), FI (Forza Italia), AN (Alleanza Nazionale), Lega (Lega Nord), PPI (Partito Popolare Italiano).

[b] Parties presented on joint election lists.

[c] Ran on PCI lists.

[d] Includes South Tyrol People's party (SVP), Sardinian Action party (PSA), Valdotaine Union (UV) and Socialist Party of Proletarian Unity. (PSUIP) SVP generally accounts for three seats; PSUIP won twenty-three seats in 1968. The Greens won thirteen seats with 2.5 per cent in 1987. After 1992 various center-right factions and the anti-mafia vote are important.

[e] New electoral system. Percentages are from proportional contests, seats are total seats from majoritarian and proportional contests.

TABLE 4.1 Political elections 1946–96, Constituent Assembly (1946) and Chamber of Deputies, per cent by party (seats in parentheses).

sociological studies of party-government and political subculture links. For reasons outlined later, none of these models is considered satisfactory.

The first involves identifying the most 'fundamental' geographical divisions in voting behaviour in terms of subcultural homogeneity. A number of taxonomies have been proposed, the earliest in 1967 (Dogan 1967), the most influential being that of Capecchi et al. (1968) and the most recent being those of Cartocci (1987) and Anderlini (1987). Over time, the taxonomies have shifted from a tripartite regional division, north-east, centre and south, with the north-west as a 'residual' region not easily characterised in subcultural terms, to an emphasis on the importance of the north-south division (Cartocci 1987) and local 'functional' regions defined partly in cultural terms (Anderlini 1987).

A second primordial model involves focusing upon local areas with a long history of political homogeneity, such as 'red areas' with strong support for the PCI in central Italy (see, for example, Bagnasco and Trigilia 1985; Baccetti 1987; Caciagli 1988) or 'white areas' with strong support for the Christian Democrats in the north-east (see, for example, Bagnasco and Trigilia 1984; Messina 1997). Emphasis is placed upon the persistence of political alignments in the face of economic and social change, suggesting that political cultures defined in the past continue to exercise control over later political behaviour (see, for example, Tullio-Altan 1986; Putnam 1993). Unlike the American literature (see, for example, Almond and Verba 1963), there is a positive tendency to see political culture as a phenomenon rooted in and emanating from local social institutions (especially clubs and associations) rather than directly 'internalised' psychologically by individuals (Caciagli 1988).

The third model focuses on the question of local institutions, particularly the dominance in them of particular political parties and particular organisational cultures. For some commentators (see, for example, Tarrow 1977; Galli 1984), when local political systems—elsewhere, as well as in Italy—are dominated by a single political party and political entrepreneurs of a particular complexion, they tend to use jobs, favours and a dominant local ideology to produce local populations with commitments to that party. The tautological nature of this position (dominance produces dominance) has led others to introduce 'subcultures' as a kind of social 'glue' or mediating variable for particular parties and their appeal. In examining the recent economic success of north-east and central Italy, for example, Trigilia (1986) and Bagnasco (1988) argue for the importance of local party dominance and social traditions in jointly creating the conditions of consensus and mediation of diverse interests necessary for the development of the dynamic small firms that have prospered in these Italian regions. Subcultures, party dominance and economic growth thus form a virtuous circle in these regions, whereas by implication they do not elsewhere, especially in the south (for detailed critiques see Bellini 1989; Blim 1990; Amin and Robins 1990).

All these models share a 'primordial' definition of culture and an orientation towards continuity rather than change in political behaviour. There are four specific drawbacks to them. First, there is little if any attention to the reconstruction of historical-geographical sequences in the development of

Italian politics. Geography is seen in static rather than dynamic terms. Once they are established at a critical juncture in the past, cultural differences simply reproduce themselves through their association with some places rather than with others. Second, there is little emphasis on the local area as a 'theatre' of activities from which social and political commitments and political change emerge. Rather, the local is seen in terms of cultural persistence, resistance to change and the overwhelming weight of tradition.

Third, only some regions or localities are viewed as 'integrated' communities with territorial subcultures. Elsewhere, again especially in the south, communities are viewed as lacking the consensus or bonds of faith and trust that are taken as indicative of 'true' subcultures (see, for example, Trigilia 1986). The problem here is that those who cannot have a subculture pinned on them are left without culture at all. Kertzer (1980) has suggested that the term 'hegemony' be reserved for those settings where political parties have acquired a certain role in consensus and institution-building, and that the term 'subculture' be dropped altogether so that all Italians can be thought of in cultural terms, rather than just those in the north-east and centre (also Feltrin 1988).

Fourth, culture—especially 'political culture'—is seen in static and deterministic terms. Opinions, captured in surveys at particular points in time, are regarded as constitutive of political culture which, in turn, becomes a 'black box' of values and beliefs used to explain the self-same opinions. To avoid this tautological dead-end, culture is better thought of as a structure or system of 'signification' (set of symbols and commitments) that defines the range of possible actions (political and other) that a group or individual can undertake in a given society (Williams 1981; Allum 1988). More particularly, a political culture can be thought of as defining the limits of the 'possible' in political life, the intersubjective framework to which individual actors bring their own attitudes, values, interests and personalities (Taylor 1985). Allum (1988, p. 265) brilliantly summarises this perspective as follows:

> It can be affirmed, by reformulating a noted saying, that, 'culture proposes, man [sic] disposes'. Further, however, I would underline that political culture is not static, even if it is persistent: it changes over time even if slowly, as taught in the 18 Brumaire of Marx, and changes above all in the course of political struggles that totally restructure practices and 'systems of signification', so that the 'sense' of yesterday is not always the 'sense' of today, and alternative politics that were unthinkable yesterday become suddenly possible today.

PLACE AND POLITICS

The critical issue for a geography of Italian politics, unaddressed by either residualists or primordialists, can be raised in terms of a simple empirical puzzle: averages are more or less representative of specific observations, depending upon the degree of dispersion of all observations. The point is more substantive than statistical. National averages disguise a variety of local differences. By way of example, Figure 4.1 shows the relationship between

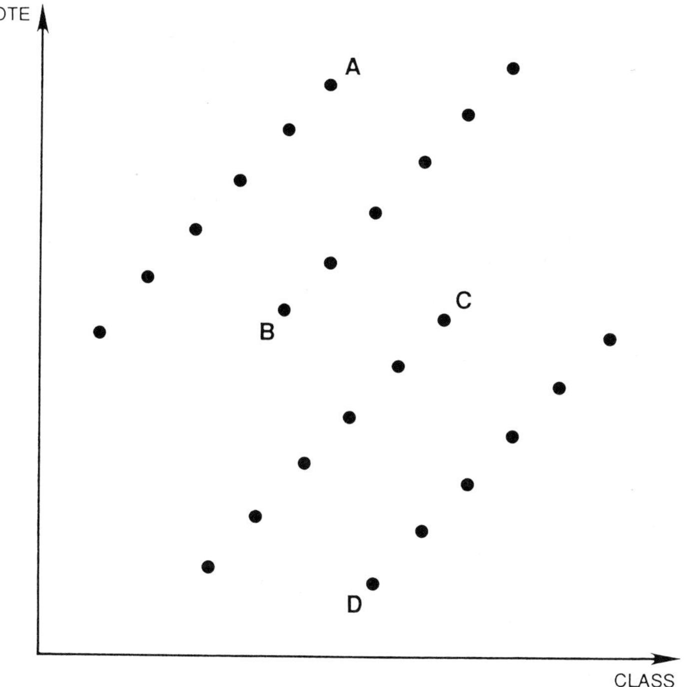

FIGURE 4.1 Regions, class and vote.
Source: Derivry & Dogan (1986, p. 158).

social class and vote in an imaginary country of four regions. In each region the correlation between class and vote is perfect, but for the country as a whole there is no relationship whatsoever. This extreme case illustrates a simple point: rather than seeing local variations as deviations from a national norm, the national norm is meaningless unless seen as constituted out of locally-specific situations (Agnew 1998).

The argument for this perspective is sociological. People are social beings rather than isolated individuals or members of census categories. It is in social contexts that people acquire the practical reasons that lead them to act in some ways rather than others. These social contexts are formed geographically. Social relations are constituted in physical settings or locales that people cross into and out of constantly in the course of their everyday lives. Such locales are embedded in a wider territorial society according to locational constraints imposed by the activities of states and the demands of geographically extensive divisions of labour. Common experiences and interests create an emotional attachment and self-definition peculiar to the specific place in which the locales of enduring social relationships are concentrated. This is a local identity or 'sense of place' (Agnew 1987).

What is possible politically is defined by the evolving cultures of specific places. Over time these can be more or less distinctive but, however similar or different, they are formed from the bottom up—out of everyday life. This does not mean to say that political dispositions are created in geographical isolation.

That has been the fallacy of so many 'community' studies (Cooke 1990). Different places have different relationships to the national state, international economy, and secondary social organisations such as churches, labour unions and political parties. These differences affect the nature of local political cultures as local life adjusts to external challenges. The outcome of this process of social structuration is the geographically differential appeal of different political parties and movements that changes over time as changing 'local cultures propose and local people dispose'.

THE GEOGRAPHICAL DYNAMICS OF ITALIAN ELECTORAL POLITICS, 1947–96

Italian electoral politics since the Second World War can be viewed in terms of either nationalisation and the rise of the individual opinion voter or regional cultures with static political profiles. Alternatively, it can be interpreted in terms of three political-geographical 'regimes' in which the places out of which Italy is made have had different degrees of similarity and difference at different times. After describing the case for the three regimes at the national level an attempt is made at explaining them by reference to two provinces in central Italy: Lucca and Pistoia.

The three regimes

The geography of Italian politics since 1947 can be characterised in terms of three distinctive geographical regimes that have dominated in different periods (Agnew 1998). The first regime, dominant from 1947 until 1963, involved a regional pattern of support for the major political parties based upon place similarities that clustered regionally. The second regime, in effect from 1963 until 1976, witnessed the expansion of the Communist Party (PCI) out of its regional strongholds into a nationally competitive position in relation to the Christian Democratic Party (DC). This had different causes in different places but the net effect was to suggest a nationalisation of the two major parties. The third regime, characteristic of the period since 1976, has seen increased support for minor parties, including regional parties such as the Northern League (*Lega Nord*), the geographical 'retreat' and political disintegration of the PCI and DC and a more localised pattern of political expression in general, reflecting the increased 'patchiness' of Italian economic growth and social change and the crisis of the system of parties after 1992.

The regionalising regime

The period 1947–63 is that of the classic electoral geography of Italy established most definitively by Galli and his colleagues (Galli and Prandi 1970). They divided the country into six zones on the basis of levels of support for the three major parties, the PCI, DC and the Socialists (PSI), and the strength of the major political subcultures, the socialist and the Catholic (Figure 4.2).

FIGURE 4.2 Italian provinces and voting regions used by Galli and Prandi (1970, p. 114). Copyright 1970, The Twentieth Century Fund.

- Zone 1, the industrial triangle, covered north-west Italy and included Piemonte, Liguria and Lombardia. This was the region in which industrial production was concentrated before the Second World War and in which most new industrial investment was concentrated in the 1950s. Socialists, Christian Democrats and Communists were all competitive in this region.
- Zone 2, *la zona bianca*, covered north-east Italy and included the provinces of Bergamo and Brescia in Lombardia, the province of Trento,

the province of Udine and all of the Veneto except the province of Rovigo. The Christian Democrats were most strongly entrenched in this region and opposition was divided among a number of parties.

- Zone 3, *la zona rossa*, covered central Italy and included the provinces of Mantova, Rovigo and Viterbo; the whole of Emilia-Romagna except for the province of Piacenza; Toscana except for Lucca (an *isola bianca*); Umbria; and the Marche, except for the province of Ascoli Piceno. In this region the PCI was most strongly established, especially in the countryside but increasingly in the cities.
- Zone 4, the south, included the province of Ascoli Piceno, Lazio (except Viterbo), Campania, Abruzzo e Molise, Puglia, Basilicata and Calabria. This zone was historically the poorest and most marked by clientelistic politics. In the 1950s the Christian Democrats and the right-wing parties dominated the zone but were faced with increasingly strong challenges from the PCI and PSI.

The final two zones, 5, Sicily, and 6, Sardinia, had more complex political alignments than the peninsular south. For example, the PCI was well established in the southern provinces of Sicily (especially the sulphur mining areas) while Sardinia had a strong regionalist party.

There were strongly rooted cultural 'hegemonies' (party-based consensus building) in only two of these zones, *la zona bianca* and *la zona rossa* (Stern 1975; Muscarà 1987). However, in electoral terms, support for specific political parties was remarkably clustered regionally in 1953 (Rizzi 1986): the PCI in the centre, the PNM (monarchists) and MSI (neo-fascists) in the south and Sicily, DC in the north-east and the south. Italian politics in the 1950s followed a regional regime reflecting a similarity at the regional scale of place-based social, economic and political relationships.

The nationalising regime

The second period, 1963–76, marks a break with the regional pattern characteristic of the 1950s. Two electoral shifts were especially clear: the expansion of support for the PCI outside *la zona rossa* (along with its consolidation inside), particularly in the industrial north-west and parts of the south, and the breakdown of *la zona bianca* as a number of small parties made inroads in the previously hegemonic support for DC in parts of the north-east. The net effect of these changes was a seeming nationalisation of the major parties, even though they still maintained traditional areas of strength.

These political changes were the fruit of the major economic and social changes Italy underwent in the late 1950s and early 1960s. A major expansion occurred in manufacturing and industrial employment, especially in the north-west, as a phenomenal boom or 'economic miracle' drew the Italian economy away from its predominantly agrarian base. At the same time that the industrial centres of the north-west were experiencing such dramatic economic and social change as a result of the economic boom and massive immigration, the rest of the country was experiencing shockwaves emanating from the north-west. The extreme south (Puglia, Basilicata and Calabria) was a major zone of emigration to the north-west and, with the exception of Taranto, without much industry. Where industry was established it created pockets of new social and economic relationships in the midst of a rapidly depopulating rural society. In all these places and among immigrants from the south in the north, the PCI expanded its support in the late 1960s and early 1970s.

The other major feature of the period 1963–76 was the so-called breakdown of the Catholic subculture in *la zona bianca* or north-east and subsequent loss of DC voters. The argument is that DC, being largely an electoral rather than a mass party with a large membership, had relied heavily on affiliated organisations, many of a religious nature, to mobilise its support. However, in the late 1960s, as a result of heavy outmigration from rural areas in the Veneto, Trento and Friuli, the constituent subregions of *la zona bianca* and the growing industrialisation of some areas such as Venice, Treviso, Trento and Pordenone, the traditional social networks and communal institutions upon which DC hegemony was based began to collapse (Parisi 1971; Sani 1977; Caciagli 1985; Chubb 1986).

The nationalising political-geographical regime peaked in 1976 when DC and PCI together accounted for 73 per cent of the national vote. Although this trend had distinctive causes relating to the geographically differentiated social and economic impacts of the economic miracle and their interplay with political and organisational traditions, it was widely interpreted as a permanent nationalisation of political life (Agnew 1988). DC and the PCI were now national political parties.

The localising regime

The 1979 election indicated a much more complex geography of political strength and variation than had been characteristic previously. Since then all parties have been less regionalised or nationalised than in the past (Rizzi 1986). The 1983 and 1987 elections suggested a trend towards a localisation or increased differentiation of political expression that has continued through the great political and electoral changes of the early 1990s. In 1983 DC lost 5.4 per cent nationally, but PCI was not the beneficiary. Rather, it was smaller parties such as the PSI and the Republicans (PRI) in the north and the MSI in the south that gained the most. In 1987, DC recovered somewhat from 1983, but without a major geographical expansion. The major loser this time was the PCI, which lost ground in the north-east, the north-west and some provinces of *la zona rossa* to the PSI and a variety of smaller parties including the Radicals (PR), the Greens and Democrazia Proletaria (DP) (Leonardi 1987).

One cause of localisation was the increasingly differentiated pattern of economic change after a previous era of concentration. While the economic boom of the early 1960s concentrated economic growth increasingly in the north-west, by the late 1960s there was considerable decentralisation of industrial activity out of the north-west and into the north-east and the centre. This new pattern of differentiated economic growth led some commentators to write of the 'three Italies'—a north-west with a concentration of older heavy industries and large factory-scale production facilities; a north-east centre of small, family-based, export-oriented and component-producing firms; and a still largely underdeveloped south, reliant on government employment but with some of the small-scale development (for example, in the vicinity of Bari or Caserta) characteristic of the 'third Italy' (north-east–centre) (see Bagnasco 1977). This terminology, though useful as a general characterisation of a new economic geography, masks both a much more uneven and differentiated pattern at a local scale and the linkages between localised development and the big firms of the north-west. High concentrations of employment in major growth industries have, in fact, been widely scattered (Cooke and Pires 1985).

Other causes have also contributed to the localising political-geographical trend from the late 1970s to the present. One was the failure of the parties to successfully adapt to social and economic change. In Trento and Udine (in the north-east), for example, DC had problems adapting to the new economy. In large parts of the south and the north-west, the PCI was unable to capitalise on earlier successes mainly because when it came to the south, it had neither control over the state resources that lubricate the politics of many parts of that region, nor was it able to build a permanent following. In the north-west its major vanguard of unionised workers was much reduced in economic importance at the same time that the other parties had become better organised and the particular problems of the southern immigrants, whom the PCI had previously recruited as voters, had largely receded from the political agenda (Sassoon 1981; Caciagli 1985; Pasquino 1985).

The emergence of effective regional-level governments since 1970 also reinforced the interests and sense of place. Where parties have achieved some strength and legitimacy through control over regional governments, they have been able to build local coalitions for national politics based upon the pursuit of local interests. The PCI, for example, benefited from its control of or participation in the regional governments of Emilia-Romagna, Toscana and Umbria, but it suffered elsewhere, and other parties such as DC or the PSI benefited because of its lack of control over patronage jobs and inability to write regional political agendas (Putnam et al. 1985).

The former successes of DC and the PCI in, respectively, *la zona bianca* and *la zona rossa* rested to a degree on the social institutions with which they were affiliated (unions, cooperatives, clubs, etc.), as well as social isolation. However, the shifting orientations of these institutions and the rise of the consumer society opened up possibilities for smaller parties. There is some evidence that, after the late 1960s, ties between DC and the PCI and their supportive organisations, especially the unions for the PCI, had weakened (Weitz 1975; Hellman 1987; Mershon 1987). The parties themselves were responsible for some of this. In order to expand nationally, they often had to abandon or at least limit the ideological appeal that served so well in areas of traditional strength. They also had to respond in some areas to 'new' movements, such as the Greens, which opened them up for both factionalism and essentially localised forms of organisation and ideology (Amyot 1981; Caciagli 1985). More generally, parties do not always travel well. Thus, in comparing north-east with central Italy, the question of compatibility between 'party style' and 'local style' arises. In a comparison of the two regions in which DC and the PCI exerted their greatest influence in the 1950s and 1960s, *la zona bianca* in the north-east and *la zona rossa* in the centre, Stern (1975, p. 223) has noted:

> [t]he evolution of two very different forms of political hegemony, each with distinct characteristics that necessitate sharply contrasting forms of maintenance. The Christian Democratic variety that flourishes in northeastern Italy is fuelled efficiently by stable social organisation that de-emphasises the place of politics in community life. In comparison the communist variant thriving in central Italy accents the urgent attention that political matters should command among the local citizenry and thereby constantly reaffirms the relatively recent sense of legitimacy that underlies PCI control.

Of course, these hegemonies always had local roots and in some localities their power has been quite visible and persistent, as studies of Bologna and Vicenza suggest (Kertzer 1980; Allum and Andrighetto 1982). Although, as Tesini (1986) suggests for Bologna, things *could* have turned out quite differently.

Finally, in 1992 the system of parties in place since the end of the Second World War came to an end. As a result of the end of the Cold War and disputes over the meaning and appropriateness of the term Communist, the PCI had already regrouped as two new parties, the larger PDS (Partito Democratico della Sinistra) and the smaller hard line Rifondazione Communista (RC). As a result of investigation of systematic corruption in their operations, the PSI collapsed and DC disintegrated into three separate parties, the Partito Popolare to the centre-left and two smaller factions to the right. The fascist MSI was reborn as a new 'post-fascist' conservative party, Alleanza Nazionale, and in 1994 a new party organised by the media tycoon Silvio Berlusconi, Forza Italia, attempted to replace DC on the centre-right. The proliferation of smaller parties continued, but a new electoral system in effect for the first time in 1994 forced parties to look for coalition partners before elections so as to run more effectively for the 75 per cent of seats decided by majority votes in single-member districts. The other 25 per cent of seats remain under the previously dominant system of proportional representation for candidates from party lists in multi-member districts. With the federalist/separatist Lega Nord a potent electoral force in many parts of northern Italy, all parties save Forza Italia and PDS are now largely local or regional in strength (Agnew 1995). Even these two parties must coalesce with some of the others to achieve national-government office. As a result of the local strength of different parties, support for all parties today is more obviously localised than it was in 1976 or in the 1950s.

LUCCA AND PISTOIA

Lucca and Pistoia are interesting provinces from the perspective of this chapter because in conventional 'primordialist' terms each represents a particular territorial subculture: Lucca, the Catholic subculture (*la zona bianca*) and Pistoia, the socialist subculture (*la zona rossa*). Although each, especially Lucca, can be reasonably portrayed as historically culturally distinctive, it is important to stress two points: first, that their political complexion has not remained static over time; and second, that different *comuni* within the provinces have changed over time politically in different as well as similar ways to other *comuni*.

The major purpose of this section is to explore these two points and suggest from the 'place perspective' how the cultural contexts of Lucca and Pistoia have changed so as to 'produce' the sequence of regimes at a national level.

The provinces of Lucca and Pistoia are located in northern Toscana, north of the river Arno to the west-north west of Florence (Figure 4.3). One of the oldest *autostrade* (four-lane highways) in Italy, dating from the 1930s, the 'Firenze-Mare', runs through the two provinces and connects them to Florence. In 1981 Lucca had a population of 388 904 and Pistoia of 267 151. The six

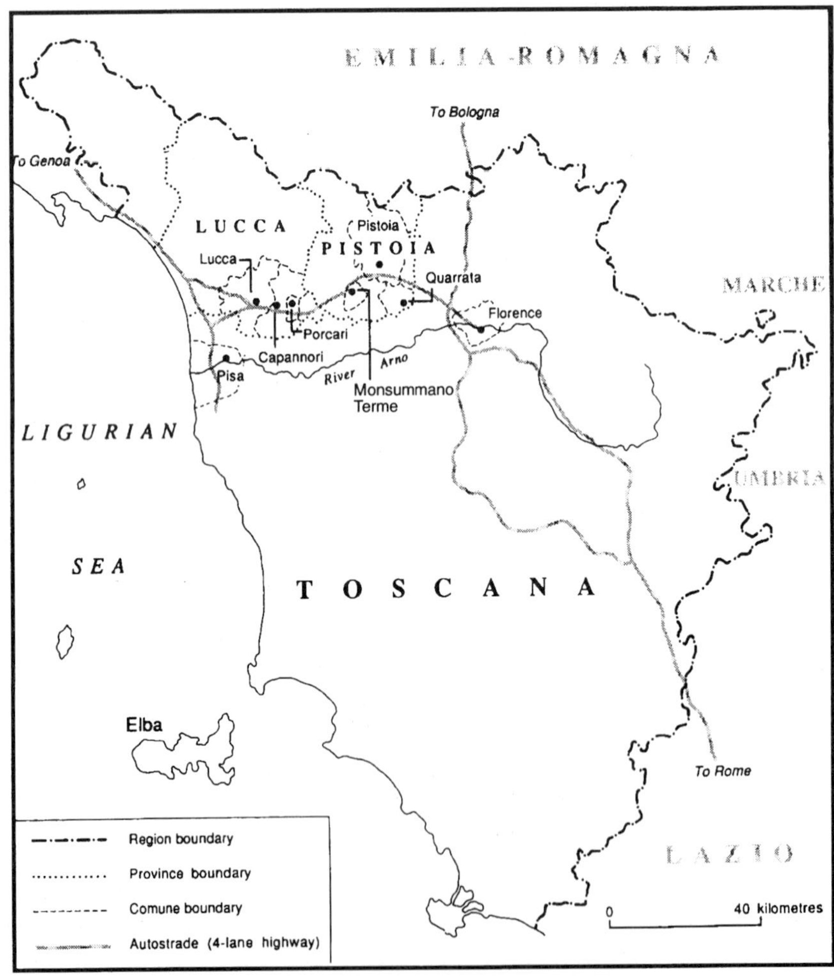

FIGURE 4.3 The provinces of Lucca and Pistoia, showing the six *comuni* referred to in the text and the *comuni* of Pisa and Florence.

comuni chosen for study, all of which grew in population and experienced considerable economic, especially small-scale industrial, development between 1960 and 1990 (Becattini 1975; Reyne 1983) had the following populations in 1981: Lucca, 91 246; Capannori, 44 041; Porcari, 6699; Pistoia, 92 274; Quarrata, 20 350; and Monsummano Terme, 16 511.

Politically the two provinces and the six *comuni* are diverse. In terms of electoral support for the two largest Italian political parties over the period from 1945 to 1992, Lucca and its *comuni* have been more dominated by support for the Christian Democrats than have been Pistoia and its *comuni* by support for the Communist Party (Table 4.2). However, each province tended to go through three phases. In Lucca, the period 1946–58 was one of consolidation of support for DC. From 1963–76 the PCI emerged as a major competitor as the DC vote initially fell, but was thereafter generally maintained. After 1976 support for the DC fell, much more in *comuni* other than the three selected here, but parties other than the PCI, especially the PSI and the Verdi (Greens), gained in support. In Pistoia the period 1946–58 was one of balance between the two major parties except in Monsummano Terme, where there was an early dominance by the PCI. From 1963–76 the PCI moved ahead of the DC, even though the DC remained the major opposition party. After 1976 the PCI vote stagnated and then declined, and the DC vote decreased substantially, with other parties such as the PSI acquiring the 'lost' votes. However, in Quarrata, DC maintained its position much more than in the other *comuni*. Since 1992 DC has disappeared in both provinces, replaced electorally to a very limited extent by Forza Italia, and the PCI has given way to the PDS and Rifondazione Comunista (RC). Though PDS is by far the dominant, RC has acquired considerable local strength, particularly in more rural areas.

Overall, these trends conform to those for Italy as a whole described in the previous section. In the 1950s DC and PCI 'hegemonies' (ascendancy in social and political life based on social consensus) were in formation, although the DC hegemony in Lucca was much the strongest. In the 1960s DC and PCI became competitive on what was previously each other's turf, even though one-party dominance was maintained or enhanced. A greater heterogeneity in patterns of support for all political parties was apparent after 1976. Today, neither DC nor the PCI exists, though each has descendants that vie with one another for popular support. The old hegemonies are gone, but differences in local identity, if of a different calibre, continue to persist.

A focus on the *comuni* can, perhaps, help explain what happened. Porcari and Quarrata changed the most politically. In 1953 DC was the majority party in each. Then it steadily weakened, largely to the benefit of the PCI, most clearly in Quarrata. In each case economic transformation and immigration played major roles. Prior to fascism Quarrata was a stronghold of the PPI (Partito Popolare Italiana), whose activists were founders of the local DC after the Second World War (Ballini 1981). However, the economy of the area changed from agricultural to industrial. Moreover, the area experienced considerable immigration, especially from other parts of Toscana and the Italian south. The PCI worked to extend its support in the area, partly through ancillary organisations such as social clubs. This strategy was

	1946			1948			1953			1958		
	T	DC	PCI	T	DC	PCI (FDP)*	T	DC	PCI	T	DC	PCI
Lucca	87.6	48.0	13.6	91.3	61.2	21.6	93.1	51.9	17.8	92.4	54.1	15.7
Lucca	85.4	49.5	12.2	92.5	63.8	16.2	94.8	54.9	15.8	94.8	56.5	12.5
Capannori	89.3	48.8	9.9	92.9	63.1	16.6	93.1	55.8	16.7	91.7	61.0	14.6
Porcari	92.6	46.5	11.8	93.7	60.9	21.4	95.3	55.8	22.8	94.0	56.6	21.4
Pistoia	94.5	29.8	34.5	95.2	40.1	47.2	96.4	35.0	37.1	96.1	34.5	37.8
Pistoia	93.4	28.7	34.4	97.1	39.7	47.2	96.9	34.4	37.3	97.0	34.4	37.5
Quarrata	94.0	24.3	42.3	95.7	50.3	39.3	97.4	46.6	28.3	97.5	46.8	29.2
Monsummano T.	94.2	20.8	46.9	96.1	32.5	55.2	96.9	26.4	49.4	96.7	24.0	50.4

	1963			1968			1972			1976		
	T	DC	PCI	T	DC	PCI	T	DC	PCI	T	DC	PCI
Lucca	93.5	47.2	17.7	94.1	45.8	21.0	94.6	47.3	23.0	95.1	47.6	29.9
Lucca	95.2	49.7	13.3	95.5	49.2	15.6	95.9	51.6	16.8	96.5	54.2	22.8
Capannori	94.6	55.7	15.7	94.2	53.6	20.6	94.6	57.5	21.4	94.2	56.5	27.0
Porcari	94.1	49.7	23.4	94.6	48.4	28.8	96.0	49.6	30.2	96.6	47.9	38.3
Pistoia	96.6	30.2	42.7	96.3	30.3	44.6	96.5	30.2	45.3	96.5	30.7	50.5
Pistoia	98.5	30.1	41.5	96.9	30.1	43.4	96.9	30.2	44.1	97.2	30.4	49.8
Quarrata	97.1	43.6	36.5	97.5	42.0	40.9	97.2	41.8	42.0	96.3	40.1	47.3
Monsummano T.	96.0	20.3	56.0	96.2	21.6	56.4	96.3	20.1	56.4	96.5	22.6	62.2

	1979			1983			1987			1992		
	T	DC	PCI	T	DC	PCI	T	DC	PCI	T	DC	PDS
Lucca	92.5	45.1	27.9	90.7	39.0	28.1	90.6	38.7	26.1	—	—	—
Lucca	94.8	50.3	21.4	91.5	42.9	21.6	90.9	42.1	19.8	83.7	36.6	11.6
Capannori	92.2	54.4	25.3	90.4	49.9	25.4	90.6	48.3	23.6	82.7	45.9	13.2
Porcari	95.4	45.2	35.1	93.4	42.6	34.3	94.0	41.5	30.8	86.0	41.4	17.9
Pistoia	94.5	29.8	48.7	92.5	25.4	48.9	93.3	25.7	45.4	—	—	—
Pistoia	94.7	29.3	47.2	91.7	25.2	47.6	94.0	25.5	44.2	85.6	21.9	27.9
Quarrata	95.2	39.3	45.6	93.2	34.6	45.8	93.5	34.9	41.7	84.3	30.3	25.0
Monsummano T.	95.1	23.6	58.6	93.8	17.8	57.7	93.1	20.1	54.0	84.9	16.9	36.1

	1994			1996		
	T	FI	PDS	T	FI	PDS
Lucca	—	—	—	—	—	—
Lucca	—	19.8	15.8	79.3	16.5	16.7
Capannori	—	21.1	17.6	75.7	17.9	18.3
Porcari	—	21.9	21.1	81.6	16.2	19.8
Pistoia	—	—	—	—	—	—
Pistoia	—	16.7	32.2	83.9	14.4	33.8
Quarrata	—	19.6	28.9	81.8	16.8	29.2
Monsummano T.	—	19.5	38.2	82.5	18.3	37.6

*FDP = Fronte Democratico Popolare (inc. PCI), 1948.
Sources: 1946,1948: Gabelli, M. 1988, 'Toscana elettorale 1946 e 1948', *Quaderni dell' Osservatorio Elettorale*, 20, pp. 199–308; 1953–68 Giunta Regionale 1972, *Dalla Cosituente alla Regione: Il Comportamento Elettorale in Toscana dal 1946 al 1970*, Florence; 1972: Giunta Regionale 1975, *Il Comportamento Elettorale in Toscana: Una Prima Interpretazione*, Regione Toscana, Florence; 1976–83: Giunta Regionale 1976, 1979, 1983, 1987, *Elezioni Senato e Camera* 1976, 1979, 1983, 1987, Regione Toscana, Florence; 1992, 1994,1996: Regione Toscana, *Elezioni 1992, 1994, 1996.*

TABLE 4.2 Results of elections to the Constituent Assembly (1946), Chamber of Deputies (1948-96), Provinces of Lucca and Pistoia and three comuni from each: turnout (% eligibles voting) and % DC, PCI, FI, PDS.

successful for a time, but today these clubs attract mainly older men and are not major instruments of political mobilisation.

Porcari is likewise an area whose economy was transformed and which has also had a large immigration from southern Italy. In this case, however, the PCI was not particularly well-organised to exploit the grievances and aspirations of new voters, perhaps because PCI organisation in the province of Lucca is much inferior to that in the province of Pistoia. However, none of these parties is well-organised in Porcari and there is a much lower level of politicisation of local and national issues than is apparent in Quarrata.

This degree of political change is less true of the *comuni* that are seats of provincial government. They have relatively more diversified economies, although Lucca has a greater preponderance of larger firms and a weaker small firm sector than Pistoia. This reflects Lucca's greater dependence on outside capital and its long history of ties with northern Italy and overseas. Pistoia's economic development has been much more endogenous in origin, based on local artisans transforming themselves into small entrepreneurs. Also, in the *comuni* of Lucca and Pistoia, affiliation to the dominant local party has been an important prerequisite for appointment to a wide range of jobs in the public sector. Local industries and local organisations such as Chambers of Commerce were strongly tied to the two major parties. For example, banks and the Chambers of Commerce in both Lucca and Pistoia were strongly DC in orientation. There is also, perhaps, the most continuity in local social-spatial identity or sense of place. In both Lucca and Pistoia, but especially in Lucca, the historical centre of the city provides an emotive reference point for identity that is missing from the amorphous *comuni* of the 'urbanised countryside' such as the other four. In Lucca the walls of the city stand as an everyday reminder of the glorious past of Lucca and its political independence (Tazartes 1987). A merging of the civil and religious in a concentration of physical symbols such as the walls and churches of the city helps to cement the self-image of *lucchesi* as citizens of a 'separate world' with its own distinctive politics (Camaiani 1979) (Figure 4.4). Given the Tuscan context of PCI dominance, DC was the major beneficiary of this Luccan 'separatism'.

In Pistoia the physical damage to the city in the last years of the Second World War, still apparent in places, is a constant reminder of the importance of those who resisted fascism. This has abundantly benefited the PCI which played the leading role in local resistance efforts (Risaliti 1976). The PCI has also been successful in Pistoia in politicising the working-class population to its advantage. This was partly due to its success among the workers of the major local employer, Breda costruzioni ferroviarie (a major producer of railway vehicles and buses), but it also reflects the ability of the local party organisation to adapt to changing economic conditions, for instance through its strong support for expansion of the small firm sector among local artisans and former share-cropping families (see Figure 4.5 which shows the announcement of a PCI conference in Florence on small and medium-sized firms).

Interestingly, DC in Lucca was all but invisible between elections, suggesting that the population there has lower aptitude than that of Pistoia

FIGURE 4.4 An aerial panorama of the city of Lucca looking west to east, the famous walls clearly demarcating the 'old' city.

for political mobilisation on an everyday basis (on this issue in general see Stern 1975). Ironically, there appears to be a lower level of activity in voluntary organisations such as social clubs and the volunteer ambulance in Lucca than in Pistoia, including DC and PCI activists and their replacements, even though Lucca has a long history of involvement with Catholic aid societies and is dominated by political language emphasising mutual aid and an active social life based around parties and neighbourhood.

In Capannori and Monsummano Terme the hegemony of one or other of the two major parties was long maintained against the trends in their respective provinces. Even though these *comuni* have changed the least electorally they have undergone tremendous economic and social change. In Monsummano Terme an established agrarian radicalism, based around the class conflict inherent in the system of share cropping which is dominant locally, was effectively harnessed by the local PCI which also successfully recruited southern immigrants into the party (Rossi and Santomassino 1981). The party was also active in promoting and supporting the local shoe industry and improving local physical infrastructure and housing.

In Capannori the industrialisation of the local economy has reinforced the dispersed settlement pattern of a *comune* which still looks to Lucca as its centre. Until 1978 the seat of the *comune* government was Lucca rather than in the *comune* itself. Many workers also still farm small family-owned plots even when they work full-time at the factory or workshop jobs. These 'peasant workers' identify closely with the city of Lucca, which is the centre for most social services. The important social role of the local priest in

FIGURE 4.5 A new communist manifesto? 'The firm as labour', a meeting with small and medium entrepreneurs, Palazzo dei Congressi, Florence, 4 February 1989.

everyday life reinforces the persistence of a social Catholicism which lent itself to support for DC. Rather than breaking down DC dominance, therefore, social and economic changes in Capannori long supported it. This is somewhat different, however, from the myth of transcendental subculture persisting autonomously to constantly recreate the politics of the past.

A range of different processes, then, operated to produce the shifts in support for the two major political parties that characterise both the provinces of Lucca and Pistoia and Italy as a whole. Rather than individualised opinion voting or primordial subcultures, therefore, explanation has been sought in the fluid, constantly reworked cultures of particular places.

CONCLUSION

The main purpose of this chapter has been to dispute dominant views of the link between local identity and politics by proposing an alternative perspective which views local identity as socially constructed and changing but ever-present rather than residual or primordial. In other words, local identity is part of the structuration of politics in place. In so doing the chapter offers a contribution to the redefinition of the culture concept occurring in contemporary human geography and social science.

The major advantages of the perspective laid out here are:

1. its ability to deal with changes in the geography (including dominant scale of expression) of electoral politics over time;
2. political culture is not equated with tradition but is seen as the intersubjective framework of practices, ideas and symbols in which political choices and activities are embedded;
3. *all* people live in cultural worlds that are made and re-made through their everyday activities, not just those who live in areas where specific political parties have created systems of consensus or hegemony; and
4. cultural worlds are grounded geographically in the experience of place. Culture, therefore, is *inherently* geographical, defined in places and through local identity, and thus *internally related* to the geographical dynamics of politics.

ACKNOWLEDGMENTS

The section on Lucca and Pistoia is based on fieldwork undertaken in the spring of 1989 and during return visits since then. A number of local people were especially helpful to me: in Pistoia, Pierluigi Bartolini, Ivo Lucchesi, Sabino Catania and the Hon. Gerardo Bianchi; in Lucca, the Hon. Sergio Dardini, Armando Carnini and Walter Lencioni. I would also like to thank Michael Shin and Christine and Katie Agnew for help with the revised version of this chapter.

REFERENCES

Agnew, J.A. 1987, *Place and Politics: The Geographical Mediation of State and Society*, Allen & Unwin, London.

Agnew, J.A. 1988, 'Better thieves than reds? The nationalisation thesis and the possibility of a geography of Italian politics', *Political Geography Quarterly*, vol. 7, no. 4, pp. 307–21.

Agnew, J.A. 1995, 'The rhetoric of regionalism: The Northern League in Italian politics, 1983–1994', *Transactions of the Institute of British Geographers*, vol. 20, no. 2, pp. 156–72.

Agnew, J.A. 1998, 'The geographical dynamics of Italian politics, 1947–1987', in *The Geography of Social Change*, eds L. Hochberg & C. Earle, Stanford University Press, Stanford, CA, forthcoming.

Allum, P. 1988, 'Cultura o Opinione? Su alcuni dubbi epistemologici', *Il Politico*, vol. 53, pp. 261–8.

Allum P. & Andrighetto, T. 1982, 'Elezioni e elettorato a Vicenza nel dopoguerra', *Quaderni di Sociologia*, vol. 30, pp. 355–97.

Almond, G. & Verba, S. 1963, *The Civic Culture*, Little, Brown, Boston.

Amin, A. & Robins, K. 1990, 'The re-emergence of regional economies; the mythical geography of flexible accumulation', *Environment and Planning D: Society and Space*, vol. 8, no. 1, pp. 7–34.

Amyot, G. 1981, *The Italian Communist Party: The Crisis of the Popular Front Strategy*, St. Martin's Press, New York.

Anderlini, F. 1987, 'Una modellizzazione per zone sociopolitiche dell'Italia repubblicana', *Polis,* vol. 1, pp. 443–79.

Baccetti, C. 1987, 'Memoria storica e continuità elettorale. Una zona rossa nella Toscana rossa', *Italia Contemporanea*, vol. 167, pp. 7–30.

Bagnasco, A. 1977, *Tre Italie: La problematica territoriale dello sviluppo italiano*, Il Mulino, Bologna.

Bagnasco, A. 1988, *La costruzione sociale del mercato*, Il Mulino, Bologna.

Bagnasco, A. & Trigilia, C. 1984, *Società e politica nelle aree di piccola impresa*, Il caso di Bassano, Arsenale, Venice.

Bagnasco, A. & Trigilia, C. 1985, *Società e politica nelle aree di piccola impresa, Il caso di Valdelsa*. Franco Angeli, Milan.

Ballini, P-L. 1981, 'La Democrazia Cristiana', in *La ricostruzione in Toscana, dal CLN ai partiti. Tomo II: I partiti politici*, ed. E. Rotelli, Il Mulino, Bologna, pp. 21–248.

Barbagli, M., Corbetta, P., Parisi, A. & Schadee, H.M.A. 1979, *Fluidità elettorale e classi sociali in Italia*, Il Mulino, Bologna.

Bartolini, B. 1976, 'Insediamento subculturale e distribuzione dei suffragi in Italia,' *Rivista Italiana di Scienza Politica*, vol. 6, pp. 481–514.

Becattini, G. (ed.) 1975, *Lo sviluppo economico di Toscana,* IRPET, Florence.

Bellini, N. 1989, 'Il socialismo in una regione sola: Il PCI e il governo dell'industria in Emilia-Romagna', *Il Mulino*, vol. 325, pp. 707–32.

Blim, M.L. 1990, 'Economic development and decline in the emerging global factory: Some Italian lessons,' *Politics and Society*, vol. 18, pp. 143–63.

Caciagli, M. 1985, 'Il resistible declino della Democrazia Cristiana', in *Il sistema politico italiano*, ed. G. Pasquino, Laterza, Bari, pp. 101–27.

Caciagli, M. 1988, 'Approssimazione alle culture politiche locali. Problemi di analisi ed esperienze di ricerca', *Il Politico*, vol. 53, pp. 269–92.

Camaiani, P.G. 1979, *Dallo stato cittadino alla città bianca. La 'società cristiana' lucchese e la rivoluzione toscana*, La Nuova Italia, Florence.

Capecchi, V., Cioni Polacchini, V., Galli, G. & Sivini, G. 1968, *Il comportamento elettorale in Italia*, Il Mulino, Bologna.

Cartocci, R. 1987, 'Ott risposte a un problema. La divisione dell'Italia in zona politicamente omogenee', *Polis*, vol. 1, pp. 481–514.

Chubb, J. 1986, 'The Christian Democratic party: Reviving or surviving?' in *Italian Politics: A Review*, vol. 1, eds R. Leonardi & R.Y Nanetti, Pinter, London.

Cooke, P. 1990, 'Locality, structure, and agency: A theoretical analysis,' *Cultural Anthropology*, vol. 5, pp. 3–15.

Cooke, P. & Pires, A. de Rosa 1985, 'Productive decentralization in three European regions', *Environment and Planning A,* vol. 17, pp. 527–54.

Derivry, D. & Dogan, M. 1986, 'Religion, classe et politique en France. Six types de relations causales', *Revue Francaise de Science Politique*, 36, pp. 157–81.

Dogan, M. 1967, 'Political cleavages and social stratification in France and Italy', in *Party Systems and Voter Alignments*, eds S.M. Lipset & S. Rokkan, Free Press, New York, pp. 129–95.

Feltrin, P. 1988, 'Le culture politiche locali. Alcune osservazioni critiche sugli studi condotti in Italia', *Il Politico*, 53, pp. 293–306.

Forgacs, D. 1990, *Italian Culture in the Industrial Era, 1880-1980*, Manchester University Press, Manchester.

Galli, G. 1984, *Il bipartitismo imperfetto. Comunisti e democristiani in Italia*, Mondadori, Milan.

Galli, G. & Prandi, A. 1970, *Patterns of Political Participation in Italy,* Yale University

Press, New Haven.

Hellman, J.A. 1987, *Journeys Among Women: Feminism in Five Italian Cities*, Oxford University Press, New York.

Johnston, R.J. 1986, 'The neighbourhood effect revisited: spatial science or political regionalism?', *Environment and Planning D: Society and Space*, vol. 4, no. 1, pp. 41–55.

Kertzer, D.C. 1980, *Comrades and Christians: Religion and Political Struggle in Communist Italy*, Cambridge University Press, New York.

King, R. 1985, T*he Industrial Geography of Italy*, St. Martin's Press, New York.

Leonardi, R. 1987, 'The changing balance: The rise of small parties in the 1983 election', in *Italy at the Polls, 1983: A Study of the National Elections*, ed. H.R. Penniman, Duke University Press, Durham NC, pp. 100–19.

Mershon, C.A. 1987, 'Unions and politics in Italy', in *Italy at the Polls, 1983: A Study of the National Elections*, ed. H.R. Penniman, Duke University Press, Durham NC, pp. 120–45.

Messina, P. 1997, 'Persistenza e mutamento nelle subculture politiche territoriali', in *Le elezioni della transizione. Il sistema politico italiano alla prova del voto 1994-1996*, eds G. Gangemi & G. Riccamboni, UTET, Turin, pp. 19–55.

Muscarà, C. 1987, 'Dalla geografia elettorale all geografia politica. Il caso italiano delle aree bianca e rossa', *Bollettino della Società Geografica Italiana*, 4, pp. 269–302.

Parisi, A. 1971, 'Il matrice socio-religioso del dissenso cattolico in Italia', *Il Mulino*, 21, pp. 637–57.

Parisi, A. & Pasquino, G. 1980, 'Changes in Italian electoral behavior: The relationships between parties and voters', in *Italy in Transition: Conflict and Consensus*, eds P. Lange and S. Tarrow, Frank Cass, London, pp. 6–30.

Pasquino, G. 1985, 'Il partito comunista nel sistema politico italiano,' in *Il sistema politico italiano*, ed. G. Pasquino, Laterza, Bari, pp. 126–68.

Pavsiv, R. 1985, 'Esiste una tendenza all'omogeneizzazione territoriale nei partiti italiani?', *Rivista Italiana di Scienza Politica*, 15, pp. 69–97.

Putnam, R. 1993, *Making Democracy Work: Civic Traditions in Modern Italy*, Princeton University Press, Princeton.

Putnam, R., Leonardi, R., Nanetti, R.Y. & Pavoncello, F. 1985, 'Il rendimento dei governi regionali', in *Il sistema politico italiano*, ed. G. Pasquino, Laterza, Bari, pp. 345–83.

Reyne, G. 1983, 'L'industrie en Toscane. Etude d'Une Region Italienne Confronteé a la Crise', PhD thesis, University of Nice, France.

Risaliti, R. 1976, *Antifascismo e resistenza nel Pistoiese*, Tellini, Pistoia.

Rizzi, E. 1986, *Atlante geo-storico, 1946-1983. Le elezioni e il parlamento repubblicana*, GSI, Milan.

Rossi, M.G. & Santomassimo, G. 1981, 'Il Partito Comunista Italiano. Introduzione', in *La ricostruzione in Toscana, dal CLN ai partiti. Tomo II: I partiti politici*, ed. E. Rotelli, Il Mulino, Bologna, pp. 757–68.

Sani, G. 1977, 'Le elezioni degli anni settanta: terremoto o evoluzione?' in *Continuità e mutamento elettorale in Italia*, eds A. Parisi & G. Pasquino, Il Mulino, Bologna, pp. 67–102.

Sassoon, D. 1981, *The Strategy of the Italian Communist Party*, St. Martin's Press, New York.

Stern, A. 1975, 'Political legitimacy in local politics: The Communist Party in northeastern Italy', in *Communism in Italy and France*, eds D.L.M. Blackmer and S. Tarrow, Princeton University Press, Princeton, pp. 221–58.

Tarrow, S. 1977, *Between Center and Periphery: Grassroots Politicians in Italy and France*, Yale University Press, New Haven.

Taylor, C. 1985, 'Interpretation and the sciences of man', *Philosophy and the Human Sciences: Philosophical Papers 2*, Cambridge University Press, Cambridge, pp. 15–57.

Tazartes, M. 1987, *Una città allo specchio. Lucca fra cronaca e storia*, Maria Pacini Fazzi, Lucca.

Tesini, M. 1986, *Oltre la città rossa. L'alternativa mancata di Dossetti a Bologna (1956–1958)*, Il Mulino, Bologna.

Trigilia, C. 1986, *Grandi partiti e piccole imprese*, Il Mulino, Bologna.

Tullio-Altan, C. 1986, *La nostra Italia. Arretratezza socioculturale, clientelismo, trasformismo e ribellismo dall'Unità ad oggi*, Feltrinelli, Milan.

Weitz, P. 1975, 'The CGIL and the PCI: From subordination to independent political force', in *Communism in Italy and France*, eds D.L.M. Blackmer & S. Tarrow, Princeton University Press, Princeton, pp. 541–71.

Williams, R. 1981, *Culture*, Fontana, London.

5

Corporate cultures and the modern landscape of New York City

Mona Domosh

> Like almost all the arts, even music, architecture has a representational function. Not only does it express the values (and land values) of a society, but also its ideologies, hopes, fears, religion, social structure, metaphysics. It may represent these facts or betray them; it may give the illusion of an unearthly realm ... or create in reality an earthly 'paradise'. This strange, double aspect of architecture—both to be and to represent a state of affairs distinguishes it from other, purely expressive arts such as painting (Jencks 1982, p. 178).

> However irrelevant to the conduct of business, a company's investment in bricks and mortar—its building—inevitably says something about its culture. After all, building investments are made or at least overseen by senior management. As much as they'd like to avoid the thought, most senior managers recognise that the buildings will likely outlive them; thus they try to create a setting that makes a statement to the world about their company, both deliberate and otherwise (Deal and Kennedy 1982, pp. 129–30).

INTRODUCTION

When corporate executives make decisions about the location and design of their buildings, they are indeed creating images of their companies; they are involved in the complex activity of communicating by symbol the culture of which they are a part. As Charles Jencks (1982) points out, those buildings both represent that culture and house it; they are functional and symbolic at the same time. In this sense, corporate buildings are no different from any other type of architecture; they both exist as and represent a state of affairs. Yet the corporate landscape is in many respects unique—given the highly-structured world of the corporation and its complicated relationship to its employees and customers, the decisions concerning architectural form are rarely simple and often involve the appeasement of seemingly contradictory needs. In addition, the corporate landscape is riddled with messages and codes that allude to the commercial nature of its enterprises, messages that are often not obvious from first appearances. What is it that corporations want to communicate to the world? Does a corporation wish to display its commercial motivations in its building, or an image untainted with the everyday workings of money-making? What other interests do corporations have in shaping the urban landscape? The answers to these questions are complex, varying through time and across the corporate world, dependent on the relationships between the business world, the architectural professions and changing societal values and ideals. This chapter will explore the answers to these questions by focusing on the creation of the business landscape of nineteenth-century New York, and, using that analysis, will suggest how that process has continued and changed throughout the early and late twentieth century. First, it is important to discuss in more detail the notion of corporate culture and its relationship to architecture and landscape.

There are, indeed, 'cultures' of corporations, but it would be difficult to argue that there is one corporate culture. Many companies have found it beneficial to develop policies that establish a type of ethos among its employees; this ethos or 'culture' is considered successful if it helps the company compete in its particular business environment. As Terrence Deal and Allan Kennedy discuss in their book *Corporate Cultures*:

> This business environment is the single greatest influence in shaping a corporate culture. Thus, companies that depend for success on their ability to sell an undifferentiated product tend to develop one type of culture ... that keeps its sales force selling. Companies that spend a great deal of research and development money before they even know if the final product will be successful or not tend to develop a different culture ... designed to make sure decisions are thought through before actions are taken (Deal and Kennedy 1982, pp. 13–14).

Thus, companies tend to develop a set of practices that serve to codify a particular value system and promote a type of self-representation. The construction of a building gives material expression to those practices and in this sense participates in the definition of a corporate culture. A faithful 'reading' of the corporate landscape requires an understanding of these internal distinctions between types of business cultures. A company that bases its success on constant innovation will assuredly construct for itself a building different in type from a business that relies on an impression of stability for its success. Yet the image that a company wishes to promote, whether it is of innovation or stability, is dependent upon the larger business environment—that is, on how the world of business fits into the prevailing social, economic and cultural relations of the time. To 'read' the corporate landscape, then, requires an understanding both of the types of companies involved—the corporate 'cultures', in the words of Deal and Kennedy—and the historical and material conditions under which that landscape was created. This chapter will discuss changes in the types of business 'cultures' and their relationship to broader social and economic contexts by focusing on the first self-conscious displays of commerce in the modern world, the early skyscrapers of lower Manhattan.

THE CONTEXT OF SKYSCRAPER DEVELOPMENT

> The modern high building, whether it is beautiful or ugly, whether it expresses pleasant or disagreeable traits and truths, is distinctively of this day and this country, and containing all the other modes of enterprise it is comprehensively typical (Steffens 1897, p. 38).

If, indeed, the skyscraper was typical 'of this day and this country', then it must have embodied at least some of the defining characteristics of its time. It did come to serve as the undisputed symbol of New York City and as such was laden with those extremes of emotion that the city has tended to generate (Strauss 1961; Trachtenberg 1979; Domosh 1985). Skyscrapers were invested with meaning by those who viewed them, but they of course were also created by people with certain intentions that developed out of circumstances particular to late nineteenth-century New York, and it is to an understanding of this context that we must first turn our attention.

As the self-proclaimed poet of Manhattan, Walt Whitman was the first literary figure to capture the essence and spirit of New York City. His poetry, in both form and content, expresses the energy, dynamism and diversity of the city that was to become the capital of the modern world. Nineteenth-century New York was a city of extremes and excess that, like Whitman's poetry, looked outward, towards the vistas of the American West for inspiration. Historian Edward Spann makes the point clear:

> Although it included a wide range of human existence, New York was best known in its extremes, as a city capable of shedding the most brilliant light and casting the deepest shadows. Perhaps no place in the world evoked such extremes of love and hate, often in the same person. In its slums, dirt, materialism, violence, congestion, rush, politics and municipal mismanagement, it could depress, degrade and offend the human spirit. In its wealth, intelligence, power, opportunities, freedom, and in the seemingly endless wonders of its streets, it could exalt, exhilarate and, occasionally, even charm strangers and citizens alike. The new metropolis was radically imperfect, but its imperfections were those of a masterwork of collective human spirit and masterful presence in the world (Spann 1981, p. 426).

By mid-century, New York had come to dominate the economic sphere of the nation, and by the 1890s, of the western world (Hammack 1982). That dominance resulted from both the city's strategic physical location—midway between the major population centres of America with access to exceptionally good and well-protected harbours—and the ability of its population to take advantage of that location and establish innovative economic initiatives. One of the earliest of such innovations was the construction of the Erie Canal, which provided the only water route from inland America to a port and thereby enabled New York to capture much of the interior fur and agricultural trade. Because of the strong ties with the British market that such trade established, New York merchants were able to take over most of the cotton trade from Charleston and New Orleans merchants. As cotton was the prime export of America at the time, such a takeover provided New York with incredible mercantile supremacy. In 1830, 36.8 per cent of all importing and exporting in America passed through the port of New York and by 1850 the percentage jumped to 71.2 per cent (Hammack 1982).

Such success in mercantile endeavours created strong ties to the capital supply controlled by Great Britain and helped New York merchants to invest in what was to become one of the most lucrative enterprises of the century—railroads. Both Philadelphia and Boston merchants had tried their hands in such investments but, for various reasons, each had failed to supply the large amounts of capital necessary for success in railroad financing. Wall Street's rise to supremacy in the railroad finance world by 1860 had significant effects on the city's economy, bringing economic dominance to New York in the mercantile, financial and eventually industrial spheres (Chandler 1977).

Such economic dominance was intimately related to New York's social fabric. New York's innovative business class was in many senses both the cause and result of the city's economic position. The tone of the city was set by the competitiveness, heterogeneity and fluidity of its social classes. From its original inception as a trading post by the Dutch trading companies in the late seventeenth century, the raison d'etre of the city was its economic functionings without any illusions of religious or social control. Even in the early eighteenth century, New York was known for its tolerance of diversity and throughout the century experienced waves of migrations from Europe that foreshadowed the massive immigration of the nineteenth century. The original Dutch and then English elite classes controlled the city for short time periods, but were not able to maintain economic or cultural control over such a rapidly-expanding population (Jaher 1982). This heterogeneity and instability of New York's population continued to characterise the city throughout the nineteenth century and helped create its competitive and innovative business culture by encouraging commercial risk-taking and discouraging conservative business policies.

It is from within this particular context that the impulse for businesses to build skyscrapers developed. Because of this instability and diversity, New York's business class in the late nineteenth century was continually striving for supremacy, looking to every possible invention or gimmick to gain the competitive edge. Skyscrapers, then, provided both a lucrative investment and a very legible advertisement for new and competitive industries. As a group whose wealth was of relatively recent vintage, New York's business class was socially unstable and was seeking signs of status and cultural legitimacy. The ornate historical-revival style skyscrapers acted as status symbols and cultural adornments for a class eager to display itself through any channel, including the landscape. Skyscrapers, then, fulfilled a combination of needs—for real estate investment, material symbolism, social status and cultural legitimacy. Close analyses of the creation of two such buildings will serve to illuminate these points.

CULTURAL MONUMENTS TO BUSINESS SUPREMACY: TWO NEW YORK EXAMPLES

> Many large companies have long since recognised the commercial advantages of a splendid building which shall give outward and visible evidence of the magnitude of their resources ... the greatest companies imagining, and with some show of reason, it must be admitted, that those who occupied the largest and highest buildings will be endowed, in the popular mind, with the most wealth (Ferree 1894, pp. 304–5).

Pulitzer *(World)* building

When Joseph Pulitzer was considering the construction of a new building to house the expanding business of his newspaper, the *New York World,* he was faced with decisions concerning its location, size, design and designer. His purchase of the relatively small newspaper in 1883 had been prompted by more than strictly mercenary aims, although the newspaper industry at the time promised to be a lucrative one. Pulitzer, a relatively recent migrant to New York and not far removed from his Eastern European ancestry, was looking for a way of communicating both his newly-found economic and cultural status. The purchase and supervision of a newspaper provided Pulitzer with a platform from which he could contribute to the political and cultural dynamic of the city, while at the same time allowing him to display his concern for the 'common people', by treating his paper as a type of 'public' service.

Pulitzer's pioneering techniques in sensational journalism, combined with his use of large headlines and illustrations, turned the *World* into an immediate success, with the paper boasting a record-breaking circulation of 250 000 by 1886 (Bleyer 1927). The rapid growth of the paper necessitated the enlargement of its quarters on Park Row, and Pulitzer decided that a new and grand building would be constructed as the home of the now famous *New York World.*

The newspaper industry in New York was a highly competitive one, with all of the daily newspapers vying for supremacy. Most of the papers were located near Park Row because it was close to both City Hall and Wall Street, and throughout the latter part of the 1870s these newspaper companies had participated in a building competition—that is, some of the newspapers began to express their status by constructing ornate and often tall structures. In 1875 the *New York Tribune* had taken that competition seriously when it constructed for itself what many consider the first skyscraper, thereby outdoing all its competitors by virtue of its height alone. It would have been difficult for anyone in Manhattan, let alone in the newspaper industry, to miss the overt symbolism of such a building. The *New York Times* had constructed for itself a new building on Park Row that was completed in 1888, and although it was no taller than the *Tribune* building, it was designed in the very latest architectural style. With his somewhat shaky ego and newly-found social status, Joseph Pulitzer was not about to let his paper be surpassed by the *Tribune* and the *Times,* and in his instructions to his architect for his new building, he made explicit his concern that the building be at least as fine as the *Times* building:

> The finish of the building is something I know very little about. I want to be sure that no false economy or niggardliness will mar the building inside. I want the finish to be creditable at least, if no more, and first-class in every respect, as the contract with Post [the architect] requires ... How is the *Times* building finished? Have you ever been through it? Can anything be suggested by which our finish can be improved?. You remember Post's contract requires it to be at least as good as that of the *Times* (quoted in Seitz 1924, p. 175).

The *World* building was meant to fulfil at least these two needs—that is, for more space for the expanded newspaper, and as a response to the building competition among the newspapers in New York. Yet Pulitzer seemed to have much more in mind when he insisted that his building be an 'architectural ornament to the metropolis' ('The Pulitzer Building' 1890). Pulitzer wanted his building to be praised for its aesthetic qualities as much as he wanted it to be noticeable on the skyline. He hired the most popular commercial architect in the city, George Post, and instructed him to design a building that would be an aesthetic tribute to the city. In addition, Pulitzer spoke of his newspaper as a public service, as a voice for the common people, and his new building was also meant to express this public nature of the paper.

Pulitzer's demands for his new building were difficult to negotiate. The building was to advertise the new status of the newspaper and therefore was meant to be a commercial statement. It was also to fulfil Pulitzer's aspirations of achieving elevated status for himself and therefore was meant as an aesthetic adornment that would be praised by the city's arbiters of taste. The building was also to represent the public nature of a newspaper and its concerns for the virtues of everyday people. To further complicate matters, George Post, the architect, also had various personal and professional agendas in designing the building.

Post's choice of the Renaissance revival style for the new building was appropriate to these demands. The allusion to the Renaissance period served to associate the paper with the cultural creations of that era, as well as the public (as opposed to commercial) nature of the newspaper. Many of the civic structures built in the latter half of the nineteenth century in American cities were designed in similar styles, completing the association with public service that Pulitzer had demanded.

Completed in 1890, the new *World* building stood six storeys above any other building in the city (Figure 5.1). The uppermost of its sixteen storeys was topped by a gold dome in which were located Pultizer's and the editorial staff's offices. The classically inspired archways, columns and pedestals that adorned the exterior of the building gave the building a distinctive appearance, as did the four large torchbearers representing art, literature, science and invention. The choice of these four realms of human invention is instructive, in that Pulitzer noticeably deleted any mention of commercial endeavours from the exterior form of the building. The building was to be a cultural monument to public service.

Given the complexity of the design process and the often conflicting demands, it is not surprising that the building had its critics. It failed most resoundingly as an aesthetic creation. The arbiters of taste in New York, mostly the architectural critics, judged the building a failure, arguing that 'for thoughtful and refined design, one looks everywhere in vain' ('The New World Building' Record and Guide, 1890). Yet as an advertisement of the paper to the public it was an overwhelming success. Thousands of people came to the elaborate opening-day ceremonies, and the building continued to attract visitors for years, many choosing to ride the elevator to the top in order to view the city from the highest vantage point available. The new *World* building was apparently the talk of the town, with *Harper's Weekly* writing: 'The success of the *World* newspaper under the management of Mr. Pulitzer is one of the most important achievements of recent years. It is fitly crowned and attested by the erection of the great building ...' ('The New York "World"', *Harper's Weekly*, 1890, p. 47).

What was not mentioned by *Harper's Weekly* is almost as significant as what was: the building was not admired for its architectural design, or floor-plan, or the feat of engineering that it represented; it was 'great' because it was tall. The connection between the owner and the building was explicit—the *World* had literally crowned itself for its success. The building, then, was a success as advertisement for the newspaper and a monument to Pulitzer, but less of a success as an aesthetic artefact.

By the mid-1890s, most of the newspapers in New York had completed the structures that were to house them for the next fifty years or so; the expansion of the industry had reached its peak. It is at this time that another type of business, the life insurance industry, became particularly involved in skyscraper development. Like the newspaper business, the life insurance industry was an incredibly competitive one, with many companies vying to capture the millions of dollars that the new urban dwellers were willing to spend to insure their newly-found wealth. Lacking other forms of material expression, and in need of larger and more offices, life insurance companies were very interested in constructing ornate and tall buildings. Between 1892 and 1896, life insurance companies were responsible for over 20 per cent of all significantly tall buildings constructed in Manhattan (Domosh 1985).

Metropolitan Life building

A relative newcomer to the industry, the Metropolitan Life Insurance Company expanded rapidly in the last decade of the nineteenth century. The

FIGURE 5.1 Pulitzer *(World)* Building, exterior view.
Source: Photo by George P. Hall & Son, n.d. Courtesy of the New York Historical Society, NYC.

company had outgrown its headquarters in lower Manhattan and in 1893 took the risky step of moving uptown to Madison Square to build its new structure. The eleven-storey marble edifice was designed by architect Napoleon LeBrun in the Renaissance revival style, complete with a marble court that had a vaulted ceiling three storeys from the floor and a stairway to the executive offices that was apparently modelled after the Paris Opera House (James 1947, p. 27). The rapid growth of the company necessitated expansion of the building only a few years after it opened and company president James Hegeman decided to hire the sons of the deceased architect to design a building appropriate to the company's rising economic status.

Similar to Pulitzer's decisions concerning his new building, the decisions about the type and design of the Metropolitan's new building were based on multiple needs. Certainly the need for more office space was a major concern, but the actual design of that space was given much thought by Hegeman himself. As a product of and participant in a particular type of corporate culture, Hegeman shared with other life insurance executives an ideological belief in the benign service role of their companies. As Equitable Life president James Alexander argued, 'assuredly, an institution which exists for the benefit of widows and orphans ... is one which ought not to be conducted on a low plane of competition' (Keller 1963, p. 26). Such an ideological stance permeated the public statements of the life insurance industry, legitimising their excess profits and lack of any apparent material product. More than many other types of businesses, life insurance could be construed as providing a public service for the good of society, and such associations were exploited artfully by the executives of the emerging industry.

When it came to the construction of a new addition to the main office building of the Metropolitan, Hegeman and his vice-president, Haley Fiske, were interested in creating a statement not only about the newly-found economic position of their company, but also of the public-mindedness of its 'mission'. Given the general Renaissance style of the main building, Hegeman decided that the addition would take the form of a tall tower that would use the campanile in St Mark's Square in Venice as its prototype. The choice was an apt one—the tower would enable the Metropolitan to continue the skyward commercial competition in which life insurance companies were actively involved, and the association with Venice and the Renaissance period would provide both cultural legitimacy and a message of civic-mindedness.

When completed in 1909, the fifty-storey tower was the tallest structure in New York (Figure 5.2) and the company wasted no time in exploiting that fact as advertisement for itself. On the exterior, from the twenty-fifth to the twenty-seventh floor was a large clock that apparently was visible over a mile away, and at the very top was an electric lantern that flashed out the time. Haley Fiske called this 'the light that never fails', making explicit the association with the company's public stature. The image of this beacon on top of the building—with those words encircling it—became the logo for the company and was placed on all of its advertisements and correspondences (Domosh 1988). At the fiftieth storey was a public lookout from which, the company claimed, were visible the homes of over one-sixteenth of the entire American population (*The Metropolitan Life Insurance Company* 1908, p. 26).

As an advertisement for the company and a symbol of its new economic power, the Metropolitan tower was a success (Dublin 1943). New Yorkers

FIGURE 5.2 Metropolitan Life Building.
Source: From a postcard, n.d.

seemed enamoured with the building and millions rode the elevator to the top to see the panoramic view from the fiftieth floor. Whether its association with the pre-capitalist, civic-oriented Venetian Renaissance registered in many of the visitors' and viewers' minds is doubtful, although such association did enhance its recognition value and allowed it to be considered seriously as an aesthetic object. The notion of the incompatibility of art and commerce was being challenged by life insurance companies like the Metropolitan, who were using art (in this case an 'aesthetically-correct' architecture) to create a public identity for a corporate entity. That identity would serve the corporation well, particularly as its internal policies came under legislative attack in the last years of the nineteenth century (North 1952), and its role as a 'philanthropic' enterprise became increasingly suspect. Metropolitan's home office building and its branch offices were meant as clear expressions of a business that had public-minded goals at the forefront of its activities. Among the many urban guide-books that proliferated in the nineteenth century, Moses King's *Handbooks* were perhaps the most influential, and his 1894 description of the notable buildings of Manhattan alludes to the complete identification of the private insurance industry with public, philanthropic endeavours:

> All kinds of benevolent, semi-benevolent and philanthropic organisations are productive of wholesome results. But chief of all these are the numerous life insurance companies—the most practical kind of philanthropy ... Beside their benevolent work, these life corporations have been the prime causes of the city's architectural growth, for the life insurance buildings of New York surpass the office structures of any city in the world (King 1894, quoted in Gibbs 1984).

The Metropolitan, along with the other life insurance companies in New York, apparently had succeeded in presenting to the public a civic-minded corporate identity, and its headquarters building was the material manifestation of that identity.

As a contender in the aesthetic game, however, the Metropolitan building was less than successful. By the time of its completion, the architectural critics were searching for a skyscraper style that would be representative of America and of the newly-emerging modern period. As a direct imitation of a structure from a different country and different time period, the Metropolitan tower was deemed inappropriate for its context. One critic compared it unfavourably to the Flatiron building (a twenty-storey structure completed several years earlier), saying that the tower 'belongs to an earlier people and a vanished race', while the Flatiron was a 'twentieth century giant' that 'stands on the threshold of vigorous new life and of vast architectural possibilities' (Corbin 1903, p. 262).

The Metropolitan tower certainly fulfilled the needs of the company for office space and for a distinctive form of material expression and advertisement, yet it did not provide a form of aesthetic legitimacy for the company. The aesthetic constructs established by the arbiters of taste in New York excluded such buildings, since its style was deemed to be simply out of date. Like Pulitzer, Hegeman's status aspirations were never fulfilled.

Such a failure must not have bothered Hegeman very much—the building was far more a corporate entity than a personal one, whereas the *World* building had been very much a personal expression for Pulitzer. In fact, personal and corporate identities were intertwined for Pulitzer. The *World* was Pulitzer's own creation and his new building was as much a statement of his personal prestige as it was an advertisement for the paper. Hegeman, on the other hand, was only one of many presidents of what was (and is) an incredibly large and complex corporation. The Metropolitan tower was more a corporate symbol than a statement of personal status.

During the relatively short time between the construction of the two buildings, a change had occurred in the type of economic structure that characterised New York. Economic historians argue that the country was moving from a mercantile to a modern, industrial form of capitalism (Chandler 1977). Corporations began to replace individually-run businesses, distancing ownership from control. Business organisations grew larger and more complex, resulting in the creation of a new class of white-collar workers. Life insurance companies are one of the best examples of this type of new organisation and the Metropolitan tower represents a transition stage between the personally-identified businesses of the mid-nineteenth century and the corporate world of the early twentieth century. In this sense, the Metropolitan Insurance Co. belonged to a type of corporate culture different from that of the *New York World*. It is representative of a type of bureaucratic and hierarchical culture that began to take control of the urban landscape at the turn of the century.

THE EMERGENCE OF A MODERNIST CORPORATE LANDSCAPE

Many of the new corporations that began to dominate the economic structure of the country in the early twentieth century had their headquarters in New York, which became the major centre for bankers, insurance workers, lawyers, engineers and managers (Hammack 1982). Skyscrapers were built to house these white-collar workers, but these buildings were neither personal statements nor corporate symbols. Instead, they were large, speculative structures built to earn the most rents from a particular piece of real estate. These massive office buildings began to provoke reaction both from architectural critics, who referred to the buildings as 'architectural aberrations', and from a newly-vitalised group of urban reformers who found their appearance and height unacceptable. Drawing their inspiration from a national reformist crusade often referred to as the city beautiful movement, this group of professionally educated middle- and upper-class people translated the new aesthetic and vision of urban order into a language that American city-dwellers could understand.

According to William Wilson, embedded in the city beautiful movement was an ideology that conflated the notions of beauty and utility (Wilson 1989). 'No structure or scene could be truly beautiful without being functional as well' (Wilson 1989, p. 83). With this conflation of interests, the large businesses that were beginning to control the urban landscape became quite vocal supporters of the attempts to 'beautify'; the functional city was to their financial benefit. New circulation routes in the city were beautiful because they were functional, and vice versa. In addition, the new city beautiful ideology spoke not only of the association of beauty and utility but also of efficiency, particularly the efficiency of the new factories and corporations. As

Wilson writes, these urban reformers believed that 'the presumed efficiency of some private-enterprise factories and offices could be transferred to nonpecuniary concerns including the aesthetic' (Wilson 1989, p. 83). This confluence of the concepts of beauty, utility and efficiency produced an alliance of big business, design professionals and many politicians that was to shape the future of the American urban landscape (Boyer 1983; Wilson 1989).

The irregularly-shaped speculative skyscrapers of the late nineteenth and early twentieth centuries certainly did not fit into this prevailing aesthetic. The new corporate world was not particularly concerned with symbols of personal or individual corporate status. Instead, it was interested in the built environment as a means of promoting a certain corporate image, and as a way of facilitating the transportation and communication systems that were essential to its functioning and profit-making. The new design and planning professions found symbols of unbridled competition such as the mammoth skyscrapers of the turn of the century inappropriate and unacceptable (Domosh 1989). Commercial buildings were permissible if they took a secondary position to civic monuments and if they participated visually in a compatible grouping of buildings. The landscape of the city beautiful was one 'where mere individualism was subordinated to the harmony of the greater good' (Wilson 1989, p. 283).

Proponents of the aesthetics and ideology of the city beautiful movement were from the beginning self-conscious about their efforts to create a rational landscape. These notions provided the underpinnings of what is today called modernism, and the modernist aesthetic became the dominant architectural style for the new corporate world. Modernism, as it was imported into American architecture from Europe throughout the first decades of the twentieth century, spoke of a fit between design and function. The now-famous dictum that form should follow function was more than a rallying cry—it indeed represented a celebration of function, of the workings of modern life. In this, modern design fitted the needs of modern industrial corporations. Instead of disguising the technological underpinnings of the modern world, modernism not only allowed for but encouraged a display of that technology. The simple, interchangeable parts of modern design reflected the structure of the new corporate world and satisfied demands of corporations for flexible and expandable spatial arrangements. An architecture that suggested the eschewal of the past in favour of future progress suited corporations that identified themselves as the harbingers of a brave new world.

Yet modernism provided corporations with more than an architectural style; it provided an aesthetic justification for the efficiency and functionalism of the corporate world. David Ley summarised this merging of the interests of big business with urban design issues in his discussion of such modernist advocates as Le Corbusier:

> For Le Corbusier ... 'big business is today a healthy and moral organism' and other contemporaries agreed that the business corporation could 'introduce into city government the standardisation and scientific management already found in industry ...' (Ley 1989, p. 50).

Modernism indeed served modern corporations yet, as is noted above, the converse is also true—modern corporations served modern architecture. Not only did corporate executives provide many of the commissions for the first major structures of modernism (Jencks 1973; Doordan 1989), but they and the companies they ran served as the model for numerous modern architects. The standardisation of products essential to modern industrial production could be seen as a democratic innovation in that it allowed for the mass production of items for middle America. By so doing, mass production did indeed provide goods to people who previously could not afford them and allowed for a rhetoric of social responsibility and democratic vision by the business world. Similarly, the standardisation of architecture made possible by new technology and celebrated by modernism could adequately provide for the many in an egalitarian society. Technology could be seen as liberating, and the machine-like functionings of the corporation provided a structure to make that possible. The business corporation was a model of efficiency, of technology used productively, of the egalitarianism of the machine, of management through an established hierarchy, and of rational order. These were the precepts of the new architects and urban planners of the 1920s and 1930s and, arguably, of the following three decades (Jencks 1973; Berman 1982). Guided by a similar ethos and armed with new machines and money, modern architecture and modern corporations created the modern city—a place of mass-produced, anonymous and interchangeable structures.

Unlike Pulitzer's *New York World*, modern corporations were not interested in using the built environment for personal statements or as advertisements. With other, more sophisticated means of advertising available, and with the degree of competitiveness somewhat dulled, the interests of corporations in shaping the built environment were perhaps more subtle. Buildings were used less as advertisements than as signs of group identity, a demand important for both employees and customers of a large, depersonalised corporation. Business corporations relied on a rational ordering of space in the city—on efficient transportation and infrastructure. Modernism fulfilled both these needs. We can think of modern architecture and the modern corporation as the products of the same cultural moment—each fulfilling the needs of the other.

CONCLUSION: TOWARDS A POSTMODERN CORPORATE LANDSCAPE

The urban skylines of most western cities and, increasingly, the suburban fringes surrounding such cities are dominated by structures built for corporations. All of these structures were meant to fulfil some basic needs for these corporations yet, as we have seen, those needs are neither simple nor unchanging, nor are they the same for all corporate 'cultures'. Many of the early skyscrapers in New York were built as much as statements of personal identity, business acumen and aesthetic legitimacy as they were to provide the space necessary for the incredible economic expansion of the city in the late nineteenth century. Although most were failures as bids for the legitimacy afforded by participation in 'high' culture, they were resounding successes as advertisements for their businesses, and as creators of the symbolic association of height with the new economic order.

As the nature of New York's economy and society changed, the landscape expression of the corporate world also changed. Corporate needs for a rational ordering of space coincided with the aesthetic of modernism, and the repetitious lines of the new glass boxes were perfect representations of the modern industrial organisations. The relationship between business elites and design professionals was altered in the early years of the twentieth century. The ideology of the city beautiful movement and the aesthetics of modernism provided an agenda for urban reformers that was in the best interests of both groups. In addition, corporations were becoming increasingly prominent participants in both the political and economic life of cities and therefore were extremely influential members of the coalitions that shaped our modern cities. The conflict between commerce and art that seemed to afflict nineteenth-century business leaders was no longer an issue. The needs of one were the expression of the other.

It is difficult to ascertain exactly how corporations will shape the postmodern world. Postmodernism speaks a rhetoric antithetical to the functional needs of the late twentieth-century corporation. New construction projects are meant to be place and culturally specific, to be small-scale, and to contain allusions to historical precedent, local vernacular styles or personal identity. Yet most large corporations have become, if anything, more powerful and internationalised since 1970, and an architecture with place-specific symbolism may not seem the most appropriate. However, if the emergence of the office park is any indication, the image that some types of corporations wish to convey is different from their modern counterparts. The imagery of office parks is decidedly anti-urban and anti-machine, representing a rural or suburban ideal, yet underlying it is a very modernist conception—the ordered and controlled world of the corporation, effectively removed from outside contact and shielded from the day-to-day encounters that an urban setting would provide. It would seem, then, that the corporate world is re-situating itself, but its cultural and economic investment in the landscape suggests a situation fundamentally the same as that of the modernist era.

In fact, we see today an accentuation of the modernist alignment of the interests of corporations with those of design professionals. As Paul Knox (1991) reminds us, many real estate, construction and design businesses have merged into large, national corporations, and these corporations are responsible for the vast majority of new office buildings and complexes constructed today. As a result, the expression of corporate culture in the landscape is now shaped by these large firms (corporations themselves), creating the homogenous zones of economic activity that now encircle our nineteenth-century downtowns. These ersatz cities, where, according to Edward Soja, 'everything is possible and nothing is real', (1992, p. 121) look the same whether they are in Orange County, California, or surrounding Kansas City. That similarity of imagery is all about one thing—'packaging' a corporation and its product. With few exceptions, architects are now called upon not to create aesthetic statements, but to market products. Architect Kenneth Frampton puts it this way: 'It is a sign of our times that aesthetic display has come to be used as a form of packaging to such an extent that architecture is often called upon to provide nothing more than a set of seductive images with which to "sell" both the building and its product' (1991, p. 23). Here we can see continuities that go all the way back to Pulitzer—his building helped him sell newspapers to the masses at the same time that it solidified his personal, cultural legitimacy. But today the imagery is more sophisticated and slippery, passing through the hands of many highly-skilled image experts. Whether we are more taken in by this sophisticated imagery than we were in the nineteenth century (as Soja would have us believe) is a question left open for discussion. For now, what we can say is that some of the same impulses that shaped the nineteenth-century city are still alive in our postmodern world.

REFERENCES

Berman, M. 1982, *All That is Solid Melts into Air: The Experience of Modernity*, Simon & Schuster, New York.

Bleyer, W.G. 1927, *Main Currents in American Journalism*, Houghton Mifflin Co., New York.

Boyer, M.C. 1983, *Dreaming the Rational City: The Myth of American City Planning*, MIT Press, Cambridge, MA.

Chandler, A.D. 1977, *The Visible Hand: The Managerial Revolution in American Business*, The Belknap Press, Cambridge, MA.

Corbin, J. 1903, 'The twentieth century city', *Scribners*, vol. 33, pp. 259–72.

Deal, T. & Kennedy, A.A. 1982, *Corporate Cultures: The Rites and Rituals of Corporate Life*, Addison-Wesley Publishing Co., Reading, MA.

Domosh, M. 1985, 'Scrapers of the Sky: The Symbolic and Functional Structures of Lower Manhattan', unpublished PhD thesis, Clark University.

Domosh, M. 1988, 'The symbolism of the Skyscraper: case studies of New York's first tall buildings', *Journal of Urban History*, vol. 14, pp. 321–45.

Domosh, M. 1989, 'New York's first Skyscrapers: conflict in design of the American commercial landscape', *Landscape*, vol. 30, pp. 34–8.

Doordan, D. 1989, 'Corporate culture as symbol and icon', paper presented at the Hagley Museum and Library corporate culture seminar series.

Dublin, L.I. 1943, *A Family of Thirty Million*, The Metropolitan Life Insurance Co., New York.

Ferree, B. 1894, 'The high building and its art', *Scribners*, vol. 15, pp. 297–318.

Frampton, K. 1991, 'Reflections on the autonomy of architecture: A critique of contemporary production', in *Out of Site: A Social Criticism of Architecture*, ed. D. Ghirardo, Bay Press, Seattle, pp. 17–26.

Gibbs, K.T. 1984, *Business Architectural Imagery in America, 1870–1930*, UMI Research Design, Ann Arbor, MI.

Hammack, D.C. 1982, *Power and Society: Greater New York at the Turn of the Century*, Russell Sage Foundation, New York.

Jaher, F.C. 1982, *The Urban Establishment: Upper Strata in Boston*, New York, Charleston, Chicago, and Los Angeles, University of Illinois Press, Urbana, Illinois.

James, M. 1947, *The Metropolitan Life*, Viking Press, New York.

Jencks, C. 1982, *Architecture Today*, Harry N. Abrams Inc., New York.

Jencks, C. 1973, *Modern Movements in Architecture*, Garden City, Anchor Press/Doubleday, New York.

Keller, M. 1963, *The Life Insurance Enterprise, 1885–1910*, Harvard University Press, Cambridge, MA.

Knox, P. 1991, 'The restless urban landscape: economic and sociocultural change and the transformation of metropolitan Washington D.C.', *Annals of the Association of American Geographers*, vol. 81, no. 2, pp. 181–209.

Ley, D. 1989, 'Modernism, post-modernism, and the struggle for place', in *The Power of Place*, eds J. Agnew & J. Duncan, Unwin Hyman, Boston, pp. 44–65.

The Metropolitan Life Insurance Company, 1908, *The Metropolitan Life Insurance Company*, New York.

'The new World Building', 1890, *Record and Guide*, 14 June.

'The New York "World"', 1890, *Harper's Weekly*, 34, p. 47.

North, D. 1952, 'Capital accumulation in life insurance between the Civil War and the investigation of 1905', in *Men in Business*, ed. William Miller, Harvard University Press, Cambridge, MA, pp. 238–53.

'The Pulitzer Building', 1890, *New York World*, 10 December.

Seitz, D.C. 1924, *Joseph Pulitzer: His Life and Letters*, Simon & Schuster, New York.

Soja, E. 1992, 'Inside exopolis: Scenes from Orange County', in *Variations on a Theme Park: The New American City and the End of Public Space*, ed. M. Sorkin, The Noonday Press, New York, pp. 94–122.

Spann, E. 1981, *The New Metropolis*, Columbia University Press, New York.

Steffens, J.L. 1897, 'The modern business building', *Scribners*, vol. 22, pp. 37–61.

Strauss, A. 1961, *Images of the American City*, The Free Press, New York.

Trachtenberg, A. 1979, *Brooklyn Bridge: Fact and Symbol*, The University of Chicago Press, Chicago.

Wilson, W.H. 1989, *The City Beautiful Movement*, Johns Hopkins University Press, Baltimore.

Constructing geographies

identities of exclusion

6

Constructions of culture, representations of race

Edward Curtis' 'way of seeing' | Peter Jackson

INTRODUCTION: REPRESENTING 'THE OTHER'

John Berger's *Ways of Seeing* (1972) provides some radical insights into the problem of visual representation. Berger demonstrates that pictorial images carry multiple meanings and that their interpretation involves political as well as aesthetic judgements. Reference to his title is particularly apt in the context of the present chapter, which deals with 'representation' in both the political and aesthetic senses of that term. Any claim by one group to 'represent' another is itself a form of power exercised over subordinate groups by those more powerful than themselves (Hall 1997). Recent years have witnessed some significant challenges to this virtual hegemony in the power of representation with the development of history-from-below (Samuel 1981), the feminist critique of masculinist forms of knowledge (Harding 1986; Rose 1993) and the growing realisation of a 'crisis of representation' throughout the human sciences (Marcus and Fischer 1986).

In his brilliant study of *Orientalism* (1978), Edward Said demonstrates the extent to which representations of other cultures reflect the 'domestic' concerns of their author's own society rather than providing a faithful portrait of those they claim to represent. Yet, with few exceptions (see, for example, Anderson 1991), geographers have shown little interest in turning their analytical gaze onto their own society's constructions of cultural difference or applying a comparative perspective to their own culture as well as to those of more 'exotic' societies overseas. Again with few exceptions (see, for example, Cosgrove and Daniels 1988; Schwartz and Ryan 1998), the problem of visual interpretation has been seriously neglected in comparison with the burgeoning attention paid to such literary concerns as landscape biography (Samuels 1979), problems of narrative (Sayer 1989) or the metaphor of landscape-as-text (Duncan 1990; Barnes and Duncan 1992). Yet the interpretation of visual images poses as many challenges as the critical exegesis of literary texts.

The present chapter focuses on representations of 'race' and constructions of cultural difference. Examining a series of photographic images of North American Indians from the early years of this century, it demonstrates how particular images of 'race' are related to historically and culturally specific forms of domination. It shows how racism changes shape according to the particular context as ideologies shift with changing material conditions (Jackson 1987). Finally, it shows that many different 'readings' of any given set of images are possible, reflecting the different interests of the observer. Rather than attempting to identify any single 'photographic message' (Barthes 1977), this chapter demonstrates a number of ways of reading Curtis' photographs, aiming to contextualise his work in terms of contemporary 'ways of seeing'. In keeping with this emphasis on complexity—on the multiple 'maps of meaning' (Jackson 1992) with which we make sense of the world—the chapter concludes with a discussion of some of the diverse ways in which the photographer has himself been represented.

The photographs in question result from the virtual obsession of Edward Sheriff Curtis (1868–1952), who set out to make a permanent record of the culture and society of the North American Indian. Curtis was born in rural Wisconsin, moving to Seattle with his family in 1887. He began to photograph Indians in the 1890s, having earlier specialised in portraiture and landscape photography. In 1899 he joined the E.H. Harriman expedition to Alaska as official photographer. The following year he devoted himself full-time to photographing Indians, taking more than 40 000 photographs over the next thirty years. In 1905 he met President Theodore Roosevelt, who became one of Curtis' most ardent supporters, providing him with an introduction to the American banker, J. Pierpont Morgan, who loaned him the capital to begin publication of his massive undertaking. Published privately over more than twenty years and sold by subscription, the work was entitled *The North American Indian, being a series of volumes picturing and describing the Indians of the United States and Alaska* (Curtis 1907–30). Each set comprised twenty volumes of illustrated text with a further twenty portfolios containing more than 700 photogravures. Never having made much money from the project, Curtis died in relative obscurity in 1952 (Graybill and Boesen 1976).

CONTEXTUALISING CURTIS

While this chapter takes the form of a case study, it would be wrong to exaggerate the uniqueness of Curtis' photographic vision. Instead, he will be approached as representative of a 'way of seeing' which was widely shared among his contemporaries. For, as Berkhofer's (1978) work has unequivocally shown, the image of the 'white man's Indian' has been an extremely persistent one, exercising a powerful effect on a whole range of issues concerning the rights of native peoples from land claims to political sovereignty, commercial exploitation to human welfare. Before evaluating Curtis' work, therefore, it is necessary to outline something of the political and economic, cultural and intellectual contexts in which it was produced.

Born in 1868, Curtis grew up in the period of westward expansion when the United States saw its national destiny in terms of the occupation of the entire continent. These territorial ambitions dictated US policy towards Native Americans which went through several phases during the nineteenth century. From an initial emphasis on removal and resettlement west of the Mississippi, policy was modified during the 1840s and 1850s under the so-called Peace Policy through which the US government took over responsibility for native education, concentrating Indians on reservations, denying them self-government and religious freedom. In 1871, after the conquest of Native Americans was virtually complete, the policy of treaty-making with particular tribes was superseded by a new emphasis on detribalisation and assimilation. Under the provisions of the *General Allotment Act 1887*, each family was 'allotted' a quarter-section of 160 acres, held in trust for twenty-five years by the Secretary of the Interior. Ostensibly designed to reduce the effects of 'tribal communalism', the Act led to a drastic reduction in Indian land over the next fifty years. When Curtis' study was being published (1907–30), many Native Americans had still not been granted US citizenship, a right that was only finally bestowed in 1924. And while several reports by the Bureau of Indian Affairs had urged the settlement of long-standing claims against the federal government arising from broken treaties and similar abuses, an Indian Claims Commission was not established until 1946.

Clearly there were economic and political imperatives to the westward extension of the frontier, but there were also cultural and ideological forces that made the American public eager to hear about the 'backwardness' and 'inferiority' of the Indian 'race'. Popular attitudes were given greater legitimacy through various forms of 'scientific' racism (Jones 1980). Victorian anthropology lent scientific credibility to the categorisation of human beings according to physical criteria such as skin colour, facial characteristics and 'cranial capacity'. By such criteria, 'races' were ordered hierarchically and inferences about social attributes (from sensuality to leadership potential) were inferred directly from physical traits. The Victorian penchant for scientific measurement and classification was soon brought to bear on the question of 'racial' origins and human evolution, providing scientific legitimation for imperial expansion overseas. It was this mind-set that Curtis inherited and applied in the context of America's expanding western frontier. Observations of physical 'type' led directly to inferences about human culture and, with equal inexorability, to judgements about moral worth. As Berkhofer has shown, scientific observers were as prone as explorers and settlers to mix ideology with ethnography:

> Ethnographic description according to modern standards could not truly be separated from ideology and moral judgment until *both* cultural pluralism and moral relativism were accepted as ideals. Not until well into the twentieth century did such acceptance become general among intellectuals, and even then only a few Whites truly practiced the two ideals in their outlook on Native Americans (Berkhofer 1978, p. 27).

Belief in the inherent superiority of the white 'race' provided ample justification for the subjugation of other 'races' including the extermination of many thousands of Indians. Only much later in the twentieth century has it come to be generally acknowledged that the concept of 'race' has no sound biological basis (Banton 1987; Rex and Mason 1986). To speak as though separate 'races' exist other than as social constructions is to perpetuate the kind of racist ideology from which discriminatory practices inevitably follow.

One final context for the interpretation of Curtis' work is the growing importance of photography for 'political' as well as for recreational and 'artistic' purposes which took place during Curtis' lifetime. While photography was still considered marginal as an art form in the 1890s, the invention of small hand-held cameras such as Eastman's Kodak increased its popularity until it rivalled that of the bicycle. The craze for popular photography was soon supplemented by more serious practitioners who (like Curtis) used the camera for ethnographic purposes or (like Jacob Riis and Walker Evans) for political commentary and social reform. Jacob Riis's *How the Other Half Lives* (1890) is often regarded as a pioneering work of photo-journalism. His studies of street life among New York's tenement poor were, no less than Curtis' Indian photographs, carefully posed for maximum impact. His work reached massive audiences through serialisation in *Scribner's* magazine and reproduction of some of the more dramatic pictures in the *New York Sun*. Walker Evans' photographic preface to *Let Us Now Praise Famous Men* (Agee and Evans 1939), a study of the lives of impoverished Alabama share croppers, also achieved considerable renown with selected highlights published in popular journals like *Atlantic Monthly*. The work has since achieved classic status within the history of photography as well as fulfilling its contemporary role within the progressive politics of the Farm Security Administration who commissioned the work. Besides their political and artistic significance, each of these studies constitutes a kind of cultural record of particular 'ways of seeing'. This is part of the context in which to approach an interpretation of Curtis' oeuvre.

PICTURES AT AN EXHIBITION

The current re-evaluation of Curtis' work began at an exhibition, organised by the Smithsonian Museum, that toured various American museums in the early 1980s. Entitled *The Vanishing Race and Other Illusions: A New Look at the Work of Edward Curtis*, the exhibition presented a critical interpretation of Curtis' photographs. The exhibition's title refers to one of Curtis' most famous images, *The Vanishing Race—Navaho* (1904) (Figure 6.1), about which he wrote: 'The thought which this picture is meant to convey is that the Indians as a race, already shorn of their tribal strength and stripped of their primitive dress, are passing into the darkness of an unknown future' (Curtis 1907). The photograph shows a group of Navaho Indians on horseback, receding from the camera and about to enter a dark canyon. One of the

FIGURE 6.1 The Vanishing Race — Navaho (E.S. Curtis 1904). Source: Smithsonian Institution, photo no. 90–14320.

Indians looks wistfully over his shoulder towards the viewer, suggesting both the Indians' uncertain future and the viewer's complicity in their fate.

Viewing the exhibition in Chicago in 1983, one could not help being both attracted by Curtis' sepia-tinted photographs and appalled at the lengths to which he had evidently gone to construct an 'authentic' picture of Indian life, amounting in some cases to complete fabrication. The exhibition was designed to draw attention to these 'illusions', which were also the subject of an accompanying book (Lyman 1982). Among the deceptions which Curtis employed, Lyman notes the use of props which the photographer himself gave his subjects (feather head-dresses, beads and wigs); posing and framing his subjects in particular ways (often inside the studio tent which he took with him on all his expeditions); cropping and retouching his photographs (with the help of his darkroom assistant Adolph F. Muhr) to obliterate every sign of 'European' influence (such as parasols and automobiles).

Similarly, for his musical celebration of *The North American Indian*, Curtis borrowed teepees and other props from the American Museum of Natural History in New York to serve as stage sets. The musical selections were not 'authentic' Indian songs but 'arrangements' specially written for the occasion by the Boston composer, H.F.B. Gilbert. As opposed to 'mere adaptations of

Indian melodies', one contemporary observer notes, they were 'original compositions ... filled with the particularly rich quality of Mr Gilbert's imagination' (Arthur Farwell, quoted in Gidley, 1987, p. 70). Far from being an 'authentic' record of Indian life, Curtis' representations are what anthropologists today call 'partial truths' (Clifford 1986): incomplete and necessarily biased accounts that tell us as much about the expectations of Curtis' viewers as about their ostensible subject matter.

The very choice of subjects, picture captions, titles and accompanying texts were all designed to portray an 'authentic' and abiding 'Indianness'. Curtis' photographs represent a highly selective and idealised version of pre-contact Indian culture and of the landscapes with which that culture was thought to be associated. One could argue that Curtis' deceptions merely involved the exercise of artistic licence—the kind of creative manipulation of the medium that gives photography its claim to the status of art. Yet Curtis himself, and his promoters, claimed that his work measured up to the strictest standards of 'scientific accuracy'. However we approach these issues, Curtis' photographs clearly merit closer scrutiny and should be judged by the standards appropriate to ethnographic evidence as well as in terms of their artistic merit. But we should also guard against the tendency to exaggerate Curtis' uniqueness. Rather, it is the extent to which he mirrors the 'way of seeing' characteristic of his day that gives his work its general significance for cultural geography.

ART AND ILLUSION

In the general introduction to volume 1 of *The North American Indian*, Curtis describes his objective as having been to make 'a comprehensive and permanent record of all the important tribes of the United States and Alaska that still retain to a considerable degree their primitive customs and traditions' (Curtis 1907, Vol. 1, p. xiii). Like many of his anthropological contemporaries, Curtis' work was infused with a sense of impending crisis which drove him to try to make a documentary 'record' of his subject matter before it 'vanished' for all time. As Curtis himself explained:

> The great changes in practically every phase of the Indian's life that have taken place, especially within recent years, have been such that had the time for collecting much of the material, both descriptive and illustrative, herein recorded, been delayed, it would have been lost forever (Curtis 1907, Vol. 1, p. xvi).

However, the goal of capturing an 'authentic' version of Indian culture led Curtis to deny certain aspects of change, leading him to 'reconstruct' what had recently 'vanished'. As a result, Curtis documents little of the impact of cultural change, creating the illusion of a relatively untouched aboriginality.

The tension between scientific accuracy and artistic licence was a feature of Curtis' work. He refers to it himself in an early letter to J.P. Morgan, soliciting funds for *The North American Indian*. Writing in 1906, Curtis describes his work as aiming for both 'scientific accuracy' and 'artistic merit' (quoted in Lyman 1982, p. 60). President Roosevelt was to express the same tension when he wrote the Foreword to the first volume, describing Curtis as 'both an artist and a trained observer whose work has far more than mere accuracy, because it is truthful' (Curtis 1907, Vol. 1, Foreword). One of Curtis' earliest critics, writing in the journal *Camera Craft* in 1901, similarly noted the 'immense ethnological value' of Curtis' photographs but also claimed that 'most of them are really picturesque, showing good composition and interesting light effects' (Arnold Genthe, quoted in Lyman 1982, p. 53). Curtis discusses this issue in his own introduction to the series where he argues that:

> ... the fact that the Indian and his surroundings lend themselves to artistic treatment has not been lost sight of, for in his country one may treat limitless subjects of an aesthetic character without in any way doing injustice to scientific accuracy or neglecting the homelier phases of aboriginal life (Curtis 1907, Vol. 1, p. xiii).

There is not simply a tension here between 'scientific accuracy' and 'artistic treatment'. The very notion of 'scientific accuracy' is itself a cultural construction and a highly significant one in the context of Curtis' work. For Curtis claimed to have photographed Indian life 'directly from Nature', showing 'what actually exists or has recently existed ... not what the artist in his studio may presume the Indian and his surroundings to be' (Curtis 1907, pp. xiii–xiv). Yet, while Curtis travelled extensively throughout North America to photograph his subjects in the field, there were clear limitations to his dedication to the principle of observation from nature. His photographs of Indians 'on the warpath', as also his pictures of the Hopi snake dance and similar rituals, were obvious re-enactments where subjects were paid to adopt militaristic poses or to perform 'secret' ceremonies in front of the camera. Thus, in an article on 'Posing the American Indian' that compares Curtis with other contemporary photographers, Margaret Blackman describes Curtis' 'romanticised view' as having been 'tempered with the ethnographer's concern for accuracy' (Blackman 1980, p. 71). She praises the 'ethnographic accuracy' with which Curtis costumed his subjects, but goes on to admit that he carried with him 'a wardrobe of museum props' in order to effect the appropriate pre-contact image of his subjects.

Curtis employed a variety of visual and textual strategies to engage his audience and to persuade them of his claims to verisimilitude. In the text he wrote to accompany his 'musicale', for example, Curtis speaks directly to the audience, emphasising the authority that comes from long first-hand experience: 'I want you to see this beautiful, poetic, mysterious, yet simple life, as I have grown to see it through the long years with the many tribes' (quoted in Gidley 1987, p. 75). It is, however, in the visual representation of Indian culture and landscape that Curtis' deceptions are most pronounced.

DOCUMENTING THE DECEPTIONS

Lyman (1982) provides a catalogue of the photographic deceptions that Curtis employed in the construction of an anthropological 'illusion'. There is only space here to illustrate a handful of Curtis' attempts to fabricate an 'authentic' view of Indian landscape and society. Curtis employed a variety of techniques to sustain the illusion of an undiluted aboriginality. In his representations of people, he frequently used air-brushing to remove signs of 'European' influence: trouser braces, parasols, manufacturers' names on 'traditional' materials, automobiles and so on. In some cases, Curtis went to extreme lengths to remove 'inauthentic' details, such as the medal or clock that appears in the negative but not in the finished version of *In a Piegan Lodge* (1910) (Figures 6.2 and 6.3). Most remarkable, however, is the transformation that Curtis worked on his translator and informant, A.B. Upshaw, depicted by Curtis in the full regalia of a 'traditional' Crow Indian (*Upshaw—Apsaroke*, 1905), but shown, some seven years earlier, in much less exotic attire by the Omaha photographer F.A. Rinehart (*A.B. Upshaw—Interpreter*, 1898) (Figures 6.4 and 6.5). Elsewhere, too, the deceptions are so crude that it is easy to catch Curtis out: in two separate photographs, a Shunkala man and a Hitdatsa appear in identical costumes, such as those that Curtis carried with him.

Landscape representations were subject to similar photographic

FIGURE 6.2 In a Piegan Lodge—(before retouching).
Source: Smithsonian Institution, photo no. 75–11978.

FIGURE 6.3 In a Piegan Lodge—(after retouching) (E.S. Curtis 1910). Source: Smithsonian Institution, photo no. 90–14319.

manipulation. In this case, the illusion that Curtis sought to sustain was of an idealised pre-contact society living in complete harmony with nature. In *Pima Water Girl* (1907), for example, Curtis used extensive air-brushing to give an irrigation ditch the appearance of a natural pool. Other landscape elements were more contradictory. The sheep in *Navaho Flocks* (1904), for example, were clearly a European introduction but apparently presented less of a challenge to Curtis' idealised 'way of seeing'. They were simply assimilated as a 'natural' part of the aboriginal landscape.

Curtis' landscapes are entirely consistent with his 'way of seeing' Indian culture, in harmonious relation with externalised nature. The way that Curtis posed his subjects in the landscape stresses their inseparability from the natural world. Curtis' caption to *A Son of the Desert—Navaho*, for example, reads:

> In the early morning this boy, *as if springing from the earth itself*, came to the author's desert camp. Indeed, *he seemed a part of the very desert* … (quoted in Graybill and Boesen 1976, p. 118, emphasis added).

The Scout—Apache similarly shows 'the primitive Apache in his mountain home'. 'Nature' and 'culture' are even more closely fused in subjects like *Chipewyan Tipi Among the Aspens* where the family group and their teepee blend in harmoniously with their sylvan setting. Curtis' Indians are depicted gaining their livelihood directly from nature. Their handicrafts are displayed as skilful transformations of natural materials. Even their portraits are captioned with Indian names that bear witness to the close association between human beings and the natural world (Slow Bull, Black Eagle, Two Moon).

The representation of Indian life as peculiarly 'close to Nature' enabled Curtis' non-Indian contemporaries to portray the Indian as an evolutionary predecessor of more 'advanced' non-Indian cultures such as their own. But the ideological construction of Indian culture as mysteriously in tune with the natural world has been extraordinarily persistent, re-emerging in the 1970s when Indian culture was being championed as part of a general rise in environmental awareness. In the introduction to a catalogue of Curtis' photographs on exhibition at the Philadelphia Museum of Art in 1972, for

FIGURE 6.4 Upshaw—Apsaroke (E.S. Curtis 1905).
Source: Smithsonian Institution, photo no. 81–8708.

example, Joseph Epes Brown argued:

> It is thus near to Nature that much of the life of the Indian still is; hence its story … is a record of the Indian's relations with and his dependence on the phenomena of the universe—the trees and shrubs, the sun and stars, the lightning and rain—for these to him are animate creatures (Brown 1972, p. 6).

Whether or not these observations are true, they enable the author to construct a picture of the Indian's 'special relationship with his natural environment' and to speak condescendingly about the 'childlike quality of the Indian's soul' (Brown 1972, pp. 7–8).

Curtis' romanticised construction of Indian culture and landscape can be discerned in his aesthetic as well as in his choice of subject matter. He adopts the same visual aesthetic in many of his Indian studies as he employed in his early landscape photographs. *The Clam Diggers* is a particularly good example. Having won Curtis various honours in a national photographic exhibition, the same photograph later reappears in *The North American Indian*. Apart from cropping the original photograph, there is no difference in

FIGURE 6.5 A.B. Upshaw—Interpreter (F.A. Rinehart 1898).
Source: Smithsonian Institution, photo no. 81–9647.

the aesthetic that Curtis employs in the two contexts despite the 'scientific' pretensions of Curtis' Indian research (for details, see Lyman 1982).

Given his claims to scientific objectivity, it is also relevant to judge Curtis' photographs by the standards of contemporary anthropology at a period when the discipline was only just beginning to emerge as a professional science. As a photographer with no formal training in anthropology, Curtis' relationship with the scientific establishment was basically deferential. Curtis was aware that he lacked the credentials of a trained anthropologist and wanted his work to be edited by 'men in the scientific field, recognised as authorities' in order to lend it 'unquestionable authenticity' (quoted in Lyman 1982, p. 60).

In the interests of 'authenticity', Curtis frequently deferred to professional anthropologists such as George Bird Grinnell, A.L. Kroeber, George A. Dorsey and Clark Wissler. In turn, several members of the anthropological establishment were lavish in their praise of Curtis' work. In his study of *The Crow Indians*, for example, the anthropologist Robert H. Lowie described *The North American Indian* as 'an excellent piece of work and while not written either by or for a professional anthropologist lives up to high standards of accuracy' (Lowie 1935, p. 355). Similarly, the *American Anthropologist* gave Curtis a favourable review, describing *The North American Indian* as a 'faithful representation of actualities', 'a noble monument to a passing race' and a 'trustworthy graphic memorial of our passing aborigines' (McGee 1910, p. 449).

Other contemporary observers were more critical, questioning the 'naturalness' of Curtis' posed subjects. Writing in the photographic journal *Camera Craft* in 1903, for example, George Wharton James questioned Curtis' practice of posing his subjects, while the anthropologist James Mooney objected to Curtis' habit of referring to Indians as 'warriors' even when they were not at war. Similarly, in his attitudes to 'race', Curtis can be clearly situated in relation to the prevailing ideas of his time.

REPRESENTATIONS OF RACE

Photography and other forms of pictorial representation played an important role in scientific deliberations about 'race' during this period (Cowling 1989). Anthropological lectures were commonly illustrated by lantern slides and expeditions regularly brought back photographic evidence of 'exotic' cultures and landscapes. Among Curtis' contemporaries, for example, Clark Wissler included several carefully posed photographic portraits of different 'racial types' in his anthropological study of *The American Indian* (1917). Various conventions were established to improve the reliability of photographic images as empirical evidence. Guidelines such as Louis Sullivan's *Essentials of Anthropometry: A Handbook for Explorers and Museum Collectors* (1923) were published, giving detailed instructions about posing anthropological subjects against a regular grid in order to ensure accurate measurements of body shape and size.

By posing his subjects in 'naturalistic' settings, Curtis generally avoided the standard full-face and profile poses of contemporary anthropometric photography, described by Green (1984) as embodying a 'technology of power'. But any notion of 'capturing' a person on film reflects an inherent inequality in the relationship between photographer and 'subject', whether or not permission has been given for the photograph to be taken and whether or not the photographer has paid for the privilege. Even today, representations of 'exotic' people, especially where these images are produced for sale, raise equally troubling political and ethical dilemmas. The description of Leni Riefenstahl's photographs of the Nuba and the Kau as 'fascinating fascism' (Sontag 1975) may be an extreme case. But readers of popular journals like *National Geographic* are regularly confronted with similarly commodified depictions of other cultures (Abramson 1987). It is the inequalities that different parties bring to the encounter (subject, photographer, publisher, viewer) that give photographic representation its political edge.

Despite his preference for outdoor settings and relatively informal poses, Curtis' work nonetheless reveals many of the contradictions of contemporary racist ideologies. For example, Curtis' habitual reference to 'the Indian' (in the singular), implying that he believed in a discrete and homogeneous Indian 'race', was frequently contradicted by his acknowledgment of 'tribal' diversity. Many of his photographs claim to represent particular Indian 'types' such as *Typical Nez Perce* (1899) or *Typical Apache* (1906) and the text is full of passages such as the following, which combine racist stereotyping with a crude form of environmental determinism:

> Physically the Mohave are probably superior to any other tribe in the United States. Men and women alike are big-boned, well-knitted, clear-skinned. Mentally they are dull and slow—brothers to the ox. The warm climate and comparative ease with which they obtain their livelihood seem to have developed a people physically superb; but the climate and conditions that developed such magnificent bodies did not demand or assist in building up an equivalent mentality (Curtis 1908, Vol. 2, p. 48).

Some of Curtis' more popular works, such as an article he wrote in *Scribner's Magazine* in June 1906, contain quite blatant forms of racism, such as his reference to the Indian's 'inbred desire for bloodshed' (quoted in Lyman 1982, p. 657). Elsewhere in Curtis' work, passages that contain a degree of circumspection, such as his argument that 'we cannot refer to the Indian as a unit ... but rather we must in a measure consider each group as a subject unto itself', sit uncomfortably beside more clearly racist stereotyping, such as his description of the Apache as 'warriors to a degree unparalleled' (quoted in Gidley 1987, pp. 76–9). The general moderation of Curtis' 'scientific' tone occasionally gives way to more unbridled remarks, exposing more 'popular' forms of racism. Thus, 'scientific' assertions that the American Indian is 'one of the five races of man' with more than fifty 'linguistic stocks' are juxtaposed with more virulent forms of racism such as his description of the Apache: 'His birthright was craving for the warpath, and his cunning beyond reckoning. His character is a strange mixture of savagery, courage, and ferocity, with a remarkable gentleness and affection for his family' (quoted in Gidley 1987, pp. 75–7).

Even his more serious work, like *The North American Indian,* is characterised by various forms of 'scientific' racism such as his description of the Apsaroke as embodying 'the highest development of the primitive American hunter and warrior. Physically these people were among the finest specimens of their race' (Curtis 1909, Vol. 4, p. xi), or by more complex (but no less racist) arguments such as the following: 'To the workaday man of our own race the life of the Indian is just as incomprehensible as are the complexities of civilisation to the mind of the untutored savage' (Curtis 1907, Vol. 1, p. xv).

For Curtis, Indian culture was primarily of interest as a reflection of 'the mind of the untutored savage', and, as Roosevelt's Foreword makes clear, this was closely linked to an evolutionary theory of 'race'. Roosevelt explicitly compares contemporary Indian life with the 'conditions thru which our own race past so many ages ago that not a vestige of their memory remains' (Curtis 1907, Vol. 1, Foreword). Despite these attempts to construct an image of a remote and idealised aboriginality tempered by an evolutionary theory of human development, Curtis clearly recognised the disastrous effects of westward expansion on 'traditional' forms of Indian life. While he rarely referred to the massacres that had taken place during his lifetime such as the slaughter of 300 Dakota at Wounded Knee in 1890 (Brown 1970), Curtis' whole project can be seen as an implicit critique of current US policy towards the Indian. Though he generally avoided explicit criticism of government policy, he described the treatment accorded to the Indians as 'in many cases … worse than criminal' (Curtis 1907, Vol. 1, p. xv). He referred to the Indians' 'unequalled struggle against inevitable subjection' (Curtis 1911, Vol. 6, p. xi), occasionally giving vent to more extended criticism, as in his condemnation of US policy towards the Californian Indians:

> All Indians suffered through the selfishness of our own race, but the natives of California were the greatest sufferers of all … By what was supposed to have been a treaty they signed away their lands, in lieu of which they were to be granted definite areas much smaller in extent, together with certain goods and chattels, and educational advantages. This treaty was never ratified, yet we took advantage of one of its proposed provisions by assuming immediate possession of the Indian lands, by which cunning the majority of the natives were left homeless. Little by little, tardily and grudgingly, action towards providing homes for the surviving unfortunates has been taken; but what has been granted them in most cases only intensifies the outrage, for many of the reservations are barren, rocky hillsides of less than an acre for each individual—land the tillage of which is next to impossible … (Curtis 1924, Vol. 13, pp. xi–xii).

If Curtis constructed a particular view of Indian 'racial' difference, his attitude towards gender roles and relations is no less noteworthy. Although he was struck by the general lack of differentiation between the roles of Indian men and women, his representations of male and female subjects still conform closely to his contemporary viewers' expectations about patterns of masculine and feminine behaviour. Typically, men were photographed in active poses (on the warpath, fishing, dancing) while women were depicted in more decorative, passive poses (day-dreaming, waiting, watching). Curtis generally avoided visual references to the alleged sexual promiscuity of Indian women, unlike the gratuitous nudity in the portrayal of Indian women by several of Curtis' contemporaries. But the titles of his photographs often give a sexual twist to their interpretation which is not immediately apparent from the visual image itself. *At the Trysting Place* (1921) is a case in point. Curtis' title refers unequivocally to a place of romantic assignation while the photograph itself carries no clear indication of such a motive. It simply shows two Hopi women in traditional costumes and hairstyles, waiting by the side of a path under a tree (Figure 6.6). The imputation of a sexual motive is entirely adventitious.

FIGURE 6.6 At the Trysting Place (E.S. Curtis 1921).
Source: Smithsonian Institution, photo no. 90–14318.

Whatever our judgement on these issues, it is evident that Curtis indulged in fewer fabrications as his work progressed. In the later phases of his project, particularly in volume 19 of *The North American Indian*, published in 1928, there is less attempt to disguise the effects of acculturation than in the early volumes. Parasols and motor cars are clearly visible in several of these photographs where they would have been removed by retouching in earlier phases of the project. European commodities were, of course, more widespread by this point. But more cynical readings are also possible. It could be argued, for example, that Curtis' later work simply represents the final phase in the 'domestication' of the Indian: having removed the potential military threat to westward expansion, the American public could now afford the luxury of romanticising the Indian, a process in which Curtis' photographs were certainly implicated. Changing images of the American Indian, from savagery to nobility, and more or less idealised representations of the Indians' relationship to the land must clearly be interpreted in terms of these changing material circumstances. So, too, must the revival of Curtis' popularity since the 1970s.

REPRESENTING CURTIS

Having discussed how Curtis represented Indian culture to the contemporary American public, it is also worth considering how Curtis has himself been represented since the publication of his work in the early decades of the twentieth century. If an examination of Curtis' work demonstrates that there can never be a 'correct' way of representing other cultures divorced from the material context in which those representations are made, then an analysis of Curtis' fluctuating fortunes demonstrates the equal impossibility of reaching a definitive judgement of the photographer's intellectual, moral and artistic worth. Soon after publication of the first volumes of *The North American Indian*, Curtis' reputation rose from that of local hero ('Seattle Man Triumphs', *Seattle Times*, 22 May 1904) to national celebrity ('the most talked of man in the United States in that line of work', *Seattle Times*, 11 June 1905). The support and patronage of President Roosevelt and J.P. Morgan ensured that Curtis' work was taken seriously, even if the project was never a great financial success.

The fate of Curtis' work was itself a reflection of the crisis of confidence through which the United States was passing during his lifetime. The Depression years were not an auspicious time for selling volumes of lavishly-produced photographs that cost several thousand dollars. But even as the country's economic fortunes improved, national attitudes towards the treatment of American Indians were also beginning to change. Once the human cost of westward expansion began to be recognised, few people wanted to be reminded of Curtis' 'vanishing race'.

During the 1960s, however, Curtis' reputation began to improve with the rise of environmental awareness, civil rights campaigns and the growth of an increasingly politicised native rights movement. In the 1970s, major exhibitions of Curtis' work appeared at the Pierpont Morgan Library in New York and at the Philadelphia Museum of Art (Brown 1972), with complete sets of *The North American Indian* selling for over US $70,000. Curtis began to be lionised by anthologists and biographers, two of whom describe *The North American Indian* as 'the most remarkable undertaking by one man in the history of books' (Graybill and Boesen 1976, p. 109). With the publication of Lyman's critical study, accompanying the Smithsonian exhibition in 1982, Curtis' reputation once again hung in the balance. Lyman himself reflects generously on Curtis' benign intentions and on the constant financial pressure under which he worked, but still considers his work to have been guilty of deception. The repudiation of Curtis as the creator of a racist illusion was under way.

If anachronistic judgements are to be avoided, it is important to assess Curtis' work in relation to appropriate contemporary standards including the emerging scientific establishment of professional anthropologists and museum curators. Here, it is worth noting that Curtis' status was never fully assured. His work was spurned by several national institutions such as the Smithsonian Museum, which never bought a subscription to *The North American Indian*. Another point of comparison might be with the leading photographers of his day. Here, a more positive assessment is possible, for Curtis' photographs bear favourable comparison with the work of many of his peers, avoiding sexist stereotyping of Indian women and bloodthirsty shots of Indian men which were all too popular with other photographers. Neither was Curtis alone in posing his subjects or lending them props in order to achieve the desired ethnographic or artistic effect. Similar practices were common among Curtis' contemporaries, including such luminaries as John Wesley Powell and Edweard Muybridge. Clearly, there are dangers in judging Curtis by the moral and professional standards of another generation. Christopher Lyman's work and the Smithsonian exhibition run this risk, giving present-day viewers a sense of moral superiority in relation to Curtis' apparently more innocent contemporary audiences. A more balanced judgement might concede that portraits of other societies always contain elements of illusion, distortion and misrepresentation, especially where the encounter is characterised by such rampant inequalities as separated the American Indian from Curtis' viewing public.

Curtis' work contains evidence of conscious manipulation and deliberate deception. But this merely highlights the extent to which all representations of other cultures are an ideological fiction (Hall 1997)—cultural constructions which reveal in their making the interests that they serve. Curtis' photographs may have their idiosyncrasies but they also reveal a characteristic 'way of seeing' that was common among Curtis' contemporaries. His romanticised portraits of Indian culture and his exaggeration of their harmony with nature helped soften the image of the primitive 'savage', but they also served to confirm the superior self-image of the white 'race'. For all their aesthetic qualities, Curtis' photographs cannot be divorced from their ideological role in the legitimation of white supremacy. In this sense, Curtis' photographic 'way of seeing' is inseparable from the imperialism that it both reflected and helped reproduce. This surely is their primary significance for cultural geographers.

CONCLUSION: CONSTRUCTIONS OF CULTURE

The interpretation of Curtis' photographs provides a good example of what anthropologists now refer to as a 'crisis of representation' (Marcus and Fischer 1986). The phrase implies that it is no longer possible to assume the mantle of scientific objectivity which Victorian anthropologists once confidently adopted in their descriptions of other cultures. The innocence that may once have informed such representations has long since been lost in the move towards a more critical sense of cultural politics.

Photography poses particular problems in this regard, with its illusion of objectivity and its beguiling sense of transparent meaning ('the camera never lies'). Uncovering photography's hidden codes is a complex and contradictory process, since the dominant code of photographic realism gives every appearance of being *uncoded* (Hutcheon 1989). However, art historians and cultural critics are becoming increasingly aware of what John Tagg has called the 'burden of representation' (Tagg 1988), challenging the notion of photography as a mere record of reality. Whether one considers the documentary tradition, the use of photography in official surveillance or the 'science' of visual anthropology (Collier 1967), photography comprises a site of struggle in which the meaning of visual images and their political significance are often fiercely contested.

How then are we to view Curtis' photographs and what lessons does his work contain for contemporary cultural geography? The essential contradiction, it seems, is that Native American culture is an integral part of US history and yet Curtis' photographs have always been valued for their evocation of a sense of cultural 'otherness'. At first, Curtis deliberately set out to record the 'primitive', to document what he saw as a 'vanishing race'. For a time his photographs were praised for their anthropological interest as portraits of an exotic 'other', while today his work is being reassessed in the knowledge that America's westward expansion was achieved at enormous human cost. To judge the cultural significance of Curtis' work requires that we see his photographs not so much as the product of one man's unique vision as representative of a broader cultural 'way of seeing'.

If Curtis' work contains elements of demonstrable falsehood, misrepresentation and deception, it also raises general questions about the extent to which members of one group can ever fully and accurately represent the culture of another group, especially when the power differential between them is so great. Anthropologists have begun to reflect critically on the politics of representation in constructing ethnographic accounts of other cultures, but even they have tended to focus on verbal rather than on visual media (see Clifford and Marcus 1986; Geertz 1988). As geographers enter the contested terrain of cultural politics, we need to sharpen our sensitivity to the visual. However, most importantly, as this analysis of Curtis' photographs suggests, we must also insist on the inseparability of aesthetic, 'scientific' and political judgements. Though Curtis and his contemporaries would no doubt have denied it, his work provides ample evidence of the extent to which the cultural is political.

ACKNOWLEDGMENTS

I would like to thank the Librarian of the Museum of Mankind (British Museum Department of Ethnography) for letting me consult a facsimile edition of Curtis' *The North American Indian* in the museum's collection. Also, many thanks to Jane Jacobs, Jan Penrose, Hugh Price, Teall Triggs, Sarah Whatmore, Peter Wood and the editors for thoughtful criticism of previous drafts.

REFERENCES

Abramson, H.S. 1987, *National Geographic: Behind America's Lens on the World,* Crown, New York.

Agee, J. & Evans, W. 1939, *Let Us Now Praise Famous Men,* Houghton, Mifflin, Boston.

Anderson, K. 1991, *Vancouver's Chinatown: Racial Discourse in Canada,* McGill Queens University Press, Kingston.

Banton, M. 1987, *Racial Theories,* Cambridge University Press, Cambridge.

Barnes, T.J. & Duncan J.S. (eds) 1992, *Writing Worlds: Discourse, Text and Metaphor in the Representation of Landscape,* Routledge, London and New York.

Barthes, R. (ed.) 1977, 'The photographic message', in *Image-music-text,* S. Heath (trans.), Hill & Wang, New York, pp. 15–31.

Berger, J. 1972, *Ways of Seeing,* Penguin, Harmondsworth.

Berkhofer, R.F. Jr 1978, *The White Man's Indian: Images of the American Indian from Columbus to the Present,* Alfred A. Knopf, New York.

Blackman, M. 1980, 'Posing the American Indian', *Natural History,* vol. 89, pp. 68–75.

Brown, D. 1970, *Bury my Heart at Wounded Knee* , Barrie & Jenkins, London.

Brown, J.E. 1972, 'Introduction: mirrors for identity in the photographs of Edward Curtis', in *The North American Indians: A Selection of Photographs by Edward S. Curtis,* Aperture, New York, pp. 6–12.

Clifford, J. 1986, 'Introduction: partial truths', in *Writing Culture: The Poetics and Politics of Ethnography,* eds J. Clifford & G.E. Marcus, University of California Press, Berkeley, CA, pp. 1–26.

Clifford, J. & Marcus, G.E. 1986, *Writing Culture: The Politics and Poetics of Ethnography,* University of California Press, Berkeley, CA.

Collier, J. Jr. 1967, *Visual Anthropology: Photography as Research Method,* Holt, Rhinehart & Winston, New York.

Cosgrove, D.E. & Daniels, S.J. (eds) 1988, *The Iconography of Landscape,* Cambridge University Press, Cambridge.

Cowling, M. 1989, *The Artist as Anthropologist: The Representation of Type and Character in Victorian Art* , Cambridge University Press, Cambridge.

Curtis, E.S. 1907–30, *The North American Indian* (20 vols. and supplements), privately printed.

Duncan, J.S. 1990, *The City as Text: The Politics of Landscape Interpretation in the Kandyan Kingdom,* Cambridge University Press, Cambridge.

Geertz, C. 1988, *Works and Lives: The Anthropologist as Author* , Stanford University Press, Stanford.

Gidley, M. 1987, '"The vanishing race" in sight and sound: Edward S. Curtis' musicale of North American Indian life', *Prospects* , vol. 12, pp. 59–87.

Graybill, F. C. & Boesen, V. 1976, *Edward Sheriff Curtis: Visions of a Vanishing Race*, Thomas Y. Crowell Co., New York.

Green, D. 1984, 'Classified subjects: photography and anthropology', *Ten.8* , vol. 14, pp. 30–7.

Hall, S. (ed.) 1997, *Representation: Cultural Representations and Significant Practices*, Sage, London.

Harding, S. 1986, *The Science Question in Feminism*, Cornell University Press, Ithaca, New York.

Hutcheon, L. 1989, *The Politics of Postmodernism*, Routledge, London.

Jackson, P. 1987. 'The idea of "race" and the geography of racism', in *Race and Racism: Essays in Social Geography*, ed. P. Jackson, Allen & Unwin, London, pp. 3–21.

Jackson, P. 1992, *Maps of Meaning*, Routledge, London.

Jones, G. 1980, *Social Darwinism and English Thought: The Interaction Between Biological and Social Theory*, Harvester Press, Brighton.

Lowie R.H. 1935, *The Crow Indians*, Farrar and Rinehart, New York.

Lyman, C.M. 1982, *The Vanishing Race and Other Illusions: Photographs of Indians by Edward Curtis*, Smithsonian Institution Press, Washington DC.

McGee, W.J. 1910, 'Review', *American Anthropologist* , vol. 12, pp. 448–50.

Marcus, G. & Fischer, M. (eds) 1986, *Anthropology as Cultural Critique*, Cambridge University Press, Cambridge.

Rex, J. & Mason, D. (eds) 1986, *Theories of Race and Ethnic Relations*, Cambridge University Press, Cambridge.

Riis, J. 1890, *How the Other Half Lives*, Charles Scribner's Sons, New York.

Rose, G. 1993, *Feminism and Geography: The Limits of Geographical Knowledge*, Polity Press, Cambridge.

Said, E.W. 1978, *Orientalism*, Random House, New York.

Samuel, R. (ed.) 1981, *People's History and Socialist Theory*, Routledge & Kegan Paul, London.

Samuels, M.S. 1979, 'The biography of landscape', in *The Interpretation of Ordinary Landscapes*, ed. D.W. Meinig, Oxford University Press, New York, pp. 51–88.

Sayer, A. 1989, 'The "new" regional geography and problems of narrative', *Environment and Planning D: Society and Space*, vol. 7, no. 3, pp. 253–76.

Schwartz, J.M. & Ryan, J. (eds) 1998, *Picturing Place: Photography and the Geographical Imagination*, John Wiley & Sons Ltd, London.

Sontag, S. 1975, 'Fascinating fascism', *New York Review of Books*, February 6, pp. 23–30; reprinted in *A Susan Sontag Reader*, Penguin, Harmondsworth pp. 305–25.

Sullivan, L.R. 1923, *Essentials of Anthropometry: A Handbook for Explorers and Museum Collectors*, American Museum of Natural History, New York.

Tagg, J. 1988, *The Burden of Representation: Essays on Photographies and Histories*, Macmillan Education, London.

Wissler, C. 1917, *The American Indian*, Douglas C. McMurtie, New York.

7

Outsiders in society and space

David Sibley

INTRODUCTION

Sigmund Freud remarked that one of the accomplishments of civilisation is to achieve a state of cleanliness and order—'The benefits of order are incontestable: it enables us to use space and time to the best advantage'. Conversely, he observed that 'Dirt seems to us incompatible with civilisation' (Freud 1930, pp. 56–7). The two assertions are connected in the sense that the ordering of space and time results in the stigmatising of some human activities and cultures because they do not fit those modes of order preferred by the dominant society. Things and people which do not fit may be represented negatively as 'dirt' or matter out of place, as Mary Douglas (1966) put it. Cultural difference may be one form of being out of place which is a consequence of the impress of order on society. Conceptions of what is clean (ordered) and what is dirty (disordered) render some minorities as discrepant and 'dirt' because their ways of organising their lives differ from those of the majority. They may be 'dirt' also in the sense that they are perceived as merging with the nonhuman world. Thus, indigenous minorities like the Inuit (Eskimo) and native North Americans have been portrayed 'at one with nature'—as a part of the natural world rather than civilisation. In the same vein, racist propaganda has effectively dehumanised people by associating them with, or representing them as, animals which are widely considered to be unclean and polluting, like rats and pigs. Frederick Douglass noted in his autobiography how slaves were dehumanised by bracketing them with animals: 'There were horses and men, cattle and women, pigs and children, all holding the same rank in the scale of being, and all were subjected to the same narrow examination' (Boime 1990, p. 211). Nature is a source of powerful metaphors for negative constructions of 'otherness'.

This chapter explores the social construction of stigmatised groups, examining both stereotyped images which have entered popular consciousness and have confirmed marginal or residual status in advanced capitalist societies, and the anatomy of the spaces to which outsiders have been relegated. The perception of some minority cultures as being beyond the boundaries of 'society' is associated not only with characterisations of the group, but also with images of particular places, landscapes of exclusion which express the marginal status of the outsider group. This argument is illustrated with reference to Gypsy communities in Britain (also known as Roma elsewhere in Europe, in the Americas and Australasia), but the ideas have some relevance to groups other than racialised minorities (Sibley 1995). There are some similarities in the response to minority cultures like Gypsies and to those who have been quite inappropriately lumped together as 'deviant', particularly the mentally ill and those with learning difficulties (Wolch and Dear 1987; Philo 1989). Similar problems of misrepresentation and a desire to exclude in a social and spatial sense have been expressed, for example, in the construction of isolated asylums in the nineteenth century. As Philo (1989, p. 284) observed: 'In the long term the practical consequence of having a network of "coded spaces" devoted specifically to mad people was to produce and then continually to reproduce a population designated as different, deviant and dangerous by "mainstream" society.'

In order to understand how socio-spatial constructions of the minority have been shaped in the case of Gypsy communities, this chapter will look first at conflicting world views, the difference between Gypsy culture as it is articulated by members of the community themselves, and the distorted representations which result inevitably from interpreting visible elements of the minority culture in the context of dominant world views.

THE ROMANTIC, THE DEVIANT AND THE OTHER

In human geography, difference, alterity, otherness and hybridity have been defining issues in the recent 'cultural turn', although this interest does echo earlier concern elsewhere in the social sciences about unsubtle accounts of humanity. In feminist writing, in particular, it has been argued that general descriptive categories like 'class' or 'woman' neglect significant social cleavages and forms of oppression. Michelle Barrett (1987, p. 30), for example, has suggested that to treat a category like 'class' as essential or universal does violence to a range of collective experiences which are actually or potentially significant in a political sense, like the experience of working-class African-Caribbean women in Britain. She suggested that 'the claims of nation, region and ethnicity, as well as age, sexual orientation, disability and religion are being pressed as important and politically salient forms of experiential diversity'. Social scientists need to be sensitive to difference and to inform debates about what constitutes 'normality' and 'deviance'. At the grass roots, singular views on what is 'normal' and acceptable and, conversely, what registers as deviance and warrants correction, contribute to community conflict. The problem is typified by a letter to an English local newspaper, the *Walsall Observer,* which expressed hostility to the presence of Irish Travellers in the locality: 'Why, in heaven's name, don't [these] members of a foreign public stay in their own country and live in houses there, like normal people?' (Sibley 1981, p. 23).

Acknowledging that there are a number of 'salient forms of experiential diversity' as Barrett puts it, it is still difficult to capture these differences because the world views of others are in varying degrees inaccessible or muted. Cultural difference implies that people communicate in different idioms and employ different categories to make sense of their world (Ardener 1975). Even without a language barrier it may be difficult to represent other world views authentically. In developing a sense of self-identity, we all engage in 'an endless series of misrepresentations, all of which share an essential quality, the quality of otherness, of being not-me' (Hoggett 1992, p. 356). These misrepresentations, or stereotypes, may become fixed as a part of a collective identity; however they may also be reproduced by written and visual media and sanctioned by law. Minorities will also misrepresent the larger society, but this is not such a serious problem. It is state agencies and antagonistic communities which have the power and the capacity to affect the lives of minority groups, and state policies for minorities can be oppressive partly because they are informed by partial and stereotyped views.

Representations of Gypsies in some academic writing, in the visual media and in novels demonstrate both repulsion and desire which Gilman (1985) has argued are essential qualities of the stereotype. Gypsies are portrayed both as romantic and deviant. The romantic image, which appears in cultural forms as diverse as opera (Carmen) and tourist brochures advertising the 'natural' attractions of the Camargue in the south of France (wild bulls, wild horses, flamingoes and Gypsies), fits a world view in which Gypsies are seen as a part of nature or of an imagined pre-industrial existence. This image draws on myths of nomadism and the exotic. Nomadism is equated with freedom, with escape from the constraints of settled society, while 'the Gypsy personality' is associated with passion, colour and mystery. The place of the romantic Gypsy in popular culture is suggested by a picture from a Monsoon clothes catalogue, with women modelling 'ethnic' fashions draped around a bow-topped wagon, the acceptable mode of shelter and transport for Travellers in Britain (Figure 7.1). The deviant consists of visible elements of Gypsy culture, associated primarily with work and shelter, which are seen out of context. That is to say, in deviant representations there is no appreciation of the practical needs of a semi-nomadic people whose survival may depend partly on recycling materials discarded by the larger society. The majority do not like to be reminded of their residues which are transferred to Gypsy culture as a malignant and polluting presence.

Ironically, a mythical, romantic Gypsy culture features as the authentic culture in popular responses to Travellers, as distinct from the 'they are not real Gypsies' reaction to those actually encountered. Visible features of modern Gypsy culture, such as chrome-trimmed trailers parked on waste

FIGURE 7.1 Use of the romantic Gypsy image in advertising. Advertisement produced by Phyllis Walters Ltd, London, for Monsoon Fashion Catalogues.

ground in cities and surrounded by piles of scrap metal and wrecked cars, pram wheels and milk-churns for storing water (Figure 7.2) clearly do not correspond to the romantic stereotype and so, in this sense, the people

FIGURE 7.2 Illegal Gypsy encampment in Hull, 1979.

observed are not 'real'. At the same time, they violate accepted notions of the appropriate use of land in cities. The 'real' Gypsy belongs in the countryside, preferably in the past, part of a cosy image of rural life (Figure 7.3) whereas the people camped on waste ground in cities are perceived as transgressive, violating an ordered urban landscape. This is reflected in English newspapers, reporting opposition to urban Gypsy sites. Consider, for example, 'City could be gipsy (sic) dump' (*Hull Daily Mail,* 7 November 1990) and similarly: 'A spokesman for [York] corporation said that it was a long standing policy to clear sites, and tipping refuse was part of that policy. "If you don't tip, you will get more gipsies (sic)", he said' (*The Guardian,* 4 September 1975). In these two instances, there is a clear association between residual matter, refuse, and a residual population. Coded terms used to describe British Travellers, particularly 'tinker' and 'itinerant', are heavily invested with notions of deviance and illegitimacy, and these ascriptions reinforce the view of the group as residual.

In popular perceptions of the Gypsy presence in Britain, the appropriate context for understanding Gypsy culture, that is, the world views which Gypsies themselves articulate, remains largely hidden. Gypsy beliefs about social organisation, about work and cleanliness, which make their use of land comprehensible, are out of sight. What is visible does not correspond to accepted ideas about social and spatial order which prevail in the larger society. Thus, their behaviour is viewed as anti-social rather than an expression of an alternative conception of social order. Difference is perceived as threatening.

FIGURE 7.3 Gypsy encampment near Hull, 1972.

It is notable that in many respects the values of the dominant society are reversed in Gypsy culture. This is a case of symbolic reversal associated with many minority cultures (Cohen 1985). For the Roma, it is manifest in the integration rather than separation of work, residence and recreation and in the maintenance of ritual taboos about cleanliness which are designed to avoid the pollution of the pure inner body. The latter include the avoidance of some domestic animals, particularly cats which are *mochadi* (unclean) because they lick their genitals, and the clear separation of space for defecation and residential space, although this is usually impossible if the family lives in a house or apartment. Whether practised or not, the boundary between Gypsy society and the larger society is confirmed through a series of reversals. While Gypsies are seen as polluting spaces controlled by the dominant society, *gauje* (non-Gypsy) practices pollute Gypsy space. The social distance between Gypsies and others is maintained by this boundary separating the pure and defiled.

This is not to say that relations between Gypsies and the larger society are immutable. Some British Gypsies interact freely with *gaujes* and there is a long history of intermarriage. Since the 1970s in England and Wales, the state has recognised that Gypsies have a right to education, although the question of what constitutes appropriate education has not been resolved, and between 1970 and 1994, local authorities were required to provide secure settlements for nomadic Gypsies in the form of serviced caravan sites. Sites are spaces of control. They can seriously constrain economic activities and social life, but families living on permanent sites do have more access to education, health care and other forms of social welfare than they would have if travelling. This may lead to greater contact between Gypsies and others which may in turn result in a greater awareness of cultural difference. In

1994, however, the introduction of some public order legislation for England and Wales in the Criminal Justice and Public Order Act relieved local authorities of the obligation to provide sites and strengthened the laws of trespass. The impact of this legislation is currently difficult to assess but it may result in increased conflict. When the presence of Gypsies is perceived as a threat to property values and amenity, the partial, distorted view of the minority is commonly articulated and its supposed deviance is amplified through the combined efforts of hostile communities and the local press.

The case of British Gypsies demonstrates an important general point in regard to knowledge. Some social groups and cultures are muted, meaning that they do not communicate in the same idiom as members of the dominant society, so their world views only partially register. To some extent, they are invisible. This applies to some aspects of the relationship between adult and child, women and men, the able-bodied and the physically disabled, for example, as well as cases where cultural difference is marked by ethnicity or language. A lack of knowledge may have unintended consequences, for example, the creation of oppressive play environments for children. However, knowledge is not the only consideration in explaining the marginalisation and oppression of nomadic and racialised groups like Gypsies. They pose a more fundamental threat to dominant modes of spatial organisation and, from the perspective of the sedentary *gauje* society, a spatial solution to the problem is required.

LANDSCAPES OF EXCLUSION

Space is implicated in the cultural construction of Gypsies as outsiders in two respects. First, marginal, residual spaces, places with which Gypsies are often associated (Figure 7.4), reinforce the outsider status of the minority. They may be places which are avoided by members of the larger society because they appear threatening—a fear of the 'other' becomes a fear of place. This is similar to the representation of the 'inner city' in some large metropolitan areas in England, where images of place are inextricably linked to the imagined deviance of black minorities (Keith 1987; Smith 1989). Stereotypes of place compound the stereotype of the group. A second role for space in the construction of marginality concerns the arrangement of spaces in the built environment. Spatial structures can strengthen or weaken social boundaries, thus extruding a minority and making it more conspicuous or, conversely, rendering the group less visible. What happens in particular instances depends on visions of society projected by the state—who belongs and who does not belong, the power of the state and capital to control space, and the capacity of those subjected to controls to be subversive and resist.

Historically, it is possible to recognise strong expressions of power in the ordering of space under particular regimes. In early urban societies such as the meso-American civilisations, for example, the imprint of priestly power was very clear. In Teotihuacan in Mexico, the bounded, enclosed central

FIGURE 7.4 Gypsies camped under a motorway in Arles, south of France, 1990.

space was clearly the locus of the priest-kings and one which should not be profaned. Similarly, Neusner (1973) suggested that in ancient Israel the rabbis could proscribe a wide range of things and activities as polluting and this effectively gave them power to exclude people not only from the temple but also the land of Israel. The list of pollutants included some animals, women after childbirth, skin ailments and other bodily conditions. In the modern European city from the Baroque period onwards, planning has commonly emphasised the cleaning or purification of urban space through the insertion of boulevards and squares. Challenges to authority in the form of popular uprisings were more conspicuous if they violated these purified spaces and they were more easily put down than they would have been in the winding alleys of pre-Baroque cities (Mumford 1961, pp. 369–70). Also, as Corbin (1986) remarked, planning was a means of removing the smell of the proletariat. In cities, which are creations of the twentieth century, particularly capital cities like Brasilia, power is still expressed in grand designs and simple geometries.

More generally, spaces which are homogeneous or uniform, from which non-conforming groups have been expelled or have been kept out through the maintenance of strong boundaries, can be termed 'pure' in the sense that they are free from polluting elements. The purification of space is a process by which power is exercised over individuals or groups who appear discrepant if they fail to conform to the values of those who have the power to exclude (Sibley 1988, 1995). Clearly, difference will be visible in a space which is uniform and where homogeneity is valued more than it would be in an area of mixed land uses and social heterogeneity. Residents in a socially and physically homogeneous neighbourhood, for example, may strive to erect barriers to exclude those who are perceived to constitute a threat to the homogeneity which the residents have been conditioned to value. The first account of this problem was probably Richard Sennett's *The Uses of Disorder* (1970), where he argued that the North American suburb, as an ideal type of social area, was both exclusive and repressive. The question is a more general one than Sennett suggested, however. We can begin to understand the connection between the organisation of space and social or cultural difference by looking at an analogous problem in education.

SPACES, BOUNDARIES AND CONTROL

In an attempt to understand the relationship between the content of school curricula and control systems in education, Basil Bernstein (1967) developed a number of schemata which focused on subject boundaries and content. As a control problem, the structuring and organisation of the transmission of knowledge is analogous to the question of regulating spatial boundaries and locating objects or social groups in spatial units. In 'Open schools, open society' (1967), Bernstein distinguished between an open curriculum, which emphasised the interconnections of different branches of knowledge and thus the blurring of subject boundaries, and a closed curriculum in which knowledge is compartmentalised and boundaries between subjects are strongly defined. The former he equated with a democratic approach to learning, where students participate in making decisions about what is taught, and the latter with a hierarchical, centralised system where decisions are made at the top and transmitted downwards with little opportunity for reconstituting knowledge through interdisciplinary work. In fact, it is in the interest of those in control of the closed curriculum to encourage the maintenance of boundaries between subjects. Their position is secured by the retention of strong boundaries and 'pure' subjects because this discourages new thinking across traditional subject boundaries which would present a challenge to authority.

Bernstein later formalised these ideas, describing the organisation of knowledge in terms of classification and framing (Bernstein 1971). Classification, according to Bernstein, can be either strong or weak. With strong classification, boundaries are clearly defined and the knowledge contained within the boundaries is identified in unambiguous terms. Homogeneity is valued and the blurring of boundaries is seen as a threat to the integrity of the subject. Thus, strong classification is characteristic of the closed curriculum. Weak classification, by contrast, signifies weakly defined subject boundaries and a concern for the integration of knowledge. Similarly, within subject areas, strong framing means that there are clear rules about what may and what may not be taught, whereas weak framing means that many possible relationships and interconnections are explored.

Open/closed or strongly classified/weakly classified curricula could also be seen as alternative models for society, one where power is diffuse and the other where power is concentrated in the hands of a few at the top of a political hierarchy. In applying Bernstein's ideas to the organisation of space, it is this connection with the distribution of power which should be recognised. Strongly classified spaces have clear boundaries, their internal homogeneity and order are valued and there is, in consequence, a concern with boundary maintenance in order to keep out objects or people who do not fit the classification. Weakly classified spaces will have weakly defined or fuzzy boundaries because they are characterised by social mixing and/or mixed land uses. Difference in these circumstances will not be obvious and, if mixture and diversity are accepted, policing of boundaries will be unnecessary. Generally, strongly classified spaces will also be strongly framed because a concern for the overall homogeneity of a locality, a suburb for example, will be mirrored in a desire for internal order and separation. Weak framing would suggest more numerous and more fluid relationships between people and the built environment than occur with strong framing. Buildings may have multiple uses, either simultaneously or at different times of day, for example. Using this schema, it is possible to see how space contributes to the social construction of the outsider as a 'folk devil'.

The spatial context of the outsider problem refers to the presence of a non-conforming group in a strongly classified space or the fear that the group will intrude into a space which is strongly classified. The desire to maintain a space as a strongly classified one will heighten anxieties. The distancing from others which is a consequence of strong classification makes it likely that these others will appear to fearful communities as negative stereotypes. To illustrate this point, Richard Sennett described an affluent suburban community in Chicago in the late nineteenth century, 'Union Park', where there was a panic following a spate of armed robberies in the city. Whatever the real circumstances of these crimes, in Union Park 'everyone knew immediately what was wrong, and what was wrong was overwhelming: it was nothing less than the power of the "foreigner", the outsider who had suddenly become dominant in the city' (Sennett 1971, pp. 228–89). The folk-devils in this case were 'Italian anarchists'. In response to a threat that was more imagined than real, 'only a state of rigid barriers, enforced by a semi-military state of curfew and surveillance would permit the suburban community to continue to function'. External threat, however, may also lead to internal cleansing, an urge to expel anyone who appears not to represent collective values. This urge to purify territory has been evident in many historical episodes and at several spatial scales. To give two further examples, first, the Salem witch trials in seventeenth-century Massachusetts showed how any woman behaving in a way which appeared to depart from an ever more narrowly defined set of community values could be accused of witchcraft and hanged; second, the conflict in the former Yugoslavia in the early 1990s showed how anxieties about neighbours marked as different by their ethnicity could spiral out of control, resulting in 'ethnic cleansing' or genocide.

It can be argued, therefore, that there is a connection between the strong classification of space and the rejection of social groups who are non-conforming. Further, there is evidence that minorities who are obliged to live in strongly classified and strongly framed environments characteristic of planned settlements, which include approximately half the Traveller-Gypsy population of England and Wales (as opposed to Gypsies living in houses or apartments) and many groups of indigenous peoples living in the Arctic and sub-Arctic, in Canada, Greenland, Scandinavia and Russia (Osherenko and Young 1989), may find the organisation of space in settlements, or on official sites in the case of English and Welsh Gypsies, constraining and alienating. In these cases the spatial organisation of settlements and the control regime conflict with traditional ways of organising space and social life. They take no account of extended family networks or the need to combine work and residence.

To summarise, space is an integral part of the outsider problem. The way in which space is organised affects the perception of the 'other', whether as foreign and threatening or simply as different. The strong classification of space, as in the archetypal homogeneous suburb, implies a rejection of difference so the difference of minority groups in such spaces is amplified. Similarly, when strong classification is imposed on a minority which has a value system different to that of the dominant society, its cultural practices are likely to appear deviant to the control agencies, thus justifying the control regime. In weakly classified space, minorities will be less visible, they may not be identified as non-conforming and, consequently, the potential for conflict over space is reduced. Because behaviour is less likely to be recognised as deviant, control will not be so much of an issue. Thus, we can generally anticipate an association between the strong classification of space and the identification of discrepant others.

EXCLUSION AND ADAPTATION: RELATIONS BETWEEN GYPSIES AND THE DOMINANT SOCIETY

The aspects of Gypsy culture described so far in this chapter are characteristic of the British population. However, Gypsies exhibit considerable cultural diversity partly due to the different ways in which they have related to the cultural practices and values of the majority population. Gypsies are a minority in all European countries (including Russia), in parts of the Middle East, particularly Egypt and Iran, in central Asia and in India and Pakistan. In addition, the Gypsy diaspora has taken them to the Americas, particularly Brazil, Argentina, the United States and Canada, and to Australia and New Zealand. Although Gypsies have an ethnic identity secured by language, economy and other cultural attributes, they have intermarried with other nomadic groups and with the settled population. Indeed, it is meaningless to talk about a racial identity although Gypsies have been racialised in the sense that aspects of their way of life viewed negatively have been described as racially inherent. This has provided legitimation for discrimination and exclusion.

In Britain and Holland in particular there are also culturally distinct semi-nomadic groups with whom Gypsies compete for resources but who are similarly represented as rather deviant outsider groups. These include Irish and

Scottish Travellers living in England and Wales as well as in their native countries, Woonwagenbevoners (caravan dwellers), who are native Dutch Travellers, and New Age or New Travellers in Britain and France. Within the European Gypsy population, communities distinguish themselves by kin-ties, place associations and occupational traditions which have contributed to the emergence of distinctive cultural identities, although complex patterns of migration have blurred any regional patterns which might have existed. Some of the larger groups include the Kalderas, traditionally metal workers from Russia who are now found in Paris, Gothenburg and other western European cities and also in the United States, notably in the San Francisco Bay area and Los Angeles; the Boyash, from Hungary and Romania, but also settled in western Europe and North America and with strong traditions in entertainment; the Sinti and Manus, widespread in Europe; and the Vlach ('Wallachian') in Romania and Hungary. However, self-ascriptions are complex and refer to different kin-groupings and national identities. Also, Gypsies may not refer to themselves as Gypsy because of the pejorative use of the word by *gaujes*. It is for this reason that many British Gypsies most of the time describe themselves as Travellers while Rom or Roma, meaning 'the people' in Romany, are self-ascriptions more commonly used by continental European Gypsies. As Liegeois (1986, p. 46) observed: 'Gypsies … are defined as such by the views and attitudes of others.'

The Gypsy economy is one of the most significant indicators of cultural distinctiveness. However, it is not occupations but attitudes to work that are defining characteristics of the economy. The economic niches occupied by Gypsies at different times and in different places vary considerably but what is distinctive is that Gypsies avoid wage labour where possible and try to maintain a dominant position in any transaction as a matter of ethnic pride. They value flexibility and opportunism, with several money-making activities such as scrap metal dealing, horse-trading and hawking often being pursued simultaneously in one family. To some extent, attitudes to work define the boundary between Gypsies and *gaujes* (although non-Gypsy traders may also exhibit similar opportunism and flexibility). Okely (1979, p. 20) suggested that self-employment was crucial in defining this boundary, but there may be circumstances where self-employment is not possible. In Communist regimes in central and eastern Europe, for example, most adults were required to work for the state, particularly in factories, but in Hungary in the late-1980s, Vlach Gypsies combined factory work with horse-trading, scavenging for metal (while employed as refuse collectors) and cultivating plots of land in 'Gypsy villages'. Since the end of Communism and the collapse of state enterprises, Hungarian Gypsies have had to compete in the informal economy with others on the margins, and smuggling, currency dealing, drug-dealing and prostitution have been added to the list of Roma occupations as they have struggled to survive. Although highly dependent on dominant economies which are themselves subject to the destabilising effects of global capitalism, Gypsies in their face-to-face transactions with *gaujes* are concerned not to get into a dependent position. They see the larger society as exploitable.

Being mobile and living on the margin allows Gypsies to exploit the residual products of the dominant economy such as domestic scrap, and to provide services where mobility and minimal capital outlay give a competitive advantage. One example given by Ann Sutherland in the 1970s (Sutherland 1975) was of Kalderas in Oakland, California, who carried on their tradition of metal working by repairing supermarket trolleys and removing dents from metal car fenders (bumpers), work which could be done with very few tools. The modern Gypsy economy is highly dependent on customers and resources produced in cities. In many countries Gypsies are primarily an urban minority yet they are located elsewhere in popular imagery. The fact that they are placed in the countryside has important consequences for urban Gypsy communities. If Gypsies are not associated with the city, it may be easier for them to pass as non-Gypsy traders. In some occupations, like second-hand car sales or house repairs, a Gypsy stereotype of unreliability would be bad for business, so it is advantageous to be able to disguise ethnic identity.

In the 1980s, the Kalderas in the working-class eastern suburbs of Paris found that presenting themselves as *gaujes*—made easier because they lived in small houses or bungalows (pavilions)—helped in getting contracts for building repairs and other work which is not usually associated with Gypsies (Williams 1982). By contrast, when Gypsies live in trailers and stop on unauthorised sites in cities, the rural association accentuates their 'deviance' in the eyes of antagonistic house dwellers. Here, they are polluting because they do not belong in an urban setting. English and Welsh Travellers may not be accepted in rural areas either because the visible features of their culture—chrome-trimmed trailers, piles of scrap metal, prams and milk-churns—represent disorder in an ordered landscape. In the past, even wagon dwellers such as those shown in Figure 7.3, were vilified in the local press because their stopping places were deemed untidy. They did not match up to the rural idyll. There is no 'proper place' for Gypsies because, according to the romantic stereotype, they are always distant in space and time.

PREJUDICE IN PRACTICE: SEPARATION, CONTAINMENT AND CONTROL

In Europe there is a long history of attempts by the state, or by local groups with government sanction, to remove Gypsies from national territory. The Nazi regime in Germany was the last to attempt this, through genocide. In some instances, there may be no attempt to expel Gypsies but their lives may be made so insecure, through the denial of citizenship, that they emigrate. During 1997 and 1998 Roma from the Czech Republic, for example, have been trying to gain refugee status in Canada and Britain because the state (in the Czech Republic and in Slovakia) has failed to accept responsibility for the minority. In modern industrialised nations the more general objective has been to settle and contain Gypsies, to remove them from locations where they are perceived as a non-conforming outsider group, violating space valued by the settled society, particularly residential space. Separation rather than integration has been the unstated goal of most settlement policies (Sibley 1987). An alternative response in central and eastern European countries during the Communist period was to deny that Gypsies had a cultural identity and to house them with other workers. In Romania, for example, the Roma did not appear in censuses of 'nationalities' even though the country has the largest Gypsy population in Europe.

Liegeois (1986) documented past attempts by European states to eliminate or remove Gypsies. In the seventeenth and eighteenth centuries, sanctions included hanging Gypsy men (in Slovakia in 1710 and Prussia in 1721), the mutilation of women and children, flogging, branding, forced labour and banishment, including deportation from Britain to North America and Australia. In France a common punishment for being a Gypsy was to be sent to the galleys for life. The harshest penalties were eventually seen to be ineffective, however, and other measures were substituted, with the same objective of removing Gypsies from sight, through physical expulsion to remote locations or cultural annihilation (assimilation).

LOCAL RESPONSES: THE CASE OF GYPSIES IN HULL

There is a connection between this history of exclusion and responses to Gypsies in modern societies. Attitudes to Gypsies in the developed world still suggest that the minority constitutes a threat to social order and, in some countries, a threat to spatial order. Thus, in a country like Britain, where the land use planning system reflects widely accepted notions of spatial order and amenity, unregulated Gypsy settlements constitute deviant landscapes. The response of the state to this deviance was, from the 1970s to 1994 when the enabling legislation was repealed, to impose order on Gypsy communities through the medium of official sites, to isolate and transform them in a controlled environment. The way in which these controls were exercised locally can be demonstrated with reference to the recent history of the Gypsy population in Hull, in the north-east of England.

Gypsies have lived in Hull for at least one hundred and fifty years. During the time when Traveller families were campaigning against evictions in the early 1970s, old people recalled spending winters during their childhood in rented houses in the inner city and migrating for agricultural work in the summer months. While some families maintained this seasonal pattern of movement and settlement until about 1975, most had by this time settled permanently in the city. They camped, illegally, on roadsides or in fields close to a large local authority housing estate on the edge of the city or on land made available by housing clearance in the inner city.

This was a period of persistent conflict. Evictions by the local authority were frequent and antagonistic comments were publicised by the local press in a series of alarmist articles. Effectively, Gypsies were the subject of a moral panic. One demonstration in the summer of 1973 by local authority tenants demanding the removal of a Gypsy camp close to their estate illustrated the enduring negative image of Gypsies protected by hostile communities. Some placards alluded to the deviant form of settlement: 'How much longer do we have to put up with this shanty town on our estate?' Others referred to unregulated industrial activity: 'Smokeless zone Gypsies burn car tyres, we would be fined.' Residents interviewed by the press at this time made adverse and rather bizarre comments about the Travellers' lifestyle: 'They smell, they have rats, they make a noise.' This protest had all the elements of a moral panic but there were also more routine acts of violence over a longer period, like bricks and metal bars thrown through trailer windows.

This conflict was defused by the construction of two sites in the city, both locations reflecting the local authority's desire to distance the Gypsies from the rest of the population in order to minimise conflict. The first was built in a heavily polluted industrial area which had been cleared of housing on the grounds that it was unsuitable for residential use. The second site was located on the edge of the city in an old quarry which had formerly been used for dumping rubbish. In both cases, the connection between Gypsies and residues was maintained. Through site development, Gypsies were consigned to residual space—a morally polluting minority was associated with physically polluted places.

These sites reinforced the boundary between the semi-nomadic Gypsy community and the rest of the city's population (there were other Gypsy families in houses who were less conspicuous). The isolation of the sites is coupled with designs which represent a geometry of control or 'strong classification', in Basil Bernstein's terms. Both site layouts were based on models proposed by a central government department (the Department of the Environment). Spaces for trailers were arranged in regular rows and this Gypsy space was clearly separated from the warden's space which was next to the site entrance. There was no work space. Families were evicted from one site for 'misusing' space, for example, by erecting sheds in the 'residential zone'. This kind of boundary enforcement caused discontent because the boundaries were imposed by authority and they were not those recognised as of any consequence in the Gypsy community where work, play and residence are spatially integrated. A common observation of site residents was: 'You might as well be in a house as living on this site.' Boundary enforcement, however, depends on effective policing. While one site was highly regulated, on the other site boundaries were blurred through the construction of chicken runs, dog kennels and storage sheds around some of the trailers. The warden did not attempt to maintain the separation of uses and, probably because of this, there appeared to be a higher level of satisfaction with the site. Thus, while it seems legitimate to characterise official Gypsy sites as landscapes of control or sites of surveillance, it must be acknowledged that the residents can act subversively and frustrate the efforts of the social control agencies.

CONCLUSION

The socio-spatial construction of certain groups as outsiders is a complex issue, but the problem can best be understood by focusing on boundary processes, particularly the ways in which distinctions are made between the pure and the defiled, the normal and the deviant. Taking a cue from Mary Douglas (1966), outsiders can be defined as those groups which do not fit the dominant models of society and are therefore seen as polluting. In social space, such groups disturb the actual or desired homogeneity of a locality and a common reaction of the hostile community is to expel or exclude the polluting group in order to 'purify' space. For Gypsies, both their unregulated occupation of land and the controlled environments to which some in Britain, Ireland and Holland have been relegated constitute 'deviant' landscapes which confirm their outsider status and reinforce the boundary between the minority and the dominant society.

The imaginary plays an important part in the construction of the minority as deviant and not belonging. Gypsies are stereotyped, romanticised and 'placed' in landscapes which are removed from the familiar, everyday residential environments of the majority. They belong in the past or at a distance. This imagined construction of people and place then provides an impossible yardstick against which those Gypsies who are encountered are measured. This renders their presence malign and illegitimate and provides a justification for exclusion. A fear of non-conformity is partly a fear of the nomad, a fear of transgression, notwithstanding the fact that many Gypsies are sedentary. Perceptions of an outsider group, however, are also conditioned by its visibility. While an inability to gain a complete understanding of the world view of the minority is part of the problem of stereotyping which academic research may hope to rectify, to remain out of the sight of the dominant society may also be to the advantage of the minority. In the case of Gypsies, attempting to survive in a modern urban society, to maintain an economic system which escapes state regulation depends on retaining a degree of invisibility, so myths associating Gypsies with a romantic, rural past may work to their advantage. In the city, romantic myths may help them to disappear. Visibility is also affected by structural factors, however. In particular, being able to disguise ethnic identity depends on opportunities related to the management of the housing market and the built environment, and these opportunities vary over space and time. Because their relationship to place varies and because of their cultural diversity, there can be no single representation of Gypsies as an outsider group. Gypsy territory might be 'invisible'—a house or an apartment in the city—or it might be highly visible—a patch of waste land or an official site—a landscape of exclusion. While a consciousness of the boundary with the *gauje* is a defining characteristic of Gypsy culture, this boundary can assume many shapes.

REFERENCES

Ardener, E. 1975, 'The problem revisited', in *Perceiving Women*, ed. S. Ardener, Routledge & Kegan Paul, Andover, Hants, pp. 19–27.

Barrett, M. 1987, 'The concept of difference', *Feminist Review*, vol. 26, pp. 29–41.

Bernstein, B. 1967, 'Open schools, open society', *New Society*, 14 September, pp. 351–3.

Bernstein, B. 1971, *Class, Codes and Control, Volume 1,* Routledge & Kegan Paul, Andover, Hants.

Boime, A. 1990, *The Art of Exclusion: Representing Blacks in the Nineteenth Century,* Thames & Hudson, London.

Cohen, A. 1985, *The Symbolic Construction of Community,* Tavistock Publications, London.

Corbin, A. 1986, *The Fragrant and the Foul: Odor and the French Social Imagination,* Harvard University Press, Cambridge, Mass.

Douglas, M. 1966, *Purity and Danger,* Routledge & Kegan Paul, Andover, Hants.

Freud, S. 1930, *Civilisation and its Discontents,* Hogarth Press, London.

Gilman, S. 1985, *Difference and Pathology: Stereotypes of Sexuality, Race and Madness,* Cornell University Press, Ithaca, New York.

Hoggett, P. 1992, 'A place for experience: a psychoanalytic perspective on boundary, identity and culture', *Environment and Planning D: Society and Space,* vol. 10, no. 3, pp. 345–56.

Keith, M. 1987, 'Something happened: the problems of explaining the 1980 and 1981 riots in British cities', in *Race and Racism,* ed. P. Jackson, Allen & Unwin, London, pp. 275–301.

Liegeois, J-P. 1986, *Gypsies: An Illustrated History,* Al Saqi Books, London.

Mumford, L. 1961, *The City in History,* Secker and Warburg, London.

Neusner, J. 1973, *The Idea of Purity in Ancient Judaism,* E.J. Brill, Leiden.

Okely, J. 1979, 'Trading stereotypes: the case of English Gypsies', in *Ethnicity at Work,* ed. S. Wallman, Macmillan, Basingstoke, pp. 17–36.

Osherenko, G. & Young, O. 1989, *The Age of the Arctic,* Cambridge University Press, Cambridge.

Philo, C. 1989, 'Enough to drive one mad: the organisation of space in 19th century lunatic asylums', in *The Power of Geography,* eds J. Wolch & M. Dear, Unwin Hyman, London, pp. 258–90.

Sennett, R. 1970, *The Uses of Disorder,* Penguin, Harmondsworth.

Sennett, R. 1971, 'Middle class families and urban violence: the experience of a Chicago community in the 19th century', in *Anonymous Americans,* ed. T.K. Haravan, Prentice Hall, Englewood Cliffs, NJ, pp. 280–305.

Sibley, D. 1981, *Outsiders in Urban Societies,* Basil Blackwell, Oxford.

Sibley, D. 1987, 'Racism and settlement policy: the state's response to a semi-nomadic minority, in *Race and Racism,* ed. P. Jackson, Allen and Unwin, London, pp. 74–89.

Sibley, D. 1988, 'Survey 13: purification of space', *Environment and Planning D: Society and Space,* vol. 6, no. 4, pp. 409–21.

Sibley, D. 1995, *Geographies of Exclusion. Society and Difference in the West,* Routledge, London.

Smith, S.J. 1989, *The Politics of 'Race' and Residence,* Polity Press, Cambridge.

Sutherland, A. 1975, *Gypsies: The Hidden Americans,* Tavistock, London.

Williams, P. 1982, 'The invisibility of the Kalderas in Paris', *Urban Anthropology,* vol. 11, no. 3–4, pp. 315–46.

Wolch, J. & Dear, M. 1987, *Landscapes of Despair,* Polity Press, Cambridge.

8

Gender in the landscape

expressions of power and meaning

Janice Monk

INTRODUCTION

It is not difficult to recognise the more obvious expressions of class, race or ethnicity in the material landscape. The quality of residences and their decoration, the signs on shop windows, the graffiti on walls, the manicured lawns or the jumble of weeds and rubble convey to us impressions of affluence or poverty, diversity or homogeneity and feelings of familiarity or strangeness, comfort or anxiety. But gender? Superficially, since for the most part men and women occupy the same spaces, it seems that an analysis of the landscape focusing on gender would not be fruitful. Yet gender is a central element of human experience. It would therefore be surprising if the landscape did not reflect the ideologies that support distinct gender roles and the inequalities of power that they embody. Further, we might expect that gender socialisation would lead women and men to experience the landscape in different ways and to attach different meanings to it. Because gender roles and relationships are largely taken-for-granted aspects of life, however, and because the experience of the masculine gender has been assumed to represent the universal rather than the particular in much geographic writing, the gendered nature of the landscape was rarely acknowledged until the development of feminist research in the 1970s (Monk and Hanson 1982).

The purpose of this chapter is to explore some of the ways in which power and meaning in the landscape are associated with gender. In dealing with gender this chapter will draw on feminist thinking which distinguishes between sex (the biological differentiation of male from female) and gender (the cross-cultural, historically and geographically varying expressions of masculinity and femininity) to illustrate the variability and malleability of gender roles and relationships. Examples are presented from a number of cultural settings, locations and historical periods. It will also indicate how differences occur within gender groups as they are inflected by other social categories such as class, caste, 'race', ethnicity, religion, stage in the life course or sexual orientation. It is argued that the often unspoken social and cultural beliefs, that is, the ideologies which people hold about gender, are important in shaping landscapes. In turn, landscapes set the contexts within which men and women act and reproduce gender roles and relationships. Much of the discussion will demonstrate how landscapes, both materially and symbolically, reflect power inequalities between men and women by embodying patriarchal cultural values. These values support the dominance of men and the subordination and oppression of women; they are often interpreted as being universal and historically pervasive, though they vary in expression and in the intensity of their impact at different times and places.

As a counter to this examination of patriarchal domination in the landscape, the ways that women have resisted it by creating their own visions of landscapes and working to bring these visions into being will be considered. The efforts of women to reform male-created architectural and urban spaces and to combat the environmental destruction they see as stemming from masculine manipulation of nature and technology are also discussed.

Dealing with oppression and resistance, however, does not tell enough of the story. Studies of women's religious beliefs and rituals, their oral and written literature and their arts suggest that they draw on the landscape in expressing a sense of female autonomy and their identity as women. In other words, the meanings women draw from the landscape may empower them not only to resist patriarchal domination but also to validate themselves. This chapter describes how some women have drawn on the landscape for such purposes. In summary, this approach is designed to show that gender and landscape are indeed connected and to argue that landscape expresses power and meaning in ways that have both negative and positive implications for women.

OF HEROES AND HORSES, MYTHS AND MAIDENS: SYMBOLIC BODIES IN PUBLIC PLACES

At the south-eastern corner of Central Park in New York, in glistening gold, General William Tecumseh Sherman, astride his majestic horse, dominates a small plaza (Figure 8.1). However, the hero of the Union Army is not alone. His horse is preceded (not led) by a winged female figure holding aloft a palm frond. She symbolises Victory. Describing this noted monument, art historian H.W. Janson comments: '(W)hat is original about Saint Gaudens's Victory is her delicate, virginal type, even the consciously awkward way she carries the palm frond, and the way she keeps pace with the forward movement of horse and rider' (Rosenblum and Janson 1984).

Though such monuments might seem to function largely as backdrops in daily life, they are intended to commemorate what we value and to instruct us

FIGURE 8.1 Saint-Gaudens monument to General Sherman, New York.
Source: Photo by Amy W. Newhall.

in our heritage through visible expressions of human bodies on the landscape. In western societies, their message of male power, reinforced by the commanding mounted position, is repeated frequently in tributes to military heroes. As Susan Gross and Mary Rojas (1986) have documented, most of the people who are commemorated by the outdoor monuments of Washington DC are male military and political figures. Among the monuments listed on the Rand McNally tourist map of the city only one represents a woman, Joan of Arc (also mounted on a horse). Three other women are portrayed in the city's outdoor monuments—Queen Isabella I of Spain, another political figure, Mary McLeod Bethune, and Olive Risley Seward. Bethune is commemorated in her own right as a black educator, though she too served as a political appointee (Gross and Rojas 1986). Even the placement of female historical figures on the landscape may signify something other than the woman herself. Seward's statue, for example, honours her family for their political work, though she is recognised for her interests in the abolition of slavery and her influence on her father (Gross and Rojas 1986). Similarly, the stern figure of Queen Victoria in the square which bears her name in Sydney presents her complete with orb and sceptre, the symbol of empire and colonial power. It bears little relation to the woman herself—one who chose to wear the black dress and bonnet of widowhood to the celebration of the jubilee of her reign though others attending were garbed in ceremonial dress (Benson 1985).

Though the few monuments commemorating individual historical women on the landscape favour the political realm, women from other spheres of life, for example those who have nursed soldiers in war, are sometimes represented in a generic way. Such commemorations are relatively rare, however. In Australia, among 2000 or more Anzac memorials to the First World War, only one local monument portrays a nurse (in Maryborough, Victoria), though figures of nurses are included in the major memorials in Melbourne and Sydney. However, as Ken Inglis notes 'you have to look hard' to see them on relief panels in Melbourne, and the official description of the memorial in Sydney turns the nurses into mothers of the race lovingly tending the weary and wounded (Inglis 1989, p. 37). Resisting the male monopoly of the commemorative landscape, the Women in Military Service For America Foundation obtained congressional authorisation in 1986 to construct a memorial at Arlington National Cemetery to honour all United States women veterans of the past; it was eventually opened in 1997. The design is remote from the concept of the heroic figure on the horse. The memorial sits behind and above a thirty foot granite wall through which cut four staircases to symbolise women breaking barriers (Military women's memorial 1997). A unique feature is a computer registry of the 1.6 million women who have served in the armed forces. The women registered may choose to have their photographs included (Vaught n.d.). 'It's positively the most fitting [memorial], said retired Air Force Major General Jeanne Holm, 'for the simple reason that our stories have never been told' (*Arizona Daily Star* 17 October 1997, p. A3).

By contrast with the realism of this monument, the representation of female figures in the urban landscape is usually of an abstract symbol, a mythical maiden, like the Victory with General Sherman. As Marina Warner writes:

> (E)ven if executed with a high degree of naturalism, female figures representing an ideal or abstraction hardly ever interact with real, individual women. Devices distinguish them: improbable nudity, heroic scale, wings, unlikely attributes (Warner 1985, p. 28).

She reports a staggering number of abstract female forms decorating official buildings in Paris, bringing together the French sense of the romantic and erotic. In Britain she notes the female guardian of virtue symbolised in many monuments—an armed woman expressing the conquest of desire in the guise of Peace, Victory, Fortitude, Justice or Truth. The association of female figures with Liberty, whether the French Marianne or the American 'Miss Liberty', can only seem ironic given the history of restriction and political exclusion of real women in male-dominated democracies.

Thus, conveyed to us in the monuments of western societies is a heritage of masculine power, accomplishment and heroism; women are largely invisible, present occasionally if they enter the male sphere of politics or militarism. Even representation of these women may only be achieved when other women work together to support construction. In their place are abstract female symbols, which may be interpreted as noble ideals for men but which reflect little of the worlds that women have made and inhabited. As indicators of patriarchal hegemony in western cultures, these monuments set and reflect the context of gender relations of everyday life.

If building monuments is one way that groups of people use the landscape to express power and meaning, another is to hold a public parade in which bodily 'performances' serve symbolic ends. Long a means by which military, ethnic, and political groups have marked their identity and claims to power, parades have recently been used to bring issues of sexuality to public attention. Such events can also help us to see how understanding the politics of gender and identity in the landscape is becoming increasingly complex. They highlight the ways in which other social categories inflect the distinctions between masculine and feminine, even as these categories incorporate aspects of this division. Lynda Johnston's (1997) research on the HERO parade in Auckland, Aotearoa/New Zealand[1] provides an example. Initiated to help raise funds for HERO, a project to support gay men living with HIV/AIDS, the name is intended to validate the courage of these men. Yet the parade includes lesbians as well as gay males, and the distinctions emphasised are those between 'gay' and 'straight' populations. 'Performers' are gay, while it is understood that the majority of the large 'audience' will be straight.

Initially, the HERO parade was held in Queen Street, Auckland's most prominent business centre. But this site became hotly contested in 1994 and 1995, with opposition from politicians and religious groups outraged by the 'public' expression of embodied 'private' sexuality in a site long reserved for parades of 'true' national heroes (apparently male ones, such as Olympic athletes, rugby players, and other sports figures). They decried men in g-strings, bare-breasted women and transvestites. Some gays responded to the attacks by protesting, on political grounds, that a proposal to move the parade to Ponsonby Road, in the heart of the city's gayest suburb, would push gays back to the private spaces of the 'closet'. Others defended the move as a way to claim a sense of pride, ownership and enjoyment of its own 'home', the friendly, embodied 'heart' of the gay community, while still seeing the parade as serving a public, political purpose. Johnston argues these discussions disrupt simple divisions between what is 'private' and what is 'public', in the process foregrounding the embodied aspects of geography.

HOME SPACE: PROTECTIVE OR CONSTRAINING?

'Home' is a concept with multiple meanings. We speak of a home country, a home community, and of the house where we live as 'home' (Bowlby, Gregory and McKie 1997). It is often represented as a protective and welcoming space—as indeed some organisers of the HERO parade see Ponsonby Road, Auckland. When we look at the home through a gender lens, however, the meanings attached to it are ambiguous. It may be protective, but also constraining. This section of the chapter will focus on the landscapes of domestic residences as 'homes' to explore, in a variety of cultures and across historical periods, how ideas about domestic architecture express ideologies about gender roles and relations. Examples across cultures reveal how patriarchal values, often ostensibly protecting women, in fact constrain them. Nevertheless, these same examples show that women may attach different meanings to home spaces than men, that they may find ways to manoeuvre in them to meet their own needs and that they make efforts to design spaces to reflect their own values. Which of these approaches women take will depend on the context.

For centuries in Imperial China, specific men's and women's spaces codified the social order of Confucian society. In the world of the middle and upper classes especially, dwellings consisted of a series of courtyards bounded by a wall. The women's quarters were isolated from the outside world, located at the rear along a windowless back wall, accessible only by passing through the other courtyards. Valued in the patriarchal culture for her reproductive capacities and central to assuring the identity of the male line, a woman was thus protected and secluded from outside contact and expected to devote her life to the household of her husband, his parents and her sons (Pollock 1981). What meanings and consequences derive from this prescribed segregation? Nancy Pollock, interpreting Chinese painting and poetry, argues that for the male artist the beautifully rendered interior rooms and gardens symbolised the ideal woman, subservient, humble and obedient. For the women poets, architectural barriers implied containment, exclusion and isolation, 'loss of mobility and individuality ... being bound to the home and a limited sphere of activity' (Pollock 1981, p. 37).

Similar segregation has characterised the dwellings of Iranian households in support of patriarchal Islamic principles which prohibit contact between women and men unless they are *mahram* (that is, ineligible marriage partners), principles that are implemented by the custom of secluding women in the home. For the devout Moslem, sharing space with people who are *na-mahram* (that is, not *mahram*) is to be avoided because it might lead to illegal sexual relationships outside of marriage. In order to entertain visitors at home, families set aside a space near the front of the house, separated from family quarters to the rear. Women withdraw from this space and are thus protected from view when male *na-mahram* visitors are present (Khalib-Chahidi 1981).

However, the rigidities of idealised seclusion may be used by women to serve their own purposes, or may be modified in daily life and by changing circumstances. Thus women use the private women's spaces for uninhibited female socialising; they also enter the publicly-visible spaces of Iranian villages and use them for their own purposes in daytime hours when men are absent (Khatib-Chahidi 1981). Urban living may also bring modifications to rigid gender separation in home space even when elements of seclusion persist. For example, the large central courtyard of the rural Iranian home from which the family could see a visitor without being seen may shrink to a modest family living area in an urban apartment so that seeing becomes reciprocal. If a separate entertaining area is maintained in the apartment, this permits the more religious family members to avoid *na-mahram* visitors by withdrawing to some other room (Khatib-Chahidi 1981).

This example should not be construed to mean that modernisation necessarily reduces the negative consequences of spatial isolation for women. In other contexts, recent economic changes have reinforced the advantages of female seclusion for sustaining male power. The situation in Narsapur, India, provides a good illustration. Penetration of global capitalism into this community has generated increasing demands for the inexpensive lace produced there. To meet these demands, secluded women work long hours for little pay in their own homes. Their exploitation is supported by an ideology which defines them as 'housewives' rather than as workers, and the principal profits of their work redound to men in the community. Underlying this situation is a social history which links social prestige and female seclusion and which illustrates how class and gender ideologies may be intertwined. The lace-makers are *Kapu*, a class in which men's status is dependent on secluding women; they contrast with the lower class, untouchable *Harijans* in which women work openly in the fields. Today, the *Harijan* women are able to earn more than the *Kapu*. According to Maria Mies, with higher incomes and the enhanced sense of confidence and esteem derived from working collectively, *Harijan* women have come to look down on the *Kapu* women. Yet she argues, the *Kapu* women, constrained by the limiting patriarchal values that identify high status with female seclusion, shun manual work outside the home. We do not know if they fail to see how these values disadvantage them or if they are powerless to resist. The result of the pressures of economic change is that these women remain isolated and have been impoverished (Mies 1982).

It is often easier to recognise the implications of spatial forms in other cultures than in our own because we take so much of the everyday world for granted. A brief study of housing policies and plans and of the writing of social critics since the late nineteenth century in the United States and Britain shows how ideas about gender roles permeate the design of domestic space. These materials also reveal how conceptions of gender roles change over time, how issues of class intersect with conceptions of gender, and provide examples of some ways women have sought to define their own visions.

In the latter half of the nineteenth century, the notion that men were most properly associated with the public sphere of life and women with the domestic held strong sway in the United States, especially among the middle class. Articles in popular magazines such as the *Ladies Home Journal* and books like *The American Woman's Home,* written by Catherine Beecher and Harriet Beecher Stowe in 1869 idealised a woman's duty as the spiritual centre and efficient manager of the home, which was portrayed as the centre of domestic harmony and a retreat from the world for the working husband. These ideas were still being promoted in the first decade of the twentieth century when the *Ladies Home Journal* published designs by Frank Lloyd Wright for homes in which high walls and leaded windows enclosed a truly protected environment while a continuous open space within centred on the family hearth, a symbolic focus of harmony and togetherness (Rock, Torre and Wright 1980).

Such designs contrast with dwellings the Utopian communities built in the United States between the 1820s and the 1840s by followers of the British reformer Robert Owen and his French contemporary Charles Fourier. Exhibiting a concern for equality within the home and a priority for reducing the burden of individual women's housework, they constructed communal housing that incorporated private space for sleeping (and sometimes family living), but shared areas for cooking, dining, and childcare. Similarly, material feminists like Charlotte Perkins Gilman and Melusina Fay Pierce, who wrote in the late nineteenth and early twentieth centuries in the United States as a reaction against the ideal of female domesticity, advocated kitchenless houses or apartment hotels with cooperative kitchens, communal cafés, and shared nurseries and play areas for children. Their goal was to free women from the isolation of full-time housework in the domestic sphere in order to make it possible for them to engage in wider social participation in the public sphere (Hayden 1981). Though their designs offered broader opportunities for middle-class women, they did not solve the needs of working-class women and their families, especially those who might be employed as providers of the collective childcare or food services. Nor did they fundamentally challenge the prevailing ideologies of the period that associated family and domestic care with women.

British feminists concerned about the needs of low-income women took a different approach in their reports for the Women's Housing Sub-Committee which was established by the British government in 1918 to plan state-built housing. Unlike earlier feminists who had been challenging women's inequality in the public sphere, the women on this committee wanted to ease women's lot within homes where the gender division of labour was accepted. Informed by detailed conversations with working-class women and seeing the inadequacies of homes in which families lived in a couple of rooms, shared sculleries, had no hot water and often were required to carry water and slops up and down stairs, they aimed to save the women expenditure of money and energy. They suggested a separate room for cooking removed from the family living area and a parlour where the woman could relax away from her unfinished work; they paid special attention to economical means of providing hot water and cooking fuel. Their final report referred briefly to communal housing, but concluded that 'English women … do not regard communal housing with favour. It is not, however, a reason for neglecting to consider schemes by which unnecessary drudgery would be saved' (quoted in Matrix 1984, p. 36). Their work contrasts markedly with that of a committee of male experts set up by the Local Government Board in 1917. Its brief recommendations were confined to ideas about building housing quickly and cheaply. One of its most influential members, Raymond Unwin, attacked the notion of a separate parlour as inappropriate aping of the middle classes (Matrix 1984).

Contemporary feminist writers and activists are again advocating design reform, but their proposals incorporate visions which seek to free women from oppressive domestic situations and to recognise their need to work outside the home. Among the projects publicised in feminist writings on the built environment are The Mothers' House in Amsterdam, the Constance Hamilton Cooperative in Toronto and the Nina West Homes in London which provide private and communal areas, spaces for childcare, counselling offices and the like (Hayden 1984; Klodawsky and Mackenzie 1987). Feminists are also working to support refuges for battered women and their children, stressing locational and design features, not only the establishment of homes. They seek sites near public transportation, schools and other services, and larger old houses that include several bedrooms on upper floors with common spaces on the ground floor so that the women will have privacy as well as community support and security (Klodawsky and Mackenzie 1987). These projects reflect a new feminist recognition of the desirability of separate spaces to protect women from male violence and demonstrate a reconceptualisation of women's social needs compared with the domestic visions of the nineteenth century and the 1950s. They illustrate one form of resistance to male domination, yet they remind us of the gender inequalities still pervasive in western societies where such refuges remain necessary. Their construction, however, is hampered by inadequate finance and obstacles like zoning laws which in many communities in the United States prohibit the building of group homes in neighbourhoods zoned for individual family residences. In general then, power over the built environment remains in male hands and women have less control over its form.

GENDERED SPACES IN URBAN PLACES

Expressions of gender in contemporary urban landscapes transcend the individual dwelling. Indeed, the distinction between city and suburb that emerged in twentieth-century western cities reflects gender ideologies writ large. Feminist geographers have located the origins of this division in urban space historically in the rise of industrialisation, when the site of paid productive work moved out of the home into the factory and the home became the locus of unpaid reproductive work. For the middle class especially, the division was supported by values which identified women with work in the home and cast men in the role of outside breadwinner (Hayden 1984; Mackenzie and Rose 1983; McDowell 1983). As the development of public transportation and acquisition of family cars made possible the greater spatial separation of home and work, and the promotion of appliances for the home reinforced this sphere as the place of the woman consumer, the distinction between the suburban home as the female domain and the urban workplace as male territory was strengthened (Miller 1983). Mortgage and zoning policies exacerbated the division, supporting the construction of single-family homes and the separation of residential and commercial areas.

The gender politics underlying the development of suburbia in western cities continues to find expression in the late twentieth century in other contexts. Lily Phua and Brenda Yeoh (1997) clearly analyse how the massive construction of public housing in Singapore over the last thirty years concretises gendered state ideologies about the 'normal' Singapore family and the 'Asian extended family'. These ideologies are evident in the criteria for eligibility, the designs of housing complexes and new towns and of the individual flats. Only 'families', not single young people, divorcees under age twenty-one and, since 1994, single mothers, are eligible applicants; applicants are assumed to be men—women can only be 'co-applicants' or 'proposed occupiers', even if they contribute to the purchase. Men are an essential in the family unit. The design of units reflects a western nuclear family model, though attempts to promote 'traditional Asian family' values of mutual support are expressed in allocation schemes such as Reside Near Parents/Married Children Scheme or Multi-Tier Family Scheme that encourage residence of two generations in the same neighbourhood. In this way the state reinforces expectations that women will serve as caregivers. In their layout, the public housing estates incorporate European 'new town' principles of the post-Second World War period; they include residences and services, but only restricted (usually low-paying, female) employment opportunities, thus reinforcing gender divisions in daily life, with women relegated to the local and men commuting to work elsewhere. The floor plans of the flats, and publications illustrating them, further support these gender expectations. Women's space, the kitchen, is usually located at the back of the flat, hidden from public view. Photographs commonly show women in the kitchen, but men relaxing in the living room.

Such designs shape not only material experiences, but self-concepts and the creation and reproduction of gender values. Phua and Yeoh (1997) report the everyday strategies of the Singapore women to accommodate their domestic isolation and restricted roles—from nagging, crying, chatting on the phone or in the neighbourhood, to participating in community groups. They note that these strategies may make daily life more tolerable, but do not challenge gender roles or create long-term prospects for social change. Similarly, in the French context, Jacqueline Coutras (1987) writes of the dilemmas of women who have recently moved to expanding suburbs in the Paris region, valuing residence there for their families, but personally caught between isolation and extended commuting. Joos Droogleever Fortuijn's (1996) research on couples in Amsterdam shows how their residential choices reflect class, lifestyle preferences and life course stages that represent diverse configurations of gender roles. Following couples from their single years into the period when they have young children, she reports that dual career couples for whom paid work is a high priority chose to live in high quality inner-city neighbourhoods with good access to services such as day care, laundries, and catering; each partner made some adjustments to their paid work and household responsibilities, but they emphasised substitution of paid services for their own domestic labour. Less affluent professional workers (such as teachers or nurses) chose residences in less expensive and less well-served inner suburban single-family neighbourhoods, valuing the space for their families and reasonable accessibility to work, but putting stress on themselves to organise sequential schedules in order to combine paid work and childcare. By contrast, the typical families in recently-built, less expensive outlying new towns are working- and lower-middle-class couples in which the woman has left paid employment (or been dismissed prior to taking maternity leave) to become a full-time housewife and mother, while the man becomes the absent father, commuting long distances daily to work. These couples value the space for their families in the new town over the convenience of services that, in any case, they cannot afford.

The examples above identify the daily inconveniences and economic costs to women of residence in the suburbs and new towns, and hint at its psychological costs. Quite widely written about since Betty Friedan identified the stultifying limitations of suburban domesticity for women in her book *The Feminine Mystique* (1963), these costs continue to be identified in social surveys and by women writers who are advocating change. Sophie Watson highlights the contrast between her life in suburban Canberra and her residence in inner Sydney:

> In my mind I see Canberra bringing the end of the relationship. I lost my sense of self in Canberra … The lack of my own space, the suburban box, the long empty streets, the difficulty of meeting people, the social life based on couples, the lunchtime affairs, the absence of community … that was Canberra. It was hard to build a life of one's own. I felt I had become the suburban wife. My centre slipped away.
>
> Sydney is another story. I've moved several times. Different arrangements. Inner city life. Community. Diversity. Possibility. Turmoil. Dirt. Waves. Beach. Breakfast on the roof at Bondi. Nino's. Enzo's. Real houses. Houses with thick walls. Bedrooms to play music in. Different coloured faces. People dropping by. Noise. Difference valued and created (Watson 1989, pp. 10–11).

Watson's celebration of disorder brings to mind Elizabeth Wilson's (1992) critique of urban planning, architecture and city life which makes a persuasive argument that much planning, as well as cultural interpretations of city life across time and cultures, has been rooted in ideologies that seek to control women. Contrary to these visions, she proposes that the city offers freedom for women, including sexual freedom, but that it also presents dangers. She advocates acceptance of the complexities and diversities of city life, but points out the involvement of women in shaping the city and its responsiveness to their needs, aspirations and strengths. Examples of women's commitments to improving urban spaces are numerous, as are examples of the failures and negative consequences of urban development schemes that attempt to control or marginalise women's autonomy. Self-help housing projects in Latin American cities have served women poorly when they relocate squatters miles from the city, isolating women from ready access to jobs they have to take as maids, yet women have also found ways to agitate for change and community services in such settings (Moser and Peake 1987). Women planners have also taken leadership in advocating for 'safe cities', promoting design alternatives that will mitigate urban crime and violence (especially against women) in the streets, parks, parking lots and subways (Wekerle and Whitzman 1995).

Efforts to change urban forms have to take multiple perspectives into account, however. Whereas for some women, suburbia may be stultifying, for others, among them low-income, single mothers who were interviewed in Providence, Rhode Island, the ideal may incorporate stereotypical, suburban visions—of privacy, peace and quiet, qualities that have been rare in their lives. Still, they value access to city services and indicate that having affordable apartments provided them by the Women's Development Corporation has given them a heightened sense of independence, confidence and control (Breitbart

1990). Despite the fact that economic and socio-demographic conditions indicate that we would be better served by more varied and flexible spatial forms which integrate home, work and services, outmoded gender assumptions continue to inform urban land use planning. The challenge is to adapt what we have to support not only the conventional nuclear unit but also diverse types of households ranging from adolescent single mothers to dual-employed couples to elderly widows trying to cope without adequate community support in houses that are overly large for their circumstances. Individuals are creating alternatives, for example, by redesigning and redesignating home spaces to operate childcare services in neighbourhoods or conduct businesses from their residences (Mackenzie 1987).

Although private groups may develop cooperative housing or women's shelters (Wekerle 1981), it is also critical to organise to claim women's rights to public spaces and to initiate institutional changes at local and national levels. Indigenous Mixtec women street sellers in Tijuana, Mexico, provide one model. Shunted from the main downtown street, Avenida Revolucion, by city authorities and police harassment because they lacked the necessary permits or credentials to gain access to authorities, the women responded by forming a street vendors association and affiliating with an established political organisation, the Regional Confederation of Workers and Peasants. This enabled them to negotiate with authorities and eventually to secure permits to trade in a nearby plaza, then an undesirable site strewn with garbage, weeds, and 'sleeping drinkers'. The women cleaned up the site, which is now a cleaner and safer place, attractive to the tourists who buy the Mixtecas' wares (Lopez-Estrada 1998). They have demonstrated the value of resistance and organisation. Similarly, Los Angeles women in 1920 successfully overthrew a downtown parking ban that implied their convenient access to stores was unnecessary because women's time was inconsequential (Scharff 1988). Women reformers in the United States in the early twentieth century brought urban changes on a larger scale, supporting the development of settlement houses, urban parks and improved sanitation (Cranz 1981; Gittell and Shtob 1981; Merchant 1984). However, as Cynthia Enloe (1990) points out, gender ideologies that have inhibited women's participation in the larger political sphere embody the same concepts of patriarchal power that favour public expenditure on militarism and policies that support international business while reducing expenditures on social welfare. Thus, future transformation of the urban landscape in a significant way will require substantial changes in the prevailing cultural ideologies that underlie political and economic life.

WOMAN AND NATURE: POWER, MEANING AND METAPHOR

Thus far, ways in which ideas about gender roles and relationships are constituted in the built environment have been addressed, with an emphasis on the implications of these expressions for the material conditions of everyday life.

The scope of the discussion will now be widened to address visions of natural as well as built landscapes and of the human transformations of nature, focusing on metaphors which link 'woman' and 'nature'. The intent is to show how different meanings attached to such metaphors have affected the ways in which diverse groups approach their relationships with the natural environment.

An array of contemporary women scholars, writers and activists, especially those who identify themselves as ecofeminists, have challenged the ways western scientific and philosophical thought over the last several hundred years have constructed and associated the concepts of 'nature' and 'woman'. They argue that the values embodied in these conceptualisations have been deleterious to nature and supportive of the domination of women. They call for modifications if humanity is to achieve sustainable life in the future, recognising that forms of consciousness are power structures that impact society, nature and space. Among the early influential works in this literature is Carolyn Merchant's *The Death of Nature: Women, Ecology and Scientific Revolutions* (1980), which examines the transition in European thinking between the fifteenth and seventeenth centuries from an organic world view in which the human, natural and spiritual are blended, to a mechanistic world view in which nature is conceptualised as an object to be manipulated and controlled by the human mind and technology. In the organic view, nature is valued and identified as a mother or goddess. In the mechanistic view it is seen as a machine to be controlled by man. Merchant claims that '(T)he removal of animistic, organic assumptions about the cosmos constitute the death of nature' (1980, p. 193).

Merchant (1980, 1987) and a variety of other writers have pointed out a second way in which 'woman' and 'nature' have been linked. Because of their capacity to bear children, women have been portrayed as closer to 'nature', while men are linked to 'culture'. By extension, if it is legitimate for men to dominate 'nature', then it is also legitimate for men to dominate women. Commonly-used metaphors for nature reveal the connections between these conceptualisations. Thus nature is portrayed as a 'virgin' to be raped, tamed or possessed. The 'mother' metaphor also continues, with nature portrayed as a fruitful mother who exists to nurture men.

Complementing this literature on the history of scientific thought is an ecofeminist literature which responds to the devaluation of nature and women by advocating conceptualisations that esteem nature as goddess and mother. Ecofeminists draw a sense of female spiritual power from their association with nature and some demonstrate this empowerment in activism against the destruction of the natural environment by male-dominated technologies. Identification as mothers is an important element of some ecofeminist protests. Targets like nuclear power plants, toxic waste dumps and polluted waters are portrayed as threats to the health of their children as well as to the survival of 'Mother Earth' (Merchant 1987). Whether 'ecofeminist' or not in self-identification, women's motivations to protest commonly integrate concerns for the environment and concerns for the health of their families and communities. Some make their domestic roles materially and symbolically visible parts of protest activities, like the women of Gibraleon, (Spain), who nightly banged their *caceroles* (saucepans) and frequently brought their domestic work (sewing, knitting, cleaning vegetables) to their public protest meetings (Bru 1996). Not all feminists concerned with environmental issues emphasise maternal roles or identification with the earth goddess, however, and neither are all women who identify as 'mothers' in their environmental activism ecofeminists in this spiritual sense. Some base their analyses in the material realm of daily work with its gender divisions of labour and gendered rights to resources (Rocheleau, Thomas-Slayter and Wangari 1996). Others frame their struggles as engaging multiple forms of domination that are deleterious for human and natural life—those of race, class and colonialism—and identify with environmental social justice movements (Kirk 1997). These also, however, often have a strong gender component. Many of the activists are women and for some groups, such as the Mothers of East Los Angeles, the identification as 'mothers' makes symbolic and practical links that justify women's participation in grassroots environmental activism for their families, neighbourhoods, and ethnic group (Platt 1997).

Third World development is also being reinterpreted by feminist writers seeking alternative metaphors to support new approaches to living with the environment. One of the best-known writers, Vandana Shiva (1989), challenges the tenets of western masculine conceptions of science and development as they are applied to environmental manipulation in the Third World. She posits that models that have been represented as embodying universal truths are, in fact, based on assumptions of power, violence, exclusion and reductionism that cast nature as woman, the passive 'other'. Shiva proposes the alternative of the feminine principle embodied in the Hindu deity, Prakriti, that, in conjunction with the male principle, Purusha, incorporates a vision of the pursuit of harmony, diversity and sustainability as the key to saving nature and human life. In contrast to the passive woman, Prakriti is an active creative force.

Shiva presents the consequences of western philosophy and behaviour as disastrous for the daily survival of women, peasants and indigenous peoples. She reviews problems in forestry, agriculture and the control of water, exploring the ways rural women, such as those in the Chipko movement, have mobilised against the commercial exploitation of forests for lumber and the planting of fast-growing alien species. Instead they support the planting of ecologically appropriate trees that will protect soils and watersheds and sustain life. She sees such efforts to reaffirm the life of nature as essential because '(T)he killing of people by the murder of nature is an invisible form of violence which is today the biggest threat to justice and peace' (1989, p. 36). For her, liberation of the person and liberation of nature will only be accomplished through integrating such dualisms as male/female and human/natural.

The metaphors women use to relate to the land are not bounded by concerns for environmental quality, however. Nor are they concerned solely with countering male visions and domination. Across cultures, women find empowering meanings in the land which validate their own gender identity. They express these meanings in their religious beliefs and rituals, oral and written literatures and the arts, in the process revealing how the specificities of place and gender identities are intertwined. I will provide only a few examples, drawing on women's creative writings about the south-western United States and Australia. They suggest the richness of such expressions by women and also reveal how other social and cultural considerations inflect the women's identifications with the landscape.

American Indian, Mexican American and Euro-American women writers in the south-west refer to the land in female terms, but the woman is not a virgin to be raped or tamed, nor is she restricted to the identity of mother. In this landscape, the vast spaces and extensive areas that seem free of human domination appear to liberate women from the traditional strictures of femininity that silence their voices. They identify the land as a woman who embodies traits that give them a sense of their own complexity, power and worth. Thus, Euro-American Mary Austin portrays the desert as a strong woman who has not been, and cannot be, mastered. Alice Corbin Henderson sees the land as an old woman, ancient and peaceful, 'Blinking and blind in the sun ... who mumbles her beads/ And crumbles to stone' (quoted in Rudnick 1987, p. 13). For contemporary Mexican-American Pat Mora, the landscape can also be an old woman, a teacher or *curandera*, the healing, wise woman of her culture who mediates between human beings and nature and brings power and magic to the woman writer.

The women's visions also reveal a sense of vital female sexuality in an erotically charged energy that emanates from the land. This is most forcefully and consistently exhibited in the writing of American Indian women, who describe women having sexual relationships with the Spirit beings that inhabit, and indeed are, the land; they draw personal and cultural sustenance from their encounters. Thus in her collection, *Storyteller*, Leslie Silko tells of Yellow Woman who goes out to rendezvous with the sun around the time of the Fall equinox:

> She left precise stone rooms
> that hold the heart silently
> She walked past white corn
> hung in low rows from roof beams
> the dry husks rattled in a thin autumn wind.
> She left her home
> her clan
> and the people
> (three small children
> the youngest just weaned
> her husband away cutting firewood)
> (Silko 1981, p. 64)

Consummation of her relationship with the sun ensures that he will not leave the earth forever locked in winter (Smith with Gunn Allen 1987). This active sense of female sexuality is also clearly revealed in Mexican-American poetry. Pat Mora, for example, writes: 'The desert is no lady ... Her unveiled lust fascinates the sun' (quoted in Norwood and Monk 1987, p. v).

Perhaps most common across the Indian, Mexican-American and Euro-American women are expressions of a sense of integration between self and land, rather than separation. It is pervasive in the Indians' communication with animate nature and illustrated by the creations of Euro-American artists Michelle Stuart and Nancy Holt who fuse their physical bodies with the land in the process of creating their works, finding spiritual communication with the land. Stuart, for example, rubs ground rocks and earth onto paper laid on the earth, then polishes the paper with her hand, through this integration allowing the earth to reveal its own patterns (Duvert 1987). Holt, in her work *Sun Tunnels,* a series of concrete pipes placed in the Utah desert in alignment with solar geometry, cuts holes in the pipes to allow the sun to play over the body of the occupant and to permit vision out to the heavens. On seeing the site she chose for the work, Holt felt 'my insides and outsides (come) together for the first time' (quoted in Duvert 1987, p. 212).

Ultimately, the meanings these women derive from the landscape empower them to survive:

> Desert women know
> about survival.
> Fierce heat and cold have burned and thickened
> our skin. Like cactus
> we've learned to hoard,
> to sprout deep roots,
> to seem asleep, yet wake
> at the scent of softness
> in the air, to hide
> pain and loss by silence,
> no branches wail
> or whisper our sad songs
> safe behind our thorns.
>
> Don't be deceived.
> When we bloom, we stun.
> (Mora 1986, p. 80)

If these women in the south-western United States find identity and autonomy in desert landscapes, Australian Barbara Hanrahan turns to the working-class suburb of her youth and the nature that exists in the wild night garden of her childhood home:

> All about me was a wild world that broke through the symmetry of prim brick borders, neat vegetable rows, tortured roses. With the night, rats wove between the creepers on the fences that divided the yards … I watched it all, and it was in the wild night garden that I discovered I did not fit the snug electric world that others did (Hanrahan 1973, p. 162).

Beyond her home, she turns to the city and the adjacent hills. The bush and outback that has been routinely invoked to define Australian (male) identity is not for her (Monk and Norwood 1990).

> But where were the hills of the history book ... the hills of sunburned earth and budgerigar grass, the azure skies and fiery mountains we sang about at school ...? Where were the flowers that wilted in blistered clay? (The hills are gentle, their trees are pale the scented paper bark with its peeling trunk, the snow-white ghost gum—warm to the touch ...) I looked about me for the sunburned land. In vain (Hanrahan 1973, pp. 90–91).

CONCLUSION

This chapter has tried to convey that ideologies about gender have shaped the form of landscapes, and that representations of gender in the landscape contribute to defining our choices in life and the constraints we confront. Nevertheless, it should be clear from the examples incorporated that gender does not function in a simple way as a dichotomy between an essentialist masculine and feminine. Gender roles and relationships are historically, geographically and culturally constructed and mutable. So is their embodiment in the landscape. Class, ethnicity, sexuality and an array of other social divisions all shape the ways that gender functions in specific times and places. Meaning and power relationships change as contexts and consciousness change.

Insofar as landscapes reflect power relationships, it is clear that patriarchal hegemonies have created spaces and places which deny or devalue women. For many women and increasingly, it appears, for the environment, such dominance has been damaging. But expressions of power do not go unchallenged. Women have found ways to manipulate restrictive landscapes for their own purposes and there are examples of women taking action to create conditions more amenable to their interests and values. Because women and men draw meaning from landscapes and use them in expressing their senses of personal and collective identity, landscapes can also empower people to creativity and action, to develop cultural alternatives that might contribute to the making of a sustainable and more socially equitable environment.

NOTE

1 The naming of this country as 'Aotearoa/New Zealand,' reflecting the political valuing of its Maori and European heritages is another issue of interest to cultural geographers, though this will not be taken up here, given the focus of this chapter on gender as the primary theme. See the chapter in this volume by Eric Pawson.

REFERENCES

Arizona Daily Star 17 Oct. 1997, 'Miltary women's memorial to tell untold stories.'

Benson, E.F. 1985 (1930), *As We Were: A Victorian Peep-Show*, Hogarth Press, London.

Bowlby, S., Gregory, S & McKie, L. 1997, '"Doing home": patriarchy, caring, and space', *Women's Studies International Forum*, vol. 20, no. 3, pp. 343–50.

Breitbart, M. 1990, 'Quality housing for women and children', *Canadian Women's Studies*, vol. 11, no. 2, pp. 19–24.

Bru, J. 1996, 'Spanish women against industrial waste', in *Feminist Political Ecology: Global Issues and Local Experiences*, eds D. Rocheleau, B. Thomas-Slayter & E. Wangari, Routledge, London pp. 105–24.

Coutras, J. 1987, *Des Villes Traditionelles aux Nouvelles Banlieues*, SEDES, Paris.

Cranz, G. 1981, 'Women in urban parks', in *Women in the American City*, eds C.R. Stimpson, E. Dixler, M. Nelson, & K.B. Yatrakis, University of Chicago Press, Chicago, pp. 7–92.

Droogleever Fortuijn, J. 1996, 'City and suburb: contexts for Dutch women's work and daily lives', in *Women of the European Union: The Politics of Work and Daily Life*, eds M. D. Garcia-Ramon & J. Monk, Routledge, London, pp. 217–28.

Duvert, E. 1987/1997, 'With stone, star, and earth: the presence of the archaic in the landscape visions of Georgia O'Keeffe, Nancy Holt, and Michelle Stuart', in *The Desert Is No Lady: Southwestern Landscapes in Women's Writing and Art*, eds V. Norwood & J. Monk, Yale University Press, New Haven/ University of Arizona Press, Tucson, pp. 197–222.

Enloe, C. 1990, *Bananas, Beaches and Bases: Making Feminist Sense of International Politics*, University of California Press, Berkeley.

Friedan, B. 1963, *The Feminine Mystique*, Norton, New York.

Gittell, M. & Shtob, T. 1981, 'Changing women's roles in political volunteerism and reform of the city', in *Women in the American City*, eds C.R. Stimpson, E. Dixler, M. Nelson, & K.B. Yatrakis, University of Chicago Press, Chicago, pp. 64–75.

Gross, S.H. & Rojas, M.H. 1986, *But Women Have No History: Images of Women in the Public History of Washington DC*, Glenhurst Publications, Inc., St Louis Park, Minnesota.

Hanrahan, B. 1973, *The Scent of Eucalyptus*, Chatto & Windus, London.

Hayden, D. 1981, *The Grand Domestic Revolution: A History of Feminist Designs for American Homes, Neighborhoods, and Cities*, MIT Press, Cambridge.

Hayden, D. 1984, *Redesigning the American Dream: The Future of Housing, Work, and Family Life*, W.W. Norton & Company, New York.

Inglis, K. 1989, 'Men, women and war memorials: Anzac Australia', in *Learning About Women: Gender, Politics, and Power*, eds J.K. Conway, S.C. Bourque & J.W. Scott, University of Michigan Press, Ann Arbor, pp. 35–59.

Johnston, L. 1997, 'Queen(s') Street or Ponsonby Poofters?: embodied HERO parade sites', *New Zealand Geographer*, vol. 53, no. 2, pp. 29–33.

Khatib-Chahidi, J. 1981, 'Sexual prohibitions, shared space and fictive marriages in Shi'ite Iran', in *Women and Space: Ground Rules and Social Maps*, ed. S. Ardener, St. Martin's Press, New York, pp. 112–35.

Kirk, G. 1997, 'Ecofeminism and environmental justice: bridges across gender, race, and class', *Frontiers*, vol. 18, no. 2, pp. 2–20.

Klodawsky, F. & Mackenzie, S. 1987, 'Gender sensitive theory and the housing needs of motherled families: some concepts and some buildings', *Feminist Perspectives Feministes*, no. 9, Canadian Research Institute for the Advancement of Women, Ottawa pp. 1–39.

Lopez-Estrada, S. 1998, 'Women, urban life and city images in Tijuana, Mexico', *Journal of Historical Geography* 26, pp. 5–25.

Mackenzie, S. 1987, 'Neglected spaces in peripheral places: homeworkers and the creation of a new economic centre', *Cahiers de Geographie du Quebec,* vol. 31, pp. 247–60.

Mackenzie, S. & Rose, D. 1983, 'Industrial change, the domestic economy, and home life', in *Redundant Spaces in Cities and Regions,* eds J. Anderson, S. Duncan, & R. Hudson, Academic Press, New York, pp. 155–200.

Matrix 1984, *Making Space: Women and the Man Made Environment,* Pluto Press, London.

McDowell, L. 1983, 'Towards an understanding of the gender division of urban space', *Environment and Planning D: Society and Space,* vol. l, pp. 59–72.

Merchant, C. 1980, *The Death of Nature: Women, Ecology, and the Scientific Revolution,* Harper & Row, San Francisco.

Merchant, C. 1984, 'Women of the progressive conservation movement, 1900–1916', *Environmental Review,* vol. 8, no. 1, pp. 57–85.

Merchant, C. 1987, 'Ecofeminism', *New Internationalist,* 18–19 May, p. 18.

Mies, M. 1982, 'The dynamics of the sexual division of labor and the integration of women into the world market', in *Women and Development: The Sexual Division of Labor in Rural Societies,* ed. L. Beneria, Praeger, New York, pp. 1–28.

Miller, R. 1983, 'The Hoover in the garden: middle-class women and suburbanisation, 1850–1920', *Environment and Planning D: Society and Space,* vol. 1, pp. 73–88.

Monk, J. & Hanson, S. 1982, 'On not excluding half of the human in human geography', *The Professional Geographer,* vol. 34, no. 1, pp. 11–23.

Monk, J. & Norwood, V. 1990, '(Re)membering the Australian city: urban landscapes in women's fiction', in *Place Images in Media: Portrayal, Experience, and Meaning,* ed. L. Zonn, Rowman and Littlefield, Savage, MD, pp. 105–19.

Mora, P. 1986, 'Desert women', in *Borders,* Arte Publico Press, University of Houston. Houston, p. 80.

Moser, C. & Peake, L. (eds) 1987, *Women, Human Settlements and Housing,* Tavistock, London.

Norwood, V. & Monk, J. 1987/1997, *The Desert Is No Lady: Southwestern Landscapes in Women's Writing and Art Yale,* University Press, New Haven/ University of Arizona Press, Tucson.

Phua, L. & Yeoh, B. 1997, 'Gendered ideologies and women's negotiation of everyday lives in Singapore's public housing landscape', *Proceedings, International Conference on Women in the Asia-Pacific Region: Persons, Powers and Politics,* Department of Geography, National University of Singapore, Singapore, pp. 453–69.

Platt, K. 1997, 'Chicana struggles for success and survival: cultural poetics of environmental justice from the Mothers of East Los Angeles', *Frontiers,* vol. 18, no. 2, pp. 48–72.

Pollock, N.L. 1981, 'Women on the inside: divisions of space in Imperial China', *Heresies,* vol. 11, no. 3, pp. 34–37.

Rocheleau, D., Thomas-Slayter, B., & Wangari, E. (eds) 1996, *Feminist Political Ecology: Global Issues and Local Experiences,* Routledge, London.

Rock, C., Torre, S. & Wright, G. 1980, 'The appropriation of the house: changes in housing design and concepts of domesticity', in *New Space for Women,* eds G. Wekerle, R. Peterson & D. Morley, Westview Press, Boulder, pp. 83–100.

Rosenblum R. & Janson, H.W. 1984, *Nineteenth Century Art,* Prentice Hall and Harry N. Abrams, Inc., Englewood Cliffs, NJ and New York.

Rudnick, L. 1987/1997, 'Re-naming the land: Anglo expatriate women in the Southwest', in *The Desert Is No Lady: Southwestern Landscapes in Women's Writing and Art,* eds V. Norwood & J. Monk, Yale University Press, New Haven/University of Arizona Press. Tucson, pp. 110–26.

Scharff, V. 1988, 'Of parking spaces and women's places: the Los Angeles parking ban of 1920', *National Women's Studies Association Journal*, vol. 1, pp. 37–51.

Shiva, V. 1989, *Staying Alive: Women, Ecology and Development*, Zed Books, London.

Silko, L. 1981, *Storyteller*, Seaver Books, New York.

Smith, P. with Gunn Allen, P. 1987/1997, 'Earthy relations, carnal knowledge: southwestern American Indian women writers and landscape', in *The Desert Is No Lady: Southwestern Landscapes in Women's Writing and Art*, eds V. Norwood & J. Monk, Yale University Press, New Haven/University of Arizona Press, Tucson, pp. 174–96.

Vaught, W.L. n.d., Letter soliciting donations to the Women in Military Service For America Memorial Foundation, Inc.

Warner, M. 1985, *Monuments and Maidens: The Allegory of the Female Form*, Weidenfeld & Nicolson, London.

Watson, S. 1989, 'Social spatial connections', in *Inner Cities: Australian Women's Memory of Place*, ed. D. Modjeska, Penguin Books. Melbourne, pp. 7–13.

Wekerle, G.R. 198l, 'Women house themselves', *Heresies*, vol. 11, no. 3, pp. 14–16.

Wekerle, G.R. & Whitzman, C. 1995, *Safe Cities: Guidelines for Planning, Design, and Management*, Van Nostrand Reinhold, New York.

Wilson, E. 1992, *The Sphinx in the City: Urban Life, the Control of Disorder, and Women*, University of California Press, Berkeley.

9

Inventions of Gender and Place in Films

Tales of Urban Reality

Kevin M. Dunn
Hilary P.M. Winchester

INVENTIONS OF PLACE AND GENDER THROUGH MEDIA

Places and identities are increasingly seen by cultural geographers as socially constructed. In other words, for many people the reality of places is derived from images and the discourses that surround them. In Australia, Dunn et al. (1995) have demonstrated how the industrial landscape and narratives of a 'dirty old town' and of a 'city in crisis' have coloured outsiders' views of the city of Newcastle. Similarly, place narratives of the Sydney suburb of Redfern as a 'war zone' and 'no-go area' have produced a dominant but contested reading of this place as a demonised Aboriginal 'ghetto' (Anderson 1993). In contemporary times, audio-visual cultural products such as film and music video are increasingly instrumental in structuring such place concepts. The images produced by these media are central to the formation of ideas about human and physical landscapes (Zonn 1984, p. 44).

Similarly, social group identities are also constructed and reproduced by media. Gendered identities are often caricatured by the media as polarised opposites, with discourses of aggressive dominant masculinities being played out in opposition to passive and vacillating femininities. Such representations are constantly reaffirmed in cultural products, in both their production and consumption. The regular characterisation of the football field as a battle ground, for example, where 'real men' struggle on heroically despite bleeding head-wounds constructs and reaffirms the value of the masculine warrior in a form which is consumed on a weekly basis by young men (and others). Importantly, gendered identities and their associated power hierarchy are also constructed by the absence of women in representations of sport, politics and public life and spaces. Feminist geographers since the early 1980s have pointed out that women were excluded not only from such spaces, but more generally from human geography. Women's roles and experiences were either assumed to be the same as men's, in which case these studies were gender-blind, or women were assumed to conform to a stereotype, usually of women as mothers and unpaid housekeepers (Monk and Hanson 1982). Similarly, the media both excludes and caricatures women, sometimes in negatively stereotyped ways, for example as sex objects for a male gaze (Moore 1988) or as the female monster (Creed 1993).

Despite the significance of cultural products in mediating constructions of social categories, geographers have paid little attention to the role of film and music in defining and naturalising the meanings of places and peoples. Jackson complained that in a time when the 'experience of place is now thoroughly mediated by what we read and what we see on television' the study of this medium has only recently received attention from geographers (Jackson 1989, p. 22). Burgess (1990, p. 157) put forward a threefold agenda for a cultural geography of media. First, such a geography should ask 'how landscapes, places and nature are encoded in the press, television, radio, cinema and advertising'. Second, it should assess the role of 'class, gender, ethnicity and locality' in the production and consumption of cultural products. Third, it should expose the ideologies that underpin and are naturalised in our media. To those ends, this chapter seeks to examine the meanings of place and gender that are encoded and naturalised within the film *Falling Down,* set in Los Angeles (Schumacher 1993). The film title implies societal breakdown and the media kit (released with the film) poses striking images of urban malaise in which an individual male is cast as victim of a declining urban and moral order (Warner Bros 1992). This chapter undertakes a critique, invigorated by the insights of both cultural studies and feminist geography, of a backlash genre of film in which men are presented as victims of women's emancipation (Faludi 1992). Backlash cultural products are flourishing in an environment of apparent urban chaos and the political ascendancy of the New Right and the moral majority (Winchester and White 1988, p. 39; Jackson 1989, pp. 6–7). *Falling Down* is a mainstream Hollywood film of the contemporary era, and as such it manifests the tensions and anxieties of our time.

GEOGRAPHY AND CULTURAL PRODUCTS

Literature, music and art

Geographers have been engaged with cultural products such as art and literature since the heyday of regional geography. Classic studies of the regional novels of Thomas Hardy (Darby 1948) and Walter Scott (Paterson 1965) examined these novelists' depictions of real places. Innovative approaches to the cultural landscape analysed art works to identify English perceptions and tastes in landscape, including the bucolic, the picturesque and the antiquarian (Lowenthal and Prince 1965). The use of creative literature in geography has developed from a literal reading of landscapes to a more individualistic view of geographies of the mind and the imagination (Lowenthal and Bowden 1976).

Most often, however, these geographies were rural or historical, reflecting geography's previous regional emphasis and a rose-tinted nostalgia for a romanticised rural past. Similar themes have been evident in the geography of music, with a historical focus on the regional development of folk, blues and country rather than popular music (Carney 1990; Gill 1993; Kong 1995).

Geography's serious contemporary engagement with cultural products is associated with the rise of humanistic geography in the 1970s, a period also viewed as the 'golden age' of music geography (Carney 1990). Humanistic geography, as part of a critique of spatial science, focused on human agency and human experience (Buttimer 1976; Tuan 1976). Humanistic geographers drew on qualitative sources and texts, such as works of art and literature, to express more fully the gamut of human experience. Geographers of music, although less embedded in the humanistic critique, also examined images of place and the affective power of landscape (Ford and Henderson 1974). The humanistic approach particularly drew on art and literature, which were quarried for the social construction and meanings of the landscape, reflecting geography's shift in focus from the geometry of space to the meanings and senses of place (Brosseau 1994, pp. 337–8).

The development of a nuanced sense of place from literary sources is well exemplified by the work of Pocock (1981). Literature offers an insight into the meaning of place, partly by vivid use of a range of language and evocative description (Pocock 1981; Meinig 1983; Teather 1990). More recently, it has been maintained that '[c]reative or imaginative literature has a power to reflect complex and ambiguous realities that make it a far more plausible representation of human feelings and understandings than many of the artefacts used by academic researchers' (White 1995, p. 21). Geographers have thus been able to use literature and other cultural texts to appreciate the meanings and experiences of place and situations for individuals.

Other geographers have focused less on the individual meaning and experiences of place and more on the immediate regional and historical context in which the works are set (White 1984, pp. 1–3). For example, Teather (1990), in an analysis of post-war fiction set in Sydney, related the place-bound depictions in her chosen novels very closely to the social and spatial context of urban change and planning. Despite these interests in the social and spatial content of cultural products, the geographical use of film has been criticised for its shallow treatment of social relations (Jackson 1989, p. 22). The criticism of superficiality is easily levelled at humanistic geography, although it was never intended to be theoretical, nomothetic or structuralist (Pocock 1983). With respect to literature, the shallow treatment of which Jackson complains is best seen in two respects. The first is the stereotyping of the identity of places and the naturalising of social structures and relations; a classic example is the depiction of the north of England, characterised as dirty, industrial working class and masculine (Pocock 1979; Shields 1991; Daniels and Rycroft 1993). Such an approach ignores the dynamic interpretations and multiple meanings of places for different individuals, as indicated in the above-mentioned study of Newcastle, Australia. More recently, the plural, competing, contingent and even contradictory interpretations of the novel as text have been recognised by Brosseau (1995, p. 91). In a quantum leap from classic sense of place studies he attempted to tease out a dialogue between city-text and reader, emphasising both the textual strategies embedded in the novel and the unfinished nature of meaning as an interactive process between reader and city-text. The second lacuna of interpretation is structural or theoretical. Very few geographical analyses of literature, with the exception of Silk (1984), have adopted a perspective which emphasises the 'collective and unconscious structures' mediated by cultural products (Silk 1984, pp. 153, 165).

Feminist analyses have been significant in bringing out from the shadow the voices and experiences of women, who have previously been suppressed. Daniels (1992) ignored the gendered nature of the textile industries of Leeds, while Daniels and Rycroft (1993) revelled in the maleness of the Nottingham depicted in the texts and genres of Alan Sillitoe's novels without pondering its partiality. Female voices, silenced, ignored or naturalised in such analyses, have been brought to the fore by feminist geographers (Avery 1988; Teather 1990). The recurring themes of place, home and travel and the hugely significant differences of those experiences for women and men have been considerably expanded and developed using a wide range of literary sources by Shurmer-Smith and Hannam (1994, pp. 35–40). On the other hand, the overt and implicit sexism and misogyny which permeate popular music have received little attention from geographers (for an exception see Moss 1992).

Cinema and place

Only a handful of cultural geographers, such as Burgess and Gold, have taken a sustained interest in television and cinema (Burgess 1987; Gold 1985). Geographical enquiry into film has taken a variety of approaches, ranging from industrial geography (Storper and Christopherson 1987) and the use of film as a source of historical data (Nicholson 1991, p. 29), to ways in which the portrayal of place constructs spatial meaning (Godfrey 1993; Gold 1985) and critiques of the ways in which spatial relations are presented (Harvey 1989). Despite this limited diversity there has been worryingly little contemplation in cultural geography of the way in which the social and spatial relations of gender are depicted in mainstream film, and a limited utilisation of recent theoretical developments within film studies.

Film should be a prime focus for cultural geographers because of its significance in constructing perceptions of place. Nicholson argued that '[f]or many of us, a perception … of place, … is conditioned primarily through films and television' (1991, p. 32). Film and, to a lesser extent, television present audio-visual images which have the power to appear as factual and objective, concealing their fabricated and socially constructed nature (Zonn 1984, p. 36; Burgess 1987, pp. 1, 5; Higson 1987, p. 9; Nicholson 1991, p. 29). However, films may be distorted by a variety of forces including directorial intent, production factors and hegemonic ideology (Godfrey 1993, pp. 438–9). The apparent authenticity of places and people depicted generally conceals a naturalisation of hegemonic and conservative values (G. Rose 1994, p. 46).

Films have been generally negative in their representation of the city. Gold argued that 'cinema has shared that intellectual bias against the city that has marked contemporary literature and the arts' (Gold 1985, p. 125), a bias reflected in much of classic urban geography (Robson 1994). This anti-urban outlook is set in opposition to a 'romantic and nostalgic' view of the countryside (Youngs and Jenkins 1984, pp. 48, 51); for example, in the original version of *Blade Runner* (Scott 1982) Deckard and Rachel escape from the postmodern city to a natural landscape of sun and greenery. Film has generally been used to portray the 'view that large cities are alienating and hostile places, in which there are enormous contrasts in wealth and living conditions and in which there is a seamy underlife all too ready to rise to the surface' (Gold 1985, p. 125). Benton's (1995) analysis of place of three films set in Los Angeles emphasises the fragmented and violent nature of urban life, while *L.A. Story* is distinctive in representing the city as a 'Disneyfied' Utopia (Benton 1995, pp. 146–8). In contrast, Young (1990b, p. 317) has argued that films 'have celebrated city life, its energy, cultural diversity (and) technological complexity'. However, from a reading of mainstream city-based films, Lewis (1991) identified the following negative city images: a place of physical and moral darkness, a prison; a place of filth and corruption, simultaneously home and toilet; and a place where nature and humankind are dominated by capitalism, resulting in exploitation, segregation and violence. Higson (1984, p. 18) demonstrated, using the gritty urban realist movies of the 'kitchen sink' genre, how cities are portrayed alternatively as either problems or spectacle. Supposed concern over urban problems provided the moral validation for gazing voyeuristically at the working class, the down-and-outs, subcultures and ethnic minorities. These films reinforce the distance between classes, and between black and white. Burgess (1985) argued that the juxtaposition of inner-city crime and physical neglect with ethnic minorities, subcultures or the working class serves as a diversion from criticism of structural racism, alienation and capitalism.

Geographers have criticised films for their conservative representations and message, often focusing on the way in which social relations are discussed. Harvey (1989, pp. 313, 322), in discussing the presentation of social and spatial relations in film, lamented that while Scott's *Blade Runner* depicted class oppression it demonstrated no sense of a counter movement or resistance. Writing on *Wings of Desire* (Wenders 1987) Harvey complained that the facts and relations of production are missing, and therefore there is no intimation of class struggle (1989, pp. 316, 322). Moreover, both films are criticised for the use of optimism and romanticism as resolutions to conflicts and contradictions, a trend which Harvey sees as 'dangerous' (Harvey 1989, p. 322). In films depicting local communities threatened by proposed development schemes, Hillier (1994) detected a ubiquitous critique of developers and planners, the planning process being represented as readily corruptible. The communities were portrayed as unknowing victims, who, having been warned by a heroic individual, successfully rallied to oppose the threatened development. The implicit message, however, is that the system does work, assuring us that democracy will prevail over capitalism (Hillier 1994, pp. 13, 15).

Notwithstanding such comments on the conservative and mollifying representations and assumptions of mainstream film, these critiques have not been extended by geographers to the portrayal of gender relations.

Harvey's film geography was exceptional in its discussion, however brief, of gender relations in *Blade Runner.* His comment on the 'tired machismo of Deckard and the submission of Rachel' referred to Rachel's need to find her identity only through Deckard rather than in her own right (Harvey 1989, pp. 312, 322). Harvey's comments on gender relations in these films have been criticised for assuming that the character Rachel should go into an alliance with Deckard and for failing to sufficiently problematise the imbalanced power relations between them (Massey 1991, pp. 43–4). More telling studies of women's naturalised socio-spatial roles and their depictions in film have appeared in the last few years (Monk and Norwood 1990; Aitken and Zonn 1993; G. Rose 1993, pp. 93–101; 1994; Avery 1988). G. Rose's application of postcolonial theory to community film, Burgess' utilisation of semiotics and perspectives from cultural studies, Harvey's class-based critique and Benton's (1995) analysis of *LA Story* are rare examples in cultural geography of serious theoretical discussion of place portrayal in cinema and television. Despite some of the work mentioned above, the geographical investigation of film and other cultural products has largely been gender-blind (although see Benton 1995). This neglect contrasts sharply with the evolution of feminist-informed cultural geography in other fields over the last decade.

This chapter analyses the representation of the quintessentially postmodern city of Los Angeles (LA) and its people through a study of Schumacher's (1993) *Falling Down.* Particular emphasis is placed on the constructions of gender and place in the mainstream media of Hollywood film. We accept Young's argument that popular cultural products universalise and naturalise dominant ideology and are a medium through which mainstream cultural imperialism is enacted (Young 1990a). In so doing, we attempt to avoid some of the pitfalls of humanistic geographical analyses of creative literature by denaturalising the hegemonic offerings of cultural products. Hegemonic representations of white heterosexual masculinity are seen as problematic; otherness is implicitly accorded to gays, lesbians, women and people of colour. As outlined in the following section, an assessment of the reception of film is an increasingly important aspect of film analysis. To this end we reveal that while there are multiple potential readings of *Falling Down,* the text has in-built limits to interpretation. The aim of these limits is to encourage preferred readings of the film. Particular segments of the audience are provided images and plots from which they can generate these preferred meanings.

DEVELOPMENTS IN CULTURAL STUDIES OF FILM

Contemporary film studies have become increasingly directed towards cinema audiences and their reception and interpretation of film productions, and have become less and less focused upon the author, the film and the production itself. J. Rose (1986, pp. 199–200) has identified two recent divergent trends in film theory. She sees the first trend, the 'explosion of studies devoted to the analysis of audience issues' (Allor 1993, p. 99) as a reaction to the focus on how social structures influence film. The second trend, which addresses the construction and representation of gender in film, is seen as a result of the influence of feminism.

Audiences rather than authors

The shift of focus of film studies away from the auteur (author/director), is a trend rather pretentiously known as the 'death of the author' (Barthes 1977, pp. 142–8). Auteur studies were the result of a deliberate effort to elevate film from the realms of whimsy and transform it into a legitimate product for serious and artistic criticism (Bordwell 1985, p. 211; Gledhill 1990, p. 31; Burgess 1987, p. 2). Auteur studies therefore viewed films primarily as texts, produced by authors, a style of study which has been heavily criticised for privileging authorial intent. The author's intentions may be mediated through the ideological apparatus of the dominant culture, the commercial constraints of the contemporary film industry and the disparate readings of various audiences. These filters are each important elements of film studies.

The analysis of film as text—textual analysis—has been an influential technique in the study of cultural products and has developed into the 'canonical method' of film studies (Jameson 1995; Stacey 1993, pp. 260–1). Film can be an especially deceptive medium that naturalises constructions of gender, place and ethnicity. Film continually demands 'the reader' to identify with the cinematic image as the 'real world', yet at the same time be aware that, despite its verisimilitude, it is in fact not real. While the 'spectator is more duped in the cinema than in any other art form, she or he is nonetheless aware of that process' (J. Rose 1986, p. 217). This allows a convenient slippage for film texts between being projections of 'reality' and being 'just a movie'. Films therefore have to be 'read' to uncover the ideological assumptions implicit in their narrative (Green 1993, p. 111). This method involves 'deconstructing of the text, or breaking it down to its constituent parts, then reconstructing it with its hidden meanings revealed' (Kuhn 1990, p. 400). Such a textual analysis moves beyond the urban reality of the plot and the characters to a focus on the messages or ideological statements of the film.

Film has been seen as essentially controlled by the dominant capitalist culture, and therefore reproducing its conservative ideology. A primary ideological function of mainstream film is the representation of the family, community and nation as natural and normal; espousing 'the integrity and necessity of conventional domestic life' and 'law and order' (Green 1993, pp. 106–8). Green argued that film generally only presents conflicts between social groups and the nasty forces of misogyny, homophobia, racism and elitism *if* these are resolved and the groups are reconciled before the credits roll, or if not, then only if the victims are thoroughly scapegoated. Marginalised ethnic groups are re-integrated or told to fix up their own act, divorcees are reconciled, the corrupt cop is weeded out, working girls get married (typically in a church) and sexually aggressive women are put to the sword (Green 1993, pp. 114–5). The influence of mainstream film is omnipresent and profound throughout the Anglo-American world (Penley 1988, p. 23). The primary role of film may be entertainment, not education or social reform. However, when a film purports to be 'just a good story', its ideological import is more often than not conservative.

The recent focus upon the audience in film studies reflects a renewed interest in the social sciences in questions of agency and interpretation (Allor 1993, pp. 99, 261–2). Cultural studies during the 1970s focused upon the way 'groups with the least power [audiences] practically develop their own readings of, and uses for, cultural products—in fun, in resistance, or to articulate their own identity' (During 1993, p. 7). With the ascendancy of an 'audience research paradigm' the traditional representation of audiences as 'cultural dupes and mindless consumers' who accept all cultural products without question has been challenged (Jenkins 1991a, p. 91). While audiences still lack direct access to, and power over, the means of cultural production, they do not necessarily accept the textual meanings offered by directors and production companies (Jenkins 1991a, pp. 91–2).

Fans of television shows and film can be an organised audience-subculture who have an established medium for discussion of product and who produce assessments and debate (Jenkins 1991a, 1991b). Viewing is a fluid process of appropriation, resistance and selection of 'mobile images that can be inhabited in many different ways' which allows 'audiences to claim their own place and perspective as the essential authority' (Corrigan 1991, pp. 6, 228–9; During 1993, p. 7). Cultural geography has itself experienced a similar post-structuralist shift of attention from academic readings of landscapes and communities towards the collection of the interpretations of everyday users (Goss 1988, p. 398; Winchester 1992, p. 140).

Feminist film theory

Over the last two decades film has undergone a sustained and coherent critique from feminist theory, challenging gender depictions and the portrayal of gender relations. Feminist film theory takes an openly political and interventionist stance to the 'ways in which woman has been constituted as a set of meanings through processes of cinematic signification' (Kuhn 1982, pp. 70, 71). Feminist critique of cultural production has concentrated firstly upon the stereotypical depiction of women, with the ideal woman portrayed as young, shapely and well dressed (Kuhn 1982, pp. 5–6). These depictions have naturalised ideologies such as the separation of gendered spheres of activity. A second related feminist film critique, emanating from psycho-analytic or semiotic analysis, has focused on the objectification of women and on male ownership of 'the gaze'. Mainstream cultural products like film support the 'ideological construction of women as objects, in particular as objects of evaluation in terms of socially predefined visible criteria of beauty and attractiveness' (Kuhn 1982, p. 6). Both of these critiques are expanded upon below.

The limited roles accorded to women reach their epitome in the *Bond* movies, where all the women are glamorous and, whatever their political affiliation, never fail to succumb to the charms of 007. Moore (1988, p. 263) considered that there has been a highly publicised change in the depiction of women in the *Bond* movies, but that this consists merely of adding a 'token feminist'. Gordon (1992) detected in American fantasy and science fiction films an overt affiliation of the family, and particularly the heterosexual patriarchal family. Creed's (1993) analysis of woman-as-monster in film showed how the monstrous-feminine is defined in terms of sexuality and explored five faces of the monstrous-feminine in relation to Kristeva's theory of the abject and the maternal. Representations of female alcoholics depict this condition as a consequence of unbridled or misused sexuality or as a result of failed relationships (usually with a man), while male alcoholics are portrayed as romantic or noble, or 'born of cosmic struggles' (Kanner 1990, pp. 183, 193, 195). A notable exception to such portrayals occurred in the feminist-inspired television product *Cagney and Lacey* (Clark 1990; Kanner 1990).

The crisis of American bourgeois patriarchy which was portrayed in the mainstream films of the 1970s and 1980s 'attempt[ed] to contain, work out, and in some fashion resolve narratively the contemporary weakening of patriarchal authority' (Sobchack 1991, p. 6). Many films now represent men as having more feminine traits but it is still the 'old, hard, assertive, violent images from *Rocky* to *Rambo* ... which continue to make box-office records' (Segal 1990, p. 292). In *Fatal Attraction* the wife is contained within the family and the blame for failings of the family structure—instigated by male marital infidelity—are displaced on to 'women as female temptresses', the crisis being resolved through a conflict between women (Singer 1990, p. 109). These ideological assertions of the patriarchal family—usually the heterosexual nuclear family—marginalise many people who for a host of reasons do not pursue such a traditional family structure.

The second form of feminist film critique has identified the subject and object positions constructed in a film. The problem is not merely that women are stereotyped, but that their depiction assumes and caters for a male spectator. The women in the *Bond* films are obviously positioned as sexual objects (Moore 1988) that can be the object of male fantasy. The gaze in cinema has been dominantly male, reflecting patriarchal cultural domination.

In a world ordered by sexual imbalance, pleasure in looking has been split between active/male and passive/female. The determining male gaze projects its fantasy on to the female figure, which is styled accordingly. In their traditional exhibitionist role women are simultaneously looked at and displayed, with their appearance eroded for strong visual and erotic impact (Mulvey 1975, p. 11).

It is possible that the male gaze is less dominant today, largely due to the force of feminist critique of film and other cultural products (Green 1993, p. 121). The ownership of the gaze is perhaps less exclusive than previously assumed, with surreptitious glances and sub-textual offerings for the non-hegemonic gaze (Arbuthnot and Seneca 1982; Brasell 1992, p. 634; Ellsworth

1986, pp. 55, 53; Gaines 1988, p. 15). Various studies of the gaze indicate both the dynamism of reception as well as the importance of the forces of cultural production in the construction of object and subject positions in cinema.

Feminist film theory ultimately drew attention to the patriarchal structures that constrain the production and consumption of cultural products. The condemnation of 'malestream' cinema's sexist practices and depictions is an essential political and social contribution of feminist film theory.

Reading film

A geography of film which wishes to take developments in the theory and practice of film studies seriously needs to be aware of a number of forces which influence the production and reception of film. Many mainstream films are positioned within the structures of capitalism, patriarchy and ethnocentrism. Women are stereotyped and objectified, the working class are patronised or criticised and ethnic minorities are either demonised or parodied. In film these processes are ever-spatial; the stigmatising of the places ethnic minorities inhabit, the gendered allocation of space and the spheres of production, and the juxtaposition/association of urban decline with the working class. Textual analysis is a method for critically unveiling the structures that support such depictions. This chapter applies a textual analysis to a film of the backlash genre with the aim of de-naturalising the ideological statements that permeate it.

Recent research has shown that film audiences do not necessarily accept the meanings offered or hinted at by directors. However, getting beyond this dualism of production and reception, it is clear that some films lend themselves to alternative readings more easily than others, and facilitate certain types of appropriation. A second aim of our review of a backlash genre cultural product is to analyse the consumption of this film; and make some comments upon the interpretations to which the film lends itself. However, before a critical reading of the film can be undertaken, the reader will require a review of the central characters and plot.

FALLING DOWN

The adventures of an ordinary man at war with the everyday world

The subtitle above is the one-line description of the story of *Falling Down* which appeared on the video cover and in much of the advertising for the cinema release. This film, however, is clearly about *two* ordinary men. The first man is D-Fens (generally named after his car number plate), sacked from his job in the defence industry a month previously and unsuccessful in finding re-employment, and divorced from his ex-wife Beth, who is now a sole parent to their young daughter Adele. The purpose of this ordinary man's traverse through Los Angeles (LA) is to get home; we soon realise, however, that his real destination is his ex-wife's home, and that symbolically his journey is aimed at reclaiming a past. His journey 'home' and his attempts to telephone Beth precipitate an array of violent and fatal encounters. The second man, Detective

Sergeant Prendergast, is beginning his last day before an early retirement, ending a career which has of late been desk-bound. Warner Bros' *Media Information Kit* explains that Prendergast is 'professionally crippled by the neurotic, overly-dependent wife he continues to love and protect' (Warner Bros 1992, pp. 1–2). Prendergast traces D-Fens' violent path across the city on the maps and computers in his office in the safety of the police station. There are only three scenes that feature neither of these characters.

D-Fens is stuck in a traffic jam with its ineffective air-conditioning system, surrounded by a cacophony of screaming kids, car radios, car horns, car phones, and car exhaust fumes which pour into the pollution haze that hangs over the city. He becomes increasingly agitated and, to the dismay of other motorists, takes the anarchic step of abandoning his vehicle and disappearing over the embankment. D-Fens' walk across the car-oriented city of Los Angeles is a spatial metaphor for his transgression of normal codes of behaviour.

Representations of place: the sick city

The representations of place and space in *Falling Down* occur at many different levels. The viewer is left in no doubt that this is the United States of America: the 'stars and stripes' fluttering above the 'Whammyburger' fast-food restaurant, hanging along the side of a school bus and draped around the shoulders of a homeless, wheelchair-bound war veteran drive home a message that this is the real contemporary USA. The *Media Information Kit* instructs potential reviewers that this is 'the face of contemporary urban reality' (Warner Bros 1992, p. 1). Los Angeles is portrayed in the opening freeway scenes as the archetypal car-clogged, freeway-bound polluted city. These freeways carry their motorists above and away from the neglected and abandoned neighbourhoods below them—neighbourhoods which are cutoff from one another by freeway embankments.

The city, however, is represented as more than just the anti-urban stereotype. As in Scott's *Blade Runner* (1982) and Altman's *Short Cuts* (1993), Schumacher's LA is a city undergoing fragmentation and incapable of sustaining a harmonious existence for its populace. There are more than hints of 'Fortress LA' (Davis 1990), of the politics of turf (Cox 1989) and of a 'shattered metro-sea of homogenised yet fragmented communities' (Soja 1989). This is a postmodern city of multiple polarities, of surveillance, of the locally global and the globally local, of a city being turned outside-in and inside-out (Soja 1993; see also Benton (1995) for a discussion of postmodern LA through film). D-Fens moves through places such as South Central and Korea Town, which have endured long-standing institutional neglect as well as disabling myths which stunt investment (Griego 1995, pp. 7–9). Institutional racism, poor services and urban malaise all underpinned the 1992 riots which followed the not-guilty verdict for the police associated with the Rodney King bashing. The most severe damage from these riots was experienced in South Central and Koreatown (Griego 1995, pp. 5–7). The representations of the city are complex. The film is at its most oppositional in its representation of place and its implied critique of the forces of global capitalism which have given rise to economic

FIGURE 9.1 White male in gangland.
Source: Warner Bros (1992) Media Information Kit.

rationalism, industrial restructuring, institutional neglect, unemployment, homelessness and a ghettoised proletariat drawn from global sources.

Schumacher's film exposes the viewer to stark juxtapositions of wealth and poverty, made more vivid by contrasts in landscape, by changes of pace in filming and by the need to scale walls and cross boundaries. In an affluent pocket of LA, D-Fens' progress is obstructed by walls, gates, barbed wire and warning signs. D-Fens, aggressively warned-off a green and pleasant golf course by two golfers, retaliates by shooting their golf cart and berating them for their excessive use of space. He ridicules their eccentric dress, chequered pants and 'stupid little hat'; the golfers are portrayed as old, greedy and decadent, and their control over space and others is ironically contrasted with their lack of control over their own bodies as one is left gasping on the ground after a heart attack. Gangland, on the other hand, is referred to disparagingly, by both D-Fens and police as 'shit-hole', 'pissing ground' and 'piece of shit hill'. These are depicted as places where a single white male will be followed, harassed and menaced (see Figure 9.1). At one stage, D-Fens sits down upon some concrete steps covered in tags and other messages. Two Latino-Americans, depicted as suspicious and vicious, then approach him, revealing themselves as gang members. They inform him that he has trespassed on their turf and point to the tags as indicators of that. D-Fens refers to the tags as illegible graffiti. The gang members demand money or his briefcase and threaten him with a knife. D-Fens responds by striking them both with the baseball bat he has acquired.

The film is overtly critical of an economic and political system which can suddenly construct an active worker as obsolete. A placard-waving small businessman outside a branch of a Savings and Loan bank protests about the refusal to give him a loan and the cavalier and uncaring attitude of an establishment he has had financial dealings with for seven years. His placard and catch-cry 'Not Economically Viable' strike a chord with D-Fens. The police handcuff the protester, and as they take him away D-Fens gives him a nod of recognition.

Elsewhere in the city, the viewer is introduced to the alienation, poverty and dysfunction of contemporary patriarchal capitalism: an unkempt man with a sign saying 'Will work for food'; a wall poster raising consciousness about child sexual abuse; a white male with a yellow cardboard sign 'We are dying of AIDS, please help us!' and a black male in a wheelchair with the sign 'HOMeLeSS VeT, NeeD FooD, NeeD MOneY'. However, the film then introduces us to the 'Seedy Guy in Park', who begs D-Fens for money. This fellow is a wheedling loafer and his conniving is placed in contrast to those genuinely in need. It allows the viewer and D-Fens to dismiss him and move away from this poverty. D-Fens has witnessed both the classes above and below him and he has not liked what he has seen. His class, the middle class, are excluded by the elite and are being pressed downward.

Both the director and the production company have focused the blame for D-Fens' rampage on society—on urban reality. In the penultimate scene of the film Beth tells D-Fens he is sick and needs help. D-Fens retorts that it is the city and society that are sick. Urban pathology in the film is associated with social changes such as the demise of patriarchal authority and challenges to 'family values'. The solution for D-Fens is a return to how things were before. Ideologically this is an argument for traditional heterosexual patriarchal norms and is based on a myth of a homogeneous cultural American past

(Ashbolt 1994, p. 43). More extreme characters are introduced in the film in order to mollify D-Fens' own outrageous behaviour. In another traffic jam, a misogynist motorist is mid-insult to the female driver in front of him when D-Fens silences him with a punch. This 'chivalrous' act of an ordinary man is another contradistinction between D-Fens and the bullies, extremists and hoods. The corruption of this 'ordinary man' is a combined result of urban reality and the 'real' extremists he meets.

Constructions of gender and sexuality

Despite the influence of feminist critique in film studies, film reviews in popular media and cinema journals remain quite gender blind (Ellsworth 1986, pp. 52–3). Typically, there was little discussion in reviews of this film of the misogyny which was depicted. Instead, where reviews were critical, attention was focused on the racism depicted. Much of the critique of *Falling Down* has been targeted at D-Fens' vigilante acts upon ethnic minorities and the extremely negative ways they have been represented, rather than at the intimidatory, aggressive and violent nature of gender relations in the film. Lowing's review (1993, p. 110) was distinctive in the Australian press in that she complained that D-Fens' history of domestic violence and his ex-wife's story were underplayed and not adequately dealt with. The producers continually assert that this film is about the contemporary city, but it is as much about the contemporary household—as much a tale of suburban brutality as urban reality.

The constructions of the female characters are very limited, almost one-dimensional. These include hackneyed stereotypes of Sergeant Prendergast's spouse as hysterical and childlike, never having come to terms with the loss of her child or her beauty and exhibiting an exaggerated over-dependence categorised as a 'change of life thing'. D-Fens' mother is an incredibly insecure and vague character who nurtures a glass menagerie. D-Fens' ex-wife, Beth, is solely domestic, locked into the role prescribed by the ideology of separate gendered spheres. Angie, the gang groupie whose attempts to modify violence are violently shouted down, is concerned about injuries and is hysterical following the car crash. Sandra, the female detective, when she finally takes to the street with Prendergast after D-Fens, is shot down. This film focuses upon men and masculinity, and its conservative, if not reactionary, constructions of violent and misogynistic masculinity require deconstruction (Connell 1995).

Both of the lead male characters are trying to revive a past. D-Fens pursues a telephone campaign of intimidation against Beth, his ex-wife, takes pleasure in the fact that he is scaring her and intimates he intends to kill her.

While the film does attempt to conjure empathy for D-Fens, his chosen path of masculinity, the condemned hegemonic masculinity, is criticised for its ultra violence and aggressiveness. However, the alternative path presented by Schumacher, the preferred model of masculinity, is Sergeant Prendergast's. Detective Prendergast's case-findings and concerns are dismissed by his Captain, who then ridicules him before his colleagues. The Captain then informs Prendergast that he has never liked him because he doesn't swear. He tells Prendergast that swearing is a mark of a 'real man' and dismisses him out of hand for this shortcoming.

Prendergast's colleagues refer to him as the 'poor deskjockey' and mockingly warn him to 'watch out for paper cuts'. His closest colleague, Sandra, tells him that he has allowed everyone to believe that he is a coward, when it was really his wife that made him 'get off the street'. With his masculinity and authority challenged and ridiculed, and in an attempt to retrieve some patriarchal power he later shouts at his wife over the phone. Dwelling in his new-found authority, he demands 'And you have dinner ready and waiting for me. OK? And Amanda, you leave the skin on the chicken, alright?' He hangs up, chuckling and swaggering. His colleagues surprise him with a farewell party, complete with strip-o-gram and cake. Prendergast thanks them all, but says he has to go. His colleagues are disappointed and two colleagues comment on his reticence to stay and 'enjoy' the stripper, mockingly explaining away his apparent fear of women with reference to his wife.

Prendergast responds by punching one of them, knocking him over and into the cake. He then abandons his maps and computers and hits the streets. In the penultimate scene, Prendergast approaches D-Fens, who has just captured his ex-wife and daughter. Prendergast counsels D-Fens that children are special, and in a particularly corny piece of family-centric dialogue, he, who himself had lost a child through Sudden Infant Death Syndrome, maintains that children are the only thing which add significance to an adult's life. D-Fens pretends to have a gun and compels Prendergast to shoot him dead.

Having hit the streets, punched a colleague, abused his wife and shot the villain, Prendergast now curses. When the Captain compliments him upon his performance, Prendergast shakes his hand and responds, 'F … you Captain Yardley, f … you very much'. The Captain smiles and says, 'You're welcome'. Prendergast then reveals that he has decided to remain a police officer and not retire. The path to salvation, for the white male in the contemporary 'sick' urban reality, is presented through Prendergast. *Falling Down* presents not only the supposed contemporary problems of middle-class white males, but also explains the solution for the insecure patriarch. From Prendergast we learn that salvation of masculinity and patriarchal authority lies in hitting the streets (exposing yourself to danger) regardless of your wife's concerns, punching, swearing, shooting and being aggressive to, and dismissive of, your wife. This is the way a man can overcome the accusation of cowardice, or of not being attracted to women.

Within the film, heterosexuality is clearly identified as the norm and the homosexual as Other. The two gay customers in the Army Surplus store are stereotyped by dress and hairstyle. They are vilified by the extreme neo-Nazi store owner as 'queers' and 'f … faggots'. The film uses violent and vilifying homophobic dialogue and attempts to legitimise that use by positioning these incitements as the statements of an extremist. At one point, where the store owner had D-Fens prisoner, he conflates sexuality, homosexuality, violence and ethnicity when he predicts that in jail D-Fens would be 'f … ed … by some big buck nigger'. Such extreme representations of the Other not only soften and normalise the views of D-Fens but can be appropriated by neo-conservative and backlash audiences.

Reception issues

For its cinema release in Australia, *Falling Down* was subtitled 'A Tale of Urban Reality'. This subtitle is fascinating in itself, revealing the ambiguous voyage the film navigates between pure fiction and reporting on society. In the *Media Information Kit,* Warner Bros explain that the story is actually based upon 'a frenzied truck driver who began ramming cars ... on the freeway' (1992, p. 2). However, all the other problems and changes in the contemporary urban landscape were the creation of Ebbe Roe Smith. Many of the reviews of this film described it as thought provoking and controversial. Indeed, Warner Bros played upon this theme in their advertising of the film (*Sydney Morning Herald* 31/5/93, p. 1). Film critic David Stratton concluded that 'Michael Douglas is riveting as the man on the edge, and this challenging, disturbing film is a worthy American entry in Cannes' (*Movie Show* 1993). *Falling Down* is a realist commentary upon urban space at one moment, and then it is allowed a convenient slippage back to being a 'tale' about reality or 'just a movie' in its depictions of social relations.

The film is clearly about two men, both of whom, for different reasons, are trying to come to terms with an early end to their working lives. The film therefore demands that the viewer see the world from the standpoint of two males. It is a story about transformations of patriarchal capitalism and the supposed loss of white male authority and is focused almost exclusively upon how men deal with these contemporary changes. The story operates to create empathy with, and often sympathy for, the two male characters.

Schumacher has produced a text that can be readily appropriated to a backlash agenda. It can easily be read as a statement of 'what's wrong with society' or 'what we should return to'. Schumacher presents two versions of 'convenient, escapist individualistic solutions' (Greenberg quoted in Penley 1991, p. ix). *Falling Down* has a reactionary sub-text that associates contemporary social problems with the following: ethnic diversity and difference (Schlesinger 1992, 43, pp. 101–38); the increasing independence of women (Faludi 1992); the reconstruction of femininity and masculinity; gay and lesbian liberation (Hughes 1993, p. 75); and the constriction of the middle class. If there is such a thing as a contemporary backlash, then this film certainly can cater for the adherents of this reactionary agenda. The past is romanticised as stable, harmonious and communal, whereas the present is portrayed as unstable, fragmented and dangerous (Ashbolt 1994). These constructions obviously serve a particular perspective—male, white, heterosexual and middle-class. Commenting with some irony on *Falling Down,* Ashbolt pointed out that '[s]urrounded by independent women and fanatical minorities, besieged by both social processes of urban decay and mounting violence ... the world of the white, middle-class male is coming apart. He is the real victim today' (1994, p. 47).

In an interview for the *Movie Show* on Australian SBS Television, Schumacher accepted that perhaps one-quarter of the LA cinema audience cheered at the grocery store scene where D-Fens wrecked a Korean's store with his baseball bat:

David Stratton	How are audiences, say in LA, dealing with scenes like that in this film? ... I mean are some of them cheering?
Joel Schumacher	Yes. My fear was that people would leave the theatre after Michael attacked the Korean, because it's appalling behaviour. It is racist, unfair, appalling behaviour. When a quarter of the audience cheered I was staggered too. I really was.

Schumacher's surprise can be read either as naivety or as a very disingenuous disguise to cover his provision of a backlash message to an eager audience segment. Feigned surprise would seem all the more incredible in light of Schumacher's authorial intent:

> We struck a nerve, obviously. Ebbe Roe Smith when he wrote this script struck a nerve. And it certainly did when I read it, it certainly did with the cast or they wouldn't have played these roles, and then it's been passed on to the media and to the audience. And I think that nerve is that most people have felt some of these feelings. Perhaps not as violent, but I think that prejudice, bigotry, anger, rage, sexism, homophobia exist—anti-semitism exists. It exists in all of us on different levels (Schumacher, interview on the *Movie Show*, SBS Television 1993).

The 'us' or 'we' to which Schumacher refers are obviously the Self—white, male, heterosexual—rather than the Others who suffer the resultant oppressions.

The selection of Michael Douglas to play the part of D-Fens is also instructive. His involvement in films like *Fatal Attraction* and *Disclosure* have positioned him as the archetypal white male of a 'backlash genre' in which male authority is challenged but reasserted and in which aggressive—even demonic—females are put in their place (Singer 1990). Warner Bros explain that 'Michael Douglas sees *Falling Down* as a tragicomedy that explores the familiar' (1992, p. 2). *Falling Down* does not present a complex reality from which we are asked to draw our own conclusions. Rather, this narrative has a direct and deliberate ideological message. The need to attract a diverse audience requires a facade of complexity and ambiguity, so the film presents homophobia and racism as acts of extremism. Nevertheless, it naturalises patriarchal ideologies of the heterosexual family, male authority and conservative constructions of masculinity, and is pervaded by ethnocentric themes.

Mainstream reviewers applauded the commentary within *Falling Down* on the dehumanising and divisive forces of capitalism. They considered the film's discussion of ethnic residential differentiation to be controversial. However, they are largely silent on the film's ideological statements on gender. *Falling Down* attempts a criticism of (sub)urban society, but it does it almost exclusively from a white, male, middle-class perspective. A significant contemporary force which impinges upon the middle-class white male is industrial restructuring and sectoral economic shifts. It is not surprising then, that the film focuses upon those aspects of modern urban society which are primarily of concern to men. This explains why the film is critical of the capitalist city, but conservative in its treatment of patriarchy and ethnocentrism, and is what prevents this product of popular culture from being described as oppositional or progressive. Indeed, this film naturalises ethnic intolerance, homophobia and sexism and serves these up with acts of aggression for an appreciative backlash segment audience. We recognise, too, that the criticisms we make of *Falling Down* are also from a white, middle-class perspective, served up with inflections of social theory, and may be entirely different from the readings made by others.

CONCLUSIONS

The film *Falling Down* represents LA, the archetypal postmodern city, where post-industrial turmoil and societal change combine to produce a fragmenting and frightening urban space. The film depicts a sick city and by implication harks back to a previously safer and healthier society. Its representation of the city forms part of a wider anti-urban tradition, but the film is at its most progressive in portraying the urban problems and landscapes of late capitalism, problems which are depicted as impinging particularly seriously on middle-class white men.

Feminist critique of this film reveals three major problems. First, its assumption of the male gaze and definition of 'Others' in relation to it; second, its naturalisation of social relations which support patriarchy; and third, its depictions of masculinity. The first problem is that the film represents the city through the gaze of two white men. The observer is constructed as the default category of white male, whereas Others are categorised: gays vilified, non-whites demonised and women objectified. It is the white male alone who achieves the status of an individual, more or less heroic. The meanings of urban reality for those Others remain ignored, unexplored and insignificant.

The second problem lies in the depiction of social relations. Whereas capitalism is criticised for failing white men, the social relations of gender, family, sexuality and ethnicity which bolster white male status are naturalised. The ideological structures which underpin the text are inherently conservative. The problems of urban living are associated with marginalised social groups and the blame for such environments is shifted onto its victims.

The depiction of masculinity which is so central to this film is the third problematic feature. D-Fens is represented as an ordinary guy pushed too far whose excesses appear less dramatic when compared with other extremists. However, his extreme violence against others, including his ex-wife and child, is contrasted with a less aggressive masculinity in Prendergast. The representation of Prendergast as the sympathetic cop, the concerned husband and bereaved parent concealing his own personal losses has been well received (C. Rose 1993). The more problematic naturalisations of masculinity within the depiction of Prendergast—his adoption of cursing, fighting, shooting and bullying to pursue his own personal and career objectives—remained unnoticed even by reviewers. The depictions of masculinity range from the extremist neo-Nazi through the supposed ordinary guy and the nice guy. Despite this range of masculinities the film naturalises many of the aggressive, violent and misogynist performances considered to be characteristic of hegemonic masculinity (Connell 1995). Furthermore, homosexuality is arrogantly presented as a subordinate and contemptible masculinity.

In this film it is the white (middle-class, heterosexual) men who are represented as victims, victims at least in part because of all those Others, the women, gays and ethnics who have claimed victim status and in so doing have taken their jobs, their turf, home, wife and family. The construction of this film allows multiple readings. On the one hand the violence, homophobia, sexism and racism can be deplored, but on the other it can be appropriated, cheered and imitated by backlash audiences.

This analysis of *Falling Down* follows feminist critiques of film in stressing the ideological structures underlying the text, which are criticised for their naturalisations of hegemonic constructions of gender, sexuality, family and ethnicity. This cultural analysis of film also focuses on the dynamic moment of reception. The combination of a structural feminist approach, which reveals naturalised dominant ideologies, together with a focus on reception issues demonstrates ways in which a particular construction of film lends itself to multiple readings of place and gender. In this chapter it has been argued that geographers have paid surprisingly little attention to film, although there has been a long-standing concern with other cultural products, notably literature. Attempts have been made to provide some answers to Burgess' (1990) agenda for a cultural geography of media by incorporating feminist critique and aspects of film studies in a new cultural geography of film that recognises multiple meanings of place and social relations which are incorporated in both the film text and in its reception.

ACKNOWLEDGMENTS

We are grateful to Jean Hillier, Curtin University; Colin Macleay, The University of Waikato; and Paul White, The University of Sheffield for their valuable comments on an earlier draft of this chapter.

REFERENCES

Aitken, S.C. & Zonn, L.E. 1993, 'Weir(d) sex: representation of gender-environment relations in Peter Weir's Picnic at Hanging Rock and Gallipoli', *Environment and Planning D: Society and Space,* vol. 11, no. 2, pp. 191–212.

Allor, M. 1993, 'Review', *Screen,* vol. 34, no. 1, pp. 99–102.

Altman, R. 1993, *Short Cuts* (motion picture), Short Cuts Productions, Inc.

Anderson, K.J. 1993, 'Place narratives and the origins of inner Sydney's Aboriginal settlement, 1972–73', *Journal of Historical Geography,* vol. 19, no. 3, pp. 314–35.

Avery, H. 1988, 'Theories of prairie literature and the woman's voice', *Canadian Geographies,* vol. 32, pp. 270–72.

Arbuthnot, L. & Seneca, G. 1982, 'Pre-text and text in Gentlemen Prefer Blondes', *Film Reader,* vol. 5, Winter, pp. 13–23.

Ashbolt, A. 1994, 'Falling everywhere: postmodern politics and American cultural mythologies', *Arena Journal,* vol. 3, pp. 42–8.

Barthes, R. 1977, *Image Music Text,* Essays selected and translated by S. Heath, Flamingo, London.

Benton, L.M. 1995, 'Will the real/reel Los Angeles please stand up?', *Urban Geography,* vol. 16, no. 2, pp. 144–64.

Bordwell, D. 1985, *Narration in the Fiction Film,* University of Wisconsin Press, Madison.

Brasell, R.B. 1992, 'My hustler: gay spectatorship as cruising', *Wide Angle,* vol. 14, no. 2, pp. 54–64.

Brosseau, M. 1994, 'Geography's literature', *Progress in Human Geography,* vol. 18, no. 3, pp. 333–53.

Brosseau, M. 1995, 'The city in textual form: Manhattan Transfer's New York', *Ecumene,* vol. 2, no. 1, pp. 89–114.

Burgess, J. 1985, 'News from nowhere: the press, the riots and the myth of the inner city', in *Geography The Media & Popular Culture,* eds J. Burgess & J.R. Gold, Croom Helm, Kent, pp. 192–228.

Burgess, J. 1987, 'Landscapes in the living-room: television and landscape research', *Landscape Research,* vol. 12, no. 3, pp. 1–7.

Burgess, J. 1990, 'The production and consumption of environmental meanings in the mass media: a research agenda for the 1990s', *Transactions of the Institute of British Geographers,* vol. 15, no. 2, pp. 139–61.

Buttimer, A. 1976, 'Grasping the dynamism of lifeworld', *Annals of the Association of American Geographers,* vol. 66, no. 2, pp. 277–92.

Carney, G. 1990, 'Geography of music: inventory and prospect', *Journal of Cultural Geography,* vol. 10, no. 2, pp. 35–48.

Clark, D. 1990, 'Cagney & Lacey: feminist strategies of detection', in *Television and Women's Culture: the Politics of the Popular,* ed. M.E. Brown, Currency Press, Sydney pp. 117–33.

Connell, R.W. 1995, *Masculinities,* Polity Press, Cambridge.

Corrigan, T. 1991, *A Cinema Without Walls: Movies and Culture After Vietnam,* Routledge, London.

Cox, K.R. 1989, 'The politics of turf and the question of class', in *The Power of Geography: How Territory Shapes Social Life,* eds J. Wolch & M. Dear, Unwin Hyman, Boston, pp. 61–90.

Creed, B. 1993, *The Monstrous-Feminine: Film, Feminism, Psychoanalysis,* Routledge, London.

Daniels, S. 1992, 'The implications of industry: Turner and Leeds', in *Writing Worlds: Discourse Text and Metaphor in the Representation of Landscape,* eds T.J. Barnes & J.S. Duncan, Routledge, London, pp. 38–49.

Daniels, S. & Rycroft, S. 1993, 'Mapping the modern city: Alan Sillitoe's Nottingham novels', *Transactions of the Institute of British Geographers,* vol. 18, no. 4, pp. 460–80.

Darby, H.C. 1948, 'The regional geography of Thomas Hardy's Wessex', *Geographical Review,* vol. 38, no. 3, pp. 426–43.

Davis, M. 1990, *City of Quartz,* Verso, London.

Dunn, K.M., McGuirk, P.M. & Winchester, H.P.M. 1995, 'Place making: the social construction of Newcastle', *Australian Geographical Studies,* vol. 33, no. 2, pp. 149–66.

During, S. 1993, 'Introduction', in *The Cultural Studies Reader,* ed. S. During, Routledge, London.

Ellsworth, E. 1986, 'Illicit pleasures: feminist spectators and personal best', *Wide Angle,* vol. 8, no. 2, pp. 45–56.

Faludi, S. 1992, *Backlash: Undeclared War Against Women,* Chatto & Windus, London.

Ford, L. & Henderson, F. 1974, 'The images of place in American pop music, 1890–1970', *Places,* vol. 1, pp. 31–7.

Gaines, J. 1988, 'White privilege and looking relations: race and gender in feminist film theory', *Screen,* vol. 29, no. 4, pp. 12–27.

Gill, W. 1993, 'Region, agency, and popular music: the Northwest Sound, 1958–1966', *The Canadian Geographer,* vol. 37, no. 2, pp. 120–31.

Gledhill, C. 1990, 'Authorship', in *Women in Film: An International Guide,* ed. A. Kuhn, Fawcett Columbine, New York, pp. 31–2.

Godfrey, B.J. 1993, 'Regional depiction in contemporary film', *The Geographical Review,* vol. 83, no. 4, pp. 428–40.

Gold, J.R. 1985, 'From metropolis to the city: film visions of the future city, 1919–39', in *Geography The Media & Popular Culture,* eds J. Burgess & J.R. Gold, Croom Helm, Kent, pp. 123–43.

Gordon, A. 1992, 'The inescapable family in American science fiction and fantasy film', *Journal of Popular Film & Television,* vol. 20, no. 2, pp. 2–8.

Goss, J. 1988, 'The built environment and social theory: towards an architectural geography', *Professional Geographer,* vol. 40, no. 4, pp. 392–403.

Green, P. 1993, 'Ideology and ambiguity in cinema', *The Massachusetts Review,* vol. 34, no. 1, pp. 102–26.

Griego, L. 1995, 'The lessons learned from Los Angeles', paper presented at the Global Cultural Diversity Conference, Darling Harbour, Sydney, April.

Harvey, D. 1989, *The Condition of Postmodernity,* Basil Blackwell, London.

Higson, A. 1984, 'Space, place, spectacle', *Screen,* vol. 25, nos 4–5, pp. 2–21.

Higson, A. 1987, 'The landscapes of television', *Landscape Research,* vol. 12, no. 3, pp. 1–7.

Hillier, J. 1994, 'Voyeurs all—or cinematic realism: the truth which conceals that there is none', paper presented at the Annual Conference of the Institute of Australian Geographers, Arcadia Resort, Magnetic Island, September.

Hughes, R. 1993, *Culture of Complaint: The Fraying of America,* The Free Press, New York.

Jackson, P. 1989, *Maps of Meaning: An Introduction to Cultural Geography,* Unwin Hyman, London.

Jameson, F.R. 1995, *The GeoPolitical Aesthetic: Cinema and Space in the World System,* Indiana University Press, Indiana.

Jenkins, H. 1991a, '"It's not a fairy tale anymore": gender, genre, Beauty and the Beast', *Journal of Film and Video,* vol. 43, nos 1–2, pp. 90–110.

Jenkins, H. 1991b, 'Star Trek rerun, reread, rewritten: fan writing as textual poaching', in *Close Encounters: Film, Feminism, and Science Fiction,* eds C. Penley, E. Lyon, L. Spigel & J. Bergstrom, University of Minnesota Press, Minneapolis, pp. 171–203.

Kanner, M. 1990, 'That's why the lady is a drunk: women, alcoholism and popular music', in *Sexual Politics and Popular Culture,* ed. D. Raymond, Bowling Green State University Popular Press, Ohio, pp. 183–98.

Kong, L. 1995, 'Popular music in geographical analyses', *Progress in Human Geography,* vol. 19, no. 2, pp. 183–98.

Kuhn, A. 1982, *Women's Picture: Feminism and Cinema,* Routledge & Kegan Paul, London.

Kuhn, A. 1990, 'Text', in *Women in Film: An International Guide,* ed. A. Kuhn, Fawcett Columbine, New York, p. 400.

Lewis, J. 1991, 'City/Cinema/Dream', in *City Images: Perspectives from Literature, Philosophy and Film,* ed. M.A. Caws, Gordon and Breach, New York, pp. 240–54.

Lowenthal, D. & Bowden, M.J. 1976, *Geographies of the Mind: Essays in Historical Geography,* Oxford University Press, New York.

Lowenthal, D. & Prince, H.C. 1965, 'English landscape tastes', *Geographical Review,* vol. 55, no. 2, pp. 186–222.

Lowing, R. 1993, 'Tripped up by attitude', *Sun Herald,* 30 May, p. 110.

Massey, D. 1991, 'Flexible sexism', *Environment and Planning D: Society and Space,* vol. 9, no. 1, pp. 31–57.

Meinig, D.W. 1983, 'Geography as an art', *Transactions of the Institute of British Geographers,* vol. 8, no. 3, pp. 314–28.

Monk, J. & Norwood, V. 1990, 'Remembering the Australian city: urban landscapes in women's fiction', in *Place Image in Media: Portrayal Experience and Meaning Savage,* ed. L. Zonn, Rowman and Littlefield, Savage, MD, pp. 105–19.

Monk, J. & Hanson, S. 1982, 'On not excluding half of the human in human geography', *The Professional Geographer,* vol. 34, pp. 11–23.

Moore, S. 1988, 'Looking for trouble: On shopping', *Gender and the Cinema,* Serpent's Tail, London.

Moss, P. 1992, 'Where is the promised land? class and gender in Bruce Springsteen's rock lyrics', *Geografiska Annale B,* vol. 74, no. 3, pp. 167–87.

Mulvey, L. 1975, 'Visual pleasure and narrative cinema', *Screen,* vol. 16, no. 3, pp. 6–18.

Nicholson, D. 1991, 'Images of reality', *Geographical Magazine,* vol. 63, no. 4, pp. 28–32.

Paterson, J.H. 1965, 'The novelist and his region: Scotland through the eyes of Sir Walter Scott', *Scottish Geographical Magazine,* vol. 81, no. 3, pp. 146–62.

Penley, C. 1988, 'The lady doesn't vanish: feminism and film theory', in *Feminism and Film Theory,* ed. C. Penley, Routledge, New York, pp. 1–24.

Penley, C. 1991, 'Introduction', in *Close Encounters: Film Feminism and Science Fiction,* eds C. Penley, E. Lyon, L. Spigel & J. Bergstrom, University of Minnesota Press, Minneapolis, pp.vii–xi.

Pocock, D.C.D. 1979, 'The novelist's image of the north', *Transactions of the Institute of British Geographers,* vol. 4, no. 1, pp. 62–76.

Pocock, D.C.D. 1981, 'Place and the novelist', *Transactions of the Institute of British Geographers,* vol. 6, no. 3, pp. 337–47.

Pocock, D.C.D. 1983, 'The paradox of humanistic geography', *Area,* vol. 15, no. 4, pp. 355–8.

Robson, B. 1994, 'No city, no civilisation', *Transactions of the Institute of British Geographers,* vol. 19, no. 2, pp. 131–41.

Rose, C. 1993, 'Falling Down', *Sight and Sound,* vol. 3, no. 6, pp. 15–16.

Rose, G. 1993, *Feminism and Geography: The Limits of Geographical Knowledge,* Polity Press, Cambridge.

Rose, G. 1994, 'The cultural politics of place: local representation and oppositional discourse in two films', *Transactions of the Institute of British Geographers,* vol. 19, no. 1, pp. 46–60.

Rose, J. 1986, *Sexuality in the Field of Vision,* Verso, London.

Schlesinger, A.M. 1992, *The Disuniting of America: Reflections on a Multicultural Society,* W.W. Norton & Company, New York.

Schumacher, J. 1993, *Falling Down* (motion picture), Warner Bros.

Scott, R. 1982, *Blade Runner* (motion picture), Warner Bros.

Segal, L. 1990, *Slow Motion: Changing Masculinities Changing Men,* Virago, London.

Shields, R. 1991, *Places on the Margin: Alternative Geographies of Modernity,* Routledge, London.

Shurmer-Smith, P. & Hannam, K. 1994, *Worlds of Desire Realms of Power,* Edward Arnold, London.

Silk, J. 1984, 'Beyond geography and literature', *Environment and Planning D: Society and Space,* vol. 2, no. 2, pp. 151–78.

Singer, L. 1990, 'Just say no: repression, anti-sex and the new film', in *Sexual Politics and Popular Culture,* ed. D. Raymond, Bowling Green State University Popular Press, Ohio, pp. 102–111.

Sobchack, V. 1991, 'Child/alien/father: patriarchal crisis and generic exchange', in *Close Encounters: Film Feminism and Science Fiction,* eds C. Penley, E. Lyon, L. Spigel & J. Bergstrom, University of Minnesota Press, Minneapolis, pp. 3–30.

Soja, E.W. 1989, *Postmodern Geographies: The Reassertion of Space in Critical Social Theory,* Verso, London.

Soja, E.W. 1993, *Postmodern cities*—transcript of conference address, Postmodern Cities Conference Proceedings, Department of Urban and Regional Planning, The University of Sydney.

Stacey, J. 1993, 'Textual obsessions: methodology, history and researching female spectatorship', *Screen,* vol. 34, no. 3, pp. 260–74.

Storper, M. & Christopherson, S. 1987, 'Flexible specialisation and regional industrial agglomerations: the case of the U.S. motion picture industry', *Annals of the Association of American Geographers,* vol. 77, no. 1, pp. 104–17.

Teather, E.K. 1990, 'Early postwar Sydney: a comparison of its portrayal in fiction and in official documents', *Australian Geographical Studies,* vol. 28, no. 2, pp. 204–23.

Tuan, Y.-F. 1976, 'Humanistic geography', *Annals of the Association of American Geographers,* vol. 66, no. 2, pp. 266–76.

Warner Bros 1992, 'Falling Down: A tale of urban reality', *Media Information Kit,* Time Warner Entertainment.

Wenders, W. 1987, *Wings of Desire* (motion picture), Road Movies Berlin & Argos Films, Paris.

White, P.E. 1984, 'Simenon, Maigret and the social geography of Paris', *Don,* vol. 22, pp. 8–14.

White, P.E. 1995, 'Geography literature and migration: introductory themes', in *Writing Across Worlds: Literature and Migration,* eds R. King, J. Connell & P.E. White, Routledge, London, pp. 1–19.

Winchester, H.P.M. 1992, 'The construction and deconstruction of women's roles in the urban landscape', in *Inventing Places: Studies in Cultural Geography,* eds K.J. Anderson & F. Gale, Longman Cheshire, Melbourne, pp. 139–56.

Winchester, H.P.M. & White, P.E. 1988, 'The location of marginalised groups in the inner city', *Environment and Planning D: Society and Space,* vol. 6, no. 1, pp. 37–54.

Young, I.M. 1990a, *Justice and the Politics of Difference,* Princeton University Press, New Jersey.

Young, I.M. 1990b, 'The ideal of community and the politics of difference', in *Feminism/Post-modernism,* ed. L. Nicholson, Routledge, New York, pp. 300–23.

Youngs, M. & Jenkins, A. 1984, 'Shell-shocked: critical film analysis and teaching strategies', *Geography,* vol. 69, no. 1, pp. 46–53.

Zonn, L.E. 1984, 'Images of place: a geography of the media', *Proceedings of the Royal Geographical Society of Australasia,* vol. 84, pp. 35–45.

Constructing geographies

culture and capital

10

Modernity and postmodernity in the retail landscape

Jon Goss

> At the heart of the New Times is the shift from the old mass-production Fordist economy to a new, more flexible, post-Fordist order based on computers, information technology and robotics. But New Times are about much more than economic change. Our world is being remade. Mass production, the mass consumer, the big city, big-brother state, the sprawling housing estate, and the nation-state are in decline: flexibility, diversity, differentiation, mobility, communication, decentralisation and internationalisation are in the ascendant. In the process our own identities, our sense of self, our own subjectivities are being transformed. We are in transition to a new era (*Marxism Today* (1988)).

INTRODUCTION

There is widespread recognition of a profound shift of cultural sensibility in western societies over the last two decades or so. The various terms used to describe these 'New Times'—'post-industrial society', 'information society', 'postfordism' and 'postmodernism'—suggest that it is complex and encompasses various dimensions of everyday life. This chapter briefly examines the relationship between the economic and cultural components of the ongoing transformation and its manifestation in the built environment, focusing on purpose-built places of consumption, that is, shopping centres or malls.[1] This is particularly appropriate, given the importance of consumption to our contemporary lives and given the fact that it is in architecture that the new sensibility attains its most visible expression (Jameson 1984, p. 54; Sharrett 1989, p. 162).

Although by no means universal, perhaps most of the world's population now participates in globalised consumption, and in the most 'developed' societies the consumption of commodities is a primary source of individual identity. From the United States to Australia, from Europe to Singapore it seems that 'you are what you buy' as much as 'you are what you do'. Shopping has become the second most important cultural activity in North America after television, but even then commercial TV's main purpose is to promote shopping, whether directly through advertising or indirectly through depiction of consumer lifestyles. The existential significance of shopping is clearly recognised in popular culture by bumper stickers shouting slogans such as: 'Born to Shop', 'Shop 'Til You Drop', and 'I Shop Therefore I Am'.

The built environment reflects material and symbolic changes in society. Mies van der Rohe, a famous modern architect, for example, thought that 'Architecture is the will of the epoch translated into space' (cited in Frampton 1983, p. 40). A good illustration is the development of the skyscraper in the nineteenth century, which was based on advances in technology (the elevator and structural steel), the organisation of production (mergers and the rapid growth of the corporation) and dominant ideas (verticality is a symbol of corporate power while classical forms were a symbol of the civic function of business). The built environment, however, does not merely reflect historical change, for both social relations and ideologies are partly reproduced by it. The skyscraper, for example, like the church and castle before it, legitimates a particular configuration of social wealth and power and materialises social relationships of power, as anyone knows who has stood on the open concrete in the cold shadow of a towering modern office block, looking up at its anonymous reflective glass. This chapter considers that the shopping centre similarly both expresses and realises the values of consumer society and the activities of mass consumption.

THE HISTORY OF THE SHOPPING MALL

The planned shopping centre had humble beginnings before the Second World War: the first recognisable as such was probably Lake Forest, built in Chicago in 1916. In 1922 Country Club Plaza, an influential prototype shopping district with stylised architecture, landscaping, unified management and sign control was opened in Kansas City (Figure 10.1). In 1931 Highland Park Shopping Village, the first centre based on a pedestrian mall, was built near Dallas. Other centres were built at busy road intersections, but the department stores which today conventionally 'anchor' shopping centres generally remained mainly downtown until the massive highway construction and residential suburbanisation of the 1950s. In 1950, therefore, there were less than 100 shopping centres in the United States (Urban Land Institute 1985, p. 16), whereas recently there were over 35 000 shopping centres—more than the number of post-offices or secondary schools (Stoffel, 1988)—offering a total of almost two and a half billion square feet of gross leasable retail space

FIGURE 10.1 Country Club Plaza, Kansas City, Missouri. Circa 1930. Source: Chris Wilborn and Associates, Photographers, 3101 Mercier, Kansas City, MO 6411.

(National Research Bureau 1990). Huge super-regional malls with up to four major department stores sprawl around suburban highway interchanges, or in some cases squeeze into the decaying fabric of downtown. The largest shopping centre is the massive West Edmonton Mall in Canada which is one mile long, covers about 110 acres, has a total floorspace of 5.2 million square feet and parking for 14 000 cars. Like Mall of America in Bloomington, Minnesota, which checks in at a more modest 4.2 million square feet, it is a major tourist attraction in its own right, a place where people congregate from around the world to shop.

The shopping centre is more than a place to shop, however—it also functions as a cultural institution that provides for entertainment, education and sociality. It houses funfairs and fashion shows; hosts community dances and concerts; promotes fitness and healthcare; and holds classes in adult literacy, even in some cases for university and high school credit. The mall also provides community for diverse users. It is a predictable, safe and sanitised alternative to the old city street, a place where families go on outings, old people idle and exercise and teenagers hang out and grow up 'mall-wise'. The geographical spread and social centrality of the shopping centre has resulted in 'The Malling of America' (Kowinski 1985) and, although conditions are different in other advanced capitalist societies (for example, due to a lack of cheap suburban land, a different structure of capital institutions and more stringent development controls), the model is being exported globally. Are we perhaps witnessing 'The Malling of the World'?

Before further examining the development of these palaces or temples of consumption, their cultural significance, and their changing characteristics and functions in these 'New Times', this chapter briefly considers the nature and role of consumption and of the built environment in advanced capitalist society.

THE CULTURE OF CONSUMPTION

Without mass-produced consumer goods everyday life would be inconceivable for most of us, not only because they sustain our high material living standards, but also because they help define our individual and collective identities. Consumer goods serve the double purpose of satisfying socially defined wants and needs and of 'materialising' cultural distinctions, providing a code that symbolically expresses and communicates personal and social difference (Sahlins 1976; McCracken 1988). This is not entirely new, as 'consumer culture' has been in the making for several hundreds of years (Braudel 1967)—the first consumer revolution, which took place in the nineteenth century, already established consumer goods as repositories of social meaning that anchor and diffuse the values and lifestyle of the middle class (Williams 1982; Miller 1981). It is only in this century, however, and particularly since the Second World War, that everyday life has been so thoroughly commodified that we can be persuaded to buy sexual attraction, happiness and personality as well as our social status in the form of consumer goods. Persuasion is the responsibility of advertising, marketing and media specialists who might be called the 'high priests' of capitalism, since their means is summed up by the notion of 'fetishism of the commodity'.

A fetish, in the anthropological sense, is an object of religion in 'primitive' cultures that is invested with spiritual powers and regarded with dread or reverence. Commodities work similar magic and consumption depends on a 'superstition' that the physical object confers upon the owner power over nature and others. The 'real' power of the owner may lie in his/her economic or political capacity as determined by social relations, but the social reality is obscured by the belief in the 'power' of the object itself. Thus Raymond Williams (1980, p. 185), a British cultural theorist, argues that advertising is 'a highly organised and professional system of magical inducements and satisfactions, functionally very similar to magical systems in simpler societies, but rather strangely coexistent with a highly developed scientific technology'. A second, materialist sense in which the commodity is fetishised is in the masking of its origins in the social relations necessary to produce it. Sensitive contemporary consumers would generally rather not be reminded of the sweatshop labour that makes their designer clothes or the assembly lines that produce their quality household goods, so commodities appear in advertisements and in the marketplace as if by magic; the ghost of human labour is thoroughly exorcised so that consumers need not give thought to their composition, or where, how and by whom they were made (Jhally 1987, p. 49).

We should not accord too much power to either the magician or the advertiser, however, for their operations only work for an audience predisposed to believe in their 'tricks', and it is this that is the real source of the 'magic' (Bourdieu 1986, p. 137). Designers, advertisers and retailers do not have to consciously conspire to deceive their audiences (although they often do), but merely highlight 'latent correspondences' between the commodity and cultural symbols (Sahlins 1976, p. 217). It is not necessary to tell us explicitly that fast cars confer extra libido upon drivers, or that a particular cigarette brand will add sophistication to the smoker—that would be to insult our cultural intelligence—but we 'read' the attractive (female) passenger or the elegant decor and make the symbolic connection. Consumers employ accumulated cultural knowledge and varying degrees of sophistication to actively weave together the natural, symbolic and social elements to create the commodity's context and meaning (Sack 1988). Significantly for geographers, a critical component of this context is the real or imagined landscape in which the commodity is presented. 'Place' suggests the appropriate attitude, ambience and audience to be associated with given commodities—the beach, for example, signifying relaxed sensuality, and the corporate office the confidence of an easy power.

If consumers make their own meanings, however, they are not always as the 'high priests' would preach them. We are able, with varying degrees of ability and success, to actively and imaginatively appropriate and subvert commodities, for example, consuming them out of context or campaigning against the manipulative content of images.[2] This means that while we may be seduced by the promises of the marketers, we are not helpless, brainwashed dupes and we can potentially take responsibility for our consumption.

THE MEANING OF THE BUILT ENVIRONMENT

The built environment is a unique cultural artefact in that it both symbolically expresses the social relations and technologies that structure ways of life, and functions physically as a spatial system that reproduces them. First, elements of the built environment are signifiers, or physical objects, which refer, through a conventional association, to abstract concepts. For example, the towering office block with its reflective skin signifies a powerful, anonymous authority, while a suburban residence signifies private property, territoriality, (nuclear) family life and economic independence. Part of the meaning lies in the function of these structures, but each corporate architect or suburban resident adds elements that express particular, often personal, values that differentiates one office block or suburban home from another so that both functional and stylistic elements of the built environment constitute a complex system of signs which we 'read' as a cultural text. Part of the goal of this chapter is to encourage a more critical 'reading' of the retail built environment.

Second, the built environment compartmentalises social spaces, for example, into public/private, day/night and backstage/frontstage, and thus separates various uses and users, presenting opportunities and constraints for interaction. Hence, the configuration of physical spaces within and between structures has socio-psychological effects and reproduces social relations. The 'geography', or floorplan and structure, of the suburban 'family', for example, is argued to play an important role in 'domesticating' women and children and defining privacy, sexuality and eating habits (Wright 1981). A second goal of this chapter, then, is to show how various architectural elements and structural plans control movement and interaction, and segregate space and particular activities in order to increase consumption of commodities.

THE PERIODICITY OF CAPITALISM

Although there are important differences in its national and regional manifestations, scholars have identified constellations of technology, division of labour, medium of communication, spatial/organisational structures and cultural values that define discrete periods in the development of capitalism. In the United States and Europe, for example, organised capitalism, which consolidated at the beginning of this century and is associated with the culture of modernism, has been giving way to the stage of disorganised capitalism over the last two decades or so, associated with the culture of postmodernism (Lash and Urry 1987). It is important to note, however, that this does not mean changes in organisation of production *cause* changes in cultural values as is sometimes implied, for there is a complex dialectical (not determinist) relationship between culture and economy.

'Organised' capitalism is based on the following: the concentration of industrial and financial capital in large corporations; the mass production of standardised commodities under Fordist regulation—so-called because large-scale assembly line production was pioneered in Henry Ford's automobile plants in the 1910s; politics of national trade unions and workers' parties; and the growth of an administrative middle class. Manufacturing dominates the economy; the main production technologies are electricity and the internal combustion engine; the medium of communication is the printed word; and the spatial structure consists of coherent regional economies focused on urban industrial complexes (Lash and Urry 1987, pp. 3–4). Modernism, the cultural correlate of this stage of capitalism, entails technical rationality, glorification of science, a futuristic orientation and mass consumption of commodities. Mass consumption was not preconceived by an abstract entity called 'capital', but was born together with mass production as a result of the struggles between the owners of capital and organised labour. As workers gained recognition of a limited working week and fairer wages in return for increased productivity, the advertising industry and institutionalised credit developed to ensure that their increased time and money would be properly spent on the acquisition and display of commodities. The corporate state regulated the national economy and social relations, thus mediating class conflict and contributing to the management of production and consumption. This is the so-called 'bureaucratic society of controlled consumption' (Lefebvre 1971, p. 60).

The Fordist regime of accumulation began to falter in the late 1960s as productivity gains turned sluggish and labour costs increased in western capitalist economies, while more efficient regimes had developed in Japan and Asia's newly industrialising economies. The result is a 'disorganisation' of capitalism, which can be characterised by the following: the fragmentation of the process of production; the incorporation of new (female and immigrant) labour markets through subcontracting and a relative shift in manufacturing towards the Third World; a relative numerical and political decline of the 'core' (unionised male) working class; a massive expansion of services and the consolidation of a professional service class; a growth of new (environmental, gender, race and urban) social movements; a relative expansion and decentralisation of financial capital; and a political and economic crisis of the state resulting from its economic and political inability to regulate the economy and meet the contradictory needs of capital and labour. The dominant technologies are nuclear power and the computer and the mode of communication is the electronically-produced image and sound byte. The spatial manifestation of 'disorganisation' is the decentralisation of industry, decline in number and size of industrial cities and disintegration of regional economies. In cultural life, identities have multiplied and destabilised and 'style' is everything. Everyday life is increasingly aestheticised and consumption personalised: even basic commodities make statements upon one's 'taste'—from soft drinks to breakfast cereals—and markets are segmented according to criteria identified and exhaustingly researched by the new 'disciplines' of geodemographics and psychographics.

MODERNITY AND MASS CONSUMPTION

The two principal commodities upon which this political-economy were based are standardised suburban housing and the automobile. Both commodities are mass produced and they are mutually dependent—suburban residence demanded a car as the car demanded the construction of highways and the suburbs. They combined to create *space* for expanded commodity consumption in the form of the refrigerator, washing machine, vacuum cleaner, lawn mower and television, all of which became essential for the conspicuous consumption lifestyle of the modern Joneses. The 'captains of consciousness' mobilised America's romantic preoccupation with the rural frontier and the normative model of the nuclear family to promote a 'new design for living'. In the suburban home the consumer-couple is surrounded by efficient, streamlined consumer durables that define the 'American Dream'—the breadwinner is trapped into a lifetime of waged labour in order to pay for it and the homemaker into a lifetime of unpaid domestic labour necessary to maintain it. Under this powerful image, qualitative cultural differences based on geography, ethnicity and social class tend to break down (although some racial minorities and the poor are still excluded) and are replaced with quantitative social distinctions based on number and value of status-assigning possessions.

THE BUILT ENVIRONMENT OF MODERNISM

The modern built environment takes two forms: the high modern, which is meticulously planned and monumental and ostensibly universal; and the modern vernacular, which is the unplanned and practical space of modern everyday life, and, at first, distinctly American. High modernism, commonly termed the 'International Style', provides an appropriate industrial architecture for Fordism. First, it celebrates modern technologies of production by incorporating elements resembling railway lines, grain elevators, stacked TV sets and missiles. Second, like other commodities it is standardised for mass production: windowless shoe-boxes functioned as factories, warehouses and shopping malls in the suburbs, while in the cities they were glazed and stood on end to house corporate offices and lower-income workers. Third, its monotonously regular geometrical forms and the hostility of its surfaces, show as much indifference to the occupier as the assembly line to the worker. Fourth, it turns its back on the city and on the past—it violates bodily scale and the sensuous experience of urban space with its vast abstract forms and harsh angles, it consciously separates itself from urban society with its impenetrable, often reflective facade, and the no-person's land of the bleak, windswept concrete that usually surrounds it, and it eliminates all historical reference, reducing buildings to rationalist, minimalist aesthetics which disregard past function and sense of place (Jencks 1987, p. 15). Ironically, the original intent of high modern architecture was to unify work and art in its structures and celebrate the human and democratic potential of modern industry to sweep away the rigidities and inequalities of past societies symbolised in national architectures. However, the aesthetic that was a metaphor for liberation and mechanical progress was appropriated by vertically-integrated and anonymous institutions of corporate and state capitalism.[3]

The popular architecture of suburban residential and retail landscapes is different, even if also practically subordinate to the machine (in this case the automobile), operating on a more human scale and acknowledging, albeit to a limited extent, the individuality of the consumer even within the context of mass consumption. Mass-produced, standardised houses exhibit variations based upon the Cape Cod, ranch, split-level or colonial styles and even incorporate 'custom' features adapted to particular tastes and lifestyles. Commercial strips developed to service the automobile public in the 1930s and 1940s were highly differentiated, with ornamental gas service stations, restaurants and shopping plazas deploying a gaudy roadside architecture of 'decorated sheds' to grab the attention of drivers (Venturi 1972).

THE MODERN RETAIL BUILT ENVIRONMENT

The shopping mall expresses both the high and vernacular forms of modernism. It grew out of the commercial strip and the plazas that first provided off-street parking for customers along urban highways by the 1930s and 1940s, but it was not until the massive highway construction beginning in the 1950s that suburbia could compete with the retail centre of the city. The new malls provided an alternative to downtown department stores and promised a sense of suburban community and market life without the old-fashioned congestion, crime, pollution (and even weather) of the real main street. Victor Gruen, the acknowledged pioneer of the shopping mall and designer of the first climate-controlled mall (in Southdale, Edina, MN, 1956), intended that they would be 'market places that are also centres of community and cultural activity'. For the suburban residents the mall would be 'more than just a place where one may shop—it shall be related in their minds with all activities of cultural enrichment and relaxation' (cited in Gillette 1985, p. 451).

We need not doubt the sincerity of the developers of the first shopping malls, but the fact remains that they are artificial environments, which, unlike main street, have no prior reason for existence and no historic rootedness in place. The first generation of planned shopping centres were simply 'planted' in 'greenfield' sites at highway interchanges (Figure 10.2) and one suburban shopping centre could quite easily be replaced by another. A 'mall rat', 'mallie' (Kowinski 1985, pp. 33-4) or 'mall-walker' (Jacobs 1984), feels as at home in Northland, Chicago, or Prestonwood, Dallas, for example, or even in Brent Cross (London), Parly 2 (Paris) and Madrid Dos (Madrid).

The shopping mall expresses an 'instrumental rationality' (Gottdiener 1986, p. 289)—its structural and architectural elements combine to construct an efficient 'machine for shopping'. Like the corporate office building, it is an introverted space, sitting in a barren desert of asphalt and presenting a bleak concrete exterior, its monotony interrupted only by the most minimal of landscaping. Customers are drawn from their cars to the prominent formal entrances of classic columns, arches, towers or canopies and are swallowed up, often swept by escalators to galleries or grottos where they lose their immediate bearings. Inside, the exits, even fire exits, are inevitably inconspicuous and unattractive. The 'machine' circulates potential shoppers in a manner designed to optimise exposure to the merchandise on display. According to one observer, 'the American out-of-town shopping centre ... came ... to define the public mall as essentially the passive outcome of a merchandising plan, a channel for the manipulation of pedestrian flows' (Maitland 1985, p. 10). The concern to keep shoppers moving is perfectly expressed in a design manual:

> Pause points for shoppers to rest, review their programmes and re-arrange their purchases etc. also need planning with care. Seating, while offering a convenient stopping point, must not be too luxurious or comfortable. Shoppers must move on and allow reoccupation of seating and the danger of attracting the 'down and outs' of various categories must be avoided (Beddington 1982, p. 36).

FIGURE 10.2 A 'greenfield' site. Les Pumerades—Saint bruno near Montreal Canada.
Source: Urban Land Institute, 625 Indiana Avenue, N.W. Suite 400, Washington D.C. 20004.

Design of the shopping centre varies with the number of department store 'anchors', but whether generic 'dumbbell' or cruciform, mall lengths are usually restricted to about 200m as it was assumed that this is the maximum distance pedestrians are willing to walk. Focal places are otherwise used to break the flow and distract the shopper from considerations of distance and time and to give the mall a sense of exterior public place. Mall widths are restricted to about six metres, with perhaps an extra three metres of obstacles—seating, fountains, plants and temporary vendors—in the central zone that direct shoppers towards the storefronts (Gottdiener 1986).

The department stores which draw the mall's customers are able to dictate conditions to the developer and they traditionally insist on straight corridors and sign control to maintain sightlines to their logos displayed across the ends of the mall. Smaller retailers depend upon impulsive purchases by customers on their way to the department store, so their storefronts are designed to maximise the area of display and, through devices such as open storefronts and mall displays, to entice the shopper inside. Plate glass, mirrors and polished metallic surfaces reflect the shopper, imperfect compared with the mannequins and magical commodities in the looking-glass world of the dressed window.

In this retail wonderland reality is suspended through a number of subtle devices: in the early malls there were no clocks to register the march of time and no windows to remind the consumer of an outside reality. Temperature control and constant lighting was used to mask the passage of daily or seasonal time. If shopping malls are everywhere, they are also in this sense nowhere. An army of maintenance and security staff ensure that the environment is kept spotless while deliveries and services are kept 'backstage' in hidden passageways so that commodities appear 'onstage' in a flawless retail context 'as if by magic'.

Although the modern mall presents itself as public space, private ownership allows a degree of management that main street retailers cannot attain: not only is the atmosphere not welcoming of the poor 'underconsumer', but those who disrupt or affront the process of consumption, such as political leafleteers, rowdy teenagers and street-people, can be escorted from the premises. Although in the United States this right has been challenged in the Supreme Court, conflict over public access versus private exclusion has been ruled a matter for individual states to decide, and in most cases private security has considerable control over everyday activity in the mall. The mall presents itself as a public place but does not accept the responsibilities and inconveniences that might be associated with real public life.

As Kowiniski (1985, p. 68) points out, the shopping mall is not so much a new downtown, as a romanticised model of the 'Main Street' like that pioneered in Disneyland—without the dangers of the automobile or the manure of horses, undisturbed by the vagaries of weather, uncorrupted by bars, liquor stores, and betting shops. The absence of laundromats, repair shops, and second-hand stores prevents the consumer from being reminded of the materiality of the commodity. Unlike downtown where the retailer and developer compete as best they can with their existing neighbours, here positive externalities, or 'spillover effects', are internalised with the appropriate 'tenant mix'.

It would be uncharitable, however, to entirely dismiss the shopping centre as merely a strategically engineered instrument of mass consumption, for a variety of users have appropriated it for their own social purpose and have forced designers and managers to recognise their needs. The 'bottom line' remains retail profit and rental income, but the mall also provides a service to the youth, elderly and homemakers of the suburbs, who have few other places to go and commune or pass time agreeably on a daily basis. The strollers and creches for shoppers with young children, the amusement arcades and fairground attractions for teenagers and rest areas and special activities for the elderly, are 'loss leaders' necessary to service these populations. Of course, we could see these innovations as part of a total design—for example, the amusement arcades 'contain' youth on the mall's peripheries, while the elderly have greatest disposable income and their presence creates a sense of safety for other consumers—but shopping centres have sometimes shown themselves to be responsive to consumer needs in ways that some local governments have not. The creative use of the mall environment has undoubtedly forced a partial compromise of the economic logic, and the struggle over the legal status of the mall's territory must be viewed in this light.

During the 1960s and early 1970s there appeared to be no limit to the construction of out of town shopping centres, and vast regional malls were constructed with speculative abandon. It is probably premature to predict that such centres 'will go the way of the dinosaur' (Gruen 1978, p. 9)—in Britain, for example, in 1997 there were still mega-malls under construction or expansion (Hetherington 1997)—but there has been a general slow-down in construction and reduction in scale. Structural constraints include increased costs of land assembly and construction, saturation of local retail markets, reluctance of suburban governments to provide infrastructure and tightened environmental controls (Frieden and Sagalyn 1989, p. 82)—trends which coincide with increased market segmentation and a changed retailing concept. Developers have adapted by renovating old shopping centres, adding food courts, galleries, soft landscaping, architectural flourishes (such as Art Deco and Victoriana) and spectacles, creating 'the hot mall [which] goes to the heart of shopping as entertainment' (Stallings 1990, p. 14). Large developers have responded by uniting the scale and technology of modernist construction with the postmodernist affection for grand, chaotic spectacle in enormous suburban megacentres. These structures—exemplified by West Edmonton Mall, Canada, and Mall of America, Bloomington, Minnesota, United States, and on a smaller scale by Metrocentre Gateshead, England—are monsters of planned spontaneity and prefabricated pleasure, total environments that seek to satisfy every consumption need. They are self-contained tourist destinations for the whole family.

The truly postmodern retail environments, however, purvey a more particular consumption experience and are typically developed downtown, for postmodernism has rediscovered the city and its history. Before discussing the form of postmodern retail landscapes, however, these must also be placed in their material and symbolic context.

POSTMODERNITY AND INDIVIDUALISED CONSUMPTION

Under 'post-Fordism', mass production has given way to flexible systems incorporating computer technologies and electronic communications that facilitate rapid turnover of products and styles. The demand for high quality information and sophisticated coordination has led to an expansion of information specialists who provide services that are essential to commodity production and distribution. These individuals constitute the 'new middle class', whose lifestyles and cultural values, as manifest in their consumption practices, are central to the aesthetic of postmodernism.

Members of the 'new middle class' are waged workers in the sense that they do not own means of production nor the product of their labour, but yet they do have certain control over the production process and often claim an intellectual ownership of their product. They occupy a somewhat ambiguous position, but because they are relatively well-educated they are able to employ cultivated distinctions in taste, lifestyle, personal expression, sexuality and quality of living environment to define their cultural territory. These invidious distinctions are of course expressed in everyday consumption and are most readily seen in the sub-group of this class popularly known as 'yuppies', who stereotypically are associated with commodities that exhibit sophisticated cosmopolitanism (such as cellular phones and expresso coffee machines), eschew ostentation (such as minimalist furniture and natural finishes), boast quality (brand names and designer labels), display privileged knowledge (gourmet coffees and the 'right' wines), and promote bodily health (low fat foods and exercise equipment). Distinction in taste, however, is tenuous since the latest fad, if not fated to die out quickly, is increasingly rapidly assimilated by the mass market, and the cultural avant garde can stay only one step ahead by constantly developing new forms of commodified experience. Class distinction is not so much quantitative—based on the amount and value of commodities consumed—but qualitative—based on type and style. In fact, one might say that it is not primarily the material object that is consumed, but the image of ourselves consuming the object (Debord 1983; Baudrillard 1981). One no longer buys to 'keep up with the Joneses', nor does one buy because the commodity is functional in some way. These days one buys a product because, as much as anything else, it has a style that is 'me'. With a practical household gizmo one gets (literally) 'The Sharper Image' and with fashionable clothes one gets 'The Look' or becomes a member of 'The Limited', a privileged class of self-actualised consumers. Identity is dynamic, with emphasis on self-discovery, growth and improvement with the help of personal improvement seminars, image consultants and, of course, the right purchases.

With the rise of this 'culture of narcissism' (Lasch 1979), some observers suggest that societal problems are conceived as personal inadequacies, social concern is translated into self-help and public life, from festivals to elections, is reduced to spectacular publicity events. Immediate sensual and material gratification are pursued instead of life-long cooperative projects such as marriage and childrearing, and quick financial 'success' replaces the steady career goal. Ironically, perhaps, having been liberated from the constraints imposed by these institutions, the postmodern individual yearns for security and authenticity. Suffering an 'unbearable lightness of being', the postmodern yearns nostalgically for security in tradition, and in an existential search for roots voraciously consumes the manufactures of the 'heritage industry' (Jager 1986; Hewison 1987).

The past is commodified in 'pop images and stereotypes' such as old 'B' movies, retro clothing and restored pinball and soft-drink machines (Jameson 1983, p. 118). Culture is museumised as past times, distant places are ransacked and the contemporary consumers accumulate images and objects of authenticity in 'well-stocked musée imaginaire' (Jencks 1987, p. 95), for example: eating muesli for breakfast and Ethiopian or Lebanese for dinner; drinking Mexican beer or Chilean wine; wearing Red Army clothing or batiks from Indonesia; listening to reggae or rai, opera or gamelan; and dancing hula or the lambada. These souvenirs mark cosmopolitan lifestyle and sophisticated taste and link us to something somehow more tangible and real than we experience in our own here and now.

POSTMODERNITY AND THE BUILT ENVIRONMENT

Flexible accumulation has a profound impact upon the cities of the advanced capitalist world. As they lose population and employment following divestment of capital, tax revenues decrease while the costs of service provision and maintenance of the built environment escalate. At the same time, central government has reduced support in an attempt to curb both its expenditures and the political power of the cities. As a result, 'entrepreneurial' cities and their 'growth coalitions' compete in marketing an image of their city to attract footloose private capital. One strategy is to subsidise the development of urban space into office complexes, festival markets, convention centres and sports stadia which provide workplaces and play spaces for the new middle class who seem to have discovered the social and aesthetic pleasures of urban living. What observers have called the 'urban renaissance' is accompanied by commercial and residential gentrification, witnessed in historic preservation and restoration, and a new sensitivity of contemporary urban architecture to history and context.

While modernism repressed symbolic expression in the built environment, postmodernism celebrates connotative imagery and decorative play, employing the rhetorical techniques and iconography of advertising (Harvey 1989, p. 80; Frampton 1983, p. 19) and the glitz and showcraft of entertainment, literally 'learning from Las Vegas' (Venturi 1972). It employs pastiche, freely mixing metaphors and playfully combining paradoxical elements, such as old and new, local and global, high culture and vernacular forms, and quoting simultaneously from baroque, classic, rococo, art deco, high modern, commercial and folk architectures. It is sensitive to regional traditions and its surroundings, positively embracing the history and diversity of the city, investing urban space with landmarks of allusion, employing sentiment and cultivating a 'sense of place' (Ley 1987, p. 44). If it is self-consciously popular, it is also self-consciously clever, for as the postmodern building nods condescendingly to the masses it winks knowingly to the elite. For 'those in the know' the pleasure lies precisely in their privileged knowledge—or the exercise of their cultural capital.

As with modernism it is possible to identify both a high and a popular form of postmodern architecture. First are the 'hyperspaces' (Jameson 1984)—complex structures that combine 'a mixture of last-gasp late modernism and interior-decorator postmodernism' (Cooke 1988, p. 75). These structures—typified by Peachtree Development in Atlanta; Beauborg in Paris; the Bonaventure Centre in Los Angeles; and the Eaton Centre in Toronto[4]—represent an aestheticisation of the finance capital that built them. They are hermetically sealed fantasy worlds, glass bubbles whose soaring atria and cavernous voids are symbols for cultural experiences of global capitalism—their transparent surfaces invite us into brightly lit worlds of motion, spectacle and theatre where the individual is said to experience a hallucinatory exhilaration, a mixture of excitement and terror felt at the instant of total alienation from historical reality (Jameson 1984). Moving through a constant barrage of imagery from advertising in various media to diverse spectacular entertainments, we experience a world of signs where the real and the imaginary blur—what has been called 'hyperreality' (Baudrillard 1983).

Popular postmodernism is more modest. It engages in restoration or reproduction of traditional and regional architectures. It is historicist and eclectic, employing a mock vernacular of exposed brick cladding and timbers, painted woodwork, wrought ironwork, brass fittings, stained glass, antique signs and gaslights. It displays the contrived spontaneity, superficial charm and manufactured chic of 'quaintspace' (Relph 1987, p. 253), free of course from the technological and social realities that would be now intolerable to the contemporary consumer—the gaslights are really electric, the windows are double-glazed and the well draws piped water. It is typified by the gentrified neighbourhoods of the post-industrial city, the reproduction small towns of New England or the Mediterranean village, and plantation-style houses of the south. The context asks the consumer to form associations with traditional values such as family and community, truth and justice, honest labour, and solid class identity and privilege, realities for which the new middle class in particular yearns.

THE POSTMODERN RETAIL ENVIRONMENT

The essential forms of postmodern retail environment—the specialty centre and the downtown 'megastructure'—reflect the vernacular and high forms of postmodernism respectively, while a hybrid form—the festival marketplace—combines elements of both. The specialty centre is an 'anchorless' collection of up-market shops and restaurants that pursues a specific retail and architectural theme. It is prone to quaintification: typical designs in North America include New England villages (Pickering Wharf, Salem, Massachusetts), French provincial towns (The Continent, Columbus, Ohio), Spanish-American haciendas (The Pruneyard, San Jose), Mediterranean villages (Atrium Court, Newport Beach, California) and timber mining camps (Jack London Village, Oakland, California). Pride of *place* must, however, go to The Borgota in Scottsdale, Arizona, a mock thirteenth-century walled Italian village with bricks imported from Rome and signs in Italian (Kowinski 1985, p. 233), and to The Mercado in nearby Phoenix, Arizona, modelled on traditional hillside villages of Mexico with materials imported from Guadalajara, and buildings given Hispanic names (Figure 10.3).

These forms are hyperreal in the sense that details may be so effective that the stylised copy appears more real than the original so that the ethnic restaurant with its stylised architecture, objects of material culture and expensive exotic cuisine seems to be more essentially Italian or Mexican than those in Italy or Mexico itself. The consumer forgets that the veal comes from 'factory farm', that the tortillas come out of a packet and are warmed in the microwave and that the decorative handicrafts are produced by piece-workers under elaborate subcontracting systems. While the consumer is presented an opportunity to display acquired exotic tastes, the commodity on sale is perfectly fetishised.

FIGURE 10.3 The Mercado, Phoenix, Arizona.
Source: Reddie Henderson, Horizon Photography, Phoenix, Arizona.

The downtown megastructure, on the other hand, is a self-contained complex including hotels, offices, restaurants, entertainment, health centres and luxury apartments. Typical examples include Water Tower Place, Chicago, the Tower City Centre, Cleveland and Town Square, St. Paul. These structures are a part of the postmodernist challenge to the fundamental separations (between moments of production, reproduction and consumption, and between work-place, living place and leisure space) on which modernist culture is founded. At the same time these small worlds ensure that the needs of affluent residents, office workers, conferees and tourists can be met entirely within a single secure, environmentally-controlled and defensively sealed space.

Several features distinguish the downtown megastructure from the suburban shopping mall, although by now many of these have been extensively 'retrofitted' in the postmodern style. After studies found that 70 per cent of all energy consumed in malls was spent on lighting, economics and fashion have combined to return daylight to glazed malls reminiscent of nineteenth-century European arcades. The natural light of atria and galleries of the megastructures allows the planting of ficus, bamboos and 'interiorised' palms to simulate the tropical environments of tourism, to indicate a respectable age for the establishment and to suggest care for the environment. Water has always been an important element in the mall as a means to soothe tensions and refresh shoppers, but now elaborate water courses and waterfalls simulate nature rather than urban fountains. These three effects combine to turn things inside-out so that pure and perfected nature, the ideal place of leisure, is ironically found indoors within the city, no longer in the suburbs beyond.

The downtown 'malls' are also no longer primarily 'machines for shopping', although the aesthetics of movement are retained in the sweep of huge escalators and the trajectory of 'bubble' elevators. Passage through the mall is now an interactive experience, an adventure in winding alleys resembling the Arabian souk or medieval town, with the unpredictability of 'pop-out' shopfronts—glass display cases which jut out into the mall—and mobile vendors. Shopping at the downtown mall is not merely the necessary purchase of goods, but is a form of retail tourism, and the individual makes her/his own itinerary.[5]

Surprisingly, clocks have returned to these retail touristic attractions and are even displayed as central ornaments in the main courts or on prominent towers. They are invariably antique analog clocks, visual puns for past time and evocative of historic public spaces. The presence of the clock is apparently no longer a threat to consumption, perhaps because postmodern time is flexible, no longer linear nor compartmentalised into specific everyday activities. The present moment expands—the time is always now—and the pleasure of consumption in these purpose-built places transcends temporality measured by the clock. Purchase for pure pleasure rather than need does not compete with, but has become a integral and regular part of everyday life.

No trip to the mall is complete without food, and malls now offer a full range of culinary experiences, from fast food to five star and from international to local ethnic cuisine. Food is a critical marker of taste, of course, and a means to experience the exotic other, but the food court is also a place from which the consumer can watch other people, compare styles and view the spectacle of the new middle class at play.

Entertainment is more than ever the key to success, and attractions such as ice rinks, carousels (antique, of course), roller-coasters, local and historical exhibits and staged 'pseudo-events' (Boorstin 1964) are an essential part of the show. The contemporary retail environment is an exercise in Disney's 'imagineering', the employment of imaginative fantasy and engineering technology (Relph 1987, p. 129), a component of the spectacle that enlivens or conceals the mundane practical activity of shopping. Also significant is the fact that shopping centres are increasingly graced by 'high' cultural activities. Developers have commissioned artists to create special works integrated into the design of the centre, have established valuable collections of artists' works in permanent displays, sponsored temporary exhibits and hosted shows of classical music. For example, the Bel Canto opera competition is held in shopping centres across the country; a Shakespearian Festival is held in Lakeforest Mall, Gaithersburg, Maryland; sculptures by Henry Moore and Jonathan Borofsky are exhibited in 'sculpture courts' at North Park Centre, Dallas; South Coast Plaza in Costa Mesa, California boasts 'one of the most important outdoor sculpture environments in the world' (Chain Store Executive 1989, p. 108); and South Coast Plaza, Faneuil Hall Marketplace in Boston, The Mercado in Phoenix, and Horton Plaza in San Diego all have art centres or museums on the premises. This aestheticisation of the shopping experience appeals directly to the sensibilities of the new middle class, enabling display of cultural capital and allaying guilt that might be associated with the perceived vulgarity of conspicuous consumption.

The festival marketplace combines these elements with an idealised version of historical urban community and the street market, typically in restored waterfront districts after the model of Faneuil Hall marketplace in Boston and Harborplace in Baltimore (Goss 1996). They reflect nostalgia for manual labour, civic life, public celebrations and the age of commerce. Buildings and sailing vessels are restored and there is usually a museum on site. The 'marketplace' evokes old forms of trade with stylised architecture, antique signage and decorative historical artefacts, creating a landscape where the contemporary consumer can act out a little bit of history and street entertainers, barrow vendors and costumed staff all play their parts.

The aestheticisation of shopping is appropriate, since the appreciation of the context of a commodity requires an increasing amount of cultural education and exposure analogous to that required to appreciate classical art. As both the audience and the techniques of the 'captains of consciousness' have become more sophisticated, the cultural symbols employed in advertising are more complex. The young professional shopping for quality and speciality goods in the boutiques of the postmodern shopping centre or in the gourmet section of the postmodern supermarket is employing perhaps as much accumulated cultural knowledge and acquired acumen to create the context of the commodity as he or she would to interpret the meaning of a creative work of art. The act of consumption itself is fetishised: the 'crude' material activity is hidden behind the functions of leisure, entertainment, education and artistic appreciation.

CONCLUSION

The history of the planned built environment of retailing is more complex than this brief sketch can show, but in general the unitary 'shopping machine' of the suburbs is being replaced by the mixed-use 'consumer spectacle' originating in the city. This shift in form and function illustrates and reproduces some of the material and symbolic determinations of the New Times, a more or less fundamental transformation in the nature of western capitalism. The logic of consumption has replaced production as the driving force of social life and the symbolic order appears to have attained dominance over the material—the cultural over the economic. The dynamic tension or dialectic connection between these dimensions of existence, however, ensures that the increased significance of consumption is linked to profound changes in the nature of production. The built environment expresses and reproduces these dimensions in all their complexity and is therefore a particularly useful object of analysis for the cultural geographer whose task it is to examine the relationship between the symbolic and material constitution of reality, that is, between 'ways of seeing' and 'ways of being' in the world.

NOTES

1 A mall is technically an enclosed or partially enclosed pedestrian thoroughfare, but in North American usage it also refers in general to the collection of connected buildings of any large shopping centre.

2 Minority groups, particularly as defined by youth, class and race may use commodities as signs of membership, while activists and interest groups expose the materiality of commodities by organising information campaigns and consumer boycotts that have been very successful in undermining the magic of commodities such as Coors beer, Burger King fast foods and Ratners gold jewellery (see also Smith 1990).

3 This contrasts markedly with the first skyscrapers which, although also headquarters for corporations, expressed the civic concern and even the personality of their owners with classical style and elaborate embellishments. It is only recently that the skyscraper has again become a fantasy form for capital (Jencks 1987, p. 131).

4 Late-modernism is best typified by the Pompidou in Paris, the Hong Kong Shanghai Bank in Hong Kong, the Lloyds Building in London and the Sainsbury Centre for the Visual Arts, University of East Anglia. It is a self-conscious modernism, an attempt to relieve the boredom of modernist aesthetic by taking it to an extreme and exaggerating the functionalism and technical elements to amuse or please (Jencks 1986, 1987), but without the pastiche and playfulness of postmodernism proper (Sharrett 1989, p. 192). Typically this involves a display of heating and ventilation ducts and cleaning gantries and an aesthetic of motion.

5 Some shopping centres have organised self-guided tours or employ tour guides (Kowinski 1985, p. 21) and others, such as the Riverchase Galleria in Birmingham, Alabama even offer weekend shoppers' specials combining hotel rooms with retail discounts.

REFERENCES

Baudrillard, J. 1981, *For a Critique of the Political Economy of the Sign,* St. Louis, Telos.

Baudrillard, J. 1983, *Simulations,* Semiotext(e), New York.

Beddington, N. 1982, *Design for Shopping Centres*, Butterworth Scientific, London.

Boorstin, D. 1964, *The Image: A Guide to Pseudo-Events in America*, Harper and Row, New York.

Bourdieu, P. 1986, 'The production of belief: contribution to an economy of symbolic goods', in *Media, Culture and Society,* eds R. Collins, J. Curran, N. Garnham, P. Scannell, P. Schlesinger & C. Sparks, Sage Publications, Beverly Hills, pp. 131–63.

Braudel, F. 1967, *Capitalism and Material Life 1400–1800,* Harper and Row, New York.

Chain Store Executive 1989, 'Entertainment anchors: new mall headliners', August, pp. 54, 56, 108.

Cooke, P. 1988, *Back to the Future*, Unwin Hyman, London.

Debord, G. 1983, *Society of the Spectacle*, Black and Red Books, Detroit.

Frampton, K. 1983, 'Towards a critical regionalism: Six points for an architecture of resistance', in *Postmodern Culture*, ed. H. Foster, Pluto Press, London and Sydney, pp. 16–56.

Frieden, B.J. & Sagalyn, L.B. 1989, *Downtown Inc.: How America Rebuilds Cities,* MIT Press, Cambridge, Mass.

Gillette, H. 1985, 'The evolution of the planned shopping centre in suburb and city', *Journal of the American Planning Association*, vol. 51, no. 4, pp. 449–60.

Goss, J.D. 1996, 'Disquiet on the waterfront: nostalgia and utopia in the festival marketplace', *Urban Geography*, vol. 17, no. 3, pp. 221–47.

Gottdiener, M. 1986, 'Recapturing the centre: A semiotic analysis of shopping malls', in *The City and the Sign*, eds M. Gottdiener & A. Ph. Lagopoulos, Columbia University Press, New York, pp. 288–302.

Gruen, N. 1978, 'Gestalt magnetism or what is special about speciality shopping centres?', *Urban Land*, January, pp. 3–9.

Harvey, D. 1989, *The Condition of Postmodernity: An Enquiry into the Origins of Cultural Change*, Blackwell, Oxford.

Hetherington, P. 1997, 'Mega-malls become a battlefield', *The Guardian*, November 5, p. 23.

Hewison, R. 1987, *The Heritage Industry*, Methuen, London.

Jacobs, J. 1984, *The Mall: An Attempted Escape from Eversday Life*, Waveland, Prospect Heights.

Jager, M. 1986, 'Class definition and the aesthetics of gentrification: Victoriana in Melbourne', in *Gentrification of the City*, eds N. Smith & P. Williams, Allen and Unwin, Boston, pp. 78–91.

Jameson, F. 1984, 'Postmodernism, or the cultural logic of late capitalism', *New Left Review*, vol. 146, pp. 52–92.

Jameson, F. 1983, 'Postmodernism and consumer society', in T*he Anti-Aesthetic*, ed. H. Foster, Bay Press, Port Townsend, WA, pp. 11–125.

Jencks, C. 1986, *Modern Movements in Architecture* (2nd ed), Penguin Books, Harmondsworth.

Jencks, C. 1987, *The Language of Post-Modern Architecture*, (Fifth Edition), Academy Editions, London.

Jhally, S. 1987, *The Codes of Advertising*, Frances Pinter, London.

Kowinski, W.S. 1985, *The Malling of America: An Inside Look at the Great Consumer Paradise*, William Morrow, New York.

Lasch, C. 1979, *The Culture of Narcissism: American Life in an Age of Diminishing Expectations*, Warner Books, New York.

Lash, S. & Urry, J. 1987, *The End of Organised Capitalism*, University of Wisconsin Press, Madison.

Lefebvre, H. 1971, *Everyday Life in the Modern World*, Harper and Row, New York.

Ley, D. 1987, 'Style of the times: Liberal and neo-conservative landscapes in inner Vancouver, 1968–1986', *Journal of Historical Geography*, vol. 13, no. 1, 40–56.

Maitland, B. 1985, *Shopping Malls: Planning and Design*, Nichols, New York.

Marxism Today 1988, 'Introduction', (Special Issue on the New Times), October.

McCracken, G. 1988, *Culture and Consumption: New Approaches to the Symbolic Character of Consumer Goods and Activities*, Indiana University Press, Bloomington.

Miller, M.B. 1981, *The Bon Marche: Bourgeois Culture and the Department Store 1869–1920*, Princeton University Press, Princeton.

National Research Bureau 1990, *Shopping Centre Directory 1990*, NRB, Chicago.

Relph, E. 1987, *The Modern Urban Landscape*, Johns Hopkins University Press, Baltimore.

Sack, D. 1988, 'The consumer's world: Place as context', *Annals of the Association of American Geographers*, vol. 78, no. 4, pp. 624–64.

Sahlins, M. 1976, *Culture and Practical Reason*, Chicago University Press, Chicago.

Sharrett, C. 1989, 'Defining the postmodern: The case of Soho Kitchen and El Internacional', in *Postmodernism/Jameson/Critique*, ed. D. Kellner, Maisonneuve Press, Washington, pp. 162–71.

Smith, N.C. 1990, *Morality and the Market: Consumer Pressure for Corporate Accountability*, Routledge, London.

Stallings, P. 1990, 'Essay—The Call of the Mall', MacNeil/Lehrer Newshour, 27 November, transcript, WNET, New York.

Stoffel, J. 1988, 'What's new in shopping malls', *New York Times*, 7 August.

Urban Land Institute 1985, *Shopping Centre Development Handbook*, Urban Land Institute, Washington DC.

Venturi, R., Scott-Brown, D. & Izenour, S. (eds) 1972, *Learning from Las Vegas*, MIT Press, Cambridge.

Williams, R. 1980, *Problems in Materialism and Culture: Selected Essays*, New Left Books, London.

Williams, R.H. 1982, *Dream Worlds: Mass Consumption in the Late Nineteenth Century France*, University of California Press, Berkeley.

Wright, G. 1981, *Building the Dream: A Social History of Housing in America*, Pantheon, New York.

11

World's Fairs and the culture of consumption in the contemporary city

David Ley
Kris Olds

INTRODUCTION

In early 1998 Toronto City Council endorsed a bid for the 2008 Olympics. If the Games come to Toronto, it will be the biggest and most expensive mega-project in the history of that city. Deliberations over this bid are taking place a mere six years after the City of Toronto failed, by one vote, to secure the World's Fair for the year 2000. Despite a promotional campaign costing almost CDN $5 million, the city's boosters were unable to dissuade an international panel from awarding the Fair to Hamburg, representative of a united Germany. Toronto was also one of the six finalists bidding for the 1996 Olympics, a bid which cost $17 million (Olds 1998). Within Canada, Toronto is not alone in its pursuit of 'hallmark events' (Hall 1989). The trend was begun by Montreal with its celebrated Centennial Exposition of 1967, followed by the notorious billion-dollar Olympic Games in 1976. Since then the Commonwealth Games have come to Edmonton, the Winter Olympics to Calgary, a World's Fair to Vancouver and in 1994 Canada hosted its second Commonwealth Games in the city of Victoria. Other cities including Calgary, London and Halifax have been unsuccessful finalists in bids for other major events (Hiller 1998).

The pursuit of the spectacle is not confined to Canada. Besides Toronto, another of the six finalists for the 1996 Olympics was Melbourne, which triumphed in a spirited contest with Brisbane and Sydney to serve as the Australian flag-bearer. In 1988 Brisbane had its own World's Fair, and other cities are in on the act. Perth was put on the map by hosting the America's Cup yacht race, while until recently Adelaide closed its streets each year to host a Grand Prix (for these and other Australian examples, see Syme et al.

1989). In 1988 it seemed as if parts of Australia had embarked on a year-long carnival in recognition of the bicentennial of white settlement. The Sydney 2000 Olympic Games will see up to 10 200 athletes from 200 countries participating in sporting events, while some 15 000 representatives of the media will 'provide for an estimated worldwide audience of 3.5 billion' (Sydney Organising Committee for the Olympic Games 1998).

The cost of these ventures is immense and raises fundamental political and moral questions about resource allocation. Estimated costs for the proposed Toronto Olympics in 1996 reached $2.52 billion and $1.3 billion for the proposed Toronto 2000 World's Fair. The estimated total cost for the Sydney 2000 Olympic Games is AUS $2.3 billion. The opportunity costs of this scale of investment are breathtaking, not least in cities with serious environmental problems and in urgent need of affordable housing. In Toronto, for example, an anti-poverty coalition, Bread Not Circuses, assailed the Toronto media and City Council about the justice and wisdom of such conspicuous consumption in a metropolis with seventy-five food banks and perhaps 20 000 homeless (Olds 1998). Needless to say, Bread Not Circuses is also contesting the proposal to bid for the 2008 Olympic Games.

The apparent multiplication of hallmark events (also knows as mega-events) is part of a broader trend towards the playful and the aesthetic in contemporary society (Ley 1980, 1983; Jackson and Thrift 1995; MacKay 1997; Yeoh and Teo 1996; Warren 1996). The places of leisure and recreation are expanding to whole regions: in developed nations a number of growth regions, including Australia's Gold Coast, California, Florida and parts of the western Mediterranean, evoke a leisure lifestyle as a major component of their human geographies; in the developing nations a number of growth regions, including China's coastal provinces and Vietnam's major cities, evoke a golf course-centred lifestyle for transnational elites working in Asia–Pacific's global cities. Regardless of region, there is every indication that these trends will accelerate in the future. In the Canadian Rockies, for example, Japanese and other Asian interests have bought into the major winter sports centres of Banff and Whistler, and are involved (or targeted) in some of the proposals to construct upwards of forty golf courses within a ninety-minute drive of Vancouver. The same is happening within the city, as new palaces to the arts and culture—Mozart in the metropolis (Whitt 1987)—new stadia for sports and recreation, and whole districts, like Sydney's Darling Harbour or Baltimore's Inner Harbor, are being recreated as emporia of the pleasure principle. The proliferation of conference centres and their attendant brood of hotels point to the growing synthesis of business and leisure (Goss 1993; Hall and Hubbard 1996). Recreational pursuits have also become major elements of a new generation of megamalls like Gateshead's Metrocentre in England or the West Edmonton Mall, a billion-dollar facility which has 600 stores and services and, under the same roof, a range of attractions including a beach and wave pool, skating rink, funfair, miniature golf course, sea aquarium with dolphins, operational submarines and a replica of Christopher Columbus' vessel, *Santa Maria* (Hopkins 1990, 1991). The same conjunction of business and fantasy has been achieved by the London marketing company Imagination, which creates a concept of marketing as theatre for its corporate clients (Whatmore 1990), a dramatic and total environment for the extolling of a corporate product.

In its manipulation of a total environment, a company like Imagination is a magic-maker committed to moulding a new way of seeing, or rather a new way of sensing, for its temporary fabrications offer a fuller sensual environment of sight and sound. In its marketing strategy the aestheticisation of space is a key concern: 'there is no such thing as neutral space' (Whatmore 1990, p. 18). A similar revaluing of *urban* space has been a feature of the past twenty years, including a heightened sensitivity to landscaping, heritage preservation and urban design. Does the urban visitor sense this newly aestheticised urban landscape as a participant or as a spectator? Is the manipulative intent of Imagination a model for new postmodern city landscapes? There are those who see only spectacle and social control in the aesthetic halo of new consumption-based landscapes (Harvey 1987, 1989; Huxley and Kerkin 1988). Others see a more active engagement between city residents and the 'liveable city' with its new range of leisure opportunities (Boyle 1997; Warren 1996). There are many questions which remain unanswered. What is the meaning of these landscapes of consumption, some temporary, some more enduring, which provide such a stark counterpoint to the industrial areas and port waterfronts of Sydney or Brisbane which they replace? How are these landscapes of a public mass culture received by their visitors? What are the intentions of the elites who shape them and how are these dominant meanings internalised or reconstructed by the majority of urban dwellers? These questions are addressed in this chapter by examining the 1986 World's Fair in Vancouver and placing this event in a broader theoretical literature which debates the meaning of contemporary public culture.

MASS OR POPULAR CULTURE?

The problem of the masses has been a central, perhaps *the* central, preoccupation of social theory for well over a century. For Kierkegaard, authentic individuality—real human nature—was being submerged in the nineteenth century before the relentless flood of the urban crowd—the masses. Gustave Le Bon's *Psychologie des Foules* (1895) was an important reflection of a widespread sentiment and an inspiration to other theorists, including Freud. 'The substitution of the unconscious action of crowds for the conscious action of individuals', observed Le Bon, 'is one of the principal characteristics of the present age' (cited in Brantlinger 1983, pp. 166–7). From the generally disapproving view of the masses emerged the generally disparaging view of mass culture. Le Bon summarised this viewpoint:

> Crowds being only capable of thinking in images are only to be impressed by images … Bread and spectacular shows constituted for the plebeians of ancient Rome the ideal of happiness, and they asked for nothing more. Throughout the successive ages this ideal has scarcely varied … The crowd state and the domination of crowds is equivalent to the barbarian state, or a return to it (cited in Brantlinger 1983, p. 168).

This is an argument with a contemporary ring, for the values of mass culture and, by extension, its consumers have been a consistent butt of criticism as television, film and (in particular) popular music have been challenged as sources of latter-day decadence.

While these sentiments are often an expression of conservative morality, they reappear in a more radical reading where mass culture, often represented as the culture or consciousness industry, is indicted as an instrument of false consciousness, as a form of social control by an economic elite in the advancement of its own interests. This depiction of mass culture as thought control was advanced by members of the influential Frankfurt School during the interwar period. The enlightenment promises of democracy and freedom were beset by a new bondage as 'the culture industry has molded men as a type unfailingly reproduced in every product' (Horkheimer and Adorno 1972, p. 127). Resistance is inconceivable, for hegemonic power from above is complete: 'The misplaced love of the common people for the wrong which is done them is a greater force than the cunning of the authorities' (Horkheimer and Adorno 1972, p. 134). The consumer is trapped, and in an alienated life 'becomes the ideology of the pleasure industry, whose institutions he cannot escape' (Horkheimer and Adorno 1972, p. 158). In *Society of the Spectacle*, Debord (1973) extends this uncompromising picture of social and mental control. His argument elaborates the initial thesis that 'The entire life of societies in which modern conditions of production reign announces itself as an immense accumulation of *spectacles*' (Debord 1970, par. 1). The scope of the spectacle is total; it has invaded 'The entire life ... Everything that was directly lived'. For Debord, the spectacle defends unequal class power, extending to the masses only 'the impoverishment, the servitude and the negation of real life' (par. 215). It neutralises resistance as 'the sun which never sets over the empire of modern passivity' (par. 13). It casts a deceptive but seductive unreality of images and signs. This is a thesis which to varying degrees has a number of advocates (Harvey 1987, 1989).

Other perspectives in popular culture challenge this watertight system of powerful elites and passive, deluded consumers (Lears 1985; Warren 1994, 1996; Williams 1977). Such a system oversimplifies. It presents the consciousness of the masses as monolithic and unproblematic, passive and without the potential for resistance. It locates mass culture ultimately in economic relations, overlooking very real status dimensions such as race, religion, gender and lifestyle. Government is either absent from analysis or treated unsubtly as an extension of dominant elites. Societal flux, the pervasive change which constantly dislocates and provides opportunity for opposition, is missing and society is portrayed as frozen and hermetic. The question of *why* the masses so readily internalise the allegedly manipulative values of mass culture is not addressed. One set of answers suggests that commodities supply a set of both material and symbolic needs deemed important by people (see Diggins 1977). Investigation of the relations between definitions of the good life by the public and the critic is, then, a significant issue, but one notable by its absence in the literature we have reviewed. Moreover, the view of mass culture expressed by its critics is distant and elitist. The interpretation of mass culture is invariably inferred rather than direct. There is a surprisingly consistent gap between the theory of social control and any empirical examination of the meaning of mass culture to its market. A web of interpretation is thrown over the experience of mass culture, but it is a web which is not informed by utterances from the consumers themselves.

A number of works in popular culture studies have reacted strongly against a posited mass culture. 'With the notion of "mass"', writes Laba (1986), 'the social reality of the forms of popular culture is either generalised and trivialised or ignored completely'. The influential view of mass culture as manipulation homogenises both the cultural product and its consumers, reduces them to passivity, and does not consider culture as an actively-negotiated process. It overlooks, for example, the common regularity that entrepreneurs follow styles as often as they create them, that commodities frequently emerge from expressive forms of popular culture (Laba 1986; Martin 1981) and the fact that the garment industry, for example, is organised on the premise that manufacturers cannot tell which of their current fashions will be successful (Scott 1988). A second perspective argues that popular culture is more complex, diverse and shifting, containing its own purposes which may be oppositional to elite intents (Warren 1996).

Many of the social movements of the past twenty years have been associated with the liberal culture and politics of the new middle class, including environmentalism, civil rights, feminism, cultural nationalism and the anti-nuclear and democracy movements. In conservation, heritage and particularly neighbourhood protest, opposition has focused on the nexus of place (Eyles and Evans 1987; Hasson and Ley 1994). Oppositional subcultures which do not present a face of passivity are also found on the margins of mainstream society. In Britain the empirical research of the Centre for Contemporary Cultural Studies in Birmingham has documented numerous examples of resistance, particularly in youth subcultures (Hall et al. 1980; Willis 1977). Similarly, in the American inner city the stylised social worlds of the street gang member and the graffiti artist include rituals which invert the value system of 'straight' society. Like mainstream models, these adolescent subcultures seek to excel but, unlike the mainstream, the contours of their own existence encourage them to excel at being outrageous, at being 'bad' (Ley and Cybriwsky 1974). Ethnic displays also present an opportunity to nurture alternative realities through the performance of an ethnic carnival (Jackson 1988) or the creation of street murals reviving folk histories. The Chicano murals of the East Los Angeles *barrio* present a particularly resilient expression of folk culture, and it is within the *barrio* that a distinctive popular music has developed, a music which like the murals includes a cultural politics of historic folk memory and contemporary community struggle against poverty and cultural prejudice (Lipsitz 1986–87).

The debates around mass and popular culture have been focused with renewed intensity on postmodern cultural forms. Employing much of the vocabulary of the critique of the culture industry, postmodern design is attacked as superficial, tasteless, deceitful and manipulative (see Foster 1985). However, this criticism characteristically overlooks the active negotiation of symbolic forms that may occur in postmodern design. The use of recognisable popular elements is a key element of postmodern design, but their rearrangement may permit an ironic or parodic interpretation which challenges their taken-for-granted status. Postmodernism offers, in short, 'a model that is profoundly implicated in, yet still capable of criticising, that which it seeks to describe' (Hutcheon 1986–87). The critical potential of postmodernism is apparent when we remember its adversarial stand against the elitist designs of modern architecture and planning and their patrons in corporate capitalism and the corporate state (Ley and Mills 1992; though see Crilley 1993a, 1993b for a differing opinion). Not the least significant of Jane Jacobs' arguments against centralised modern planning thirty years ago was her challenge of its elitist way of seeing, against which she posed a radical populism based in part upon the everyday experience of the sights, sounds and rhythms of her own street in New York (Jacobs 1961). Her new appreciation of the strength of folk and personal knowledge was extended politically to the advocacy of a participatory method which established direct communication between everyday life and planning practices. In this manner the ways of seeing and doing from below were reformulating the perception from above. The success with which Jacobs' argument infiltrated public planning challenges any view of hegemony which denies the place of active negotiation in popular culture, the capacity for opposition and penetration from below.

WORLD'S FAIRS: INSTRUMENTS OF SOCIAL CONTROL?

Like mass culture, the modern World's Fair has a nineteenth-century origin, and has invariably been the project of social elites. Their intent, it is held, was to consolidate '"ideologically coherent" "symbolic universes" confirming and extending the authority of the country's corporate, political, and scientific leadership ... (they were) triumphs of hegemony as well as symbolic edifices' (Rydell 1984, pp. 2–3). Walter Benjamin was more specific in his denunciation of the nineteenth-century Parisian expositions, which:

> opened up a phantasmagorical world, where man entered to be entertained. The amusement industry made this easier for him by elevating him to the level of a commodity. He had only to surrender himself to its manipulations, while enjoying his alienation from himself and from others (Benjamin 1970).

Let us examine more closely this interpretation of the World's Fair as an instrument of social control. In the United States, the initial sponsors of a major exposition invariably hailed from the municipal boosters of the chamber of commerce, but the role of the state should not be oversimplified. The public sector in the United States underwrote in grants and bonds 76 per cent of the cost of San Antonio's 1968 Fair, over 80 per cent of Spokane's 1974 Fair and

74 per cent of Knoxville's 1982 Fair. Indeed, senior government funds have commonly been procured through expositions to finance lasting public legacies, such as a new transportation system (e.g. Montreal 1967, Knoxville 1982), urban redevelopment on the margins of downtown (San Antonio 1968, Spokane 1974, Knoxville 1982, New Orleans 1984, Atlanta 1996) and cultural, sporting, recreational and convention facilities (Seattle 1962 and many others). However, besides the dominant economic and municipal objectives of increasing trade, tourism and public infrastructure, international objectives have added a separate dimension to a number of World's Fairs. The Anglo-French Exhibition of 1908 celebrated the *entente cordiale* between the two nations, and the 1855 Fair in Paris had the major objectives of fostering a *rapprochement* between Britain and France and consolidating the legitimacy of Louis Napoleon (Chandler 1986).

Trade, local support and political ambitions are insufficient to draw a mass public to an exposition site. Here we encounter the second theme in the social control argument—the place of spectacle, fantasy and entertainment in enchanting and diverting the masses from more serious matters. From the beginning the fairs were certainly a dramatic expression of mass society, and grandeur was a ubiquitous theme. The main building of the 1867 Paris Exposition was 1.5 km (1 mile) in circumference, while the 1889 Fair built heavenwards with the Eiffel Tower. A beaux arts White City of considerable splendour at Chicago in 1893 propelled American planners toward 'city beautiful' principles for a generation. A jewelled tower was the glory of the 1915 San Francisco Fair, while by 1939 pervasive modern design tendencies prescribed the primitive geometries of a 185 m (610 ft) high triangular tower, the Trylon, and a globular Perisphere as the New York Fair's central symbols. The aesthetics of architecture, colour, decoration and lighting added to the sense of spectacle, particularly at night (Harrison 1980). However, a tone of moral and educational improvement has challenged too simple a view of spectacle. In 1893, the Chicago midway included extensive ethnological exhibits and public education 'ran riot' at the Exposition (Rydell 1984, p. 46; Harris 1978). It was at the same Columbian Exposition that Frederick Jackson Turner presented his frontier thesis to the American Historical Association meeting which was only one of many congresses and conventions coincident with the Exposition and conveying an erudite tone to the proceedings. By 1915, over 900 congresses convened at the San Francisco Fair, representing medicine, science, religion, social policy and the arts. Indeed, display of the arts was a major feature of international expositions. In the Parisian fairs, arts and education commonly ranked first. Both Gauguin and Picasso were inspired in their own artistic experimentation by the presence of 'primitive' art at the Paris expositions (Greenhalgh 1988).

It would seem that while the trading function is central it is incorrect to see the fairs as only merchandise marts. Education and entertainment have also been high-ranking goals, as have municipal, national and international political objectives. Nor should we oversimplify the response of visitors. We need then to broaden our understanding of fairs and their visitors beyond a simple bread and circuses metaphor: 'The fairs were not only selling goods, they were selling ideas: ideas about the relations between nations, the spread of education, the advancement of science, the form of cities, the nature of domestic life, the place of art in society' (Benedict 1983).

Does this simply broaden the potential scope of hegemony to a wider range of social experience? The ethnological exhibits pre-1914, for example, were strongly influenced by Social Darwinism and as such reinforced racist attitudes. Moreover, the values displayed in the fairs were contained within the limits of middle-class society. Part of the fantasy of the expositions was their optimistic portrayal of a middle-class present and future—aesthetic, hygienic, pleasurable, self-improving and consensual where conflict and scarcity were no more evident than in any other middle-class setting. Indeed, the fairs were primarily stories a middle-class society told itself about itself. Admission charges barred large elements of the poorer population from entry. At Philadelphia's Centennial Fair a 'poor man's day' with reduced admission was held. In 1939 a Gallup poll indicated that 63 per cent of respondents who had not visited the New York Fair had stayed away because they could not afford the costs of attendance (Susman 1980). The obstacle of high admission charges to the entry of large sections of the population has been cited as recently as the ill-fated 1984 Fair in New Orleans (O'Brian 1985).

Imputations of hegemony and social control remain, moreover, inferences from above, and even detailed studies include minimal evidence of the actual ways of seeing of the public (Greenhalgh 1988; Boyle 1997). The New York exposition set out self-consciously to be 'the People's Fair' for 'the average American', but even here few documents have survived to assess how the people themselves perceived the Fair and the degree to which they internalised its values (Susman 1980). In this context the existence of a large (if imperfect) data set of visitors' perceptions of the 1986 Exposition in Vancouver is of particular interest for the light it throws upon the meaning of this landscape of heroic consumption to its audience.

EXPO 86: LEARNING WITHIN A CONTEXT OF FUN

As much as any recent fair, the 1986 World Exposition in Vancouver opened an instructive window on its time and place (Figure 11.1). It represented both an integration of themes common to most World's Fairs with the personalities, interests and opportunities of a unique setting (see the varying accounts in Anderson and Wachtel 1986; Government of Canada 1986). Expo 86 was planned and operated by the provincial government of British Columbia and managed by the Expo 86 Corporation, a crown corporation responsible to cabinet. The theme of the Fair was transportation and communications (originally its title was 'Transpo 86'), to commemorate the centennial of the City of Vancouver and the arrival of the first transcontinental passenger train. In an initial press release in June 1979 the provincial government declared that 'The primary purpose of the Exposition is not, however, to make money. It is to mark this important double anniversary' (Province of British Columbia

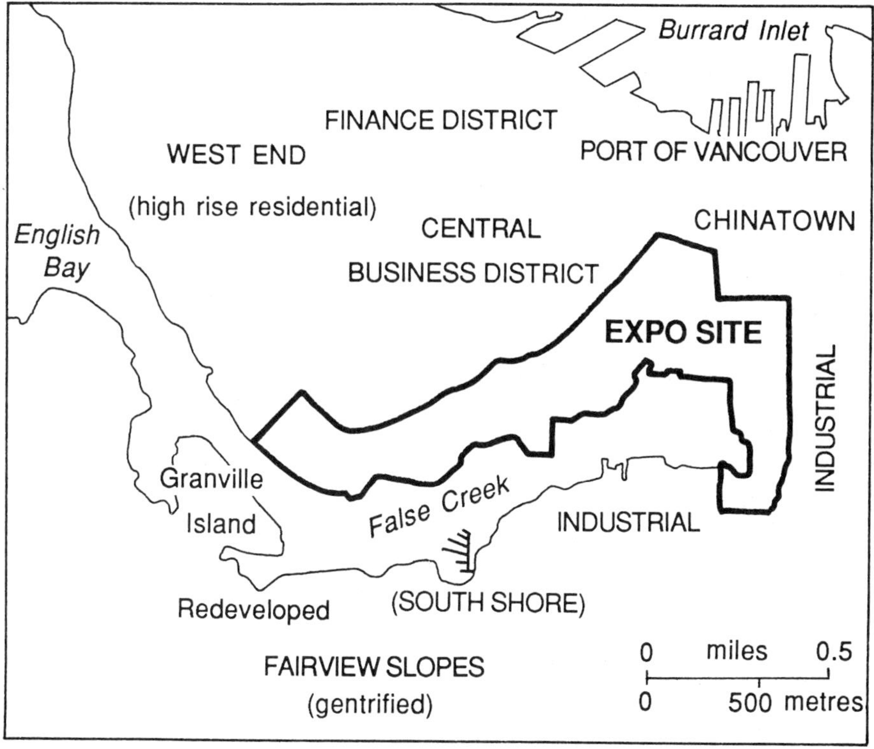

FIGURE 11.1 Location of Expo site and surrounding land use.

1979). The objectives of Expo 86 were varied and changing. At an early stage, an important objective was to secure federal funds for urban redevelopment, including a convention centre, a sports stadium and a rapid transit line. The best chance of gaining these funds was through their amalgamation in a package including a World's Fair. Promotion of the Fair was also intended to raise the sagging fortunes of the provincial government (Ley 1987). As the economic recession deepened, job creation and economic development were given pride of place in government press releases.

The organisation of Expo 86 captured a number of pervasive regional themes. Bitter disputes raged between all three levels of government about the financing and even the holding of the Fair, with the Mayor of Vancouver in opposition, and by early 1982 these conflicts seemed likely to lead to its cancellation. A second crisis followed, concerning labour disputes. Upon the insistence of the right-wing provincial government, the Expo Corporation awarded construction contracts to non-union firms, despite the high level of unionisation in the building trades (Mickelburgh 1986). With building contracts valued at between $600 and $900 million, the stakes were high for the unions, and disputes including work stoppages and demonstrations led to renewed crisis. On this second occasion, the Chairman of the Expo Board recommended cancellation of the Fair but was overruled by a deeply-divided cabinet. At this stage, the Fair, far from establishing social order, was deepening social conflict. A third theme, symptomatic of the neo-conservatism of British Columbia during the 1980s, was the dominant private enterprise orientation. The Chairman of the Expo Board (also President for the final fifteen months) was the province's most eminent entrepreneur, a rags-to-riches multimillionaire (Kelly 1986). The Board itself was dominated by businesspeople, though on a number of occasions it was overruled by direct intervention of cabinet. The true architect of the Fair was the Premier of British Columbia, who publicly announced the concept in January 1980 and who became ever more closely identified with it. By 1984, facing a growing deficit and labour unrest on the site, he described himself as 'the father of Expo suffering through its birth' (*Toronto Globe and Mail*, 12 April 1984).

The political mandate of the Fair gave it remarkable powers. The legal status of a Crown corporation conferred empowerments upon Expo 86 greater than those of a private corporation. It enjoyed the freedom to raise and disperse its own funds (under the advantageous credit rating of the provincial government), the power of expropriation and authority to override all city by-laws, zoning regulations and planning policy. With easy access to the public purse, a megaproject mentality towards spending readily arose. Any comparison between Expo 86 and the calamitous 1984 Fair in New Orleans was, according to an Expo director, 'like comparing the Queen Mary to a canoe'. The distinction he saw was significant: while the New Orleans Fair 'had a total budget of $400 million to work with, Expo 86 and its participants are spending more than three and a half times that—$1.5 billion' (*BC Business Bulletin* 1985). Of this figure, $800 million was to be spent by the Expo Corporation, $300 million by the federal government and the remainder by other Fair exhibitors. Government control gave a new meaning to the bottom line, as it had earlier to Expo 67 in Montreal. The project deficit grew from $1 million in 1980 to $75 million in 1982 and $311 million at the beginning of 1985. In the Fair's closing ceremonies, the Chairman of the Expo Corporation triumphantly announced that Expo 86 had been achieved on budget—what he had in mind was the projected deficit of over $300 million.

Advertising material highlighted entertainment rather than science and education, though the latter were certainly included. However, the matrix of the Fair, into which other activities were cast, was having fun, putting on and enjoying a good show (Kahrl 1986). Its Creative Director described the concept as 'learning within a context of fun' (Murray 1986, p. 6): 'I try to bring people to a teachable moment. To charm and delight and make them laugh while introducing some new information' (Orr, Deaton and Sturmanis 1986). The planning theme which emerged was intended to integrate pleasure and knowledge in a celebration of individual and social creativity. Against the spectre of social disillusionment, the message of the Fair was to be the achievement of human ingenuity in all fields. As such the Fair would counterpose its historic context: 'The look, feel and content of Expo 86 above all responded to the event's moment in time. It was imperative that this expression transcend the reality of a troubled decade' (Government of Canada 1986, p. 75).

Expo 86 had the air of a carnival, a colourful animation of space and time whirling in the density of its stimuli. For its site design 'images rather than words were stressed, with colour as the backbone of the vocabulary' (Government of Canada 1986, p. 9). Here, perhaps, is the disembodied realm of fantasy, the persuasive architecture of the sign, achieved to perfection. The design theme was 'festive technology', its vocabulary 'Exuberance. Festivity. Exhilaration. Charisma. Fantasy. Vibrancy. Surprise. Optimism. Spirit. Joy. The objective was to satiate the site with a level of colour and kinetics so intensely stimulating that the resulting memory would last a lifetime' (Government of Canada 1986, p. 76).

The pavilions themselves carried on the mix of 'learning within a context of fun'. The sixty-five pavilions included international, regional and corporate sponsors (Figure 11.2). They varied widely in their exhibits: some offered little more than national gift shops and travel promotion. Others were resolutely serious and scientific. A few showed considerable artistic flair. A number displayed themes which revealed more diversity than a tightly-woven view of hegemony might accommodate. Of the forty national pavilions, seven came from socialist states, including China, the Soviet Union and Cuba—a catholic selection for a free-enterprise host government. The United Nations pavilion was devoted to the achievement of peace, the perils of war and the capacity of individuals to effect positive change. Two pavilions offered strong religious themes: Christian and Muslim (Saudi Arabia). Two regional pavilions presented significant themes from local popular culture: a sensitive examination of native culture (Northwest Territories) and the human face of outmigration (Saskatchewan). The folklife area focused on different aspects of ethnic, native and popular culture. Most interesting of all was the ambivalent view of technology included in two of the corporate pavilions. The Canadian Pacific exhibit had two imaginative shows presenting social impacts of new technology and user conflicts. Equally unpredictable was General Motors' 'Spirit Lodge', a reflection on the meaning of new technology. In a pavilion which included an automobile display, the narrator of 'Spirit Lodge', an old Native Indian, challenged the claims of new technology and offered his own standard: 'Are our machines making us more like humans? Or are they making us more like machines?' (Fulford 1986). The final report of the Expo Corporation suggested in retrospect that the Fair's 'mood was post-technological' (Government of Canada 1986, p. 75). Oppositional themes may appear in the most improbable of sources—hegemony does not appear without paradox and inconsistency. So how stupefied were the visitors?

THE MEANINGS OF EXPO 86: PUBLIC PERCEPTIONS OF A HALLMARK EVENT

In the final weeks of Expo a city newspaper included a questionnaire asking readers to send in their perceptions of the Fair. Five questions appeared.

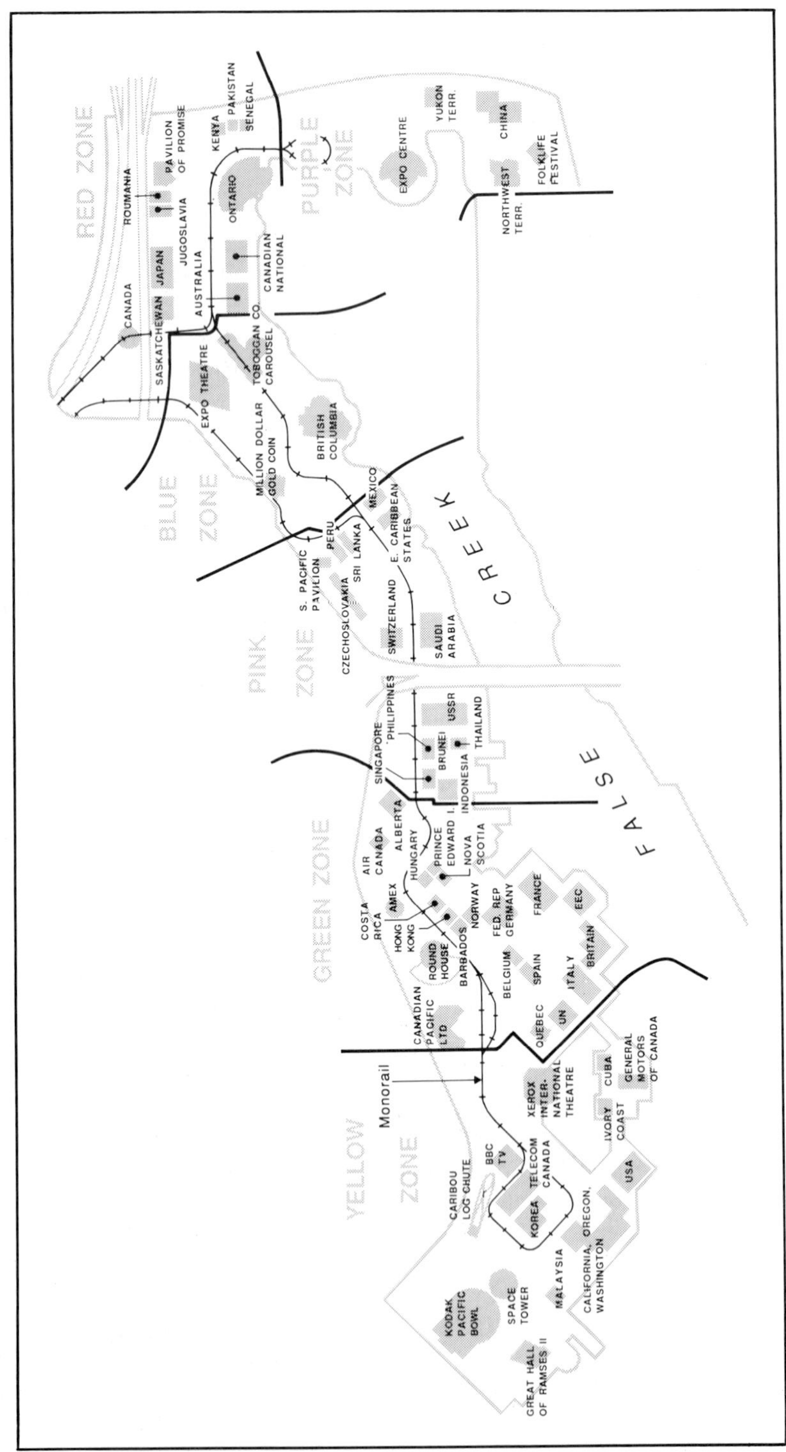

FIGURE 11.2 Expo 86 site map with pavilions.
Source: Murray, D. ed. 1986, The Expo Celebration, Whitecap Books, North Vancouver, BC.

1 What will you remember most about Expo?
2 Has it made us a world-class city?
3 What was its single best aspect?
4 Its worst?
5 Expo's deficit is now estimated at $300 million. Was it worth it?

To the editor's surprise over 2200 replies were submitted. About a quarter were received from the City of Vancouver and about half from its suburbs; 99.5 per cent had attended the Fair. While the representativeness of this sample cannot be gauged, the results indicate a group well disposed to the Fair, with 85 per cent claiming that its large deficit was well justified. The perceptions of so large a group are significant in their own right for any insights that might be offered on the nature and extent of hegemony and social control over the public.

For the respondents the single best aspect of the Fair had little to do with the economic goals the government had been declaring repeatedly for several years. Fewer than 10 per cent mentioned economic objectives and only 3.5 per cent of replies saw education as the Fair's major achievement (though educational themes did appear as a secondary theme elsewhere). Instead of these lofty goals, the majority of respondents measured Expo in more personal terms, reflecting their own experience of the Fair, its activities and people.

The most memorable features of Expo have been classified and appear in Table 11.1. Positive reaction to a 'successful' fair monopolises the categories—to a sympathetic eye even the line-ups could present an opportunity to speak to strangers and watch street entertainment ('the wonderful line-ups which enabled me to meet the world'). Perhaps the most predictable group of responses refer to the aesthetic quality of the site (categories 5, 6, 8, 11, 12). References to the waterfront setting, the rainbow colours, landscaping and sculptures indicated that the design process had been effective: 'The whimsy and colour of its beautiful land, sea and air plazas ... the smell of the sea from the quiet promenades.' 'The combining of colour and architecture with local landscape in beauty, fantasy and wit.' Expo 86 had also learnt the lessons of successful theme parks in the cleanliness of the site and the courtesy of staff: 'The cleanliness of the entire Expo site. The clean cut appearance of the staff gave the province a definite classy look.'

A second major theme explored a suspension of reality, Expo as a time and a place that was enchanting, set aside from a humdrum world. Consider the following: 'It has shrunk this year. This year didn't start till May 2 and will end in mid October'; 'Going through the entrance turnstile and being touched by the magic ... Going through the exit turnstile and it's back to reality, the real world'; 'I had so much fun. It was a fantasy place where you sensed people had left their problems outside the gate. There was a carefree atmosphere.'

There are a number of questions to ask about this spell. How permanent was it? To what extent could people make the separation between the fantasies and the real? To what extent did the world of Expo invade life outside the fairgrounds? For a large number the spell was that of a carnival

TABLE 11.1 'What will you remember most about Expo?'

		Numbers	Per cent (n = 2216)
1	Friendliness of people/happiness	758	34
2	Atmosphere/excitement	392	18
3	Entertainment/party	382	17
4	International/national meeting place	322	15
5	Pavilions/exhibits	295	13
6	Colour/colour coding	241	11
7	Pride/sense of community	241	11
8	Cleanliness	234	11
9	Courteous staff	234	11
10	Well organised	105	5
11	Setting/site itself	103	5
12	Beauty/aesthetics/architecture	100	5
13	Fireworks and lasers	98	4
14	Line-ups	70	3
15	Education received	60	3
16	Miscellaneous (30 other features)	482	22

spirit, it was entertainment, fun, a party. As such, it was the deficit, not the show, which had an air of unreality: 'Yes Expo was worth it ... worth it above all, *because we had fun*!'; 'Emphatically, yes! The fair gave literally millions of hours of pleasure. The deficit is an unbeatable entertainment bargain'; 'A party always costs us some and this was an incredible party.'

For some respondents the party became their party, and their identification with the exposition became almost obsessive. Here, most clearly, a confusion of realities was occurring: 'What a fantastic five months we have had—Expo has indeed been one big party and we shall miss it very much. I wish we could keep more of it intact ... I hate the thought of more high-rises going up on our beloved Expo site.' Note the personalisation of the Fair which occurs in the final sentence. As such, no cost it seems could be too high: 'What deficit? It is like putting a price on every hug we get from a child.' 'With the closing of Expo 86 I personally feel sad to have to say good-bye to such a dear friend, but this friend has left me with such wonderful memories that I will cherish forever.'

Such personification of the Fair is possessive, and indeed obsessive. One writer sent in a poem extolling 'My beautiful, colourful enchanting lady'. Another wrote:

> The feeling remembered is the excitement, the expectation, the pride that I got as opening day approached. A great love affair was happening, to me, to Vancouver, to the World. A sound and sight so wonderful that only the music and fireworks could come close to expressing it. EXPO 86, I remember you with passion, colour, lights, music and most of all giving the World exactly what you said you would: the biggest party of the century.

A number of respondents held season tickets and some attended frequently: 'It was a fantastic once-in-most lifetimes' experience and I'd do it all again. To date I've been 85 times.'

Such obsession is symptomatic of the spectacle. Augustine relates the seduction of a friend by the Roman games (in Brantlinger 1983, pp. 79–80). Initially resistant, its sights, sounds and excitement became an opiate blinding his moral judgement. While allusions to bread and circuses were made only by correspondents critical of Expo, it is in such obsessive perceptions that the responses came nearest to the theoretical portrait of willing victims of the culture industry. The distraction of the public from broader issues is accompanied by a preoccupation with amusement and spectacle and its elevation to 'a dear friend', an 'enchanting lady'. There are further questions to ask: How abiding is this seduction? How lasting is the spell? For a number of respondents the boundaries of fantasy and reality were clearly defined: 'Let's not worry about the deficit. Let's just accept it. The party's over. Let's pay for it now.'

A third group of categories (1, 4, 7, 9, 15) in Table 11.1 reflect a more active and positive engagement with the Fair. They refer to intersubjective relations of happiness, friendship, a sense of community and mutual learning. Very few visitors attended Expo 86 alone. They came in clusters of friends and relatives, and the Fair was an occasion, a forum for *advancing* these social bonds. Many households in the region organised family reunions during 1986: 'We invited 60 members of the family and friends; 42 said they were coming, so far we had 52 ... we enjoyed every one of them and had the greatest summer of our life. We are in our 70s.'

The Fair was an opportunity for binding family relations in learning and pleasure: 'I'll remember the leisurely hours we spent there—walking around the grounds, enjoying the entertainment, absorbing the information in the displays, watching the happiness of our children's faces.' The Fair's events and memories were *social* occasions: 'Remembering the time I sang with my friends in front of the world live in a studio was something extraordinary for me.' The Fair provided an opportunity for visitors to promote their own social purposes, to engage in the spectacle from *their own* way of seeing. Social bonds extended also to strangers and to other societies and cultures in a celebration of multiculturalism. Mutual learning offered many benefits: 'How educational it was. You could get a real feel for life in other countries and for their people. Prejudices were replaced with friendships'; 'The cultural events presented by international communities ... These have not only been a banquet for eye and ear, but have also helped to promote greater appreciation of one another's culture. Nations clearly have more in common than differences, and the audiences have felt this'; 'My 9 year old daughter will have a view of the world as a whole. Whatever else she learns, the world will remain a community.' Within responses such as this are conveyed not only the active engagement of people with the opportunities presented by a mass event. Perhaps there is also indication of learning which may engender independent world views, an example of Jameson's (1979) 'utopian potential' within all mass culture which can challenge hegemonic values.

CONCLUSION

Expo 86 offers a further example of the increasingly ludic nature of urban life, the growing intrusion of leisure and the aesthetic into the urban landscape. The culture of consumption has an important playful dimension. What do we make of this tendency? How is it to be theorised? How intoxicating are these landscapes to their audience, to what extent are they a diversion and a delusion, an instrument of social control imposed upon an uncritical public? We should note that the planning of Expo was fraught with conflict. Indeed, it exposed and aggravated the deepest regional tensions: conflict between different levels of government and, above all, labour unrest with the decision to make Expo an open work-site. While the extravaganza of Expo was being planned, the deep cuts of a provincial restraint program led to the formation of a popular opposition movement, the Solidarity Coalition, and carried the province within a few hours of a general strike. The deflection of funds into Expo aggravated these tensions. During the pre-opening period the Fair was a source of social unrest rather than social control.

We have seen that among our respondents, memories were vivid and positive, indeed for some the Fair became virtually an obsession. In this displacement of reality, the data come closest to describing the manipulation of consciousness posited by mass culture theorists. How permanent though, was this psychosis? Moreover, another large group of respondents were far less spellbound. They engaged the Fair more actively, used it as a resource for advancing family and friendship ties, were less riveted by its fantasy and were more intent on learning, including the more expansive issues of global citizenship posed by some of the pavilions. Among this group we have no basis to assume a displacement of reality. The cultural dupes posed by mass culture theorists are much less visible on the ground.

The hallmark event has become a major tool of economic development, and in some circumstances plays a role similar to that anticipated for heavy industry in earlier decades. The successful event may act as a regional multiplier, propelling waves of investment and economic activity (Hall 1997; Hall and Hodges 1997; Hiller 1998). Overseas tourism to British Columbia, which had remained sluggish from 1980 to 1985, increased by 25 per cent in 1986, the year of Expo, and has sustained this higher level since. The growth of tourists has occurred particularly in Pacific Rim source countries, notably Japan, Hong Kong and Australia. Since 1986 there has also been a significant growth of 'business category' immigration to British Columbia, over half of it from Hong Kong. While other factors are no doubt at work, Expo's role in advertising Vancouver to the Pacific Rim market seems to have achieved its objectives. Indeed, Bob Williams, a senior provincial politician with the opposition democratic socialist New Democratic Party remarked:

> Expo 86, of course, gave us an international presence. As a result we were probably catapulted a decade or two ahead in terms of global economic interest. Our verandah is now crowded with suitors from Asia and Europe, changing the nature of our town irrevocably ... Bill Bennett moved Vancouver along a decade earlier into Jane Jacob's city state (Williams 1990).

The significance of a major hallmark event is indicated by the 1992 World's Fair in Seville. With a budget of $7–8 billion to improve regional infrastructure, the Fair was regarded as, in the words of a senior bureaucrat 'the motor that will enable the economy of Andalusia to take off' (Riding 1989). The provision of public infrastructure and a plan for regional economic development did not, however, exhaust the objectives of Expo 92. Both the Prime Minister and his Deputy were from Seville and well aware of the advantages of consolidating their own power base. Beyond party politics there was also a national objective—incorporating politics, economics and culture in order to project the image of a new Spain into a newly united Europe. According to the chief engineer at Expo 92, 'Spain wants Expo 92 to show it as a modern country that is more than just bulls and flamenco' (Riding 1989). The hallmark event is anything but trivial. With its political, economic and cultural dimensions it has the capacity to remake human geographies.

NOTE

An earlier and longer version of this paper 'Landscape as spectacle: World's Fairs and the culture of heroic consumption' appeared in *Environment and Planning D:Society and Space*, vol. 6, no. 2, 1988, pp. 191–212. It is reprinted with the kind permission of the publisher, Pion Limited.

REFERENCES

Anderson, R. & Wachtel, E. (eds) 1986, *The Expo Story*, Harbour Publishing, Madeira Park, BC.

British Columbia Business Bulletin, 1985, 'Expo 86: a business with a future', vol. 1, no. 5, pp. 1–2.

Benedict, B. 1983, 'The anthropology of world's fairs', in *The Anthropology of World's Fairs*, ed. B. Benedict, Scolar Press, London, pp. 1–65.

Benjamin, W. 1970, 'Paris, capital of the 19th century', *Dissent*, vol. 17, pp. 439–47.

Boyle, M. 1997, 'Civic boosterism in the politics of local economic development—"institutional positions" and "strategic orientations" in the consumption of hallmark events', *Environment and Planning A*, vol. 29, no. 11, pp. 1975–97.

Brantlinger, P. 1983, *Bread and Circuses: Theories of Mass Culture as Social Decay*, Cornell University Press, Ithaca, New York.

Chandler, A. 1986, 'Fanfare for the new empire: the Paris Exposition Universelle of 1855', *World's Fair*, vol. 6, no. 2, pp. 11–16.

Crilley, D. 1993a, 'Megastructures and urban change: aesthetics, ideology and design,' in *The Restless Urban Landscape*, ed. P. Knox, Prentice Hall, Englewood Cliffs, New Jersey, pp. 127–64.

Crilley, D. 1993b 'Architecture as advertising: constructing the image of redevelopment,' in *Selling Places: The City as Cultural Capital, Past and Present*, eds G. Kearns & C. Philo, Pergamon Press, Oxford, pp. 231–52.

Development Action Group 1996, *The Olympics and Development: Lessons and Suggestions*, Development Action Group: Observatory, South Africa. (Available by email from dag@wn.apc.org)

Debord, G. 1970, *Society of the Spectacle*, Black & Red, Detroit.

Diggins, J. 1977, 'Reification and the cultural hegemony of capitalism', *Social Research*, vol. 44, pp. 354–83.

Eyles, J. & Evans, M. 1987, 'Popular consciousness, moral ideology, and locality', *Environment and Planning D:Society and Space*, vol. 5, no. 1, pp. 39–71.

Foster, H. 1985, *Recodings: Art, Spectacle, Cultural Politics*, Bay Press, Port Townsend, Washington.

Fulford, R. 1986, 'Only fair', *Saturday Night*, October, pp. 9–12.

Goss, J. 1993, 'The "magic of the mall"; an analysis of form, function and meaning in the contemporary retail built economy', *Annals of the Association of American Geographers*, vol. 83, no. 1, pp. 18–47.

Government of Canada 1986, *The Expo 86 General Report*, Department of External Affairs, Ottawa.

Greenhalgh, P. 1988, *Ephemeral Vistas: The Expositions Universelles, Great Exhibitions and World's Fairs, 1851–1939*, Manchester University Press, Manchester.

Hall, C. 1989, 'The definition and analysis of hallmark tourist events', *GeoJournal*, vol. 19, no. 3, pp. 263–8.

Hall, C.M. 1997, 'Mega-events and their legacies', in *Quality Management in Urban Tourism*, ed. P. Murphy, Wiley, Chichester pp. 75–87.

Hall, C.M. & Hodges, J. 1997, 'The Party's great, but what about the hangover?: the housing and social impacts of mega-events with special reference to the 2000 Sydney Olympics', *Festival Management & Event Tourism*, vol. 4, no. 1/2, pp. 13–20.

Hall, S., Hobson, D., Lowe, A. & Willis, P. 1980, *Culture, Media, Language*, Hutchinson, London.

Hall, T. & Hubbard, P. 1996, 'The entrepreneurial city: new urban politics, new urban geographies, *Progress in Human Geography*, vol. 20, no. 2, pp. 153–74.

Harris, N. 1978, 'Museums, merchandising and popular taste: the struggle for influence', in *Material Culture and the Study of American Life*, ed. I. McQuimby, W.W. Norton, New York, pp. 140–74.

Harrison, H. 1980, 'The fair perceived: color and light as elements in design and planning', in *Dawn of a New Day: The New York World's Fair 1939–40*, ed. H. Harrison, The Queens Museum and New York University Press, New York, pp. 43–55.

Harvey, D. 1987, 'Flexible accumulation through urbanisation', *Antipode*, vol. 19, pp. 260–86.

Harvey, D. 1989, *The Condition of Postmodernity*, Blackwell, Oxford.

Hasson, S. & Ley, D. (eds) 1994, *Neighbourhood Organisations and the Welfare State*, University of Toronto Press, Toronto.

Hiller, H. 1998, 'Assessing the impact of mega-events: a linkage model', *Current Issues in Tourism*, vol. 1, no. 1, pp. 47–57.

Hopkins, J. 1990, 'West Edmonton Mall: landscapes of myths and elsewhereness', *Canadian Geographer*, vol. 34, pp. 2–17.

Hopkins, J. 1991, 'West Edmonton Mall as a Centre for Social Interaction', *Canadian Geographer*, vol. 35, no. 3, pp. 268–79.

Horkheimer, M. & Adorno, T. 1972, 'The culture industry: enlightenment as mass deception' in *Dialectic of Enlightenment*, Herder & Herder, New York, pp. 120–67.

Hutcheon, L. 1987, 'The politics of postmodernism: parody and history', *Cultural Critique*, vol. 5, pp. 179–297.
Huxley, M. & Kerkin, K. 1988, 'What price the Bicentennial? A political economy of Darling Harbour', *Transition*, Spring, pp. 57–64.
Jackson, P. 1988, 'Street life: the politics of Carnival', *Society and Space*, vol. 6, pp. 213–27.
Jackson, P. & Thrift, N. 1995, 'Geographies of consumption'', in *Acknowledging Consumption: A Review of New Studies*, ed. D. Miller, Routledge, London, pp. 204–37.
Jacobs, J. 1961, *The Death and Life of Great American Cities*, Random House New York.
Jameson, F. 1979, 'Reification and utopia in mass culture', *Social Text*, vol. 1, pp. 130–48.
Kahrl, W. 1986, 'Vancouver and the hall of dynamos', *World's Fair*, vol. 6, no. 4, pp. 1–5.
Kelly, R. 1986, *Pattison: Portrait of a Capitalist Superstar*, New Star Books, Vancouver.
Laba, M. 1986, 'Making sense: expressiveness, stylisation and the popular culture process,' *Journal of Popular Culture*, vol. 19, no. 4, pp. 107–17.
Lears, J. 1985, 'The concept of cultural hegemony', *American Historical Review*, vol. 90, pp. 567–93.
Ley, D. 1980, 'Liberal ideology and the post-industrial city', *Annals of the Association of American Geographers*, vol. 70, pp. 238–58.
Ley, D. 1983, *A Social Geography of the City*, Harper & Row, New York.
Ley, D. 1987, 'Styles of the times: liberal and neoconservative landscapes in inner Vancouver, 1968–1986', *Journal of Historical Geography*, vol. 13, pp. 40–56.
Ley, D. & Cybriwsky, R. 1974, 'Urban graffiti as territorial markers', *Annals of the Association of American Geographers*, vol. 64, pp. 491–505.
Ley, D. & Mills, C. 1993, 'Can there be a postmodernism of resistance in the built environment', in *The Restless Urban Landscape*, ed. P. Knox, Prentice Hall, Englewood Cliffs, New Jersery, pp. 255–78.
Lipsitz, G. 1986–87, 'Cruising around the historical bloc–postmodernism and popular music in East Los Angeles', *Cultural Critique*, vol. 5, pp. 157–77.
MacKay, H. (ed.) 1997, *Consumption and Everyday Life*, Sage, London.
Martin, B. 1981, *A Sociology of Contemporary Cultural Change*, Basil Blackwell, Oxford.
Mickelburgh, R. 1986, 'A fair wage', in *The Expo Story*, eds R. Anderson & E. Wachtel, Harbour Publishing, Madeira Park, BC, pp. 125–48.
Murray, D. (ed.) 1986, *The Expo Celebration*, Whitecap Books, North Vancouver, BC.
O'Brian, B. 1985, 'Going bust: a case history', *World's Fair*, vol. 5, no. 2, pp. 7–10.
Olds, K. 1998, 'Hallmark events, evictions and housing rights: the Canadian case', *Current Issues in Tourism*, vol. 1, no. 1, pp. 2–46.
Orr, S., Deaton, S. & Sturmanis, D. 1986, 'The Expo 86 gamble', *Western Report*, 21 April, pp. 49–51.
Pile, S. & Keith, M. Eds 1997, *Geographies of Resistance*, Routledge, London.
Province of British Columbia, 1979, 'Transpo 86: BC seeks 1986 international exposition to mark Vancouver centennial', (news release), Ministry of the Provincial Secretary, Victoria, BC.
Riding, A. 1989, 'World's Fair a new world in Andalusia', *New York Times*, 20 August, p. 5.
Rydell, R. 1984, *All the World's a Fair*, University of Chicago Press, Chicago.

Scott, A. 1988, *Metropolis*, University of California Press, Berkeley.
Susman, W. 1980, 'The people's fair: cultural contradictions of a consumer society', in *Dawn of a New Day: The New York's World 's Fair, 1939–40*, ed. H. Harrison, The Queens Museum and New York University Press, New York, pp. 17–27.
Sydney Organising Committee for the Olympic Games 1998, 'Welcome to the Official Site of the Sydney 2000 Olympic Games', http://www.sydney.olympic.org/welcome.shtml, accessed 12 February 1998.
Syme, G., Shaw, B., Fenton, M. & Mueller, S. eds 1989, *The Planning and Evaluation of Hallmark Events*, Avebury, Aldershot, UK.
Tafler, S. 1984, 'Abandon $1.2 billion fair, Expo head tells BC Cabinet', *Toronto Globe and Mail*, 12 April, p. 1.
Warren, S. 1994, 'Disneyfication of the metropolis: popular resistance in Seattle', *Journal of Urban Affairs*, vol. 16, pp. 89–107.
Warren, S. 1996, 'Popular cultural practices in the "Postmodern City"', *Urban Geography*, vol. 17, no. 6, pp. 545–67.
Whatmore, C. 1990, 'Marketing as theatre', *TD & T*, Summer, pp. 14–18.
Whitt, A. 1987, 'Mozart in the metropolis: the arts coalition and the urban growth machine', *Urban Affairs Quarterly*, vol. 23, pp. 15–36.
Williams, B. 1990, 'Our verandah is crowded, but the view is still hazy', *Business in Vancouver*, 8 January, p. 9.
Williams, R. 1977, *Marxism and Literature*, Oxford University Press, Oxford.
Willis, P. 1977, *Learning to Labour*, Saxon House, Farnborough, Hants.
Yeoh, B. & Teo, P. 1996, 'From tiger balm gardens to dragon world: philanthropy and profit in the making of Singapore's first cultural theme park', *Geografiska Annaler, Series B, Human Geography*, vol. 78, no. 1, pp. 27–42.

12

Cultures of the past and urban transformation

the Spitalfields Market redevelopment in East London

Jane M. Jacobs

INTRODUCTION

Preserving and celebrating aspects of the past are persistent and variably manifest tendencies within contemporary western societies (see Lowenthal 1986). The past is not simply 'given'—it is refracted through the value systems and power structures of the present. Those histories and artefacts of the past that are claimed as being of importance or value in the present give testament to a range of differently empowered interests and ideologies—not just of 'then', but also of 'now'. Some versions of the past may assume dominance and even become part of the way whole nations imagine themselves, while others may be suppressed, ignored or marginalised. At times, certain interests may emphasise specific versions of the past in order to consolidate their position of power and authority in the present. The historical narratives and artefacts that are associated with these sanctioned versions of the past acquire a certain level of legitimacy—they are reiterated through ritual, enlivened by popular consensus, and protected by heritage legislation. That which comes to stand as the past is never entirely static; it can be embellished, transformed and even challenged (see Hobsbawm and Ranger 1983). In Britain, for example, the national heritage once centred around events and artefacts associated with dominant interests. The icons of British (actually English) heritage were the grand events of Empire and the monuments of the powerful, like the country house. But the national identity of today's Britain is equally constituted around an (albeit sanitised) industrial heritage or more diminutive village heritage. What is officially or popularly sanctioned as a valued past has implications for those groups who are, or are not, represented; for those settings which are, or are not, preserved. Thus understood, the past is politically weighted and has an impact on the geography and form of our cities.

In recent years the interest in the past has taken a peculiar new form in western capitalist societies. Museums burgeon, the tourist industry actively promotes and enhances history, shopping malls are designed to look like village high streets and products of all kinds are marketed, wrapped in the imagery and rhetoric of past times (Hewison 1987; Horne 1984; Lumley 1988; Wright 1985; Urry 1990, 1995). It is within the expanding service sector—particularly tourism and retailing—that the link between heritage and capital is most clearly manifest (Thrift 1989). The past is an important resource for these consumption-based industries, now such a standard feature of late capitalism. The past has become commodified and its incorporation into new modes of consumption has even been dubbed as the emergence of a 'heritage industry' (Hewison 1987).

This chapter takes as its focus this politically weighted and increasingly commodified heritage and explores the role it played in processes of urban transformation in 1980s London. The specific case of urban redevelopment dealt with, is one stage in the now long-running proposal to redevelop the former site of the Spitalfields Wholesale Fruit and Vegetable Market located on the eastern fringes of the financial centre of the City of London. The redevelopment was initially proposed in order to meet the office and service requirements of the adjoining City. This chapter assumes that there is a mutually constitutive relationship between capital and culture: that capital is not simply the determining force for things cultural; that culture is not simply incidental to the logic of capital. At the most fundamental level this assumption is evident in the way the following analysis self-consciously works away from the narrow emphasis on political and economic processes evident in many conventional studies of urban transformation. Instead, this chapter builds on the work of some recent analysts who have consciously sought to highlight the constitutive role played by culture in urban transformation. Culture, once seen as the superstructural icing on the Marxist economic cake, is now accepted as central to the process of urban transformation (Agnew, Mercer and Sopher 1984; Harvey 1989; Jacobs 1994, 1996; Ley 1987; Zukin 1986, 1988, 1995).

Heritage has received considerable attention from those seeking to instate cultural factors in explanations of urban process. Heritage, particularly the effort to conserve the historic built environment, is routinely interpreted as an explicit example of forces contrary to the logic of capital accumulation in cities. Advocating conservation of the historic built environment, as opposed to demolition and new-built development, seems to clearly express the ascendancy of cultural values over economic values in the shaping of the urban scene. For example, a number of studies have documented the rise of a conservation mentality in both popular opinion and in planning ideology and practice (Ford 1979; Fucsh and Ford 1983; Relph 1987). These studies provide much insight into the way in which the historic built environment holds meaning and has become an important part of the planning agenda through conservation policy. They chart the heroic struggles of those who have advocated conservation rather than development. Often enough the impulse to conserve the historic built environment is depicted as an unquestionably positive and exclusively 'cultural' process which operates separately from, and as a check on, the changes wrought by the cycles of investment and reinvestment in urban space. This chapter demonstrates that the depiction of the heritage impulse as the beleaguered cultural counter force to the dominant logic of capital accumulation is increasingly inadequate.

In Britain, the country which forms the backdrop to this chapter, conservation of the historic built environment gained increasing legitimacy as a planning concern during the late nineteenth century. Early legislation such as the *Ancient Monuments Act of 1882,* was concerned with only a limited number of building types: the oldest and grandest. Preservation of the historic built environment tended to glorify the sanctioned histories of the nation-state or the specialist architectural and archaeological concerns of the fledgling preservation lobby groups. During the twentieth century the type of building considered worthy of preservation changed. New pressure groups like The Georgian Group (1937), The Victorian Society (1958) and, more recently, The Thirties Society, stated the case for preserving buildings from more recent times. Planning and heritage legislation was reformed to embrace an increasing variety of building types and ages. Under the 'thirty year rule', introduced into policy in 1988, it became possible to list some of the more typical glass and steel structures of the 1950s and 1960s. Another important development in the broadening of conservation practice was the emergence of the idea of townscape and its legitimation through Conservation Area legislation (the *Civic Amenities Act 1967).* This provided the basis for identifying and designating whole areas of special architectural, historical and visual character.

The emergence of conservation legislation provides an example of how one form of the heritage impulse can gain legitimacy through government policy. The broadening of the legislation to take in newer and more modest building types parallels the growing popular interest in preserving the artefacts of the past, including the full spectrum of built environment heritage. Certainly the late twentieth century saw the support for heritage preservation move well beyond the educated elite of historians and architects who had spawned the building preservation movement in Britain. The image of built environment conservation being a middle- and upper-class concern changed especially with the emergence of pressure groups which consciously sought to popularise and democratise the conservation agenda.

The new democratic and populist tone of conservation in Britain, and its emergence as planning commonsense, means that the relationship between empowered interests and conservation are not always as clear as they have been previously. While industrial and working-class buildings are more widely valued and more routinely listed, this does not mean that the process of conserving the built environment is purged of its ideological and political implications. The Spitalfields case to follow will demonstrate that the conservation of the built environment and the heritage values associated with this process continue to empower certain interests above others and reify certain pasts above others. Further, the focus of planning legislation on preserving the artefactual past—the historic built environment—has worked to marginalise and disempower those who seek to protect and enhance pasts which are not grounded in the built environment. These pasts are no less real in their contribution to the character and functioning of the city, but their protection in the context of continual cycles of capital reinvestment and urban transformation is often far more problematic.

A number of studies of heritage values in the urban scene undertaken in the 1980s made explicit the hegemonic potential of a heritage impulse—its capacity to express and legitimate the status and power of certain interests. At least some of this work attended to the relationship between heritage and capital (Bommes and Wright 1982; Knox 1987; Hewison 1987; Wright 1985). An exemplary study was Sharon Zukin's account of the revalorisation of redundant loft space in New York's SoHo (Zukin 1986, 1988). Her study was remarkable in its detailed depiction of the way in which the economic revalorisation of urban space and built fabric in this locality worked through and was dependent upon transformations associated with a range of cultural dimensions. In particular, it highlighted the co-dependence between gentrification of the area and the initial use of the historic warehouse 'lofts' by artists and art dealers. Others too (Dear 1986; Harvey 1989; Jager 1986; King 1990; Knox 1987; Mills 1988) began to document the increasing interdependence between heritage values and the more flexible cycles of capital accumulation which characterise late capitalism. Heritage values are now acknowledged as playing a constitutive part of processes of urban transformation such as gentrification, in which older parts of the urban fabric are 'revalorised' both aesthetically and economically.

The research which forms the basis of this chapter has built upon this work and sought to highlight the nexus between capital accumulation and heritage values in city transformation. It also located this notion of a commodified past within the continually renewed and variably manifest power implications of the heritage impulse. The urban environment is not simply a site of capital accumulation, be it flexible or not. Other interests, such as conservationists, seek the preservation of the historic built environment. Others still may seek to protect the local community or a way of life. Each of these interests draws a different history and past from the city. Each seeks to preserve and enhance that past in the context of, and in differing relationships with, the continual cycles of capital reinvestment and urban transformation associated with the city.

Seeing the city as a product of contests and negotiations between differently empowered interests which ascribe to it different meanings, values and intents raises important issues of method. To understand the circulation of meaning in this variably empowered context it is necessary to look beyond the cityscape itself to the discourses and representations associated with it and to their producers or authors (for an example, see Duncan and Duncan 1988). As Knox (1982, p. 294) suggests, it is important not simply to know that the environment is meaningful, but to know who is communicating through the environment, to what audience and to what purposes. Townscapes and urban localities must be seen as part of a discursive communicative realm and research should replace the idea of a 'language *of* the city' with an understanding of the 'language *on* the city' (Choay 1986, p. 173). In undertaking this methodological program it is also necessary to contextualise the discourses thus explored through an attention to history, ethnography, politics and economics. Acknowledgment of the fruitfulness of this emphasis has produced a number of studies which look specifically at contextualised urban discourses such as the views of planners, architects and social visionaries (Bagguley et al. 1990; Jacobs 1996; Knox 1987; Ley 1987; Schorske 1980). This chapter explores the contextualised discourses produced by a selection of interests generated by the proposed redevelopment of the Spitalfields Market site in the inner East End of London.

SPITALFIELDS: PASTS AND PRESENTS

Spitalfields is one of the most deprived areas in London, yet it abuts the eastern edge of the City of London, one of the three main financial centres in the world (see Sassen 1991). It retains a popular reputation as a deprived and, at times, depraved place. It is part of the infamous East End, site of the Jack the Ripper murders and a stronghold of petty criminals (Samuel 1981). It was to the East End and to areas like Spitalfields that many of the Victorian social reformers turned to provide documentation of the appalling conditions of urban life for the labouring poor (Booth 1892). Yet Spitalfields also has other connotations.

In the 1950s and 1960s, when British sociology was recovering the idea and the reality of 'community' in the urban scene, it was to the East End that they looked to confirm the persistence of the close-knit community in the city (Young and Wilmott 1957). In the contemporary popular imagination too, the idea of a persistent, if troubled, community spirit lives on in the television soap opera *East Enders*. Spitalfields' role as a home for successive waves of immigrants who often formed distinctive ethnic enclaves added much to its community reputation. Since the early eighteenth century there has been a succession of immigrant settlers to the East End, beginning with the settlement of the French Huguenots who fled the Edict of Nantes. The Huguenots were followed in the nineteenth century by the Irish and then Polish and Russian Jews. Most recently Spitalfields has become home for Bengalis from the Sylhet district of Bangladesh. One eighteenth-century building in the area has, during its lifetime, served as a church, a Jewish synagogue and a Mosque. Also associated with the community image of Spitalfields is the long-standing market culture. The Wholesale Fruit and Vegetable Market, the focus of redevelopment, was central to the area and had operated from virtually the same site for three centuries. Equally long-standing are the large number of informal street markets. On weekends many of the streets of Spitalfields are given over to the jostle, noise and colour of such markets. This vibrant street life reiterates contemporary perceptions of a surviving urban community (Berman 1982; Jacobs 1964).

Spitalfields (and the East End in general) is equally renowned as a site of radical left politics. The local borough of Tower Hamlets, of which Spitalfields is a part, was a Labour stronghold for decades. It is the East End that provides the grand events of popular socialist resistance in London's history: the battle of Cable Street, the Poplar resistance and the anti-sweating protests (Fishman 1988; Rose 1988). Raphael Samuel, radical historian and founder of History Workshop, moved to the area in the 1960s in search not only of his own Jewish ancestry but also his radical intellectual ancestry.

The Spitalfields thus far described disguises a grander Spitalfields that once was. During the eighteenth century the Huguenot silk weavers brought to the area an economic prosperity and a way of life based not only around industry but also intellectual societies, Royal patronage and a rather elaborate and grand social life. Some of the more influential and prosperous of London families today trace a lineage to the Huguenot weavers of Spitalfields.

Spitalfields is a place and a community of many histories: immigrant, radical, informal trade and respectable Georgian. The Spitalfields of today shares much with the Spitalfields of old. The prime source of employment is still the garment trade that remains confined to overcrowded backstreet workshop spaces. The local population is primarily Bengali, continuing the area's role as a home for racial minorities. The ward of Spitalfields remained, until the late 1980s, a Labour stronghold. The street markets continue to operate with Petticoat and Brick Lane markets now attracting large numbers of foreign tourists. The prosperous Georgian Spitalfields retains a presence through a substantial stock of the original eighteenth-century terrace houses.

The last two decades have also brought a number of significant changes to the area. The first of these changes came in the mid-1970s with the emergence of an active conservation presence that sought to restore the remaining Georgian built fabric. A more recent change has been a shift in local political behaviour. While the ward of Spitalfields remains a stronghold for radical left politics, the Borough of Tower Hamlets of which it is a part has increasingly shifted to the right in party political terms.

The most dramatic change has resulted from the push eastwards of functions previously confined to the 'square mile' of the City of London (Figure 12.1). In 1986 the 'Big Bang' and deregulation expanded and transformed the financial practices of the City. New technology required new types of office space with open plan and large floor/ceiling heights to accommodate cabling. The new financial sector sought out up-market office space with an architectural style that enhanced corporate image. At the end of the 1980s there were over 60 acres of large-scale redevelopment proposed for the Spitalfields area. The Market redevelopment was at the vanguard of this massive speculative push eastwards. Since the early 1980s there were serious efforts to relocate the Spitalfields Wholesale Fruit and Vegetable Market and place on the 10 acre site a 1.5 million square foot development, predominantly for City service sector use (offices and retailing), but with some housing and local amenities.

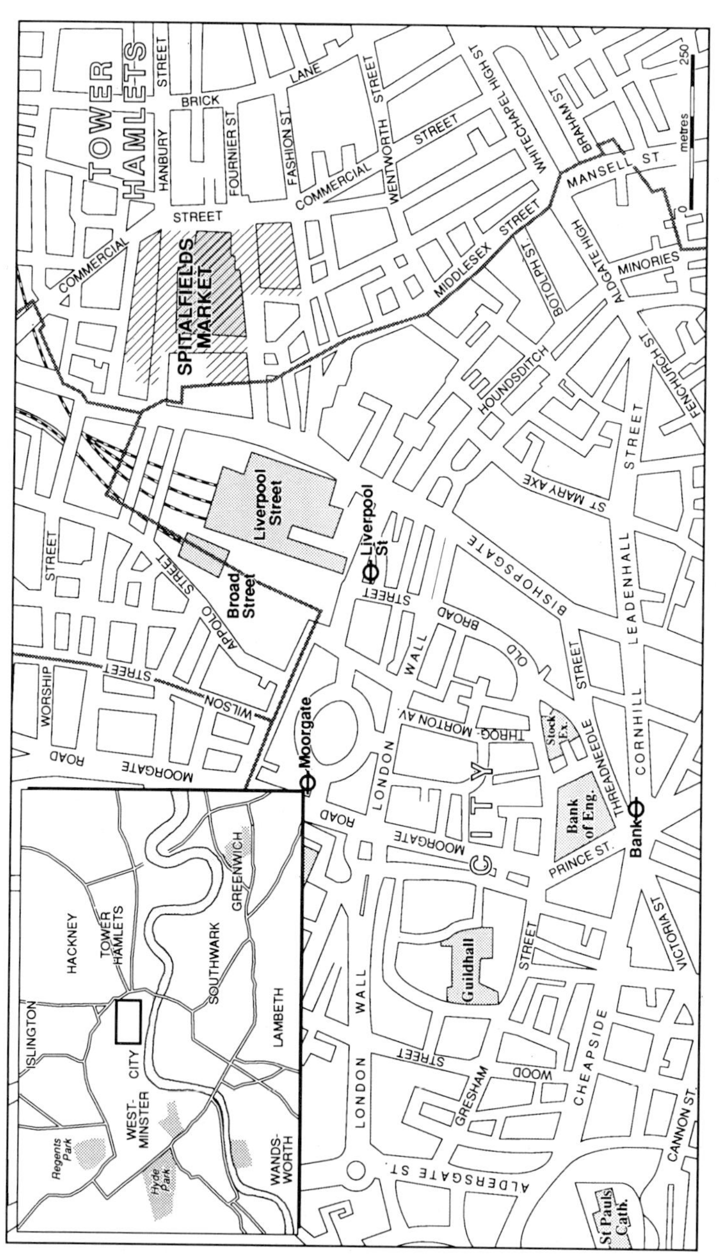

FIGURE 12.1 Spitalfields and surrounds.

The Spitalfields area sees the coming together of a number of deeply contradictory tendencies: a radical left political tradition closely associated with the long-standing racialised working-class population of the area and the persistently poor living conditions; a more recent conservationist push led by professional middle and upper classes; and an even more recent transformation of the area into a prime office redevelopment site. The proposal to relocate the Spitalfields Wholesale Fruit and Vegetable Market and redevelop the site for offices and retailing brought these varying strands of Spitalfields together in open conflict and collusion. In what follows, one small chapter in this now long-running case of urban redevelopment is explored. Attention is given to the discourses produced by three divergent interests involved in the initial debates about the relocation of the Market and the redevelopment of the site: the conservationists, the developers and the local left. The case reveals the pervasiveness of 'heritage' values in urban change, for the conflict in Spitalfields is not so much a conflict between the old and the new but between competing notions of valued pasts.

SPITALFIELDS I: THE CONSERVATIONISTS' PAST

Spitalfields was one of the first areas of London to be developed outside of the confines of the original City boundaries. During the early eighteenth century a substantial enclave of terraces was developed. Their original occupants, the French Huguenots, were weavers and added work-space lofts to many of the houses. These lofts are considered a distinctive architectural feature of the Georgian houses in the area (Figure 12.2). During the post-war years there has been increasing official recognition of the area's historic built form. In the 1950s the Survey of London, the first systematic record of London's historic built fabric, produced a volume on Spitalfields (Survey of London 1957). When official listing procedures were introduced soon after, the majority of the Georgian terraces in Spitalfields were immediately placed on the register. In the late 1960s and early 1970s the local authority designated three Conservation Areas in Spitalfields. The controversial Market site is surrounded by these designated Conservation Areas and the listed Georgian terraces.

Over time the official recognition given to the architectural merit of Spitalfields' historic fabric was transformed into passionate direct action. In the mid-1970s a small group of architects and architectural historians formed the Spitalfields Historic Buildings Trust. When the Survey of London recorded the built fabric of Spitalfields in the 1950s, they recorded 230 eighteenth-century buildings in the area. By 1977, when the Spitalfields Historic Buildings Trust was formed, only 140 remained (*Spitalfields Trust Newsletter* 1978, p. 1).

From the outset the Trust followed a unique course of direct action, unseen in British conservation societies of the time. Their first highly publicised and successful effort in 1977 was to squat in two Georgian houses earmarked for demolition. Such direct action has become a favoured and much publicised Trust strategy but it belies a more systematic effort to ensure

FIGURE 12.2 The gentrified Fournier Street showing the distinctive weaver lofts. Source: author.

the historic housing stock of the area is restored to its former Georgian glory. The Trust became an active agent in the process of transferring the historic housing stock in the area into the hands of sympathetic and strictly vetted buyers who undertook a voluntary obligation to restore the houses in accordance with guidelines laid down by the Trust. The Trust did this either by directly purchasing houses and selling them on to selected buyers or by advertising houses on the market under private estate agents in their Trust newsletter. The Trust newsletters read like an estate agent brochure. As one of the founders noted, the Trust has operated less like a conventional conservation group and more like an 'unofficial inner city development organisation' (Blain 1989, p. 9).

The Trust's project of conserving the built environment of Spitalfields relied upon buyers who were both financially and aesthetically equipped to conform with the Trust's vision of a restored Georgian Spitalfields. The Trust consciously sought to attract the 'right sort of people' to the area. The newsletters are very explicit in informing the readership of who was moving in and their 'credentials' to undertake the task of sympathetic restoration. Thus the Trust were not only active in creating a revalorised urban fabric but also in the creation of a new social and cultural enclave. The Spitalfields case is one of self-conscious, engineered gentrification.

The impact on the area has been dramatic. The revalorisation and restoration of the Georgian housing has created a primarily residential enclave of writers, artists, architects and other professionals, some of whom are quite literally of the British gentry. All of the new community lovingly restore their houses and some even make a living from the neo-Georgian enclave created. One resident offers private dinner parties with eighteenth-century cuisine. Another has transformed his home into an off-beat museum where the more adventurous tourist or Georgian enthusiast can experience the smells, the noises, the conversations and the surrounds of a Huguenot silk weaving family. Each offers a form of commodified heritage for consumption by exclusive niche markets.

The most significant impact has been on the Bengali garment industry. Prior to the conservation interest in the Georgian buildings of Spitalfields, most were in a poor state of repair. They were either so dilapidated they were uninhabitable or they were rented out cheaply as workshop space to the local garment industry. The conservation of the built environment has resulted in the displacement of Bengali users. The restoration efforts of the gentrifiers and the new life those interested in these houses gave to the property market have added to the marked rises in property values in the area. This market trend was consolidated through local authority conservation policy which introduced a specific-use policy for buildings within the designated Conservation Areas. From the late 1970s onwards there was a systematic rejection of all light industrial use applications, while 'traditional' and 'more sympathetic' residential use was encouraged. The Spitalfields Trust was highly influential in ensuring such stringent local conservation policy was followed. It actively lobbied local planners to ensure all activities in the area abided by national conservation laws. It also advocated a number of local initiatives to enhance the Conservation Areas surrounding the Market, such as the reinstatement of street cobbles and the addition of 'period' street fixtures.

The conscious restoration of a material and a social world around the Georgian aesthetic placed the Trust in conflict with the Spitalfields Wholesale Fruit and Vegetable Market. Initially the Trust saw the Market as part of the 'local colour' of the Spitalfields area. However, as the Trust's Georgian Spitalfields became increasingly fixed in the built and social fabric—as more houses were restored, more streets cobbled, more (Victorian) lampposts installed, more property interests accumulated—its tolerance of the Market as a source of 'local colour' diminished. Extensions made to the Market site this century have been responsible for the loss of some of the original Georgian housing stock. The traffic, congestion, noise and litter problems associated with the increasingly modern trading practices of the Market have become a concern for the Trust, as they are seen to damage and deface the increasingly restored residential enclave. The Trust repeatedly tried to buffer the surrounding Conservation Areas from the activities of the Market by building walls, planting trees and purchasing buildings on the borders of the Market. When the proposal to relocate the Market and redevelop the site for offices and retail use were first mooted in 1986 the Trust responded thus:

> ... [d]espite its long history and its colour and picturesqueness, the residents and the Trust will happily wave it goodbye provided it is replaced by something the design of which is worthy of this important and historic site (*Spitalfields Trust Newsletter* 1986, p. 2).

The removal of the Market and the redevelopment of the site was seen as providing not a threat but an opportunity for the further enhancement of the Georgian environment so treasured by the conservationists. The opportunity to see a particular historical vision of Spitalfields re-invented through the Market redevelopment opened the way for a relationship of cooperation between the conservationists and the developers. The redevelopment came to be seen as an opportunity in the Trust's ongoing efforts to transform Spitalfields into a restored monument to early Georgian London and to rid the area of a local feature which was seen as increasingly incongruent with this vision.

In part, Trust negotiations with the developers centred around assisting with the restoration of the existing Georgian fabric. The Trust asked that the developers provide funds for the ongoing restoration of Hawksmoor's Christ Church, the only grand-scale Georgian building amongst the otherwise diminutive domestic architecture of the area. The Trust also asked that any new scheme for the Market site reinstate Spital Square, which had had its northern edge demolished during an earlier phase of Market expansion. However, as will be shown in the following section, a considerable amount of Trust attention was given over to influencing the style of the proposed redevelopment. So fixed were the conservationists on recreating Georgian Spitalfields that they were willing to see other 'contradictory' elements of the area's past, such as the Market, eradicated. They were willing to cooperate and trade with the developer in the pursuit of their Georgian vision. The full extent of this cooperation is only clear when the developers' views and their treatment of Spitalfields 'heritage' is fully explored.

SPITALFIELDS II: THE DEVELOPER'S PAST

The developers who initially contended for the Market redevelopment contract were more than willing to respond to the requests made by the Spitalfields Historic Buildings Trust. They readily incorporated the ambitions and aesthetics of the conservationists in the area in pursuit of their own vision of transforming the Market site into an extension of the City of London. There were two main contenders for the Market redevelopment: Rosehaugh Stanhope and the Spitalfields Development Group. Each had as their base objective the transformation of the Market site, on the edge of the financial core of the City, into a commercial and retail centre which would offer high returns. Yet the architectural and urban design language in which this process of capital accumulation was encased were highly sensitive to the conservation status of the local area. Faced both with a local authority predisposed to protecting the Georgian architecture of the area and encouraging its transfer to residential use, as well as an influential and vocal conservation interest, the developers were only too aware of the importance of addressing this aspect of the heritage of Spitalfields in their quest for planning approval. Both developers tendering for the site consciously drew upon Spitalfields' history, but it was not just any aspect of the multivariate and at times contradictory

Spitalfields of old. The developers addressed that part of the Spitalfields' past which was already empowered by the conservationist lobby, already functioning in terms of the economic revalorisation of Spitalfields, and already legitimated by local and central state planning policy.

For example, Rosehaugh Stanhope actively sought a design team which addressed the conservation status of the area, and specifically the aspirations of the active and influential local conservation interests. One of the first actions undertaken by Rosehaugh Stanhope was to seek the advice of the Spitalfields Trust and the Spitalfields-based Georgian Group on the architects they should appoint. The conservationists provided a list of architects who worked exclusively in a neo-Georgian, neo-classical style. The developers followed the advice of the conservationists and retained architects who would produce designs 'in the genuine Georgian vernacular'. The collection of architects were to 'ensure the creation of a new architecture, totally in sympathy with the surrounding Conservation Areas' (Rosehaugh Stanhope, press release, 7 August 1986). The final Master Plan was produced by Quinlan Terry in a bold and uncompromising classical style (Figure 12.3). The Quinlan Terry scheme imposed on the Market site a rigidly formal and at times grand street pattern, including wide streets and large spacious squares. The scheme instated this Georgian recreation at the cost of a group of Grade II Victorian buildings on the eastern edge of the existing Market. These were to be demolished in the proposed scheme to make way for the creation of a street which would open out a grand vista of the baroque centrepiece of the area, Hawksmoor's Christ Church.

In its selection of architects, Rosehaugh Stanhope had clearly attempted to

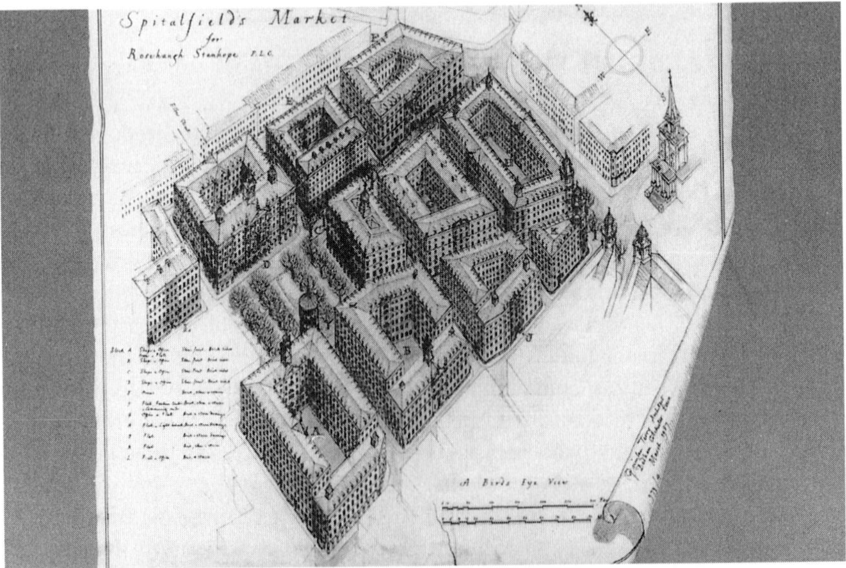

FIGURE 12.3 The grand neo-Classical scheme of Quinlan Terry.
Source: 'Spitalfields Redevelopment Scheme 1987', from Jencks, C. 1988, *The Prince, The Architects and New Wave Monarchy*, Academy Editions, London.

address the Georgian aesthetic so promoted by the Spitalfields Trust and which had been consolidated and supported by the planning policies of the heritage-minded local authority. Ironically, while the local authority was prepared to grant provisional planning approval, the conservationists were less enthusiastic about the results. The Trust felt the scheme was too grand and it disapproved of the proposed demolition of the listed Victorian buildings, despite this facilitating a new vista of Hawksmoor's Christ Church. The Rosehaugh Stanhope scheme failed in the eyes of the conservationists not because of its disregard for the Georgian aesthetic but its too formal and too grand appropriation of it.

The successful contender at this stage of the Market redevelopment was the Spitalfields Development Group (SDG). SDG also attempted to provide a development scheme that was sympathetic to the surrounding Conservation Areas, fully aware that this would help ensure planning permission. To this end it initially commissioned a design from an architect who was both a founding member of the Spitalfields Historic Buildings Trust and a resident of one of the Trust's 'rescued' buildings. Richard MacCormac's design style explicitly worked with local motifs and idioms derived from historical forms and patterns. The architect was familiar with conservation and conversion work as well as new building, and had long expressed his own vision for the area. The vision had no loyalty to the Spitalfields Market and viewed relocation of the Market and redevelopment of the site as an important step in the reconstitution and revitalisation of the area.

The MacCormac scheme (Figure 12.4) was more diverse in design and

FIGURE 12.4 The Richard MacCormac scheme.
Source: Drawn by Richard MacCormac of MacCormac, Jamison & Prichard, for the Spitalfields Development Group.

conception than the grand Georgian recreation proposed by Rosehaugh Stanhope. It provided a series of 'architectural conversations' between the different buildings on the site and the surrounding townscape. In plan, the scheme paid much attention to recreating a fine-grained block and street pattern which was compatible with that of the surrounding Conservation Areas. It reinstated the controversial north side of Spital Square and provided for additional small-scale squares and open spaces. The architectural style drew upon local architectural idioms but 'teased' with them, creating new architectural forms. The Grade II listed buildings on the Market site were incorporated into the scheme.

It was not only in design that SDG consciously adopted the conservation aesthetic. As part of a community gain package SDG earmarked funds for the restoration of Christ Church. The promotion of the scheme was also strongly influenced by historical references. The logo of SDG was based on the friendly domestic form of the nineteenth-century listed buildings on the site. Their pitched roofs and chimney stacks provided a logo with an almost village quality which disguised the massive scale of the development planned behind the facade (Figure 12.5). A special promotional booklet entitled *Spitalfields: A Continuing Story*, adorned with the village logo and soft focus photographs, presented the scheme as the most recent chapter in the ongoing history. The text implied that the new development would slip into the Spitalfields area almost unnoticed:

> ... the people of Spitalfields will still be doing much the same things as before. Spitalfields will be somewhere to live, relax, be entertained and shop; a place for people to work and prosper. All traditional pursuits, watched over by the weavers' houses, medieval precincts and Dickensian alleys and, above all, Hawksmoor's Christ Church (SDG 1986, p. 12).

Thus, in rhetoric and action, development interests were quick to appropriate the conservation agenda—and the Georgian Spitalfields it celebrated—into the design and promotion of their schemes. Such a strategy was essential to legitimate the development in the eyes of the influential conservationists and the conservation-minded local authority. Although the Trust had some reservations about the MacCormac design (in particular about its height and bulk), they did publicly endorse the scheme, which was granted planning permission.

Critical to the cooperation between the developers and the conservationists was the potential of the conservation agenda and aesthetic to serve the interests of capital. It worked to provide an acceptable facade (both architectural and rhetorical) to a large-scale redevelopment which was anything but compatible with the historical character of the area and which could only proceed at the cost of relocating the Market operations. It was one aspect of Spitalfields' history which could be appropriated without seriously jeopardising or compromising the development agenda. Furthermore, cooperation was possible because the developers were willing and able to speak in a language familiar to the conservationists: the language of architecture, urban design and townscape.

FIGURE 12.5 The quaint facade of development does not go untouched by local protest.
Source: author.

Other interests in Spitalfields found the development, regardless of its architectural form, deeply contradictory to their vision of the area and the local pasts that they valued. These alternative interests did not express their views in the language of architecture, aesthetics and urban design, but brought to the planning controversy a different Spitalfields' history, expressed in a different language. This was a past more deeply challenging to and less easily incorporated into the processes of capital reinvestment which generated the Market redevelopment proposal.

SPITALFIELDS III: THE LEFT'S PAST

The proposals to relocate the Market and redevelop the site for office and retail use was opposed by the local left, working under the title 'The Campaign to Save Spitalfields from the Developers' (see Figure 12.5). The active membership of the campaign was essentially white local left activists and a handful of Bengali people living in the area and active in local left politics. The campaign was not concerned with the Georgian architecture of the area. Indeed, in other forums its participating members had consistently opposed the gentrification occurring at the hands of conservationists. The campaign did not see the redevelopment as providing opportunities for the area but as an expansion of City interests into the East End. The campaign sought to protect the local community against this 'invasion'. The historic Spitalfields evoked in the rhetoric of the campaign was ascribed an innately radical, working-class character. From their point of view Spitalfields was a 'natural' counter to the forces of capitalism as represented by the proposed office redevelopment and the conservation-minded gentrifiers alike. The campaigners were protecting an 'indigenous' local community, the type of which was seen to hold the key to socialist reform in the city. As such, their opposition to the Market redevelopment was as deeply invested in a romanticised idea of the locality as was the historicism of the conservation movement.

It was through the evidence of Raphael Samuel, socialist historian and local resident, that the special character of the Spitalfields community was most clearly elaborated. Samuel and the campaign were united in seeing Spitalfields as:

> ... that unique and historic area ... a community of working class and industrious people: a multi-ethnic community ... a historic place which for over three centuries has harboured both refugees and immigrants ... that has given the area a distinctive working character (CSSD, Briefing for Labour MPs May 1988).

In Samuel's often romantic evocations, Spitalfields is represented as being almost untouched by the forces of modern life. The Spitalfields he found in 1962 when he moved to the area was decidedly rustic in its social and cultural practices. There were one-room pubs which sold only beer, grocers still sold kindling and coal for fires and there were two functioning dairies (Samuel 1989, pp. 138–39).

The past evoked by the campaign centred around Spitalfields as a village-like working and trading community. The garment industry, which has been the prime economic base of Spitalfields since the Huguenots, in many ways defies the image of modern industry. Most businesses are still small-scale and many run on a family basis. People still walk to work in Spitalfields. The campaigners did not deny the poor conditions suffered by many of those employed in the garment industry. However, they did laud the informal, anti-modern feel of the garment industry and were pleased with its recent revival at the hands of the Bengali community. In this sense, the campaign's case for protecting the garment industry also became, somewhat paternalistically, a case for the protection of the most recent immigrant population of the area.

The campaign also tied the working character of Spitalfields to the tradition of marketing in the area, both the Wholesale Market and the street markets. In a protest statement the campaign described Spitalfields as having 'perhaps the best open air market in the world' (House of Commons 1987). As an arena of private enterprise, marketing does not fit so readily into the traditional concerns of the left. But the market tradition of Spitalfields was depicted by the campaign as small-scale, colourful, informal and at times vaguely criminal. It is depicted as a site of anarchic and subversive opportunity and initiative, the 'natural home of the working class' shopper (Campaign protest exhibition, Bishopsgate Institute 1988). Spitalfields' marketing tradition, as represented by the campaign, was more redolent of the village market than the High Street retailing proposed in the redevelopment scheme.

The Spitalfields Wholesale Fruit and Vegetable Market is hardly of this informal, village nature. Its 10 acre site is served by giant lorries bringing produce from around the world. Yet this larger-scale version of the market enterprise was given its own intrinsic charm by the campaign and depicted as reiterating (in function, if not in form or scale) the broader market character of the area. The campaign stressed that until the 1960s the practices of the Wholesale Market were decidedly 'pre-industrial': fetching was done by barrow or pony and cart and loads of produce were carried on the head (Samuel 1989, pp. 135–36).

Thus the left valued a past which was a complex intersection of industry, local ethnic character and trade—a way of life, as opposed to a built form; a living history as opposed to a conserved history. The traditional socialist Spitalfields is not captured in the built environment but in the people and practices of the area. The Wholesale Market was depicted by the campaign as crucial to the retention of both the garment industry and the more informal street market tradition. These differing local functions were seen as being in 'harmony' and having an 'elective affinity' in which one worked to protect and sustain the other. More importantly, the Wholesale Market kept more antagonistic or less tolerant land uses at bay. Its continued presence on the existing site was seen as essential to the maintenance of the industrial/trading base of Spitalfields, that is, the working-class Spitalfields.

For the campaigners, the Market battle reiterated the traditional battle of socialism. The campaign enemy was not the wrong architectural aesthetic, but capitalism itself. The enemy was seen as 'big money' and its local expression through the Market redevelopment proposal. More potently, in this particular struggle capitalism was manifest through the forces of a grand national symbol of capital, an expansion of the City of London in its capacity as financial heartland of Britain. It was feared that Spitalfields would be transformed under the 'enemy' into the home of 'millionaire corporations' and 'international banking'. The unique, organic community would become 'just one more line on the computer screen linking Wall Street and Tokyo' (*Spitalfields Defender* 1987).

The local left which formed the basis of the campaign against the Market redevelopment imagined a past Spitalfields clearly different to that treasured by the Trust and later appropriated by the developers. They spoke of this past in an entirely different language. The conservation Trust's ideology was one of reverence for a past expressed primarily in architectural and urban design terms. The left shared a reverence for the historical character of Spitalfields, but it was a different past which it revered, represented in the present through people and practices as much as buildings. The campaign's loyalty to an idea of the Spitalfields community which was deeply contradictory to the development agenda worked ultimately to its disadvantage. Views about the protection of the social and economic fabric of the community had to compete against a more widely legitimised discourse of urban change which drew on the language and logic of historicist architectural aesthetics and urban design.

CONCLUSION

The examination of the cases for and against this stage of the Spitalfields redevelopment reveals that while the conservationists and the developer ultimately had different agendas, they shared a common desire to see the Spitalfields area rid of the Market. The developers were in pursuit of a centrally located office development which could provide enormous returns. The conservationists were in pursuit of a vision to recreate a Georgian enclave. The shared desire to relocate the Spitalfields Fruit and Vegetable Market provided the basis for cooperation and collusion between the traditional 'enemies' of developer and conservationist. The collusion was further consolidated by their use of a shared language of architecture and urban design.

Opposition to the Spitalfields Market redevelopment came from the local left who lauded and guarded a radical and racialised working-class Spitalfields. This group were marginalised in their opposition because their interests were deeply contradictory to those of the developers. They opposed the redevelopment outright and sought to keep the Market on its present site. Their arguments in defence of the Market were couched within the language of community rather than architecture and urban design. The opposition group in the Spitalfields case was concerned not with the preservation of historic buildings but with the preservation and protection of a particular social and cultural character in the area which was essentially radical and oppositional to the processes of capital.

The preceding examples of conflict and cooperation associated with this specific phase in the prolonged Spitalfields Market redevelopment reveal how heritage tendencies are variable. Different interests hold different pasts to be of value and at times these pasts are deeply contradictory. Further, these pasts have differing degrees of legitimacy depending on the power and interests of those who promote or revere them and on the extent to which they contradict processes of capital accumulation.

The Spitalfields case also demonstrates that heritage is not always the sole possession of those opposing development and change in the city. It can equally act as the agent of change. The conservation efforts of the Spitalfields Trust brought changes to the area in the form of gentrification well before large-scale development arrived. It forced out garment workshops in the revalorised areas and changed the social, economic and cultural character of the population. The developers were able to appropriate and exploit the heritage values asserted by the influential conservationists to legitimate and facilitate even more wide-reaching and dramatic change in the form of a large-scale commercial redevelopment. The Spitalfields example shows how interests which speak in an overt and conscious rhetoric of conservation and heritage can actually pose a threat to alternative, challenging and resistant pasts.

The Spitalfields Market controversy was in part a conflict of differently empowered pasts and discourses about those pasts. In British planning at that time, those aspects of the past which were embodied in the built environment and which were less challenging to redevelopment objectives were clearly privileged. Pasts with more deeply oppositional character which were present in forms and practices less readily appropriated into redevelopment objectives were marginalised from the future visions for the city. Such pasts could only be incorporated into urban processes of capital reinvestment if bleached of their radical and oppositional character. Increasingly, such 'oppositional' pasts are finding a place in the transforming cities of late capitalism: not as ongoing practices or ways of life, but as sanitised artefacts or contrived memorials for the benefit of tourists and shoppers.

ACKNOWLEDGMENTS

I would like to thank the following: Peter Jackson, Jacqueline Burgess, Kay Anderson, Fay Gale, the cartographers at University College London and The University of Melbourne, the Spitalfields Trust and Jil Cove and others from the Campaign to Save Spitalfields from the Developer.

REFERENCES

Agnew, J.A., Mercer, J. & Sopher, D.E. 1984, *The City in a Cultural Context*, Allen & Unwin, Boston.

Bagguley, P., Mark-Lawson, J., Shapiro, D., Walby, S. & Warde, A. 1990, *Restructuring: Place, Class and Gender*, Sage Publications, London.

Berman, M. 1982, *All That Is Solid Melts Into Air: The Experience of Modernity*, Verso, London.

Blain, D. 1989, 'A brief and very personal history of the Spitalfields Trust', in *The Saving of Spitalfields*, eds M. Girouard, D. Cruickshank & R. Samuals, Spitalfields Historic Buildings Trust, London, pp. 1–19.

Bommes, M. & Wright, P. 1982, 'Charms of residence: the public and the past', in *Making Histories: Studies in History Writing and Politics*, eds R. Johnson, G. McLennan, B. Schwartz & D. Sutton, Hutchinson, London, pp. 252–302.

Booth, C. 1892, *Life and Labour of the People of London: Volume. 1 East London*, London.

Choay, F. 1986, 'Urbanism and semiology', in *The City and the Sign: An Introduction to Urban Semiotics*, eds M. Gottdeiner and A. Ph. Lagopoulos, Columbia University Press, New York.

Dear, M.J. 1986, 'Postmodernism and Planning', *Environment and Planning D: Society and Space*, vol. 4, pp. 367–84.

Duncan, J.S. & Duncan, N. 1988, '(Re)reading the landscape', *Environment and Planning D: Society and Space*, vol. 6, no. 2, pp. 117–26.

Fishman, W. 1988, *East End 1888*, Duckworth, London.

Ford, L.R. 1979, 'Urban preservation and the geography of the city in the USA', *Progress in Human Geography*, vol. 3, no. 2, pp. 211–38.

Fusch, R. & Ford, L.R. 1983, 'Architecture and the geography of the American city', *The Geographical Review*, vol. 73, no. 3, pp. 324–39.

Harvey, D. 1989, *The Condition of Postmodernity*, Basil Blackwell, London.

Hewison, R. 1987, *The Heritage Industry: Britain in a Climate of Decline*, Methuen, London.

Hobsbawm, E. & Ranger, T. 1983, *The Invention of Tradition*, Cambridge University Press, Cambridge.

Horne, D. 1984, *The Great Museum: The Re-Presentation of History*, Pluto Press, Sydney.

Jacobs, J. 1964, *Death and Life of Great American Cities*, Pelican, London.

Jacobs, J.M. 1994, 'The battle of Bank Junction: the contested iconography of capital', in *Money, Power and Space*, eds S. Corbridge, R. Martin & N. Thrift, Blackwell, Oxford, pp. 356–82.

Jacobs, J.M. 1996, *Edge of Empire: Postcolonialism and the City*, Routledge, London and New York.

Jager, M. 1986, 'Class definition and the aesthetics of gentrification: Victoriana in Melbourne', in *Gentrification of the City*, eds N. Smith & P. Williams, Allen & Unwin, Herts, pp. 78–91.

Jencks, C. 1988, *The Prince, The Architects and New Wave Monarchy*, Academy Editions, London.

King, A. 1990, *Global Cities: Post-Imperialism and the Internationalisation of London*, Routledge, London.

Knox, P.L. 1982, 'The social production of the built environment', *Ekistics*, vol. 49, pp. 291–7.

Knox, P. L. 1987, 'The social production of the built environment: architects, architecture and the post-modern city', *Progress in Human Geography*, vol. 11. no. 3, pp. 354–78.

Ley, D. 1987, 'Styles of the times: liberal and neo-conservative landscapes in inner Vancouver, 1968–1986', *Journal of Historical Geography*, vol. 13, no. 1, pp. 40–56.

Lowenthal, D. 1986, *The Past is a Foreign Country*, Cambridge University Press, Cambridge.

Lumley, T. 1988, *The Museum Time Machine: Putting Cultures on Display*, Comedia, London.

Mills, C.A. 1988, '"Life on the upslope": the postmodern landscape of gentrification', *Environment and Planning D: Society and Space*, vol. 6, no. 2, pp. 169–90.

Relph, E. 1987, *The Modern Urban Landscape*, Croom Helm, London.

Rose, G. 1988, 'Locality, politics and culture: Poplar in the 1920s', *Environment and Planning D: Society and Space*, vol. 6, pp. 151–68.

Samuel, R. 1981, *East End Underworld: Chapters in the Life of Arthur Harding*, Routlege and Kegan Paul, London.

Samuel, R. 1989, 'The pathos of conservation', in *The Saving of Spitalfields*, ed. M. Girouard, Spitalfields Historic Buildings Trust, London.

Sassen, S. 1991, *The Global City: New York, London*, Tokyo, Princeton University Press, Princeton, NJ.

Schorske, C.E. 1980, *Fin-de Siècle Vienna: Politics and Culture*, Alfred A. Knopf, New York.

Survey of London 1957, *Spitalfields and Mile End New Town*, Vol. XXVII, The Althone Press for LCC, London.

Thrift, N. 1989, 'Images of social change', in *The Changing Social Structure*, eds C. Hamnett, L. McDowell & P. Sarre, Sage, London, pp. 272–9.

Urry, J. 1990, *The Tourist Gaze: Leisure and Travel in Contemporary Societies*, Sage, London.

Urry, J. 1995, *Consuming Places*, Routledge, London and New York.

Wright, P. 1985, *On Living In An Old Country*, Verso, London.

Young, M. & Wilmott, P. 1957, *Kinship and Family in East London*, Routledge and Kegan Paul, London.

Zukin, S. 1986, 'Gentrification: culture and capital in the urban core', *Annual Review of Sociology*, vol. 13, pp. 129–47.
Zukin, S. 1988, *Loft Living: Culture and Capital in Urban Change*, Radius, London.
Zukin, S. 1995, *The Cultures of Cities*, Blackwell Publishers, Cambridge, Mass.

Original sources

Spitalfields Trust Newsletters, 1975–1989.
The Spitalfields Defender, campaign broadsheet.
Records, The Campaign to Save Spitalfields From the Developer.
Bishopsgate Exhibition, Text, Letters and Public Statements, 1986–1989.
House of Commons Select Committee Proceedings, Spitalfields Market Bill, 1987.
SDG/Rosehaugh Stanhope *Promotional Material*, 1986–1989.

Constructing geographies

culture and nature

13

A 'green' vision

the evolution of Australian environmentalism

Kevin Frawley

INTRODUCTION

In 1989 the (then) Australian Prime Minister Bob Hawke, responding to political polling which had recorded a dramatic rise in environmental awareness (Lothian 1994; Papadakis 1997), launched a substantial Commonwealth government commitment to environmental protection over the next ten years (Hawke 1989). This first ever comprehensive statement on the environment by an Australian Prime Minister was an indication of how, two hundred years after the European settlement of Australia, environmental matters have become prominent on the national political agenda. By the early 1990s both main political contenders in Australia—the Labor Party and the Liberal-National Party coalition—were attempting to outbid one another on their environmental policies.

The rise of the environmental movement and 'green politics' in Australia, while appearing to be almost entirely the product of the last few decades, has deeper roots that need to be explored from a historical/cultural perspective. The growth of Australian environmentalism can be related to a particular national historical experience and cultural context as well as continuing international influences. It has evolved out of a process of learning about and coming to terms with the environment since the relatively recent European settlement of the ancient Australian continent. Visions and expectations brought by successive waves of immigrants who were faced with establishing new cultural identities in a country of highly unfamiliar environments have also been influential. Very recently, long rejected, ignored or unrecognised Aboriginal conceptions of the land have begun also to permeate the European Australian consciousness. Still-evolving Australian images of environment and sense of place involve, therefore, a blend of Eurocentric images of environment, a distinctive colonial or Australian view, uneasy adaptations to a harsh sprawling landscape, an equally uneasy relationship with an ancient culture which both modified but sustained the land through thousands of years prior to European settlement and continuing international influences both on the environment and environmental ideas. Overseas capital and associated political influence has shaped much of the pastoral, mining, forest and central urban landscape post-1788 (Jeans 1987; Dargavel 1994, 1995).

This chapter first considers some conceptual considerations relevant to environmentalism. It then outlines the history of Australian environmental ideas and the development of a public policy framework related to the environment, with a broad division of legislation into 'protective' and 'exploitative'. Finally, it considers the political struggle between opposing development and conservation paradigms in the recent period (Figure 13.1).

CULTURE AND ENVIRONMENT

The central focus of this chapter is the relationship of the Australian people to their environment. It examines some of the interactions of culture and environment that have, over time, moulded the current Australian landscape as well as a complex set of environmental attitudes, ideas and concepts which influence the interaction with the environment. While this environmental interaction strongly relates to current political, economic and social forces, it has deeper roots which are an inheritance of culture and its traditions.

Abstract ideas about the human relationship to the natural world progressively developed into a body of intellectual thought on the interactions of 'nature' and 'culture', traced for the west by Glacken (1967). Through this history not only have the nature-culture interactions remained problematic, but so have the meanings surrounding the terms themselves. Discourse regarding the natural world is inseparable from cultural constructions of reality. For example, European Australians continue to debate what is meant by the 'natural environment' or 'wilderness' when the continent was occupied by Aboriginal people for as much as 60 000 years prior to European settlement (see Griffiths 1996; Mulvaney 1990). However, it is indisputable that a major discontinuity in landscape change occurred after 1788 as former landscapes, their biota, and, in many areas, the Aboriginal people were obliterated (Taylor 1990, p. 413).

Glacken identified three main questions that humans have persistently asked about the earth and the relationship between nature and culture. One of these, the effects of human action in changing the earth from its hypothetical pristine state, has become central to modern environmental concerns. It has been most strongly articulated since the nineteenth century, when the potential for devastating human effects on the environment could be seen in the combination of a confident rational spirit of resource development and advances in the technological means to achieve this with the products of the Industrial Revolution. The second question concerning the influence of environment on people and culture has had a much longer currency, reaching its peak in the

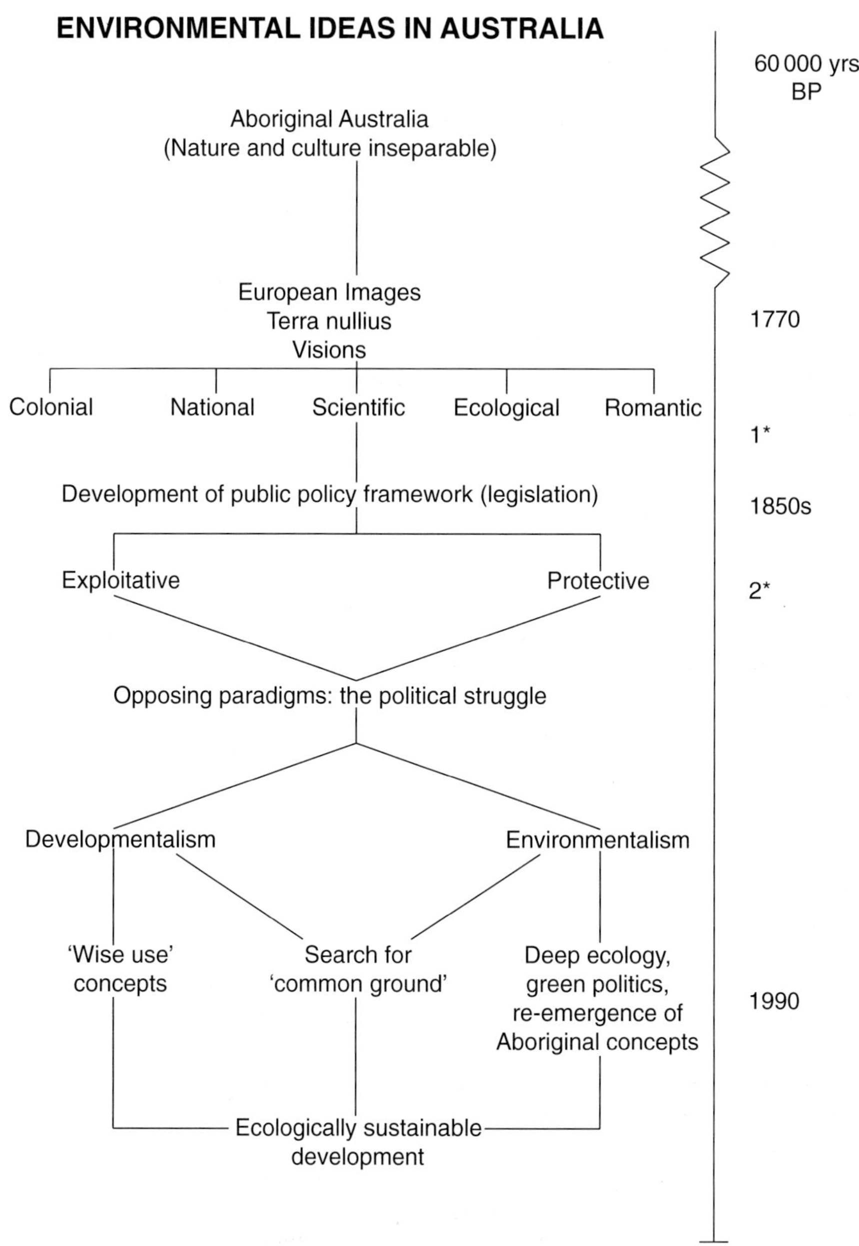

1* See Figure 13.2
2* See Figure 13.4

FIGURE 13.1 Structure of environmental ideas and public policy development, Aboriginal Australia to present.

nineteenth-century view that the environment determined the course of human development. There is a strong element of determinism in the world view of the modern environmental movement which at the global scale sees the limits of human economic activity determined by biophysical parameters (Simmons 1989).

In western intellectual traditions a persistent feature of the human-environmental relationship has been the idea that the human species stands apart from the rest of the animal world and nature in general. Christianity, the dominant western religion, provided the foundation of beliefs in this regard, but there is no single world view. Philosophers have identified three major positions, and the environmental relationships of European Australians can be framed within them at the broadest level (Attfield 1983). They are: the belief that there are no constraints on the way in which humans may treat nature; the concept of stewardship (humans have obligations to care for nature); and the idea that humans can work with nature to perfect it. The latter is relevant to the Anglo-Celtic view in which perfectibility and the rural landscape (blending nature and human design) often appear to be synonymous. This notion is expressed by W.G. Hoskins in his *Making of the English Landscape* (1955) when he describes the 'perfect landscapes' of the English countryside prior to the impacts of large-scale mechanisation.

Perhaps the most important element in the cultural constructions that provide the filter between people and environment in the west has been science, seen as both a body of established knowledge and a method of enquiry into real world phenomena. The empirical method of science has been instrumental in constructing the modern view of the world. There could have been no greater contrast between the world views of the Aborigines and those who settled mainly from Britain in colonial times. The newcomers' leaders were products of the Enlightenment—that period centred on the eighteenth century when earlier religious-based cosmologies were replaced by a view of nature and human society based on scientific principles (Lines 1991; Pepper 1996). In a consideration of modern environmentalism, the role of science is complex—trusted to provide unbiased answers and insights, but treated with suspicion due to its complexity, ambiguity and apparent links to establishment views. Pepper (1996) sees a postmodern mistrust of high science and technology, which Enlightenment thinkers championed, as central to green ideology. The Enlightenment promise to control and manipulate nature to improve everyone's lot has not materialised. Schnaiberg and Gould (1994) deliver a similar message—that better science will not solve our environmental crises. Processes of destruction have actually accelerated while the process of establishing a new environmental science has been under way. In the last decade of the twentieth century there is now enough scientific knowledge of air, land, water, flora and fauna to form the basis for managing the Australian environment sustainably. This end must be determined, however, through the political process. Scientific knowledge can only provide the means.

The foregoing has aimed to show that the relationship between people and their environment is ultimately founded on certain beliefs which may not be explicitly articulated, but are absorbed through a cultural framework which itself is being constantly remade by the outcomes of the relationship. From a philosophical perspective, environmentalism is concerned with bringing moral judgements and questions of moral duty (as in human relationships) to bear on activities traditionally seen as morally neutral (such as rural land management). A consideration of environmental ethics is fundamental to understanding modern environmentalism, at the heart of which is the quest for a change in those ethics. A key aspect of this is the belief that nature, or parts of it, has intrinsic worth, which humans ought to respect (the idea of 'rights') (Nash 1990; Passmore 1980).

ENVIRONMENTALISM

To develop an understanding of modern environmentalism it is necessary to move beyond familiar and simplistic mass media stereotypes of environmentalists. Environmentalism embodies a range of thought and action concerned with the relationship between people and their environment—both the natural and built environment. It is directed in the widest possible sense to the protection and conservation of that environment. On a global scale it has also become increasingly concerned with equity, especially with regard to resource transfers, environmental quality and the ecological sustainability of regional economic systems. It shows a mistrust of modernism—the globalisation of the world into one large commercial, electronic and cultural system with technologies which people are bewildered by and feel powerless to control. Environmentalism is the basis of a social and political movement which advocates a new philosophy of human conduct towards both nature and the cultural artefacts of human civilisation, as well as towards other human beings. Much of the 'green' world view is about society and the 'green' critique focuses on the domineering and exploitative attitudes to nature which remain a feature of most societies (Pepper 1996).

A generalised pattern of environmental ideologies has been presented by O'Riordan (1981, p. 376). One end of the spectrum is characterised by the 'technocentric' mode. Essentially this remains a developmentalist viewpoint, but one in which some consideration is given to the environment. Ideas of material progress, efficiency in managing resources, rational or objective approaches to that management (often relying upon scientific expertise) and faith in human ability to control physical, biological and social processes are hallmarks of the technocentric mode. In western countries, including Australia, governments have begun to move from this position to further accommodate environmental concerns, on the assumption that economic growth and resource exploitation can continue, provided regulatory and public participatory structures are established. The concept of ecologically sustainable development finds its place largely within this 'accommodating' mode. Authors such as Sandbach (1980) and Rowell (1996) argue that this move to accommodation is the limit of pluralist style reform in democratic systems as the agenda for change has been co-opted by dominant political and economic interests. These are able to repel or deflect more radical approaches to change and so maintain the 'treadmill of production' which seduces citizens with the constantly expanding range of material goods it offers (Schnaiberg and Gould 1994).

The opposing end of the spectrum, the 'ecocentric' mode, is based on concern that the earth's life support systems are already overtaxed and threatened. It contains the view that no habitable future is possible without a fundamental change away from the belief in technological mastery of the planet to more humble lifestyles in harmony with ecological processes. It requires some level of ethical consideration and commitment in interactions with the environment. As Singer (1995) has discussed, it implies decision-making which goes beyond self-interest and may involve relative inconvenience or lesser satisfaction, for example, refusing certain consumer goods or respecting the views of indigenous people that certain actions are inappropriate on their traditional lands. The ecocentric view is a radical one, opposed to the dominant values and institutions of industrial society. Perhaps the most fundamental difference is the view of nature, which in the ecocentric mode is held in reverence, considered to have intrinsic value or worth rather than being valued only for serving human ends, and is deemed to command certain moral obligations on the part of humans. One of its most obvious manifestations is the animal rights movement (Singer 1990). Marrying ecocentrism with political theory to chart a practical political path to reform has proven more problematic. In Australia, ecosocialist ideas based on integrating ecological challenges into democratic socialism have sound currency (Eckersley 1992), but are at a considerable distance from current mainstream political thought.

The opposing technocentric and ecocentric modes of environmentalism presented here connect as a continuum. Organisations and individuals within them commonly embrace elements of both the technocentric and the ecocentric modes, invoking contradictions which are not easily resolved or conceptualised.

Modern environmentalism challenges both the ecological relationships and the social organisation that characterise the industrialised, energy-intensive high military-spending economies which have developed over the last one hundred and fifty years, partly as products of the Industrial Revolution. As a differing world view, it has been clearly articulated only from the 1960s and mainly in western countries. However, as Pepper (1996) notes, the type of society which many see as ecologically sustainable, and therefore socially desirable, would be based on ideas and values which may have existed already for a very long time, but now run counter to the prevailing economic ethos and conventional wisdom. Central to this is a questioning of the assumption about societal progress, which simply equates greater well-being with material prosperity.

'READING' THE ENVIRONMENT: AN APPROACH

It is evident from the above that the unravelling of diffuse environmental ideas and their expression in the landscape is not a simple task. We can begin by trying to delineate significant visions of the environment, seeing these as cultural constructions of reality which draw on the long traditions outlined. These are given contemporary sanction by reigning economic and political forces or stand in opposition as competing sets of ideas. The way in which these visions gain ascendancy over one another and become the force behind private and public policy and action in the landscape must be related to power relations in society and its productive basis. Ultimately this contest of ideas and power finds expression in landscape form and meaning, but the landscape always remains contested space embedded with past ideas overlain by newly emerging ones. In attempting to read the landscape (or the environment in general) we find that despite the messages which emanate from it, it still remains obscure as if written in a form of code (Lewis 1979). Landscapes must also be seen as dynamic and transitional in form and meaning, requiring great care in interpretation of the motivations shaping them. This is because differing visions may produce similar landscape consequences; the ascendancy of particular visions may disguise the conflicts that were involved; and there is the great danger of transferring current ideas and concepts out of context and into an analysis of past environmental decisions.

The view taken here is that a people's cultural identity is forged and evolves in part through the interactions with the environment, part of which becomes existential or 'lived in space' (Relph 1976, p. 12). In a circular process, the cultural identity so established contributes to new visions which influence future environmental interactions. An important element of environmental concern is a sense of place developed at different scales. Encompassing a range of emotions, sense of place expresses oneness or connection with environment rather than its externality, and hence availability for capricious manipulation.

HISTORY OF AUSTRALIAN ENVIRONMENTAL IDEAS

Australia, as one of the 'Settler Empires' of the New World, provides a rich source for the study of environmental images and the imprint of European ideas and concepts on the landscape. Modern concern for the environment is all the more significant because of the way it represents a dramatic overturning of previous images in which derogatory views of, or indifference to, the natural environment dominated and public policy was driven by an ideology of development. The central paradox in Australian environmental attitudes relates to the post-1788 peopling of the continent by those whose cultural traditions, aspirations and environmental knowledge derived from a fundamentally different physical environment (Seddon 1976). It was inevitable that it would take generations for a new view to emerge, an affinity with place, but for all that time the European (especially Anglo-Celtic) perceptions were continually reinforced by immigration. This was particularly significant in the case of Australian elites in the churches, schools and universities whose ranks were continually replenished from Britain (Birrell 1987).

Aboriginal Australia

For Aboriginal Australians, nature and culture are inextricably bound together in the Dreaming—the time when the world, including Aboriginal people and their law, was created. Belief systems associated with the Dreaming link specific places with Dreaming events, and give every person, living and dead, a place within a physically and spiritually united world (White and Lampert, 1987). The landscape is not, therefore, a composite of external physical objects, but is made up of culturally defined features of mythical significance (ancestors of the Dreaming).

A most significant European vision of the Australian continent was that of *terra nullius*—a land belonging to no-one (being 'unoccupied' or without recognisable sovereign control). English law persisted with the description of the continent as 'waste and uninhabited' (Reynolds 1987). In 1992 this legal fiction was formally unseated by the High Court of Australia in the famous *Mabo and others vs Queensland* case, which declared that the common law of Australia could accommodate native title. In a situation paralleling some of the gruelling environmental conflicts in Australia, the result largely derived from the heroic tenacity and conviction of one man, Eddie Koiki Mabo, a traditional land owner in the Torres Strait whose lands had been annexed earlier by the State of Queensland.

The dispossession of Aboriginal Australians from their land after an occupation which prehistorians believe could date to 60 000 years was remarkably swift and violent—a violence which continued well into the twentieth century and over which a silence descended. Bernard Smith, in his 1980 Boyer Lecture 'The Spectre of Truganini', suggested that Australian culture is haunted by this dispossession and violence. In the 1990s these matters have surfaced and, particularly through native title, will have implications for a number of aspects of land and broader environmental management in Australia.

Europeans found an Australian landscape which, by their standards, lacked apparent evidence of a human past. There were none of the familiar artefacts of established civilisation, such as buildings and ruins, cultivation or domestication. Aboriginal impacts, by contrast far more subtle, would await detailed scientific unravelling much later. The new settlers did notice the common occurrence of bushfire—observations sharpened perhaps by prior experience of a landscape where such fires were uncommon. The role of fire in Australian biological systems and the practice of Aboriginal burning would eventually become a key question in Australian ecology, and feature prominently in debates over how protected natural areas should be managed (Horton 1982; Pyne 1991; Flannery 1994; Tilau 1996).

European images

Five significant visions or 'ways of seeing' the Australian environment since European settlement have been identified by Heathcote (1972) and provide a useful general schema for simplifying complexity (Figure 13.2). These visions are culturally constructed lenses which have evolved through time, sometimes in combination with one another. Scientific visions, for example, complement both the colonial and the ecological. The image categories intersect three overlapping eras in the evolution of environmental visions: exploitative pioneering; national development and 'wise use' of resources; and modern environmentalism (Figure 13.2). Throughout the three eras the dominant social paradigm has been developmentalist—focused on economic growth and the instrumental evaluation of the environment as 'resources', the exploitation of which formed the basis of economic development policy.

The scientific vision

Within the scientific vision there was initially a spirit of enquiry into the natural phenomena of the continent motivated by intrinsic interest and curiosity. Exploration of the South Pacific inspired much thought on the relations between humans and nature in both science and art (Smith 1960). The period also saw the ascendancy of empiricism in science and rejection of neo-classical representations of nature. Colonial science, as expressed by bodies such as the Royal Society of London, combined the interests of science, capital and the state, asserting a utilitarian aim for science—the domination of nature allied to the national interest (Lines 1991). In the nineteenth century scientific knowledge assisted in resource development but also began to appear in critiques of development, especially pioneering exploitation. By 1900, scientific knowledge and research methods were being applied to natural resource industries such as forestry and agriculture. In the recent period, scientific values have been central to the argument for the preservation of natural ecosystems such as the reservation of national parks for World Heritage Listing (examples are Rainforest Conservation Society of Queensland 1986; Adam 1987). New and positive images of the Australian environment are strongly based on a marriage of scientific discovery in fields such as palaeontology and biology (Archer et al. 1991; DEST 1994) and aesthetic sensibilities. The powerful position of science in our culture has led some to view it as a final arbiter in environmental conflicts. However, these conflicts demonstrate how science cannot be divorced from values, as pro-development 'establishment' science and an 'oppositional' science have stood opposed on some issues, especially forest management (Mercer 1986; Toyne 1994, Ch. 4).

The Romantic vision

The Romantic vision encapsulates the aesthetic responses to the landscape. Initially the vision engendered a sympathetic response to both the Aborigines and to the 'uncivilised' landscape that was apparently unmodified by human activity. This vision owed much to the picturesque movement which formed part of the flowering of Romanticism in the late eighteenth and early nineteenth centuries. The picturesque was closely related to empiricism in science. Nature was to be seen in all its roughness and irregularity, not reconstructed to conform to some classical ideal. The related concept of the 'sublime' brought enthusiasm for vast, chaotic and wild scenery. From about

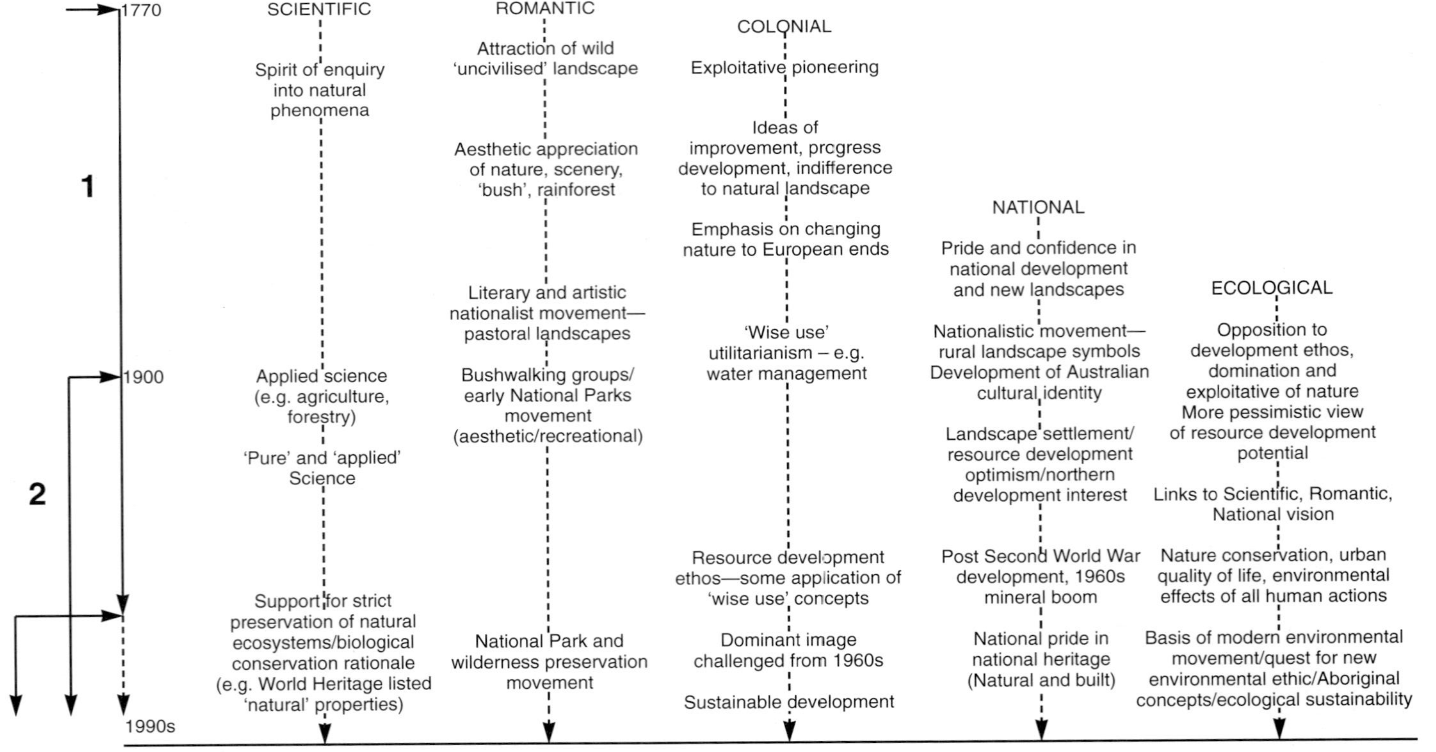

FIGURE 13.2 Images of the Australian environment 1770–1990s.
Source: Adapted from Frawley (1987), image categories from Heathcote (1972).
Eras: 1. Exploitative pioneering: from late 18th century
2. National development and 'wise use' of resources: from 1900
3. Modern environmentalism: from 1960s

1900 the Romantic image motivated the bushwalking/conservation and later national park and wilderness preservation movements. This vision with its mystical and spiritual extensions has become increasingly significant. The exceptional beauty and mystery of particular Australian landscapes and their widespread visual presentation have been instrumental in building conservation concern and the significant public commitment to preserving natural environments. Outstanding examples in recent times have been the photographs and audio-visuals of Olegas Truchanas for the ill-fated campaign to save Lake Pedder in Tasmania (Angus 1975) and later, those of Peter Dombrovkis, including the famous photograph of Rock Island bend on the Franklin River, widely used in the 1983 federal election campaign (Cadzow 1997) (Figure 13.3).

The colonial vision

The colonial vision has been the dominant one throughout Australian history since 1788. Its characteristics are an emphasis on economic development, progress and improvement of nature, as a corollary to which the vision is notable for its indifference to the natural landscape. It most strongly shows the lack of affinity for the native landscape of the immigrant European population who sought to transform it to be more like the landscapes with which they were familiar. Part of the rejection of the native flora and fauna derived from their perceived lack of economic value. This colonial vision was

FIGURE 13.3 Evocative campaigning in the 1983 federal election for protection of the Franklin River in south-west Tasmania.
Source: *Habitat Australia* 15, 5, 1987, p. 8.

also supported from abroad. Much Australian development was ultimately controlled from Britain, serving the needs of Empire and British capital (Jeans 1987; Dargavel 1994). Until recently, generations of young Australians learnt through the education system of the priority of Empire and the uselessness of the bush which—it was taught—needed to be developed and improved.

The three eras shown in Figure 13.2 can be further considered within the colonial vision. The first era was one of unregulated exploitative pioneering which through the nineteenth century increasingly applied the products of the Industrial Revolution to the exploitation of resources. Steam power, for example, in sawmills, shipping and railways revolutionised raw material processing and transport. The second era involved some tempering of this exploitation by the application of the concept of 'wise use' of resources and increasing government intervention in environmental management for both development and conservation purposes and to protect capital investment and sectoral interests. The 'wise use' conservation philosophy focused on rational planning and scientific management of natural resources. In Australia, 'wise use' concepts came to underpin state intervention in resource management only very slowly. For example, land opening for farming continued to the 1960s with little prior economic or environmental analysis. Similarly, forests were cut at a level beyond long-term sustainability into the 1970s (Resource Assessment Commission 1992). Water management projects (especially dam building and river regulation) were one of the most visible examples of 'wise use' of scarce resources—only many decades later would the disastrous ecological effects of this become apparent. In the third era, from the 1960s, the development ethos has been consistently challenged. There are also tensions within the colonial vision amongst resource-based industries competing for limited resources (Mercer 1991, p. 18) and new participants in decision-making in some industry sectors in the form of newly enfranchised native title holders. However, 'wise use concepts' remain highly influential, and a century after their introduction are being written anew under the mantle of 'sustainable development'.

The national vision

The national vision is related to a sense of pride in the achievement of development goals and confidence in Australian potential. It is both nationalistic and expressive of the establishment of a cultural identity. By the latter part of the nineteenth century, financial success in pastoralism, farming and mining brought confidence in and changed attitudes towards the land (Heathcote 1972, p. 91). Integral to the vision was a new optimism and patriotism which would be expressed through the twentieth century in closer settlement schemes, water resource developments and plans for northern Australia. The literary and artistic nationalist movement of the 1890s also affirmed an Australian view of the landscape in which the bush featured prominently. The national vision was tied in with reconstruction plans after both world wars, particular development ideologies such as hydro-industrialisation in Tasmania, large development projects such as the highly symbolic Snowy Mountains Scheme and the mineral boom of the 1960s. However, the vision also began to take an alternative, non-developmentalist form at this time, with growing pride in Australian natural and cultural heritage.

The ecological vision

The ecological vision has enjoyed popular support only since the Second World War and forms the context for the modern environmental movement. However, it is clearly linked to the scientific, Romantic and national visions with their earlier origins. The ecological vision is characterised by its opposition to the development ethos and rejection of the domination and careless exploitation of nature. It has also challenged the original national vision with a more pessimistic view of Australian resource development potential. The ecological vision is now increasingly focused on ways of achieving an ecologically sustainable economy.

Within this 'visions' framework it is essential to stress the profound shift in images of Australia which has occurred over the last three decades and has had a major public policy impact. Two factors have been instrumental in this: scientific discovery related to the natural environment, and enormous advances in archaeology and prehistory with their links to the resurgence of Aboriginal cultural identity. In his book, *The Future Eaters* (1994, p. 16) which discusses both of the above, Flannery suggests that the passing of the (Commonwealth) *Native Title Act 1993* 'brings to a close a period in our history when we possessed a purely European view of the land'. The conservation and land rights campaigns of the last thirty years have been significant in bringing this new knowledge into the public domain.

THE EVOLUTION OF AUSTRALIAN ENVIRONMENTAL THOUGHT AND PUBLIC POLICY: A BRIEF REVIEW

The link between these visions of the environment, their incorporation in public policy and their effects on the landscape can be examined in the progressive accumulation of a large body of State and federal legislation. Conceptually, environmental law is considered to embrace all legislation covering human interaction with the environment. This legislation can be broadly classified as 'protective' or 'exploitative' (Figure 13.4). The 'protective' component is legislation which has the aim of protecting the environment from undue degradation by human activity as well as that which provides for the conservation of natural and cultural resources, and largely dates from the last thirty years (Bates 1992). The 'exploitative' component is legislation for the disposal (sale, lease, granting) of natural resources and for facilitating development activity. In some instances, a specific piece of legislation incorporates both components (AEC 1986).

From earliest European settlement, the Australian landscape has been space contested by different and competing claims. Contemporary environmental conflicts are the most recent expression of a continuum of changing views as to how the environment should be used and managed. These views are cultural

AUSTRALIAN ENVIRONMENTAL LEGISLATION

	PROTECTIVE		EXPLOITATIVE	
	LEGISLATION FOR CONSERVATION OF NATURAL AND CULTURAL HERITAGE	ENVIRONMENTAL PLANNING AND PROTECTION LEGISLATION	RESOURCE LEGISLATION	DEVELOPMENT LEGISLATION
	Extends special protected status/limitations or prohibitions against development/safeguards to protect areas once reserved	Diverse measures for protecting environment from adverse effects of development	Allocating ownership and rights to resources (land, water, minerals, petroleum, fisheries, forests)	Authorises or facilitates development projects often of a large scale; indenture or franchise agreements; fast-track legislation
	EXAMPLES OF LEGISLATION			
Commonwealth	• Australian Heritage Commission Act 1975	• Environmental Protection (Impact of Proposals) Act 1974	• Seas and Submerged Lands Act 1973	• Koongarra Project Area Act 1981
Commonwealth	• World Heritage Properties Conservation Act 1983	• Ozone Protection Act 1989	• River Murray Water Agreement Act 1983	• Snowy Mountains Hydro-Electric Power Act 1949
State	• National Parks (Alpine National Park) Act 1989 (Vic)	• Environmental Planning and Assessment Act 1979 (NSW)	• Forestry Act 1959 (Qld)	• Integrated Resort Development Act 1987 (Qld)
State	• Territory Parks and Wildlife Conservation Act 1976 (NT)	• Pollution of Waters by Oil and Noxious Substances Act 1987 (Tas)	• Mining Act 1978 (WA)	• Roxby Downs (Indenture Ratification) Act 1982 (SA)

FIGURE 13.4 'Protective' and 'exploitative' categorisation of Australian environmental legislation. Source: AEC (1986), Bates (1992).

constructions deriving from both long traditions and particular visions as previously outlined. European conflict with Aborigines over the basic resource of land was the source of the first fundamental conflict. In the nineteenth century we can see the influence of British culture in the deliberate attempts to emulate both the physical form of the closely settled rural landscape and its class structure, dominated by a landed gentry. The contest, in the form of a class struggle between pastoral interests and small farmers (agrarians) is one of the enduring themes of nineteenth-century Australian social history. British cultural influences related to property rights can also be seen in the high value placed on the ability to obtain freehold land and reinforced in the view that no-one owned the land prior to the arrival of the white settlers, as it lacked visible evidence of ownership boundaries and recognised artefacts of civilisation. However, there were also adaptations of ideas to Australian conditions. These solutions to Australian problems contributed to the national vision noted earlier. Given the dryness of the Australian continent, for example, the British-derived common law rights to water were replaced at the turn of the century by State control (Bates 1992, p. 154).

Colonial Australia became part of the new capitalist world economy established between 1750 and the First World War, which was characterised by the spread of railways and empires (Dargavel 1995). Australia became a source of raw materials for industrialising Britain, a market for manufactured goods and a place for profitable investment of surplus capital. Colonial (later State) governments and, after 1901, the federal government facilitated this overseas investment with resource concessions and large-scale infrastructure works.

It is in the second half of the nineteenth century that the first roots of what was to become Australian environmentalism are identifiable. There were two distinct influences. The first was a growing concern about reckless exploitation and waste of resources, in particular the effects of rural settlement and forest clearing. Some of this concern was reinforced by the highly influential book *Man and Nature* by G.P. Marsh (1864) which gained a wide Australian readership. The second aspect related to the affirmation of Australian cultural identity, nationalist sentiment and the attempt to see the landscape through Australian rather than European eyes, evident in the Australian literary and artistic movement of the 1890s (Birrell 1987).

From the 1880s through to the First World War there was the beginning of some systematic critique of the development ethos and pioneering exploitation. A number of new ideas and movements for change in environmental management practices took hold in Australia. For example, significant steps were taken in water management and all States had established forestry administrations by 1920. Also, following the first initiative in 1879, all States accepted the idea of reserving areas of land as National Parks. Inspired by the Romantic vision, there was an expansion of 'protective legislation' for nature conservation and for the establishment of parks and reserves.

Government involvement in resource management between the 1880s and the First World War was subject to two important and distinct overseas influences. The first was the experience in other British Empire colonies. The second was the North American 'wise use' conservation philosophy noted earlier. Wise use concepts were promoted for industrial or development imperatives. Dam construction and river regulation, for example, supported the hope of realising the agrarian dream of a more closely settled rural Australia. In the case of the timber industry, 'wise use' provided a rationale for state intervention to safeguard the large capital investments being made in steam sawmilling. The state could allocate the resource among competing mills, regenerate the forest crop and reserve the forest against competing agricultural claims. The interests of millers were aligned with the public good, expressed as the supply of timber in perpetuity.

These initiatives were not followed, however, by sustained reform of environmental management practices or public agitation for such. Throughout the interwar and post-Second World War period of reconstruction, resource development linked to population growth—in turn related to defence of Australia's 'open spaces'—remained the central national vision. This period saw the beginning of specific 'development legislation' to facilitate large-scale projects, such as the Snowy Mountains Hydro-Electric Power Scheme (Figure 13.5). Nevertheless, there were some questioning voices and even stalwart opponents to the direction of development. Foresters, for example, drew attention to the need to reserve forested areas against the agricultural

FIGURE 13.5 Guthega Dam on the Upper Snowy River, New South Wales. The Snowy Mountains Hydro-Electric Power Scheme was one of Australia's largest post-war development projects and a powerful symbol of the 'wise use' of resources.
Source: *Australian Panorama*, Pictorial Collection, National Library of Australia.

advance. Dam construction brought a concern for catchment protection and, allied with growing concern for soil conservation, resulted in the first soil conservation legislation (Roberts 1989). Such questioning remained largely within the colonial vision but was motivated by concepts of wise use promoted by professionally trained resource managers.

Following the Second World War, Australia entered a period of substantial economic growth, boosted by the immigration programme and national development objectives. However, social and political changes were also afoot which would lay the basis for the modern environmental movement of the last three decades. Australia became a culturally more diverse society, more affluent, better educated, less tied directly to natural resource-based occupations and more open to the international flow of ideas. At the international level a particular unease was beginning to develop by the late 1950s regarding the application of the products of expanding science and technology to the environment. The major shadow was the threat of nuclear holocaust, but another threat was widely publicised in 1962 in Rachel Carson's biting polemic *Silent Spring* which attacked the unwitting destruction of life and habitat by massive pesticide use. In effect, Carson's book was a critique of narrow reductionist science, and triggered the expansion of alternative holistic thinking with regard to the environment.

In considering the social origin of Australia's environmental movement, Birrell (1987) has explored the role of nationalistic sentiment and the development of an Australian cultural identity. Australian nature had to be valued by Australians before they would campaign for its preservation, but for so much of the nation's European history, thought was conditioned by obeisance to all things British and inculcation of the view that Australian nature was worthless. The role of nationalist sentiment in promoting interest in the Australian heritage in the modern period is traced by Birrell to left and reformist nationalist intellectuals of the 1930s and 1940s. After the war this interest expanded, but from the 1960s Australian nationalism was increasingly identified by social critics as aligned with the right of politics, for example, in concern for defending the 'Australian way of life'. Nevertheless, an underlying current of nationalistic feeling that was to some extent separate from other nationalistic expression, but linked to the Romantic image, motivated ideas of a 'national heritage'. This feeling was closely associated with landscape symbols such as the distinctive flora and fauna and the harsh beauty of the inland. Nationalism is now a limited component of the conservation ideology expressed by the major organisations. At the grass roots level, however, identification with and caring for the landscape, flora and fauna as well as the country's cultural heritage is the way that many Australians have found sympathy with conservation goals.

While the immediate post-war period in Australia was largely 'business as usual' from the resource development viewpoint, changes in community attitudes were being expressed through conservation groups which lobbied for improvements in the provisions for nature conservation. By the late 1960s Australia was experiencing a minerals boom. Logging in the overcut forests was continuing to expand into remote country. There were new land development and dam construction schemes. In a short space of time a number of conflicts arose, with mining being prominent.

A major early campaign was against proposed mining and exploration drilling for oil on the Great Barrier Reef. This developed after the Queensland government secretly leased most of the reef area to oil-prospecting companies, some of which named members of the Queensland government as shareholders (Wright 1977; Bowen 1994). The 'Save the Barrier Reef' campaign was the earliest of the modern conservation campaigns in Australia, drawing in newly formed conservation organisations such as the Australian Conservation Foundation. It was to eventually result in Commonwealth involvement through the *Seas and Submerged Lands Act 1973* and in 1975, the formation of the Great Barrier Reef Marine Park Authority. A range of other issues were also being taken up—sand mining on the east coast, limestone quarrying in the Blue Mountains of New South Wales, brigalow woodland protection in Queensland and conservation of the Norfolk Island Territory. In Victoria, opposition to proposed clearing of the Little Desert in the north-western mallee country resulted in abandonment of the scheme in 1970 and a watershed in the uncritical acceptance of development in that State (Powell 1988, pp. 234–45).

This period witnessed the birth of modern environmentalism in Australia related to a wider tide of cultural change in the western world. Some of the movement was allied to critiques of capitalism, protest about Australian and American involvement in Vietnam and a counter-culture which rejected the materialism produced by the post-war economic boom. Most of the organisations (such as the Australian Conservation Foundation and various national parks organisations) were made up of the educated middle class which did not draw its livelihood from the industrial or commercial sectors of the economy. In some instances extraordinary campaigns were mounted by, and for many years remained focused around, particular individuals, as in the case of John Sinclair and Fraser Island (Toyne 1994; Sinclair and Corris 1994). In this period the earlier utilitarian conservation concept of 'wise use' was increasingly seen as deficient, as it allowed the destruction of other values. There was also growing cynicism about whether the professed scientifically-based wise use management of resources was in fact being practised—evidenced by the rundown of productivity in the native forests. Environmental groups, along with other movements for social change, were no longer satisfied to leave resource decisions with the 'experts' or accept passively the outcome of the close relationship between governments and development interests. Instead they demanded public involvement in resource decision-making and were prepared to use direct protest as well as more conventional means to achieve their goals. A growing proportion of the Australian population was employed in the tertiary sector and lived urban lives remote from the bush and primary production such as farming, forestry and mining. Increasingly, the bush became a place for recreation with more distant access made possible by the widespread availability of the motor car. Australians began to question whether all the continent, especially areas of great natural beauty, needed to be sacrificed to the development ideology. Could some not be saved for posterity? The immediate necessity, however, was to place environmentalism on the political agenda and legitimise environmental protection and planning in the Australian political process. This was central to changes in public policy from 1970 when there was substantial expansion of the other 'protective' category of legislation—that which established structures for environmental planning and protection.

In summary, Australian environmentalism has evolved through three main stages. The foundations were laid early this century in the adoption of 'wise use' concepts in resource management and the beginnings of advocacy for nature conservation inspired by the Romantic and scientific visions of the environment. The second stage, dating from the mid-1960s, was one of placing environmental matters on the political agenda so that they would be a continuing concern of government. Part of this involved establishing the legitimacy of the cause. The third stage, reflecting the maturing of the movement, has been one of professionalisation and direct involvement in the political process: attempting to influence votes at election time, standing 'green' candidates for election, and forming 'green' political groupings or parties.

ENVIRONMENTALISM ON THE POLITICAL AGENDA: POST-1970

Viewed in the historical context outlined above, the distinctive feature of the post-1970 period has been the formal involvement of Australian governments with environmental matters. Since the early 1970s, environmental protection and planning have been progressively incorporated into State and Commonwealth government policy-making in the form of both legislation and administrative measures. Environmentalism now forms an opposing social paradigm to the long dominant developmentalist view and is also critical of many of its technocentric and 'wise use' modifications.

Contemporary environmentalism is a complex movement incorporating a great diversity of goals and methods for their achievement. In the Australian context a number of key elements of modern environmental consciousness can be identified. The first is international in coverage, involving a major contrast with the 'core values' of industrial societies which centre around materialism (economic growth), instrumental valuation of the environment (resources), the domination of nature, the globalisation of production and exchange and the promotion of free market economics (Cotgrove and Duff 1980; Schnaiberg and Gould 1994; Pepper 1996). The alternative environmental paradigm focuses on non-material benefits (self-actualisation and quality of life), intrinsic valuation of the environment and harmony with nature. In the 1990s both paradigms have found some common ground in the concept of sustainable development or ecologically sustainable development (ESD) (Meadows et al. 1992; Foster 1997; Krockenberger 1997). The second element relates to the culturally-situated intellectual traditions outlined in the first part of the paper. Environmentalism promotes the environmental impact of society's actions as a key question and stresses deterministically biospherical limits to human action. It also raises the need for a new environmental ethic in which moral judgements are extended to the human-environmental relationship. The third element is the continuation of visions of the Australian environment since European settlement and the re-emergence of Aboriginal conceptions of the land. While the ecological vision is the most significant, modern 'green' consciousness incorporates elements of all the visions earlier outlined, including some acceptance of the 'wise use' concepts of the colonial vision in particular contexts.

The most significant development in Australian environmental thought and practice since 1970 has been the emergence of 'green politics' at all levels of government. The green political movement has grown out of dissatisfaction with existing political philosophies which are either human-centred or see the environment as simply available to be exploited for human ends (Hutton 1987). While traditional class-based conflict has been mainly about the share of the productive cake, which both sides have an interest in expanding, the problems which environmentalists identify are seen as deriving from that ever-expanding cake. A key focus of environmentalism has been a critique of developmentalist ideology and an argument that economic growth should be checked because of its increasing raw material inputs and environmentally degrading and life threatening outputs. However, as unemployment has risen in the 1980s and 1990s due to structural and technological change, while consumer expectations have continued to rise, there has been a backlash (in some instances, well organised) against environmental campaigns which threaten employment (Rowell 1996). This has required environmentalists and government policy-makers to give much more explicit recognition to social and economic impacts, hence the appeal of the concept of ecologically sustainable development.

The rise of Australian environmentalism and its mounting political force since 1970 can be traced through a number of key issues and events. Influential in the early 1970s was a flood of consciousness-raising literature which for the first time in human history took a global perspective on the state of the earth and its capacity to sustain an ever-growing population. In Australia a number of conflicts over proposed or actual exploitation of the natural environment was under way: Cooloola and Fraser Island, Queensland (sand mining); the Great Barrier Reef (mining, oil drilling); Lake Pedder, Tasmania (flooding for hydro-electric power development); the Little Desert, Victoria (agricultural clearing); as well as kangaroo management and whaling (Toyne 1994; Bonyhady 1993; Sinclair and Broadbent 1996). Taking a wider view of Commonwealth constitutional powers under the Australian constitution, the reformist Labor government elected in 1972 legislated in ways which enabled it to become involved in some of these conflicts.

Perhaps the most significant event in the birth of modern Australian environmental politics, however, was the 'Green Ban' movement in Sydney and Melbourne in the early 1970s (Figure 13.6). This linked a range of concerns including quality of life issues, urban politics, class struggle and

FIGURE 13.6 'Green Ban' graffiti on railway pillar, Woolloomooloo, Sydney, portraying some of the prominent protagonists in the conflict. Source: Anton Cermak/John Fairfax Group.

union attempts to take greater control over the labour process (Jakubowicz 1984). The social and political action involved was underlain by a radical critique of capitalism and the bureaucratic state. Though ultimately crushed, the movement was highly significant in demonstrating the usefulness of direct protest action in the democratic political process.

In 1972 the flooding of the aesthetically acclaimed Lake Pedder in Tasmania for hydro-electric power generation marked a turning point for the dominance of the colonial vision. Tasmanian developmentalist ideology and the technocratic arrogance and lack of public accountability of the Hydro-Electric Commission incurred conservationist wrath and hardened resolve that such 'desecration' would not occur again. There was a deep sense of loss and grief which is still expressed. Lake Pedder was the issue which most clearly brought out the sense of national identification with the Australian landscape. It was a symbolic site for a changed Australian environmental consciousness and became a rallying point for later massive campaigns to preserve the rugged western wilderness of Tasmania from development.

In the following years a wide range of issues were pursued by conservation and heritage organisations. Forest management, protection of the Tasmanian wilderness, mining (including uranium mining and export and mining in Antarctica), nature conservation and national parks, urban and regional planning, energy and population issues were prominent (Figgis 1996). By 1980 conservation organisations had a membership of 250 000. There was also considerable legislative activity. Between 1975 and 1982, 102 pieces of environmental legislation were passed (seventy-nine state, twenty-three federal) with about 80 per cent of this being 'protective' (Figure 13.4) (Grinlinton 1990).

The *cause celebre* of the early 1980s was the conflict over the proposed Gordon-below-Franklin dam in south-west Tasmania. While the campaign to protect the Tasmanian wilderness was initially focused on the natural environment, the discovery and documentation of thirty-seven Aboriginal cave shelters dating back 30 000 years and the rich site at Kutikina Cave added a strong cultural heritage dimension to the argument for preserving the area (Toyne 1994). In 1982 the Tasmanian World Heritage Area (Stage 1) was inscribed on the World Heritage List. Anti-dam campaigning prior to the 1983 federal election, which saw the election of the Hawke Labor government, raised campaigning to new heights in Australia and gained widespread public support. Following the election the Commonwealth government, drawing on its external affairs and other constitutional powers, passed the *World Heritage Properties Conservation Act 1983* which provided for the protection of places on the World Heritage List in the form of prohibitions of actions that might damage or destroy the property. When challenged by the State of Tasmania, the validity of the exercise of Commonwealth power was upheld by the High Court of Australia. Ironically, by the 1990s the hydro-industrialisation ideology which had driven Tasmanian public policy for decades was widely discredited and Tasmanian government tourism publicity unashamedly now gives prime focus to the Tasmanian natural environment—including 'rafting the rapids of the mighty Franklin River'.

The other major issue which gained widespread national attention was the future of the remaining rainforest in New South Wales and north Queensland. By the 1980s, rainforests assumed a prominent place in changing aesthetic appraisals of the Australian natural environment and this response was deepened with the popularisation of scientific discoveries. Rainforests became assimilated into emerging holistic and ecological views which stood in opposition to long-standing exploitative attitudes towards the forests. Following protracted political disputes, especially in Queensland where there was Commonwealth-State hostility (Frawley 1991; Toyne 1994), both areas of rainforest were eventually inscribed on the World Heritage List.

In the 1990s environmentalism is established on the political agenda, raised from being a matter of limited or peripheral concern to government by a significant and growing constituency for environmental reform. However, there is little evidence of the widespread shift to an ecocentric culture which authors such as Eckersley (1992) see as crucial to achieving a lasting solution to the ecological crisis. Political parties are willing to embrace reform of environmental policy and take action only to the extent of the perceived constituency for such change. The first national framework of conservation principles was presented in the *National Conservation Strategy for Australia* (1983). However, little action was taken to implement this. By 1990, responding to the rise in community environmental concern in the late 1980s, the Australian government was embracing the concept of '(ecologically) sustainable development' that gained wide publicity with the publication of the report of the World Commission on Environment and Development (Brundtland report) in 1987 (WCED 1987; Beder 1993).

The concept of ecologically sustainable development has appeal to governments trying to chart a course through the often contradictory messages coming from the community. It does provide some common ground for traditional development and newly ascending conservation views. In the early 1990s the Commonwealth government established an ESD working group process which resulted in a number of reports on major resource sectors and preparation of the *National Strategy for Ecologically Sustainable Development* (Commonwealth of Australia 1992). This sets out three key objectives:

- i to enhance individual and community well-being and welfare by following a path of economic development that safeguards the welfare of future generations;
- ii to provide for equity within and between generations (that is, intragenerational and intergenerational equity); and
- iii to protect biological diversity and maintain ecological processes and systems.

The translation of these generalised objectives into policy and action remains a difficult task. Cocks (1992, p. 253) describes sustainable development as 'a goal without guaranteed means' and sees the major failing of the Brundtland report (and the reason many countries endorsed it) as its lack of focus on the key issues of population growth and the inequitable distribution of wealth. Population growth is a key development pressure in Australia, but has proven difficult to establish on the environmental agenda in the form of a national population policy (Cocks 1995).

Sustainability, despite its difficulties, has become the key concept for a pragmatic Australian environmentalism facing diverse social and economic challenges (Yencken 1996). It is the focus of Australia's first national state of the environment report (State of the Environment Advisory Council 1996), underpins the National Landcare Program (Campbell 1994), the Regional Forest Agreement process between the Commonwealth and State governments, and has been incorporated into urban planning where government agencies are developing ESD-based urban planning guidelines (for example, NSW Department of Urban Affairs and Planning 1995).

In summary, the concept of ecologically sustainable development provides some common ground for traditional development and newly ascending conservation views. While the developmentalists, however, appear to see the concept largely as a more sophisticated extension of the pragmatic, managerial 'wise use' principles established through this century, many of the conservationists are sceptical of the ability of government to recognise the fundamental ecological constraints within which, it is believed, economic development must be restructured.

CONCLUSION

This chapter has examined the development of Australian environmentalism from the historical perspective of still evolving culturally-framed understandings of the environment. Within the framework of these western cultural traditions, environmental relationships of Australians from the first European settlement have been traced through three eras: exploitative pioneering, a belief in national development and wise use of resources and, more recently, the growth of modern environmentalism. 'Ways of seeing' the environment through these eras have been discussed using the framework of visions outlined by Heathcote (1972). Complex Aboriginal understandings of the environment were not recognised or were rejected except where they were valuable in establishing the rural economy. Aboriginal concepts have now re-emerged and, particularly through native title, will have implications for future environmental management. Many non-Aboriginal Australians have also begun to develop an affinity with the landscape—to 'think themselves into the country'—and in turn are better able to appreciate Aboriginal environmental knowledge, which is formally recognised in the management of some major national parks.

While modern environmentalism is often considered mainly in its contemporary political and social dimensions, it can only be fully understood by examining its challenge to long traditions in the way nature has been treated in western societies. It brings new ways of seeing to the relationship between people and their environment, which result in conflict as they clash with attitudes and values derivative of longer-standing exploitative traditions. Australian environmentalism has been shown to be linked to international environmental concern and a wave of social change which dates from the 1960s. Viewed historically, there are parallels to other profound social changes in western society such as the rise of the labour movement, the emancipation of women and universal suffrage.

To a greater or lesser degree (stressing again the great diversity of environmental thought), environmentalism presents an alternative, competing, though as yet minority social paradigm to that which dominates in developed western countries such as Australia. Over the last two decades it has formed an oppositional culture to centralised, materialistic, industrial society—creating fragile alliances with other minority and marginalised groups as well as the mainstream left of politics. In Australia, as elsewhere, the movement tends to draw its most politically active members from that well-educated section of the middle class who do not draw their livelihood from the industrial or commercial sectors of the economy.

From the 1960s, the movement in Australia struggled to place environmental matters permanently on the political agenda. The evidence—politically in the form of legislation and administrative procedures, and socially in the form of changed community attitudes and modes of behaviour—suggests that much has been achieved in this regard. Many of the areas strongly contested in the past (such as Fraser Island, the Queensland Wet Tropics and the mountainous west of Tasmania) are now formally protected, even though mass tourism presents new threats. Across the country, States and Territories have built up extensive systems of reserved lands including national parks and similar reserves. Eleven areas are on the World Heritage List, some covering extensive areas, for example, the Queensland Wet Tropics, which occupy 896 500 hectares. The Register of the National Estate contains almost 12 000 places and many more places are on State or Territory heritage registers.

There are, however, serious environmental problems, many of which are growing worse. They include loss of biological diversity; the impact of motor vehicles, stormwater and sewage disposal in the major cities; the poor state of inland waters in southern Australia and soil erosion (and other forms of land degradation) in rural Australia (State of the Environment Advisory Council 1996). Many of these environmental changes and effects (such as bacterial and nutrient contamination of water, gradual loss of species, feral animal and weed invasion and decline in air quality) are not immediately apparent and may reach a serious level before being recognised. This threshold has been reached in many parts of the country and local communities now see degraded ecosystems around them (White 1997). One result has been an upsurge in community involvement of which the Landcare movement is exemplary (Campbell 1994). However, it is difficult to be confident about the future when environmentally damaging schemes such as the recent proposal to extract water from the Paroo River in Queensland, which is part of the highly stressed Murray-Darling Basin, still appear regularly.

After more than two hundred years of European settlement there is still a limited understanding of the Australian environment on the part of many decision-makers and of the difficulty posed by instituting reforms which alienate established political constituencies in the various resource sectors. The political force of environmentalism now enters the debate around these matters, though it will be too late in many instances, for example species extinction through habitat loss or degradation. The path of green politics in Australia will remain highly volatile, being influenced by changing economic, social and political factors as well as continually evolving images of the Australian environment and its place in national cultural identity. These constraints are likely to mean that 'sustainable development' (or 'ecologically sustainable development'), despite its difficulties, will be the key concept for a pragmatic Australian environmentalism into the next millennium.

REFERENCES

Adam, P. 1987, *The New South Wales Rainforests: The Nomination for the World Heritage List,* National Parks & Wildlife Service of NSW, Sydney.

Australian Environment Council 1986, *Guide to Environmental Legislation and Administrative Arrangements in Australia,* 2nd edn, Australian Government Publishing Service, Canberra.

Angus, M. 1975, *The World of Olegas Truchanas,* Olegas Truchanas Publication Committee, Sandy Bay, Tas.

Archer, M., Hand, S.J. & Godthelp, H. 1991, *Riversleigh: The Story of Animals in Ancient Rainforests of Inland Australia,* Reed, Balgowlah.

Attfield, R. 1983, *The Ethics of Environmental Concern,* Blackwell, Oxford.

Bates, G. 1992, *Environmental Law in Australia,* 3rd edn, Butterworths, Sydney.

Beder, S. 1993, *The Nature of Sustainable Development,* Scribe, Newham.

Birrell, R. 1987, 'The social origin of Australia's conservation movement', *Journal of Intercultural Studies,* vol. 8, no. 2, pp. 22–38.

Bonyhady, T. 1993, *Places Worth Keeping: Conservationists, Politics and Law,* Allen & Unwin, Sydney.

Bowen, J. 1994, 'The Great Barrier Reef: towards conservation and management', in *Australian Environmental History: Essays and Cases,* ed. S. Dovers, Oxford University Press, Melbourne, pp. 234–56.

Cadzow, J. 1997 (22 March), 'A lasting image', *Good Weekend: Age Magazine,* pp. 32–9.

Campbell, A. 1994, *Landcare: Communities Shaping the Land and the Future,* Allen & Unwin, Sydney.

Carson, R. 1962, *Silent Spring,* Penguin, Harmondsworth.

Commonwealth of Australia 1992, *National Strategy for Ecologically Sustainable Development,* Australian Government Publishing Service, Canberra.

Cocks, D. 1992, *Use with Care: Managing Australia's Natural Resources in the Twenty First Century,* New South Wales University Press, Sydney.

Cocks, D. 1995, *People Policy: Australia's Population Choices, University of New South Wales Press,* Sydney.

Cotgrove, S. & Duff, A. 1980, 'Environmentalism, middle class radicalism and politics', *Sociological Review,* vol. 28, no. 2, pp. 333–51.

Dargavel, J. 1994, 'Constructing Australia's forests in the image of capital', in *Australian Environmental History: Essays and Cases,* ed. S. Dovers, Oxford University Press, Melbourne, pp. 80–98.

Dargavel, J. 1995, *Fashioning Australia's Forests*, Oxford University Press, Melbourne.

Department of Home Affairs and Environment 1983, *A National Conservation Strategy for Australia*, Australian Government Printing Service, Canberra.

Department of Environment Sport and Territories 1994, *Australia's Biodiversity: An Overview of Selected Significant Components*, Biodiversity Series, Paper No. 2, Department of Environment Sport and Territories, Canberra.

Eckersley, R. 1992, *Environmentalism and Political Theory*, University College London Press, London.

Figgis, P. 1996, 'ACF in the eighties: extending its influence', *Habitat Australia*, vol. 24, no. 6, pp. 15–19.

Flannery, T. 1994, *The Future Eaters*, Reed, Chatswood.

Foster, J. (ed.) 1997, *Valuing Nature: Ethics, Economics and the Environment*, Routledge, London.

Frawley, K. J. 1987, *Exploring Some Australian Images of Environment*, Working Paper 1987/1, Dept of Geography & Oceanography, University College, Australian Defence Force Academy, Canberra.

Frawley, K.J. 1991, 'Queensland rainforest management: frontier attitudes and public policy, *Journal of Rural Studies*, vol. 7, no. 3, pp. 219–39.

Glacken, C.J. 1967, *Traces on the Rhodian Shore*, University of California Press, Berkeley.

Griffiths, T. 1996, *Hunters and Collectors: The Antiquarian Imagination in Australia*, Cambridge University Press, Melbourne.

Grinlinton, D. 1990, 'The "environmental era" and the emergence of "environmental law" in Australia—a survey of environmental legislation and litigation 1967–1987, *Environment and Planning Law Journal*, vol. 7, no. 2, pp. 74–105.

Hawke, R.J.L. 1989, *Our Country Our Future: Statement on the Environment*, Australian Government Publishing Service, Canberra.

Heathcote, R.L. 1972, 'The visions of Australia 1770–1970', in *Australia as Human Setting*, ed. A. Rapoport, Angus & Robertson, Sydney, pp. 77–98.

Horton, D.R. 1982, 'The burning question: Aborigines, fire and Australian ecosystems', *Mankind*, vol. 13, no. 3, pp. 237–51.

Hoskins, W.G. 1955, *The Making of the English Landscape*, Penguin, Harmondsworth.

Hutton, D. 1987, 'What is green politics', in *Green Politics in Australia*, ed. D. Hutton, Angus & Robertson, Sydney, pp. 1–33.

Jakubowicz, A. 1984, 'The green ban movement: urban struggle and class politics', in *Australian Urban Politics: Critical Perspectives*, eds J. Halligan & C. Paris, Longman Cheshire, Melbourne, pp. 149–66.

Jeans, D.N. 1987, 'The incorporation of Australia', in *Australia—A Geography, Vol 2, Space and Society*, 2nd edn, ed. D.N. Jeans, Sydney University Press, Sydney, pp. 1–23.

Krockenberger, M. 1997, 'ACF in the nineties: broadening the issues', *Habitat Australia*, vol. 24, no. 6, pp. 20–5.

Lewis, P.F. 1979, 'Axioms for reading the landscape', in *The Interpretation of Ordinary Landscapes*, ed. D.W. Meinig, Oxford University Press, New York, pp. 11–32.

Lines, W.J. 1991, *Taming the Great South Land: A History of the Conquest of Nature in Australia*, Allen & Unwin, Sydney.

Lothian, J.A. 1994, 'Attitudes of Australians towards the environment: 1975 to 1994', *Australian Journal of Environmental Management*, vol. 1, no. 2, pp. 78–99.

Marsh, G.P. 1864, *Man and Nature: or Physical Geography as Modified by Human Action*, Scribner, Armstrong, New York.

Meadows, D.H., Meadows, D.L. & Randers, J. 1992, *Beyond the Limits*, Earthscan, London.
Mercer, D. 1986, *Institutional and Counter-Institutional Forces in Australian Environmental Decision-Making*, Working Paper No. 21, Department of Geography, Monash University, Melbourne.
Mercer, D. 1991, *A Question of Balance: Natural Resource Conflict Issues in Australia*, Federation Press, Leichhardt.
Mulvaney, D.J. (ed.) 1990, *The Humanities and the Australian Environment*, Occ. Paper No. 11, Australian Academy of the Humanities, Canberra.
Nash, R.F. 1990, *The Rights of Nature: A History of Environmental Ethics*, Primavera Press, Leichhardt.
NSW Department of Urban Affairs & Planning 1995, *Environmental Planning for ESD: Guidelines for Compliance with the Environmental Guidelines for the Summer Olympic Games*, Department of Urban Affairs & Planning, Sydney.
O'Riordan, T. 1981, *Environmentalism*, Pion, London.
Papadakis, E. 1997, 'The environment', in *New Developments in Australian Politics*, eds B. Galligan, I. McAllister & J. Ravenhill, Macmillan, Melbourne, pp. 196–210.
Passmore, J. 1980, *Man's Responsibility for Nature*, 2nd edn, Duckworth, London.
Pepper, D. 1996, *Modern Environmentalism: An Introduction*, Routledge, London.
Powell, J.M. 1988, *An Historical Geography of Modern Australia: The Restive Fringe*, Cambridge University Press, Cambridge.
Pyne, S. 1991, *The Burning Bush: A Fire History of Australia*, Henry Holt, New York.
Rainforest Conservation Society of Queensland 1986, *Tropical Rainforests of North Queensland: Their Conservation Significance*, Australian Government Publishing Service, Canberra.
Relph, E. 1976, *Place and Placelessness*, Pion, London.
Resource Assessment Commission 1992, *Forest and Timber Inquiry: Final Report*, Australian Government Publishing Service, Canberra.
Reynolds, H. 1987, *The Law of the Land*, Penguin, Ringwood.
Roberts, R.W. 1989, *Land Conservation in Australia: A 200 Year Stocktake*, Soil & Water Conservation Association of Australia, Sydney.
Rowell, A. 1996, *Green Backlash: Global Subversion of the Environment Movement*, Routledge, London.
Sandbach, F. 1980, *Environment, Ideology and Policy*, Blackwell, Oxford.
Schnaiberg, A. & Gould, K.A. 1994, *Environment and Society: The Enduring Conflict*, St. Martins, New York.
Seddon, G. 1976, 'The evolution of perceptual attitudes', in *Man and Landscape in Australia: Towards an Ecological Vision*, eds G. Seddon & M. Davis, Australian Government Publishing Service, Canberra, pp. 9–17.
Simmons, I.G. 1989, *Changing the Face of the Earth: Culture, Environment History*, Blackwell, Oxford.
Sinclair, J. & Corris, P. 1994, *Fighting for Fraser Island*, Kerr, Alexandria.
Sinclair, J. & Broadbent, B. 1996, 'ACF in the seventies: coming of age', *Habitat Australia*, vol. 24, no. 6, pp. 8–14.
Singer, P. 1990, *Animal Liberation*, 2nd edn, Cape, London.
Singer, P. 1995, *How are we to Live? Ethics in an Age of Self-interest*, Mandarin, Port Melbourne.
Smith, B. 1960, *European Vision and the South Pacific 1768–1850*, Oxford University Press, London.
State of the Environment Advisory Council (eds) 1996, *Australia: State of the Environment 1996*, CSIRO Publishing, Melbourne.

Taylor, S.G. 1990, 'Naturalness: the concept and its application to Australian ecosystems', in *Australian Ecosystems; 200 Years of Utilisation, Degradation and Reconstruction*, eds D.A. Saunders, A.J.M. Hopkins, R.A. How, Surrey Beatty, Chipping Norton, pp. 411–18.

Tilau, M. 1996, 'Firestick fictions', *Habitat Australia*, vol. 24, no. 4, pp. 12–13.

Toyne, P. 1994, *The Reluctant Nation: Environment, Law and Politics in Australia*, ABC Books, Sydney.

WCED (World Commission on Environment and Development) 1987, *Our Common Future*, Oxford University Press, Oxford.

White, J.P. & Lampert, R. 1987, 'Creation and discovery', in *Australians to 1788*, eds D.J. Mulvaney & J.P. White, Fairfax, Syme and Weldon Associates, Sydney, pp. 3–24.

White, M.E. 1997, *Listen—Our Land is Crying: Australia's Environmental Problems and Solutions*, Kangaroo Press, Kenthurst.

Wright, J. 1977, *The Coral Battleground*, Nelson, Melbourne.

Yencken, D. 1996, 'Looking ahead: ACF in the twenty-first century', *Habitat Australia*, vol. 24, no. 6, pp. 26–9.

14

Claims-making in environmental conflict

a case study of the battle over 'Hollywood-on-Thames'

Jacquelin Burgess

INTRODUCTION

Massive growth in public awareness of the impacts of human activity on the planet's physical and natural systems has occurred over the last fifteen years or so. Reflecting these changes, geographical studies of environment and society relations have been greatly enriched by the contributions of sociologists, anthropologists, philosophers and political scientists. Among significant theoretical insights to emerge from these multi-disciplinary approaches, 'social constructionism' is particularly valuable (Bird 1987; Redclift and Benton 1994). Rather than working from the belief that objective reality exists, waiting to be faithfully recorded by science or media, social constructionism asserts that different 'realities' are constructed through discourses which embody the ideas, beliefs, languages, power relations, and institutional practices of different social groups.

Sociological studies have concentrated primarily on the production and representation of environmental claims in the mass media. There has been little research addressed to questions of how different audiences make sense of the different rhetorical appeals addressed to them. Here, cultural geography has much to contribute, being concerned with understanding the full 'circuit' through which meanings are produced, circulated, consumed and (re)produced (Burgess 1990). Through an ethnographic study of a battle to build a movie theme park on a nature conservation site, this chapter attempts to explore the production of opposing economic and scientific claims, how they circulated in national and local media and how local people evaluated and appraised these competing claims in the contexts of their everyday lives.

ENVIRONMENTAL CLAIMS-MAKING

Geographers have found it helpful to conceptualise the conflicts between social constructions of nature as a form of cultural politics, as different groups representing sectional interests struggle over the meanings, values and uses of plants, animals and landscapes threatened by development (Whatmore and Boucher 1993; Harrison and Burgess 1994). The crucial point is that such groups are differentially empowered, depending, for example, on whether or not they have access to political elites or whether they are able to draw upon finance or other forms of institutional capital to support their proposals. For geographers, the specific places within which conflicts arise also matter and play a material role in their interpretations.

Sociologists discuss similar issues in terms of the social constructions of different claims (Hilgartner and Bosk 1988; Cracknell 1993; Hannigan 1995). Environmental claims are the discursive statements made by social groups/ interests which seek to persuade others of the veracity and legitimacy of the claim (and its sponsors), and to stimulate actions of some kind. Influential social movements succeed, within the terms of this argument, because they are able to mobilise institutional and popular discourses in such a way that their preferred meanings, values and actions become accepted as the right way to proceed. Redclift and Benton (1994) identify one of the fundamental processes by which environmental knowledge is acquired and environmental policy progressed as the 'differential "take up" of scientific knowledge claims.' They go on to ask 'what are the processes of communication, discursive "processing", normative orientation, moral entrepreneurship by which these public antagonisms get formed and transformed?' (1994, p. 9). This question is fundamental to analysis of the public understanding of environmental issues and cannot be answered fully here (see Irwin 1995). It is possible, however, to explore some aspects of the process by focusing on the ways in which the mass media are implicated—both as channels of communication and as active players, framing and shaping environmental meanings (Lowe and Morrison 1984; Burgess 1990; Hansen 1991; Mazur and Lee 1993).

Environmental events do not map easily within traditional news values and representational practices. Apart from spectacular natural disasters like earthquakes or hurricanes, environmental changes are complex, long-term and slow-acting. In recognition of this fact, an increasing number of authors (Schoenfeld et al. 1979; Yearley 1991; Hannigan 1995; Anderson 1997) have argued that the environment has been constructed as a social problem through the claims-making activities of a variety of institutions and agencies. As Hansen argues 'rather than focusing on the time scales of individual environmental problems in relation to a conventional notion of news value, it is necessary to focus on claims-making activity in relation to environmental issues' (Hansen 1991, p. 449). Claims-makers seek to persuade others, whether institutions or members of the public, of the veracity of their position and to encourage a particular course of action. Claims-making thus encompasses the tactics of organisations seeking coverage, the definition and launch of campaigns, staged events and other media management strategies (Greenberg 1985; Anderson 1991) which have been the mainstay of environmental protest groups for many years.

In focusing on claims, therefore, three questions which address the political and discursive processes of claims-making are important. First, who are the claims-makers and what are their objectives: are they official organisations, oppositional groups, commercial interests, or self-seeking individuals? Second, what is the rhetorical content of the claim—how the case is made in terms of the nature of evidence? What are the justifications given to support the case and what are the conclusions drawn about what actions need to be done? Third, how effective are the claims in persuading others of the veracity of the case, and the trustworthiness of the claim-maker—to what extent can particular courses of action be described as an outcome of the claim? (Best 1987; see also Myerson and Rydin 1996). The rhetorical processes of environmental claims-making are revealed particularly clearly in instances of conflict where the lines between different interests are sharply delineated.

The processes of determining plans for development projects are a particular form of claims-making in which different media play a central role. From initial sketches and physical models through to articles and debates in the mass media, proposals about alternative futures for a site involve different claims which need to be evaluated. In the critical pre-construction phase of any large commercial development, the idea or concept of the project is literally that—an idea, an imagining. Nothing tangible exists on the ground. At that stage, people are dealing exclusively with images and representations, and with projections of economic, social and environmental impacts. Battles are won and lost; planning permissions granted or denied; millions of pounds committed or withdrawn on the basis of rhetoric—images of the future which are to be weighed and tested against current realities—and the perceived trustworthiness of the claimants.

HOLLYWOOD-ON-THAMES?

For many years Universal Studios, owned by the Music Corporation of America (MCA) has invited tourists into its studios in Hollywood and Orlando, Florida to see how films are made and to participate in what the company calls 'themed attractions'. These are technologically sophisticated rides which replicate key scenes from some of Universal Studios' most famous movies such as *Jaws*, *ET*, *Raiders of the Lost Ark* and *King Kong*. In late 1988 MCA began to search the world for two locations—one in Europe, the other in Japan—to replicate their leisure concept. The choice of European location was quickly reduced to two options: arable fields to the south-west of Paris, France, and grazing marshes on the eastern edge of London, UK.

MCA chose a location some 24 km (15 miles) east of the centre of London (Figure 14.1). The site comprised some 650 hectares (1600 acres) of low-lying pastureland on the north bank of the River Thames. This green space was

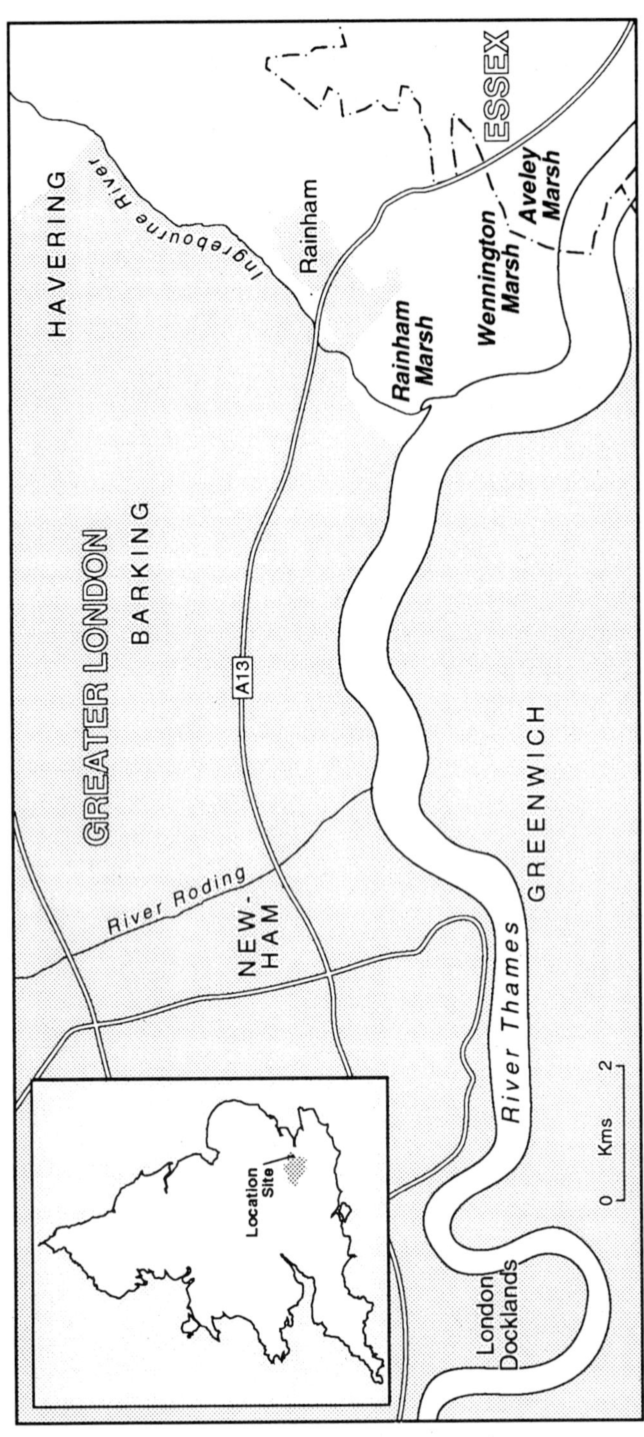

FIGURE 14.1 Location of Rainham and the site of the proposed MCA development.

sandwiched between the huge Ford motor car factory at Dagenham and the industrial/shipping activities of the Port of London going downstream to Tilbury. The UK site abutted a small unprepossessing town called Rainham. With a population of approximately 3000 people, Rainham was situated immediately north of the site. This settlement grew rapidly during the middle decades of the twentieth century as families moved out from the slums of East London. The most significant feature affecting the quality of life in Rainham at the time of the MCA proposal was very heavy traffic flows on the major trunk road (A13) which bisected the town.

The nature conservation value of Rainham marshes

Rainham, Wennington and Aveley Marshes (hereafter Rainham marshes) cover some 500 hectares (1200 acres) to the south and east of the town. The whole site was designated a site of special scientific interest (SSSI) in 1986. At the time of the MCA proposal, Aveley marsh and part of Wennington marsh (225 hectares; 560 acres) were used by the Ministry of Defence as an army firing range. Cattle and sheep grazed the pastures, but the public had very limited access to them. The remainder of Wennington marsh and part of Rainham marsh (140 hectares; 350 acres) were covered by three 'silt lagoons'—large embanked areas in which silt dredged from the main channel of the River Thames was dumped. Factories along the river-bank were engaged in engineering, food processing and container transportation. These were protected by a 210 cm (7ft) high flood wall which effectively prevented access to the river foreshore. There was also a large landfill site (100 hectares; 250 acres) where domestic waste from central London was tipped and compacted prior to being landscaped. At the western side of the site, Rainham marsh (93 hectares; 230 acres) was no longer managed for agricultural use and was being used by young men—illegally—as a motorcycle track.

The conservation value of Rainham marshes resided in their status as the largest remnant of what once was extensive estuarine marshlands, periodically enriched with the sediment of naturally occurring floods and which traditionally afforded high quality natural grazing land for domestic stock and wildlife. The pattern of land use on the marshes was established between the twelfth and seventeenth centuries. Sixty five per cent of the inner Thames grazing marshes had been lost either to industrial and housing development or to more intensive agriculture since the 1940s. Scientific research revealed that there were thirty species of invertebrates on the site—butterflies, moths, dragonflies, water beetles and snails—which were nationally scarce, and seven species of invertebrate which were in danger of extinction in the British Isles. The Emerald Green damsel-fly was thought to be extinct until it was rediscovered on Rainham marshes in 1983. Finally, the site was considered important for its breeding and over-wintering birds. One hundred and seventy different species had been recorded here, including merlins, hen- and marsh-harriers and short-eared owls. Thus, Rainham marshes were of major importance to conservationist groups and they fought hard to stop them being destroyed by MCA (Figure 14.2 and Figure 14.3).

FIGURE 14.2 Protesters outside Romford Town Hall, 27 February 1990. Source: *Romford Recorder*, 2 March 1990.

Universal City: MCA's proposal for the development of Rainham marshes

The developers proposed spending £2.4 billion on their scheme, an investment second only to that spent on the development of Canary Wharf in London Docklands (see Dane 1991). The costs were high because the site was badly contaminated and would require major remediation before any building could start. The key elements of the plan included film and television studios, a theme park, cinemas, an arena, hotels with 4000 beds, and 30 000 m^2 (320 000 ft^2) of 'festival retailing'. The company estimated that five million tourists a year would visit Universal City. However, these would not be sufficient to ensure an economic return and so the project also included a significant amount of additional development: 46 500 m^2 (500 000 ft^2) of office space, 418 000 m^2 (4.5 million ft^2) of industrial and warehousing space, 2000 dwellings, 2800 m^2 (30 000 ft^2) of shopping and community facilities and a new river pier. MCA forecast that 20 000 jobs would be created, of which 14 000 would be new to the local economy. The initial plan also included nature conservation interests: MCA proposed leaving 129 hectares (310 acres) of Aveley marsh as a nature reserve, and creating an ecology park on 74 hectares (178 acres) of the landfill site.

The political and economic contexts of the MCA proposal were important. Since the 1960s, successive UK governments had sought to regenerate the economy of the East Thames Corridor. MCA's proposal was therefore extremely welcome, a downstream extension of the new economic development associated with the London Docklands. Within UK legislation, SSSI designation does not

RECORDER/ADVERTISER, FRI., MAR. 9, 1990 (R) 5

CALL FOR MARSH PLAN INQUIRY

MCA slammed by groups

●*An old watch tower on the Thames marshes found itself a few metres offshore as last wee spring tides flooded over the banks.*

ROY WEAL REPORTS

CONSERVATION groups have stepped up their calls for a public inquiry into Havering Council's decision to grant planning permission for the £2 billion theme park and film studio complex proposed by American entertainment giants, MCA for Rainham Marshes.

And they have attacked MCA's own pledge to plough £16m into providing a wide ranging package of environmental projects.

London Wildlife Trust conservation officer Mr Jeff Edwards said: "The planning committee was dominated by a bunch of part-time politicians more at home dealing with trivial planning matters such as porches and house extensions.

"I was *not surprised* they approved the destruction of the largest and most impressive wildlife sanctuary within London.

"The Trust will be demanding that Mr Chris Patten, the Secretary of State for the Environment, calls in the application for examination at a full public inquiry."

Dr Chris Miles, conservation officer with the Essex Naturalists' Trust, said: "Havering's decision is a great setback for nature conservation.

"The trust believes the reason developers have chosen Rainham Marshes is because it is a cheap option, land of high conservation importance but low land value.

'Not acceptable'

"If Chris Patten refuses to call a public inquiry the Government's commitment to nature conservation will be seen to be completely hollow."

The £16m MCA conservation package was condemned by the Royal Society for the Protection of Birds. RSPB conservation officer Mr Kevin Bayes said: "MCA thinks it can buy off the conservation movement. Doing deals with irreplaceable natural habitats is not acceptable."

But leader of Havering Council, Cllr Roger Ramsey, said an inquiry was not needed.

"We feel all the points made by ecological interests have been fully explored."

'Sea may swamp £2bn site'

A £2 BILLION business and leisure "city" on Rainham marshes could end up under water within 25 years unless massive new sea walls are built to protect the area, it has been claimed.

A report to Anglian Water says experts predict a rise in sea level of anything between one and four metres, with disastrous effects on coastal areas and marshlands.

"As the sea level rises, erosive forces will become greater, with considerable land loss," the report says.

"It is estimated that in Essex, a rise of 0.8 metres would result in a reduction of at least 20 per cent in the area of mud flats.

"Any greater rise would lead to a near-total loss of marsh, and a reduction of up to 50 per cent in the area of mud flats."

Essex county councillor George Miles said: "Within 25 years we could be in serious trouble, with Rainham marshes certainly under water unless major works are done to protect them."

But Mr Ron Dane, British consultant for MCA, said: "I think the report's figures are rubbish."

'O ALFRED

has paid tribute to Mr Road, Collier Row, a died last week. eral years. Vice- loss will be in-

FIGURE 14.3 'Call for Marsh Plan Inquiry, MCA slammed by groups', *Romford Recorder*, 9 March 1990.
Source: *Romford Recorder*, 9 March 1990.

guarantee protection for nature sites. The national conservation agency (then the Nature Conservancy Council (NCC)) could only comment on changes and make suggestions about more sensitive management. It could not legally enforce protection of SSSIs (see Harrison and Burgess 1994). Under the terms of designation of an SSSI, land owners are willing parties and agree not to undertake operations damaging to the biological capital of the site. In the Rainham case, the largest land owners were in the public sector—the local authority, the Port of London Authority and the Ministry of Defence. Following eight months of secret negotiations between the developers, national government, the local authority and the institutional land owners, agreement was secured to sell the land for development. The SSSI designation was overridden.

Since the abolition of the Greater London Council in 1986, which had been responsible for strategic planning in London, each of the thirty-two London boroughs have had primary responsibility for determining their own local plans. Central government was involved through the function of the Secretary of State at the Department of the Environment, who had responsibility for deciding whether development proposals which were not within the scope of local plans, should go to public enquiry. The local plan for Havering had not foreseen the possibility of a development such as that proposed by MCA. The only potential site marked for development was the 100 hectares (230 acres) at the western edge of the marshes, owned by the local authority. In such cases, when a planning application of the scale of MCA's was submitted to the local authority (which has powers to grant or refuse development) it would be possible, through the behest of the Secretary of State for the Environment, to review the proposal at a public enquiry.

These legal niceties provided the campaign strategies for both the nature conservation groups and MCA. The former fought to force central government to call the proposal in for public enquiry. This would result in long delays that would damage the economic viability of the scheme, as well as involving the company in expensive legal fees and unwelcome publicity. From MCA's point of view, therefore, an enquiry was unacceptable and the company made it clear that if such were to be decided, then they would take the Paris option instead. They fought to gain planning permission from the London Borough of Havering (LBH) to go ahead and do the scheme without recourse to government or a planning enquiry.

ANALYSIS OF THE CLAIMS-MAKING PROCESS

The significant challenge for researchers is how to access the processes of claims-making—the strategies determining the rhetorical content of communications, uncertainties in securing media coverage, and the unpredictable ways in which claims (and claims-makers) will be judged by different audiences. The decision was taken in the Rainham case study to develop on ethnographic research strategy. Ethnographic research should combine observational and participatory activities with the production of an analysis of oral-visual and written texts, everyday speech and communications to elucidate the bases of local knowledge and experience within a given locality. Further, ethnographic research requires a focus on the practical actions taken by members of the culture over time.

In developing an ethnography of the conflict over Rainham marshes, the research tracked the ways in which different individuals, institutions and groups—construed both as 'producers' and 'consumers' of media communications—determined their strategies, developed their claims and progressed their goals. At the same time it was important to explore how members of the local community evaluated the developers' and the non-government organisations' (NGO) cases, and the extent to which their beliefs and attitudes about environmental changes were reinforced or challenged by different media communications.

A complex research design allowed these different goals to be achieved. Briefly, the research strategy covered the period April 1989–April 1991 by which time it was obvious that the parent company in America was no longer interested in the site. The *continuous* elements of the research programme included participant-observation at all the staged media events and local public meetings; repeated informal interviews with the key actors including the consultant for the developers, local authority planners, campaigners of the NGOs, and local journalists; and monitoring/transcription of national and local press and broadcast coverage of the Rainham marshes issue over two years. *Discrete* research activities were mapped onto this basic frame and were focused primarily on working with the local population in Rainham. A household survey was conducted in January 1990 to ascertain local opinion about the scheme (see Burgess 1992). Following the household survey, two in-depth discussion groups were recruited: each met for six, one and a half hour sessions during the spring and autumn of 1991 (Burgess et al. 1991, pp. 502–4). The first 'lay' group comprised ten local men and women who largely supported the MCA scheme; the second was also composed of ten men and women who lived in the locality, but these were all paid-up members of nature conservation and environmental organisations. Finally, a series of semi-structured interviews were conducted with the environmental correspondents of national newspapers in the early part of 1991 (see Harrison and Burgess 1992).

The economic case

The proposal by MCA was the latest in a series of options for the marshes all of which had been contested by the NGOs. This pre-existing oppositional context put pressure on MCA, at least in the crucial early stages of project development. The overall strategy of the developers was determined by the need to gain time and ascendancy in the debate about the SSSI. The reality was that the developers proposed to *destroy* approximately 890 acres of the 1200 acre SSSI. How were they to achieve political and public acceptance for that destruction without being forced into a lengthy public enquiry about the costs and benefits of their application?

The parent company in the USA had an overall strategy based on competition between the London and Paris sites. By funding two separate development teams to take the proposals through to completion, the American company put intense pressures on the UK government, the local authorities, the development consortium and its contracted consultants and the local community in Rainham. The threat was always present: if the UK government agreed it would be necessary to hold a public enquiry into the application, then MCA would choose the Paris option. But the major uncertainty for the UK development consortium was whether the NCC, with statutory responsibility for SSSIs and the NGOs, would be able to mobilise public opinion sufficiently so as to compel the local authorities to turn down the application, or to force central government to concede an enquiry.

MCA never deviated from the position that it was still considering the two sites while working hard to justify that the economic benefits of their scheme outweighed the environmental costs. In all its public statements, economic claims for the development were based on a numerical rhetoric—the scale of the investment (£2.4 billion), the number of jobs (14 000), the number of tourists (5 million a year) and the range of attractions (better than Florida). The reputation of the companies involved and their different expertises were lauded; the support of major commercial and media institutions, including the BBC and British film industry and widespread political support for the scheme at national level were cited; the importance of the development for the locality, the London region and the country as whole was stressed. The competition between London and Paris was blended with Hollywood celebrities in the national media. Locally, the press was exultant—*MEGA STARS MEGA JOBS,* the banner headline shouted on 9 June 1989 (Figure 14.4).

In public there was little dispute about the economic benefits of the proposal. National NGO campaigners found it difficult to argue against the economic case. To say publicly that such a development was not needed would have been foolhardy politically, so the NGOs were forced into a defensive stance of accepting the economic case for the development but arguing about where it should be located. As an activist said at the public meeting between MCA and conservationists: 'It's not what you want to do but where you want to do it.' Similarly, the Royal Society for the Protection of Birds (RSPB) issued a press release on 11 November 1989 in which their campaigner said: 'It is insane to replace the last vestige of London grazing marsh with a development which could just as easily be sited on derelict land or surplus farmland.' The press release provided the main elements of a story in the *Evening Standard* under the headline 'Park plan could sink marshland sanctuary' (2 January 1990). The above quote was used in the report and functioned to give legitimacy to the economic claims. And yet, as the MCA consultant admitted many months after the scheme had died, the economic claims were 'theoretical', as they were based on projections of future economic trends. He commented that it would have been difficult to substantiate some of the figures had he been challenged.

The nature conservation case

While the power to define economic benefits resided with MCA, the authority of claims over the environmental and nature conservation case resided with the NGOs and NCC. Despite this, MCA had several advantages: surprise, exceptionally strong contacts throughout central government, a local authority anxious to see a development on the site, a large budget and the NCC reeling from the shock announcement in July 1989 that it was to be split into three. The strength of the scientific claims for the marshes were never fully explored, in public at least, because the upper levels of NCC refused to enter any public debate. One of the London regional officers of NCC did play an important role, however, by attending NGO meetings and providing scientific material for press briefings.

Only after planning permission was given did NCC representatives appear on television to object that the development would destroy the scientific interest of

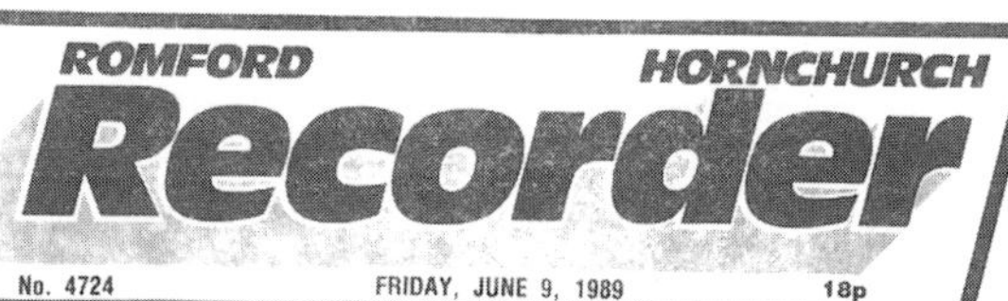

The BIG Weekend Paper For The Borough of Havering

112 PAGES
TOO GOOD TO MISS

Big marshland magnet for five million visitors a year

MEGASTARS, MEGA JOBS!

By ROY WEAL

THE CURTAIN WENT UP this week on a stunning billion-pound venture to bring the glamour of Hollywood to Rainham and Aveley Marshes by 1993.

Just 10 days after the Recorder exclusively revealed plans to create a massive film studio and theme park on the marshland site, details were unveiled.

The huge project would not only turn the area into one of the world's top tourist attractions, but would also give it international significance, and boost the economy with 14,000 new jobs.

Dubbed "Universal City", it would cover hundreds of acres, stretching three miles along the Havering and Thurrock river frontage.

● *Legendary producer and director Steven Spielberg, Universal Studios' creative consultant — pictured with his famous character ET — could be a regular visitor to Rainham and Aveley Marshes if the billion-pound studio and theme park plan takes root.*

Californian screen giant MCA Enterprises International is behind the moves, having teamed up with a consortium of 11 of Britain's top industrial companies.

MCA's film, television and leisure empire includes Universal Studios in Hollywood, responsible for mega-movie characters like ET, King Kong and Jaws.

Next year it will be opening a new studio complex and associated theme park in Orlando, Florida.

Choice

It has decided to create just two more — one in Japan and one in Europe.

The European location has been narrowed down to a straight choice between Paris and the Rainham/Aveley Marshes.

Hotels, housing, leisure-based retail outlets, a business park, a massive amphitheatre and a nature reserve would be added attractions.

MCA's consultant, Mr Ron Dane, said: "The area will have international significance.

"It would be the sixth or seventh largest tourist attraction in the world, with five million visitors a year."

● FULL REPORTS — SEE PAGES 3, 4 AND 5.

You read it in your Recorder FIRST...

Recorder

Movie moguls check area for studios and park plan

FILM GIANTS ROLL IN

Channel rail link shock

● *How the Recorder broke the news — exclusively.*

First-aider saves victim — Back Page

FIGURE 14.4 Front page news, 'MEGASTARS MEGA JOBS!', *Romford Recorder*, 9 June 1989.
Source: *Romford Recorder*.

66 per cent of the Inner Thames Marshes SSSI. The acute observation made by a journalist writing in the specialist journal *Planning* suggests an amazing ability to read the future: '*Planning* understand that the Nature Conservancy Council may not ultimately object as long as a number of key safeguards are incorporated into the project' (9 June 1989, p. 1). These 'safeguards' ultimately became enshrined in a mitigation package negotiated between MCA and NCC which was worth £16 million and retained 428 acres of the SSSI.

The main elements of the NGOs' case were established in a series of press releases over the period. These were backed up by an authoritative briefing paper on the flora and fauna of the marshes produced by the NCC officer who had done the work which led to site designation in 1986. The case combined scientific evidence with assertions about the significance and value of the site. The NGOs also resorted to a numerical rhetoric. Much was made of the size of the site (1200 acres), the number of species of birds recorded (170), the number of rare and threatened species of invertebrates (30) and wetland plants (20). A number of claims are to be found in the press releases: the marshes are described as 'the last substantial area of a now rare habitat', possessing 'a very rich population of birds and plants'. The reduction in size of the SSSI is described as being 'catastrophic for the capacity of marshes to support its rich variety of wildlife'. In the June and September press releases, Rainham was described as 'one of the best wildlife sites in Greater London', 'the most important wildlife site in London' and 'one of the largest SSSIs in London'. The scale of destruction was said to be 'unprecedented' and 'catastrophic for nature conservation', while MCA's expressed concern for nature conservation was described by the NGOs as 'cosmetic'.

MCA establish their green credentials

It could be argued that the NGOs did have one advantage in the crucial early stages of the proposal. The lead consultant of MCA responsible for finding the site and achieving planning permission did not have any environmental experience and was on a rapid learning curve. On the other hand, the NGOs and the NCC regional officers were already mobilised to fight a separate public enquiry about the marshes. They had good local intelligence and the scientific field evidence to substantiate the case for the SSSI. The MCA consultant commented privately that he would not debate with a campaigner in the media because 'I'd lose hands down. He's an expert and I'm not'.

Aware of their vulnerability on conservation issues, MCA quickly appointed a specialist firm of ecologists to collect and evaluate the biological data on the SSSI and to prepare a package of measures to ensure the overall acceptability of the scheme. But, while buying time, the developers also needed to reduce the possibility of local and national public opinion hardening against them. The tactic was to play down the conservation status of the site while somehow acquiring sufficient expertise to suggest they were sensitive to environmental concerns and competent to deal with them. First, MCA made no mention in their June press release that the site was an SSSI or had nature conservation value. Second, and more importantly, they manufactured a set of green credentials by claiming halfway down the second page of the three page release: 'MCA, *which also manages Yosemite National Park* in the United States, and BUD are sensitive to the need for full consideration of local existing environments and amenities around the chosen site' (emphasis added).

The implication was that MCA had direct responsibility for managing nature in Yosemite, one of the prime wilderness parks in the USA. This was not strictly true. In fact, a subsidiary of MCA owned a concession for visitor services in the park which included hotels, restaurants and camp-grounds subsequently valued at 300 million dollars in the takeover of MCA by Matushita (*Guardian*, 2 January 1991, p. 12). Thus, MCA did not 'manage' Yosemite. It was responsible for the commercial operations which included some environmental input in terms of visitor safety and preventing disturbance of animals, but not the day-to-day ecological management of the park. This resided with the US National Park Service. This sleight of hand was never challenged by any of the NGOs or environmental correspondents. It served MCA well in the critical early stages of the development.

None of the national press in June 1989 even mentioned the environmental issue. By contrast, the local weekly paper (*Romford Recorder*) dealt very fully with environmental and conservation issues from the beginning. Factual information about the status of the site as an SSSI and reasoned arguments from NGOs were published regularly and the discourses of the paper were biased in favour of the developers. 'Yosemite' was of major significance in the local campaign as it was fought out in the pages of the local paper. Specifically, it gave the company the green credentials they needed. On 9 June 1989, for example, the *Romford Recorder* ran a story about opposition to the scheme under the headline 'Group slams "barbarism"'. The second story on the same page had the headline 'Nature is safe say company' and substantiated the MCA assertion that the ecology of the marshes will be 'protected' by reference to the Yosemite claim.

The following week the Editor of the paper came out more strongly. Referring to 'emphatic opposition from local conservation bodies' he wrote: 'I feel their reaction is a typical "knee-jerk" one. The Hollywood organisation has vast experience of managing nature reserves, for which it has won awards' (*Romford Recorder*, 16 June 1989, p. 4). This 'fact' comes from an attributable briefing by the development consultant published as a separate story—'Plan will boost marsh: award winners slam attackers'. The MCA consultant is quoted as saying that the environment will be enhanced by the development because 'Our record in America shows MCA cares for the environment. We have managed the Yosemite National Park since the 1930s and have won numerous awards for our work there' (*Romford Recorder*, 16 June 1989, p. 7).

The transformation in MCA's case over the critical six months between the first public expression of interest in the site and the submission of a planning application at the beginning of December was revealed in their November press conference. The environment had moved up the agenda and was mentioned in the first paragraph of the MCA press release. The development 'will be the centre of a conserved landscape, given over to ecological and recreational use'. Nationally, this increased attention was politically expedient to reduce opposition in parliament. Locally it represented a response to the debate which had run throughout the summer and autumn in the weekly paper at a time when the plan was due to go to public consultation.

Further, MCA had to demonstrate that the local authority were taking the conservation case seriously and were responding to the demand by the strategic planning agency for London (LPAC) that NCC should be consulted on how much land was needed to maintain a viable SSSI within the development. Based on detailed evidence from their ecological consultants, the main claim of the company for the project had expanded dramatically. Now the development apparently would offer a greatly improved quality of life for both people *and* nature. The grounds of this claim were based on evidence that the site was currently used largely as an official and unofficial rubbish and silt tip and as a military firing range. The warrants for the claim were acceptance that the development would be an improvement aesthetically—it would offer the controlled use of the land—and that MCA could deliver this improvement—another allusion to the Yosemite credentials.

The site's status as an SSSI was mentioned halfway down page five of the release: 'a considerable area of the existing site is designated as a Site of Special Scientific Interest (SSSI), but there is substantial pollution and deterioration of the environment'. Speakers at the press conference reiterated claims made in the press release which emphasised plans for the 'enhancement and restoration of natural landscapes and habitats together with plans for keeping 310 acres of Thames Grazing Marsh. This is to be kept in perpetuity and managed as a nature reserve in order to protect and enhance the existing habitats of the area. These are currently deteriorating.' The rhetorical purpose of these claims was to challenge the assertion of the NGOs that the *whole* site, as an SSSI, was important and valuable. The consultants managed to shift the grounds of the argument to consideration of the *relative* importance of different *parts* of the SSSI.

The press conference was very well-attended. Journalists' questions not surprisingly, given that the majority were financial correspondents, concentrated on the London–Paris competition and precisely when, why and how MCA would chose one site in preference to the other. The conservation issue arose only towards the end of the conference and in muted terms. There were twelve reports in the national press with all but one emphasising the Hollywood connection in their headlines and the competition with Paris in the body of the text. Only one paper (the *Independent*) framed the story in terms of the conservationist's fight: 'Marshland fight likely over £2bn theme park' (30 November 1989).

Over the next few months there were hectic rounds of public meetings and many private negotiations between MCA, NCC and other interested parties to agree a mitigation package so the scheme could go ahead without formal objections from the NCC. Meanwhile the NGOs began a letter-writing campaign to senior MCA representatives in America and began pressuring Patten (then Secretary of State for the Environment) to call a public enquiry.

They staged an event on the steps of the Department of the Environment to submit a petition to the Secretary of State. Individuals dressed up in costumes from Universal Studio films and although the event attracted little media coverage, the event brought the issue of an enquiry up the agenda and attracted more attention from environmental correspondents. Although the NGOs lost their case—LBH approved the application and Patten finally decided against a public enquiry—they had the eventual satisfaction of seeing the case framed as an environmental conflict. Virtually all the national reports of events between February and April 1990 led with the wildlife designation of the site. Paul Brown, the environment correspondent of the *Guardian,* wrote in his report of 23 March 1990: 'The development would be on the biggest site of special scientific interest (SSSI) in the London area and is seen by wildlife groups as a fundamental test of principle on whether such statutory designations give real protection to the environment' (p. 4). The NGOs' case was finally made.

How local people made sense of competing claims

To interpret the ways in which different audiences made sense of the conflict, it is essential to understand the changing political, social and media contexts within which they were situated. Crucially, the MCA proposal was not produced in a geographical and cultural vacuum. Indeed, the whole case history demonstrates the profound importance of understanding how the global—in this case, a multinational conglomerate with a huge amount of symbolic as well as material capital—is incorporated in, and transformed by, the local. The following attempts to illustrate how the claims identified above were articulated and refracted through the experiences and lived-cultures of local people in Rainham.

Claims about the benefits of the proposal and its impact on the environment were in the local public arena in a variety of different communicative forms throughout the period: plans, diagrams, promotional videos, an expensive glossy brochure, press releases and conferences, press reports, radio interviews, television broadcasts, magazine features and public meetings. Camera crews visited local schools, helicopters filmed the marshes, people were asked to sign petitions, they wrote to their MPs and some participated in this study. These different communications permeated the locality and the lives of local residents who, in turn, gossiped and argued about them at home and in many different social contexts. People evaluated the cases of the developers and the environmentalists on the bases of their local culture, local knowledge and practical everyday experiences. For several months the pros and cons of the MCA scheme were the most important item on the local agenda. Much of the argument and debate focused on the current value of the site for 'nature' when weighed against the economic, social, cultural and environmental benefits that would apparently accrue from the MCA scheme.

These debates must also be understood within a historical context. There had been a history of struggle over the site which had a significant bearing on the ways in which local people and their political representatives responded to MCA and the conservationists. Briefly, the key moments of immediate relevance here are that the SSSI had been designated in 1986 after several years of dispute between the local authority (who wished to develop part of the site they owned) and the NCC/NGOs. Additionally, the Department of Transport proposed to re-route a major trunk road over the marshes and away from the village of Rainham itself. The A13 has a damaging effect on the quality of life of local residents. The great majority had welcomed the road proposals despite an intensive campaign by conservation groups to save the marshes from the road. These events had all received extensive coverage in the weekly paid and free local press.

This recent history was highly influential in determining the strategies of MCA and the NGOs, and the ways in which local people made sense of media coverage of the scheme. Most importantly, the NGOs were already positioned by local people as being more concerned to save the wildlife and habitats of the marshes than improving the quality of life of local people. As a woman said at the start of the first public meeting: 'What about the people who live here? What about us? Talking about conservation, don't forget, we need to be conserved, too!' Although there was considerable antipathy towards the local authority for allowing part of the riverside site to be used as a refuse dump for Westminster, and doing nothing to control illicit motorbike scrambling on Rainham marshes itself, the desire by the authority to attract inward investment to improve local prospects was largely welcomed.

A household survey of 251 Rainham residents conducted in January 1990 showed that public awareness of the MCA proposal was high and that most people (61 per cent) had first heard about the proposal through the local press (Burgess 1992). By contrast only 8 per cent of respondents had attended any of the public meetings. The two in-depth group discussions held through the summer and winter of 1990 revealed a pattern of media consumption in which the local press was unself-consciously incorporated into discourse on an equal footing with other forms of social interaction and exchange. 'They say' and 'people say' were phrases used routinely in discussions when group members were in fact drawing on information given in the local press, but there was much more often an acknowledgment of national media sources which 'distanced' them from everyday life in the locality. Often, this would surface in critical reaction to the ways in which the place itself was being represented. Referring to the proposed LWTv documentary, for example, Kate said:

> It will be interesting to see how they portray Rainham because I know the back page of the *Guardian* about 6 weeks ago, had a picture and it said: 'Rainham Marshes, where they might be building this theme park'. And it was awful because they'd taken it through a horrible wooden box that's all broken or something. And it just looked like a dump. Although it's not entirely misleading, it is somewhat misleading because it isn't ALL that dumpy and it could be quite nice. It was a deliberate ploy.

This comment articulates a more general mistrust of the national media which was evident in the discussions of both our groups and supports observations from audience reception studies (Corner et al. 1990; Wren-Lewis 1985). Individuals rely on the media for much of their information about the world but do not trust them, and tend always to privilege their own practical everyday experiences and knowledge over the 'public' comments of national media.

Evaluating the economic case

At one of public meetings, a local resident commented that 'this development will secure the future of the area. It won't be chemicals and industries. It's a nice development. It will secure the future for ever.' His views were widely shared. The members of the lay discussion group were also prepared to accept the developers' arguments about the anticipated economic benefits the scheme would bring, not least because they resonated with their own perceptions of the economic needs in the locality. Reflecting widely-held views, members were angry and anxious about the lack of existing employment opportunities available locally for both themselves and their children. The new jobs associated with the development were construed as tangible and realisable benefits that would otherwise not be available. They were prepared to believe that the scheme was soundly based, would work and would improve the image of the area. But they also remained resolutely sceptical about the real motives of the developers.

However, the in-depth discussion group of residents (the lay group), again reflecting comments made often in the community, were well aware of the futuristic nature of the claims being made and indulged in humorous fantasies about film-stars talking to local people 'over the garden fence'. The group based its assessment of the economic claims primarily on accounts of members' personal experiences of visiting Disneyland and Universal Studios in the United States. In all these discussions, the media provided a pervasive background of information and impression formation, but only very rarely would people refer directly to an item in the media, unless to establish a common ground for debate.

By contrast the in-depth discussion group of local environmentalists were not prepared to accept MCA's economic claims. Much of their discussion was devoted to demonstrating why the vision of society advanced by the developers conflicted with the world envisioned by environmentalists. Group members challenged the assumptions, underlying motives and goals associated with promoting economic growth rather than sustainable development. For these members of the public, the MCA scheme represented the height of consumerism which in turn was identified as *the* problem underpinning MCA's case. At the same time, these committed conservationists were much more willing to question the basis of MCA's economic claims. For example, members agreed with Sarah's view when she said:

> I read ... that jobs would be created, but they would be on a short term basis. While the thing was being built. Once it WAS built, we're then looking to specialist people coming in from outside. So the actual job creation would be very short-lived. And I thought that was pulling the wool over the eyes of the local population.

In this sense, environmentalists contested the economic claims of the developers from a standpoint of conviction. But they were also by drawing on their own considerable competence in contesting the validity of media reports through their cumulative lived experiences as active campaigners.

Evaluating the environmental case

Members of both discussion groups shared a healthy scepticism about the environmental claims made by MCA. Neither group were prepared to uncritically accept the claim that 'nature would be safe with MCA' as the local headlines had professed. For example, members of the lay group were dubious about MCA's ability to 'create nature' out of the huge rubbish tip covering part of the site. The company had promised to turn this into a new ecology park by creating a variety of different habitats. That was almost as fantastic as having Steven Spielberg walk down Rainham High Street.

> *Tom*: 'This is the area they're going to make their Ecology Park, isn't it?'
>
> *William*: 'That's right.'
>
> *Tom*: '(laughing) Well they've got a job there haven't they?!'
>
> *Vicky*: 'They'll have to import the insects!'
>
> *Tom*: 'If they can make an Ecology Park out of that, then I think it's worthwhile doing it to get rid of that tip.'

Similarly there was scepticism about MCA's general expertise in the field of conservation and, interestingly, no-one in either group ever made explicit reference to the 'Yosemite' claim. Kate, for example, said:

> I'm not convinced about this ecology bit. Because I know somebody that's seen the proposal plans and HE says—I mean he was talking to some conservationist fella. And he says, on the plans the lake appears to be half way up a hill. Which doesn't seem very practical to me. Which tells me that may be their heart's not in it.

The group of committed environmentalists were also completely dismissive of the developer's mitigation package. Using sophisticated arguments which exposed the limitations of attempts to put a price on what was to be lost, the notion that one unique site could be substituted by other sites and that creative conservation could provide equivalent opportunities to those which would be lost, this group gave no credence to MCA's environmental claims. Pippa expressed the central concern of the group when she said:

> 'I think the thing that makes me MORE angry—I mean, obviously the fact that these things are disappearing—but the fact that future generations aren't going to know they were there in the first place. So they're never going to have the benefit that we've got now. And I think that's sad.'

True to beliefs and concerns of the nature conservation movement in the UK, the group of committed environmentalists did not contest the claims made by the NGOs about the threat to species and habitat the development posed. Familiar with the justification for the SSSI designation by the NCC, there was consensus within the group about the need to conserve the site in its entirety. By contrast, members of the lay group were much less ready to accept the environmental claims made by the NGOs, especially those arguments associated with the site's designation as an SSSI. It has been argued elsewhere that the conservationists were remiss in not committing more time and effort to working with the local community and sharing what is widely perceived to be their 'secret knowledge' about nature (Burgess et al. 1991).

The local paper, with its in-built bias against the conservation case, was in fact primarily responsible for conveying information about the site. As Gillian said: 'I never knew that this was err, umm—is it SI?—until all this started up about MCA ... I had no idea that I had that on the doorstep.' Most of the lay group rejected the conservationists' arguments, widely reported in the local paper and rehearsed in the LWTv documentary, that there was wildlife on the site worth preserving. Further, they refused to accept the claim that species would be lost if the development were to go ahead. As Lucy remarked: 'How do they really know that these birds and insects and everything are just going to disappear? How do they know?'

During the life of the lay group, each member had watched the LWTv documentary in their own home. The film had illustrated the range of plants and animals living on the marshes and after watching it all the members of the group were prepared to admit that there was more wildlife on the marsh than they had previously believed. Similar comments were made by some of the committed conservationists, too. But on its own this information and the arguments advanced by the environmentalists did not persuade the group that the development should be opposed. Drawing on their local knowledge of the site as a rubbish dump populated only by rats, mice and mosquitos, and taking a lead from arguments advanced in the local press by environmentalists which took little account of the concerns of local people, the lay group marginalised both the scientific claims and the general veracity of the conservationists. As Vicky put it:

> That's why I can't understand the big fuss that people are making—about how wonderful these marshes are. Because most of them have never been here. They've never seen what a mess it is. So at least, if they build this and they build the ecology bit, you'll be able to walk around that and at least *see* the wildlife, which is more than you can do now!

CONCLUSIONS

The principle of 'mitigating' habitat losses in one place by creating nature elsewhere has become accepted practice over the decade (Adams 1996). The conclusion of the case of Hollywood-on-Thames, however, did not result in local people being able to see the wildlife, either on the marshes or in MCA's proposed ecology park. MCA were granted planning permission by the local authority—the Secretary of State called the plans in to review, then decided the scheme could go ahead without a planning enquiry, but nothing happened on Rainham marshes. In the autumn of 1990 it was announced that MCA had been taken over by a Japanese entertainment conglomerate in November and their Hollywood studios burned down soon afterwards. The Disney theme park in Paris (MCA's bitter rivals in the USA) opened in 1992 and the economic recession in the UK made the project's finances unworkable.

Nature is far from safe on the Rainham marshes, however. The A13 trunk road is being built and plans are far advanced to route the Channel Tunnel Rail link across the site. The local authority, secure in the certainty that the majority of its local population support the idea of development, has continued its search for a developer for the 230 acres of land it owns. A newspaper story published on the 18th of January 1998 depicted moody, romantic shot of reeds set against a wide blustery sky, with light reflecting in a watery dyke. The article poses a rhetorical question, 'Is it worth destroying this wildlife site to build another petrol station?' Some of the claims discussed in this chapter are present in the story, although a new, more appealing mammal—the water vole—is added to the conservationists' case. It is now LBH in partnership with a government agency who want to do the development to create more jobs and improve the image of the area, but the mood of the times has changed. In the last five years or so in the UK the car has become emblematic of environmental degradation and the tenor of the newspaper report clearly supports the conservationist case. This is a reminder not only that environmental claims are socially constructed, but also that cultural politics are highly contingent to particular times and places.

ACKNOWLEDGMENTS

This research was funded by the Economic and Social Research Council and the Nature Conservancy Council (grant no. W110251001). Dr Carolyn Harrison was co-researcher, and Mr Paul Maitney the Research Assistant for the project.

REFERENCES

Adams, W.M. 1996, *Future Nature: A Vision for Conservation*, Earthscan, London.

Anderson, A. 1991, 'Source strategies and the communication of environmental affairs,' *Media, Culture and Society*, vol. 13, no. 4, pp. 454–76.

Anderson, A. 1997, *Culture, Media and Environmental Issues,* UCL Press, London.

Best, J. 1987, 'Rhetoric in claims-making: constructing the missing children problem', *Social Problems*, vol. 34, no. 2, pp. 101–21.

Bird, E. 1987, 'The social construction of nature: theoretical approaches to the history of environmental problems', *Environmental Review*, vol. 11, pp. 255–64.

Burgess, J. 1990, 'The production and consumption of environmental meanings in the mass media: a research agenda for the 1990s', *Transactions of the Institute of British Geographers*, vol. 15, no. 2, pp. 139–61.

Burgess, J. 1992, 'On the cultural politics of economic development and nature conservation', in *Inventing Places: Studies in Cultural Geography*, eds K. Anderson & F. Gale, Longman Cheshire, Melbourne, pp. 235–51.

Burgess, J., Harrison, C.M. & Maiteny, P. 1991, 'Contested meanings; the consumption of news about nature conservation', *Media, Culture and Society*, vol. 13, no. 4, pp. 499–520.

Cracknell, J. 1994, 'Issue arenas, pressure groups and environmental agendas', in *The Mass Media and Environmental Issues*, ed. A. Hansen, Leicester University Press, Leicester, New York pp. 3–21.

Corner, J., Richardson, K. & Fenton, N. 1990, *Nuclear Reactions: Form and Response in Public Issue Television*, John Libby, London.

Dane, R. 1991, 'Rainham marshes: the process and the lessons', *Ecos*, vol. 12, pp. 47–50.

Greenberg, D.W. 1985, 'Staging media events to achieve legitimacy: a case study of British Friends of the Earth', *Political Communication and Persuasion*, vol. 2, pp. 347–62.

Hannigan, J.A. 1995, *Environmental Sociology: A Social Constructionist Perspective*, Routledge, London.

Hansen, A. 1991, 'The media and the social construction of the environment', *Media, Culture and Society*, vol. 13, no. 4, pp. 443–58.

Harrison, C.M & Burgess, J. 1992, 'Rainham marshes in the media', *Ecos*, vol. 13, pp. 20–6.

Harrison, C.M. & Burgess, J. 1994, 'Social constructions of nature: a case study of the conflicts over Rainham Marshes SSSI', *Transactions of the Institute of British Geographers*, vol. 19, no. 3, pp. 291–310.

Hilgartner, S. & Bosk, C.L. 1988, 'The rise and fall of social problems: a public arenas model', *American Journal of Sociology*, vol. 94, no. 1, pp. 53–78.

Irwin, A. 1995, *Citizen Science: A Study of People, Expertise and Sustainable Development*, Routledge, London.

Lowe, P. & Morrison, D. 1984, 'Bad news or good news: environmental politics and the mass media', *Sociological Review*, vol. 32, no. 1, pp. 75–90.

Mazur, A. & Lee, J. 1993, 'Sounding the global alarm: environmental issues in the US national news', *Social Studies of Science*, vol. 23, pp. 681–720.

Myerson, G. & Rydin, Y. 1996, *The Language of Environment: A New Rhetoric*, UCL Press, London.

Redclift, M. & Benton, T. (eds) 1994, *Social Theory and the Global Environment*, Routledge, London.

Schoenfeld, A.C., Meier, R.F. & Griffin, R.J. 1979, 'Constructing a social problem: the press and the environment', *Social Problems*, vol. 27, pp. 38–61.

Whatmore, S. & Boucher, S. 1993, 'Bargaining with nature: the discourse and practice of environmental planning gain', *Transactions of the Institute of British Geographers*, vol. 18, no. 2, 166–78.

Wren-Lewis, J. 1985, 'Decoding television news', in *Television in Transition*, eds P. Drummond & R. Paterson, British Film Institute, London, pp. 205–34.

Yearley, S. 1991, *The Green Case: A Sociology of Environmental Issues*, Arguments and Policies, Harper Collins, London.

The land in cultural context

15

Hunter-gatherer concepts of land and its ownership in remote Australia and North America

Elspeth Young

INTRODUCTION

The physical landscapes around us, their topography, aesthetic appeal and the evidence of human ingenuity which they present to us in a visual sense mirror our societies. In observing and interpreting the landscape, we are often immediately aware of the human use of the resources within that particular environment. We can see the results of the development of its soils and water supplies for agricultural purposes or the exploitation of its minerals, and we can assess its locational value for human settlement and activity. However, such an observation of the landscape is only one component of the picture, a visible scene existing at a particular point in space and time. The landscape also consists of 'layers', reflecting historical processes which have resulted in its continuous transformation and which stem from changing economic, political, cultural and demographic factors affecting a particular society. Visible evidence for the existence of these factors may be almost non-existent and people tend to ignore their presence in the landscape. Cultural geographers concerned with landscape interpretation have been aware of this hidden 'authorship', however, and no longer approach the landscape primarily from a descriptive, visually oriented point of view (Ley 1983). Duncan and Duncan (1988), in discussing the idea of landscape as a 'text', stress that the reading of that text should encompass the idea of how it is linked both historically and in the present to social and cultural organisation.

It is not only recognition of the influence of hidden cultural processes on landscape construction, however, which is important. It is also the realisation that social groups do not necessarily observe and interpret environments in the same way. Our own experiences, along with those which we have learnt and accepted through contact with others, affect our interpretations and reveal something of the particular social and cultural environment within which we exist. Thus 'landscape is defined by our vision and interpreted by our minds ... [it] displays us as cultures' (Meinig 1979). It 'is an ideological concept' (Cosgrove 1984); 'a way of seeing' (Jackson 1989); an 'unwitting autobiography', revealing the tastes, values, aspirations and fears and the very structure of society into which we fit (Lewis 1979). For social scientists interested in understanding people's different reactions to and interpretations of their world, recognition of this subjectivity requires them to decipher how the actors themselves see and arrive at such understandings.

Cultural geographers have for decades attempted to demonstrate that our landscapes are reflections of the cultures that perceive and mould them. More recently, such geographers have introduced a more dynamic perspective to their approach to landscape interpretation, arguing that landscapes 'exist' in contingent—not static—relation to the images and actions of the beholder. One effective approach that demonstrates this point—that the landscapes we 'see' around us are formations undergoing cultural construction—is that of intergroup comparison. In cultural terms some of the clearest contrasts today occur in remote parts of Australia and North America, where hunter-gatherer groups, such as Australian Aborigines, North American Indians, Eskimo and Inuit share the same geographical spaces with non-indigenous members of their societies. This chapter first outlines the major elements in the landscape interpretation of hunter-gatherer and industrialised societies; secondly, it identifies sources of conflict between these two visions; and finally, with the use of a central Australian case study, demonstrates how contemporary Anmatyerre constructs of the land are themselves fluid and changeable, adapted to the geographic, economic and political contexts within which different groups of these people are situated.

HUNTER-GATHERER CONCEPTS OF LAND AND OWNERSHIP

The landscapes of hunter-gatherer societies and those of the industrialised world differ because of contrasts in their interpretation of the origin and structure of the universe, and in their economic and political structures. A major cosmological contrast concerns the perceived relationship of people and land. For most hunter-gatherer societies the land has been an inextricable part of their lives; it provides not only their sustenance in the form of game, fish and vegetable foods, but also the foundation of their spiritual beliefs and hence of their social control mechanisms. Thus Watkins (1977) comments that the reason for the Dene Indian land claim to Canada's Mackenzie Valley is not only a settlement of their desire for legal recognition of present and future hunting and trapping rights, but is also a political statement—a declaration of their long-standing cultural beliefs and their right to practise them. Usher and Bankes (1986) confirm the intimacy of the people-land relationship for the neighbouring Inuit of the eastern Arctic by their description of the people being of the land rather than owning it, and stress that Inuit cosmology explained that relationship. Even the animals hunted by the Inuit were perceived not solely as food sources, but as entities with which the people were closely related, and the husbandry of them was a prime Inuit responsibility.

Similar concepts emerge in considering the people-land relationships of Aboriginal[1] Australians. For Aborigines the landscape, as Peterson (1975) and Strehlow (1970) have emphasised, provided nourishment and also expressed their spiritual beliefs, power relationships and relative group and individual statuses. Within the Aboriginal landscape ancestral beings, including human, flora and fauna, and natural phenomena such as water, lightning or thunder, acted to create physical features and to ensure the continuance and productivity of the land's resources. In that process they travelled across the country along clearly defined routes marked by experiences and actions occurring at different points and recorded through song, dance, painting and ceremony. These routes are today commonly referred to as the 'Dreamtime Tracks' and in popular literature as 'Songlines' (Chatwin 1987). Present-day Aborigines, particularly those who still have some links with traditional society (see Edwards 1998), trace their descent from these beings and identify wholly with them so that in performing the rituals associated with their own particular tracts of country they effectively become the ancestors. Thus, when discussing the activities of ancestral 'bush plums' with an elderly Anmatyerre woman on Ti Tree station in Australia's Northern Territory in 1984 it was firmly stated that the informant's grandfather, camping at the spring at Aliyawe, was himself a 'bush plum'. In those circumstances it is clear that the linkages between people and landscape are inseparable, and not surprising that, as Stanner (1979, p. 230) wrote:

> No English words are good enough to give a sense of the links between an Aboriginal group and its homeland ... When we took (from them) what we call 'land' we took what to them meant hearth, home, the source and focus of life, and everlastingness of spirit.

While all hunter-gatherer groups appear to hold these strong ties with the land, the actual expression of these linkages on the landscape has varied with the resource base, and hence with population density. In what follows, some examples of this local adaptation and internal variation of hunter-gatherer visions are outlined.

In Australia, distant and environmentally distinct parts of the country, such as monsoonal Arnhem Land, the central desert and the Bight coasts of South Australia were spiritually linked by these Dreamtime tracks along which the ancestors moved freely. However, the traditional territories used by living Aboriginal groups, particularly in economic terms, were much more restricted and were delineated somewhat differently according to the natural environment. In the northern monsoonal country of Arnhem Land, where the resource base was much richer and more reliable, traditional territories seem to be more firmly circumscribed by boundaries than those of the desert people, where food supplies were often far less abundant. Thus, although Arnhem Land people ranged on a seasonal basis between the seashores, riverine wetlands and escarpment, the region within which they moved was recognised as the responsibility of a specific group (Altman 1987). But in the central desert, where the seasonal round was less predictable, people ranged very widely, especially in drought periods. In such times those from resource deficient areas ranged into the country of their better endowed neighbours. Such incursions were wholly acceptable as a survival mechanism with which all might ultimately be faced. Usher and Bankes (1986) comment on the existence of a similar basis of mutual support and understanding in the harsh northern environments of Inuit hunters. In contrast, in the richer boreal forest country of their Athapaskan Indian neighbours, specific traplines clearly mark where, for generations, hunters have sustained their families through their use of the land's resources. Each family's country can therefore be clearly described in terms which all understand, and using another's trapline without permission would be culturally unacceptable. Evidence of land ownership presented in the Mackenzie Valley enquiry (Berger 1977) and the Dene land claim (Department of Indian and Northern Affairs (DIAND) 1988) relies heavily on information about the location and continuing use of such traplines.

Such differences, because they affect the definition of land responsibilities, also have spiritual significance. In arid central Australia different countries are identified with extended family groups rather than with leading individuals (bosses) within those groups, and permission to use territory is sought collectively rather than individually—in Arnhem Land the request must be made to the appropriate individual. Moreover, in the desert, where country is delineated by criss-crossing and intersecting 'Dreaming' tracks rather than by continuous boundaries, people hold joint responsibility for many sites and regions. For non-Aborigines such overlaps complicate the process of understanding Aboriginal perception of the landscape and, for resource developers such as mining companies, are seen to create such uncertainty of ownership that their commercial enterprise is undermined. Resolution of such uncertainty, either by mapping Aboriginal land boundaries in a manner which fixes them publicly in space (Davis and Prescott 1992; Davis 1993) or, more recently, by enacting legislation which eliminates Aboriginal native title claims within particular types of land-holding, is loudly supported both by developers and by many sectors of government. As Sutton (1995) points out, such approaches not only demonstrate ignorance of Aboriginal concepts of land-holding but also do Aboriginal people a severe injustice. For aboriginal people, both in Australia and in Canada, these overlapping responsibilities are, in contrast, reconcilable without resorting to legislation. In his study of overlapping native claims in the Mackenzie Valley in Canada, Wonders (1983), for example, noted that the Dene/Metis, Inuvialuit and Nunavut people did not seem to see lack of clarity of ownership as a barrier to the resolution of land claims; it was the non-aboriginal Canadian bureaucrats who anticipated that this would create problems.

The principles by which hunter-gatherer land responsibilities are handed on add further complications. Inuit and Dene, mindful of the problems of survival in harsh northern environments, have not only totally accepted people of different native origin who have married into their groups, but have also been sympathetic towards the needs of non-native settlers who display an understanding of native customary behaviour. As Usher and Bankes (1986, p. 14) point out, they have often allowed them access to traditional resources, such as caribou, for skins and meat.

Australian Aboriginal land-related groups have also absorbed individuals and families with inherited spiritual responsibilities which they exercise elsewhere. This has involved a deliberate process of education, through which the incomers have been taught the stories and rituals appropriate to the country in which they were living. In the past such practices were probably extremely important, particularly in the desert where groups were small in number and might on occasion die out. By transferring spiritual responsibilities to others the continued health of the land, and hence the health of future generations of its people, was assured. In more recent times (Young 1987), these mechanisms have helped people to deal with the social and economic disruptions arising from the dispersal of Aboriginal population groups whose country has been taken over by non-Aboriginal settlers. People who have been forced to live elsewhere have been deliberately taught to carry out the spiritual responsibilities relevant to their new abode.

Land inheritance and lineage add further complexities to Aboriginal concepts of land ownership. Despite earlier assumptions that land was inherited patrilineally, and hence that women had a subordinate role in caring for land, the evidence from land claims in the Northern Territory shows that people inherit land responsibilities through both maternal and paternal grandparents. This also appears to be the case elsewhere, for example in Queensland's Cape York peninsula, and in the Kimberley region of Western Australia. Each individual therefore looks after more than one country, albeit in different ways. Those who trace their responsibilities through the paternal line are commonly called 'owners' (Warlpiri: *kirda*) and those with maternal links are referred to as 'guardians' (Warlpiri: *kurdungurlu*). In rituals *kirda* perform the ceremonies while the *kurdungurlu* organise and direct them, ensuring that the songs and dances are correctly presented and the paintings properly executed. Without people of both genders none of these components of the ceremony can be properly performed. Moreover, if land is to be properly cared for both in the economic and spiritual sense, it is expected that members of both paternal and maternal groups live on it.

CONCEPTS OF LAND AND OWNERSHIP IN INDUSTRIALISED SOCIETIES

The intrusion of non-aboriginal settlers—miners, traders, pastoralists, missionaries and public servants—into remote territories such as Canada's Arctic and the rangelands of Australia's deserts has transformed the land, often visibly. Both the boreal forests of the Mackenzie River Valley and Australia's arid interior are carved up by criss-crossing seismic lines surging away into the distance; networks of roads traverse the landscape; boundary fences divide properties from one another and a sparse spread of small towns, isolated station homesteads and mining camps provides evidence for a very different type of human occupation from that of the past, one of visible resource exploitation. Many non-aboriginal people perceive these spaces principally as sources of potential material wealth, to be used for both individual and collective monetary gain. Thus commercially valuable minerals are to be developed, forests and marine products to be harvested and rangelands to be grazed by domesticated stock. Despite the fact that some sections of the non-aboriginal people population now question such resource uses, the underlying concepts of the worth of the land and its resources still remain dominant. Non-aboriginal settlers who have, through time, developed a less materialistic attachment to the land which they have come to control, are in a minority. When such people leave the desert or the Arctic they may well feel a wrench at losing contact with familiar and loved places, but their departure does not signify a social and spiritual fission threatening the future survival of their group. When they describe these places most of them emphasise their barren nature rather than their beauty, their dearth of resources rather than their wealth of fish, game or other foods. To them such areas are the 'outback' rather than the 'homeland', places to be tolerated, hopefully for only a short period of their lives.

TWO VISIONS IN CONFLICT

The main contrasts between hunter-gatherer and industrialised society concepts of land and resources lie in the emphasis on spiritual as distinct from economic worth. Hunter-gatherers stress spiritual values. Many hold the culturally binding conviction that land is not a commodity which can be bought, sold or used as a means of creating profits, and in their assessment of economic values they emphasise husbandry for the future and the use of resources for human survival rather than increasing material advantage. Industrialised societies, on the other hand, stress economic values, with exploitation of resources for continuing material gain as the perceived route to 'development'; spiritual values receive scant attention.

Such contrasts inevitably lead to conflict. Because of the superior technology, political and economic power of the industrialised societies the main losers in these conflicts have been the hunter-gatherers. Their understanding of the land in both spiritual and material terms, has been submerged by that of the incomers. That does not mean that it has been entirely eliminated, but signs of its presence are hard for many non-aboriginal people to recognise. Many of the attributes of Aboriginal and native Canadian land responsibility and use are not actually visible on the landscape. Unless asked, Inuit and Indians do not disclose the patterns of their hunting and trapping territories to outsiders and it is only pressures such as those imposed by intrusive development projects or by the need to justify their land claims which will force them to do so. Brody's fascinating study of Beaver land use and occupancy in north eastern British Columbia (1981), the monumental Inuit Land Use and Occupancy study of the 1970s (Freeman 1976) and the Mackenzie Valley pipeline enquiries (Berger 1977) all stem from such pressures. More recently, settlement of comprehensive claims for Inuvialuit and Nunavut in Canada's Northwest Territories has not only extended non-aboriginal understanding of aboriginal land and resource use, but has also focused attention on the benefits gained by adopting a co-management approach to the fragile wildlife resources of such regions (Young 1995; Usher 1996). In Australia, much of what the outside world has learnt about the complexities of traditional Aboriginal land ownership has emerged in the course of land claims, both those lodged under various State and Territory legislation since 1976 and those now under way under the more recently introduced native title legislation (Young 1995, pp. 61–5). More than ever we are now aware that, whether visibly or invisibly, many contemporary hunter-gatherers today retain their traditional concepts of land and its ownership, but that retention of culture has required enormous strength and determination. It has occurred in the face of great pressures exerted by economic, social and political interests which are part of the industrialised world which now, irrevocably, affect Aboriginal people. As the contemporary debate over the federal government's efforts to legally extinguish Aboriginal native title from Australia's extensive pastoral lands shows, those pressures continue and recent efforts to reconcile Aboriginal and non-Aboriginal visions of land may still prove to have been fruitless.

Changes in the landscape and resultant conflicts between hunter-gatherers and non-aboriginal settlers are part of relatively recent history in many remote parts of Australia and North America. In semi-arid areas of central Australia, for example, where there was sufficient water for stock, much of the land was alienated for the pastoral industry by the early twentieth century. A new physical landscape of fence lines, cattle and vehicle tracks, dams, ponds, tanks and windmills for water and homesteads appeared. Straight lines marked by barbed wire separated neighbouring properties and created physical barriers to the journeys of the modern day representatives of the Dreamtime ancestors. They were hindered from following the tracks marked by song and ceremony and hence also failed in their spiritual duties, both to their predecessors and to their children. Ultimately, as evidence presented in land claims has graphically illustrated, they believed that the whole viability of the land as their spiritual home and subsistence resource base would be threatened. Witnesses have expressed this in different ways, talking of their fears that the land would lose its fertility and of how their continued presence on the land 'holds it up'. By this they mean that through the appropriate ceremonies the edible plants and animals on which they depended would be sustained. Their presence also ensured that important land management practices, such as mosaic burning of vegetation to ensure the continuation of suitable wildlife habitats, would be carried out. The depth of these feelings has become very obvious in recent times when Aborigines, having once more obtained secure tenure to their ancestral land, have moved back to establish small outstations in their traditional country. Often their first deliberate action has been to 'burn the country', because, after many years of abandonment, the spinifex grass has grown out of control and other more palatable species have virtually disappeared. To them, country in that state has become 'rubbish'.

In economic terms the major conflict in these rangeland areas concerned access to water. Permanent springs and soakages, such as the original spring at Alice Springs, were important meeting places for Aboriginal groups which, especially in drought times, might come from distant areas to camp at such spots. They were also major focal points for the pastoralists, wanting water for their stock. Many of the station homesteads were built close to these sites, and Aborigines were actively discouraged from camping nearby either to collect water or to carry out the relevant ceremonies associated with the location. Resultant disagreements led directly to violence on both sides, with the Aborigines—despite attempts at resistance—invariably the overall losers. In the Coniston massacre, which occurred in 1928 on a remote cattle station about 300 km (185 miles) north-west of Alice Springs, around one hundred Aborigines are thought to have been shot by cattlemen and police in retaliation for the murder of Brooks, a dingo scalp collector who camped on the waterholes and was also said to be interfering with Aboriginal women (Cribben 1984).

Such violence today would be unlikely. But the conflicts remain and the old people have not forgotten. Many Aboriginal 'refugees', forced to live in the town camps of Alice Springs because of the seizure of their land, have been thwarted in their efforts to obtain suitable excisions of small living areas back in their own country because they usually request those locations of both spiritual and economic importance to them—the water sources. Most have had to accept compromises.

Another source of conflict, common to hunter-gatherer groups in Australia, Canada and the United States, has arisen because some natural resources which form part of the native subsistence base are also perceived to be valuable by the incomers. This has particularly affected Indian and Inuit communities in Canada and Alaska, where, through the hunting and trapping and tourist industries, aboriginal and non-aboriginal interests may be in opposition. Fish such as salmon or big game such as moose, grizzly bear or wolf are targets for white hunters as well as food and clothing for hunter-gatherers, and control over the use of these resources affects both groups. Within native land, subsistence priorities can be stressed. There is, however, no guarantee that this will occur elsewhere. Different perceptions of the value of these natural resources have caused conflict in the case of the harvesting of seals and other fur-bearing animals. Total bans on such activities by animal rights and conservation groups in Canada have effectively destroyed the livelihood of northern aboriginal communities. These attitudes reveal a complete lack of understanding of Indian and Inuit modes of resource use, or a deliberate refusal to acknowledge the existence of such practices (Keith and Saunders 1989).

Perhaps the most visible evidence of conflict between hunter-gatherer and industrialised society concepts of land ownership and control lies in the settlement patterns themselves. Both in northern parts of America and in outback Australia, formerly fluid patterns of human occupation, reflecting semi-nomadic societies, have been largely replaced by fixed, centralised settlement patterns. These changes were primarily deliberate, aimed at fostering the assimilation of surviving hunter-gatherer groups into the wider society, both through enforced resettlement in permanent shelters and incorporation into the wage economy. Large mission and government settlements, both in Australia's Northern Territory and in Canada's Northwest Territories, became the main 'towns' for remote-dwelling Aborigines, Inuit and Indians. Smaller nucleated settlements developed around the homesteads of the new pastoral properties and mining camps, where people could exchange their labour for prized goods such as tobacco, flour, tea, sugar and blankets. Only in recent decades has there been a resurgence of more dispersed settlement patterns. This change stems from the resumption of aboriginal control over the land, directly attributable to land rights legislation. It clearly indicates the lifestyle preferences of many aboriginal people and reveals the continuing underlying struggle to assert their rights and beliefs. Indeed, it suggests that, despite the superior power and technology of the incomers, the original inhabitants of these remote areas have been able to retain much of their knowledge and understanding of land and resource use.

What we see today, therefore, are landscapes which reflect not only differing concepts of land ownership and control, but also their ever-changing interaction with political and economic factors. The visible signs—roads which follow straight boundary lines, connecting white settlements and ignoring other places which to the hunter-gatherers might be significant; water supplies which are harnessed through complicated introduced technology even although this might disrupt the natural attributes of the resource; and schools, health clinics and stores which are located at points of central importance to non-aboriginal rather than to the aboriginal people—suggest that the land ownership concepts of the industrialised society have been overwhelming. However, signs of hunter-gatherer valuations of land are also present and, with the granting of indigenous land rights in many of these remote areas, increasingly visible. The existing 'mix' of land 'paradigms' from hunter-gatherer and industrialised society is not uniform, but varies geographically, culturally and linguistically, and according to the operation of different political and economic factors at different times. Moreover, neither aboriginal nor non-aboriginal constructs of the environment are static embodiments of some timeless essence. Rather, they display internal variation, and capacity for change, adaptation and struggle. The following case study illustrates this point as it relates to the Anmatyerre people of Central Australia.

LAND TENURE AND ANMATYERRE RESPONSES: CONTEMPORARY EXAMPLES

To the north and north-west of Alice Springs lies the country of the Anmatyerre people, a relatively small Aboriginal linguistic group which today numbers over 1000 individuals. Although semi-arid, their territory is well-endowed with surface and ground water and its outcropping ridges and sheltered valleys provide an attractive environment for a wide range of native flora and fauna. Not surprisingly this country was also attractive to incoming non-Aboriginal settlers. From 1916, when Coniston station was first established, Anmatyerre country was progressively alienated for pastoralism, and by 1950, when the Mt Allan[2] property had finally been declared, the people had lost direct control over most of their land (Figure 15.1). Instead of ranging freely over their family territories, most people camped in semi-permanent fashion around the station homesteads where they formed the

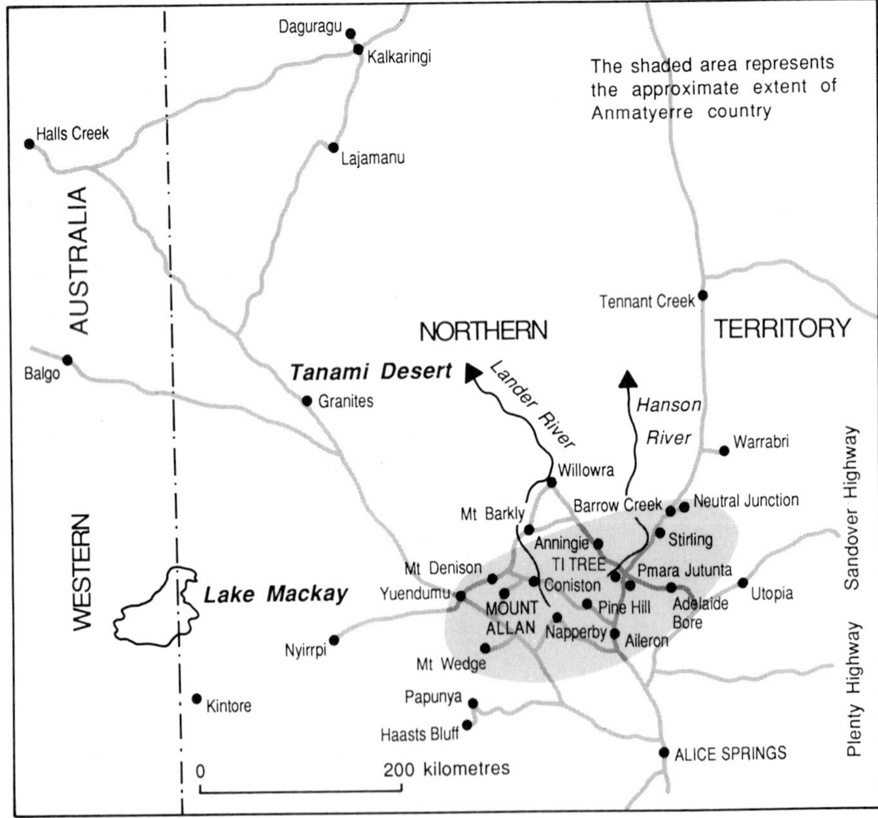

FIGURE 15.1 Anmatyerre country, Central Australia.
Source: *Aboriginal History*, vol. 11, 1987, p. 159.
Courtesy Elspeth Young.

backbone of the labour force for each stock-camp. Quite quickly, their landscape became visibly transformed by land-use practices that reflected a different environmental perception and economic system. It was crossed by roads and tracks of various grades ranging from the main road to Darwin, the Stuart Highway, to smaller access roads to homesteads and bores and tanks providing water for the cattle; and it was bounded by paddock fences. Less immediately obvious, but ultimately of great importance, were the effects of heavy grazing by hard-hoofed animals—changes in drainage patterns, development of erosion channels, introduction of new vegetation species and the disappearance of some types of native flora and fauna. Nevertheless, Anmatyerre interpretations of land ownership, while largely dormant, did not disappear. Since the mid-1970s these have re-emerged, particularly in those communities which, through government purchase programs and the implementation of land rights legislation, have regained full control over their ancestral territories. Other Anmatyerre, whose land lies within the boundaries of adjacent non-Aboriginal held stations, lack such decision-making power and have not been able to reassert their concepts of land ownership and occupation to the same extent.

Two pastoral properties, Ti Tree and Mt Allan, were purchased for their traditional owners by the federal government in 1976 and were subsequently the subject of land claim investigations for conversion to Aboriginal freehold title under the Northern Territory *Land Rights Act 1976*. Both claims were subsequently granted and thus the Aboriginal owners of both of these properties can now determine how to use their land. Aborigines living on neighbouring stations in Anmatyerre country, such as Napperby, Coniston or Anningie may be heavily restricted in their choice of modes of land use. Thus, although they share language and culture, belong to the same kinship 'mob' and move freely between each other's camps, the cognitive and physical relationships of contemporary Anmatyerre to the land vary.

Anmatyerre social organisation still forms the basis of their land ownership system. In social terms all Anmatyerre are classified into one of eight major subsections, with membership being determined patrilineally by parentage. Thus the children of Mpetyane fathers belong to Ngale subsection, while those of Peltharre fathers belong to Kngwarraye subsection (Table 15.1). These pairs of subsections are called patricouples. Subsections are also arranged into two groups of four, called moieties, between which preferred marriages occur. Thus Mpetyane people, men or women, should marry Pengarte, and Kemarre are expected to marry Peltharre.

TABLE 15.1 Anmatyerre subsection terms and linkages.

Mpetyane	=	Pengarte
Kemarre	=	Peltharre
Perrwerle	=	Penangke
Ngale	=	Kngwarraye

= This symbol links first choice marriage partners
[This symbol links fathers with children

FIGURE 15.2a Photograph of a painting by Jeannie Nungarrayi Egan (1989) from Yuendumu, Northern Territory. It shows the tracks of ancestral faunal beings (possum, goanna, kangaroo and emu) and human ancestors (Jungarrayi and Nangala), to and from Yurnipirli waterhole. The artist's explanation of the painting, in Warlpiri and English, follows:
Nyampuju kuruwarri yirrarnurna janganpkurlu manu kuyu panu kari kuja kalu yanirni ngapa kurra. [This Dreaming is about possum and other meat (edible animals) or animals coming to the waterhole.]
Yangka kardiyarlu manu yapa karirli yungulu milya pinyi junga nyarni kuruwarri yapa kurlangu ngurrararla, kuja karlipa purami manu kijirni. [(This painting is made by) all the 'bosses' so other people in their families can know the dreaming properly and learn.]
Yamuju jukurrpa Jungarrayi Nungarrayi kirlangu manu Japaljarri Napaljarri kirlangu. [This Dreaming belongs to all these family skin groups (Jungarrayi/Nungarrayi and Japaljarri/Napaljarri).]
Source: Reproduced by permission of the artist.

Patricouples such as *Mpetyane/Ngale* or *Pengarte/Penangke,* hold ritual responsibility for specific Dreaming tracks which cross Anmatyerre land. Marriages between subsections create linkages between Dreaming tracks and associated countries. The stories describing this system have been orally transmitted through many generations and are illustrated through dance, song and painting. Paintings are therefore essentially Aboriginal 'maps' of country, describing the association between the people and the land. They graphically illustrate Aboriginal cosmology. Figures 15.2a and b presents one such map of an area immediately to the west of Mt Allan, on the former Yuendumu Reserve. It shows the journeys of the ancestral faunal beings (goanna, kangaroo, native cat/possum, emu) and the human ancestors (*Kngwarraye* and *Ngale*) who cared for *Yurnipirli*, a waterhole still of great spiritual significance to the present representatives of these moieties.

Anmatyerre perceptions based on this land ownership system bear little relationship to the proofs of ownership imposed by non-Aboriginal pastoral use. The fences bounding Mt Allan, for example, cut straight across Anmatyerre delineations of the property (Figure 15.3). In the northern section the station is traversed by the honey ant ancestral track, associated with *Penangke/Pengarte* subsections; on the west lie the tracks made by the possums and native cat ancestors of *Kngwarraye* and *Peltharre*; and to the south is the emu track of *Ngale* and *Mpetyane*. Diagonally from the south-west

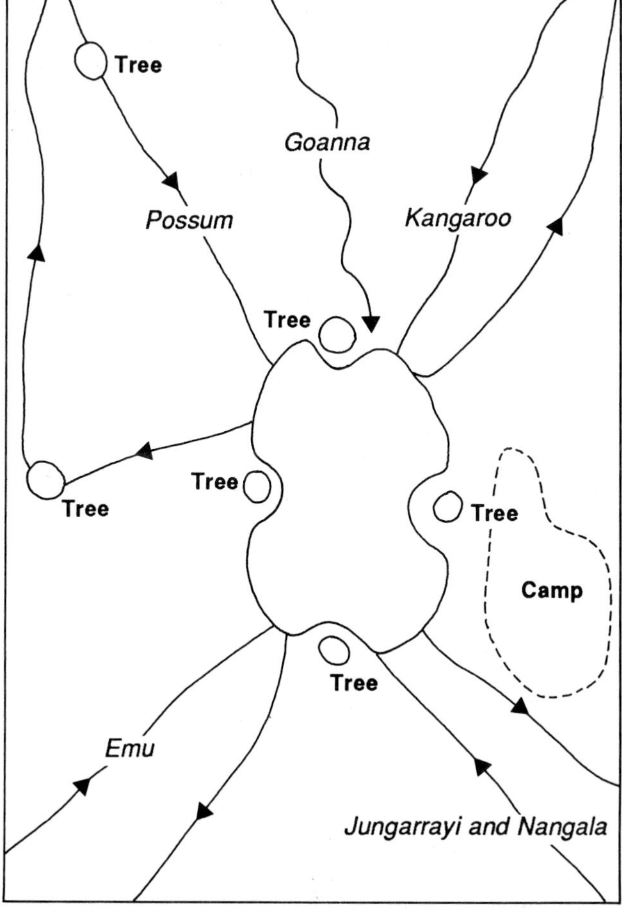

FIGURE 15.2b Diagram explaining the characteristics shown in Figure 15.2a.

to the north-east travelled the sand goannas, also ancestors of *Kngwarraye* and *Peltharre* groups. All these tracks intersect at certain points and all also continue beyond Mt Allan's boundary fences. As was clearly demonstrated during hearing of evidence for the Mt Allan land claim in 1982, the co-existence of these Aboriginal and non-Aboriginal systems of delineating land can cause some confusion. Because the actual land claim was legally restricted to the area included within the boundary fence of the pastoral lease, witnesses were asked to describe their ancestral countries in a somewhat artificial fashion, as if these territories ceased to exist at the fence line. Knowledge of country beyond the boundary fence was in many cases essential to understanding the details of their stories. Thus many witnesses did find it necessary to talk about land outside the actual claim, particularly if that land included places of great spiritual significance. As one key witness stated, that country needed to be described to the judge, both because it was linked to the actual area under consideration and also because, being on a non-Aboriginal held property (Napperby), it was more vulnerable. He, and other witnesses found it very hard to accept that, while evidence proving ownership of the land under claim was presented according to Anmatyerre concepts, the land itself was spatially delineated according to non-Aboriginal concepts.

Because Mt Allan and Ti Tree are now Aboriginal-owned, their residents can use the land as they wish. They can accord with traditional Aboriginal modes of land use, they can accept non-Aboriginal conventions, or they can combine the two. In both cases they have chosen this last course. These are working cattle stations with significant Aboriginal populations (about 150 on Mt Allan and 350 on Ti Tree). They carry Aboriginal labour forces of around fifteen during the mustering season and have the potential to provide significant community incomes when prices are favourable. Inevitably this means that some of the non-Aboriginal landscape icons are reinforced. These include the fences, bores, tanks and roads. There is also evidence for a re-emergence of more traditional Aboriginal values in land use. Mt Allan's Aboriginal residents no longer all congregate in the camp beside the station homestead. Some families have dispersed and established small outstations (or 'homeland centres') near sites of spiritual importance to them. For example, groups associated with honey ant dreaming quickly established an outstation near the western boundary of Mt Allan, within easy access to Yuelamu. This site is of great significance not only to them but also to all their other classificatory kin, including Anmatyerre, Warlpiri and Alyawarre who trace their descent from honey ant ancestors. Similarly, people who are spiritually descended from emu and dingo ancestors have moved to the east, to the country for which they are responsible.

This type of population dispersal, apparent on both Mt Allan and Ti Tree, not only changed the human occupation patterns but has both social and economic implications. Residents of these smaller settlements belong to closely linked extended families. Hence social conflicts, commonly observed when people from different groups were forced to live close to each other in large centralised settlements such as neighbouring Yuendumu, have declined. The move to smaller settlements has improved people's access to bush tucker and game. These natural resources had been heavily depleted near the central homesteads because, with the large concentrated populations, too many people were trying to make use of them. Thus the reassertion of Aboriginal concepts of land use and protection has helped to improve people's quality of life.

Population dispersal following the legal reacquisition of traditional land may, however, have other apparently less favourable implications. This is particularly noticeable when the use of the land still follows the non-Aboriginal mode, in this case commercial pastoralism. The former non-Aboriginal owners of both Mt Allan and Ti Tree stressed large-scale, centralised management. This included forcing Aborigines to live beside the station homesteads, both because they provided the labour for the stock-camps and because the owners felt that if they camped elsewhere on the property cattle operations might be disrupted. The present Aboriginal owners, however, seem to be less concerned about such disadvantages. Ti Tree station, both during its previous European history and in its more recent period of Aboriginal ownership, provides an interesting example of the kind of dilemmas which arise from overlapping concepts and uses of land.

The area covered by the present Ti Tree station includes two formerly separate smaller properties, Ti Tree on the west and Woola Downs on the east. Each of these had distinct Aboriginal populations who were drawn from the traditional land-owning group and provided the local workforces. After the

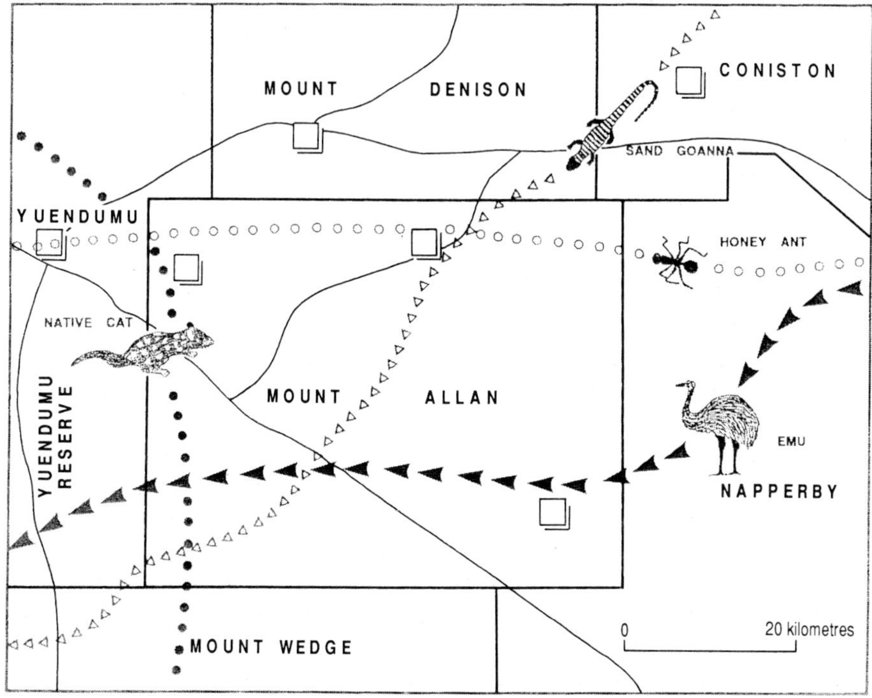

FIGURE 15.3 Anmatyerre and non-Aboriginal delineations of property on Mount Allan.

stations were amalgamated in 1950 the eastern Woola Downs Aboriginal camp disappeared, and families dispersed to Utopia station, to the east, and to the western homestead camp at Ti Tree itself. The new Ti Tree station then had only one Aboriginal camp, and was run as a large-scale, centralised enterprise. However, following the purchase of Ti Tree by the Aboriginal Land Fund Commission in 1976 the former Woola Downs mob expressed a desire to move back on to their country and established their Adelaide Bore camp in 1979. This move arose partly from the need to reassert Aboriginal concepts of land-ownership. However, the new settlement also became linked to the cattle operations. Once the camp was set up the Woola people intimated that they wanted to split the control of the pastoral enterprise, with the erection of a new boundary fence between themselves and the remainder of the group at Ti Tree station. This fence, interestingly enough, followed the Aboriginal concept of the boundary, marking the hand-over point on the *ahakeye* (bush plum) dreaming track where western families in the *Ngale/Mpetyane* group transfer spiritual responsibility to their eastern kin. In this case the Aboriginal concept of land boundary coincided in space with one which was essentially associated with non-Aboriginal ideas of land ownership. Arrangements for the two separate enterprises were also to include an allocation of funds from Puraiya, the Ti Tree station cattle company, and the granting of their own cattle brand. Although the two Aboriginal groups agreed and the boundary fence was completed in 1982, the split was not then finalised. Because of threats from government agencies, primarily the (then) Aboriginal Development Commission, that funding would be cut off unless commercial viability was the main priority, the plans for the split were not implemented. Although the issue was once more raised during the process of collecting evidence for the presentation of the Ti Tree land claim in 1985 no major changes have occurred. Nevertheless, the settlement of the land claim, under which the Aboriginal freehold tenure of the land has been recognised, gives the people the freedom to choose their preferred option for future development—large-scale centralised pastoralism, smaller-scale fragmented pastoralism or subsistence, with little or no commercial pastoralism. These complexities affecting both Ti Tree settlement patterns and land use demonstrate the problems arising when Aboriginal and non-Aboriginal concepts of ownership are combined.

Most other Anmatyerre people form smaller population groups than those on Mt Allan and Ti Tree. In Yuendumu they account for only about fifty individuals out of a total population of six hundred. The former reserve, recognised as lying at the interface between the Anmatyerre and their Warlpiri neighbours, is Aboriginal freehold land and people can exercise their land use rights freely. The Yuendumu Anmatyerre, all closely related to Mt Allan families, are involved with Ngarliyikirlangu, the Yuendumu cattle company; they also use the area for subsistence purposes and maintain their ceremonial responsibilities. The western Mt Allan boundary fence is seen only as a barrier separating the two herds of cattle. The amalgamation of Aboriginal and non-Aboriginal concepts of land ownership is harmonious, and the compromise has posed no real problems.

Anmatyerre with interests elsewhere, on non-Aboriginal owned stations such as Mt Denison, Coniston, Napperby or Anningie (Figure 15.1), are much more restricted in how they can use land. Only two of these stations, Napperby and Anningie, still have resident Anmatyerre populations (respectively numbering about two hundred and seventy). Both groups live on small leases of land excised from the properties. These areas, no more than 3 km^2, provide only for living space. There is little or no potential for the development of a community economic base and the allocated land may also lack social and spiritual significance. In the case of Napperby, the original Anmatyerre application for a living area near a place of great spiritual value was refused because the non-Aboriginal pastoralist felt that it was too close to the homestead and would have to tap into the same permanent water supplies. The excision which was finally agreed upon is some 5 km distant, on a piece of undisputed and neutral country.

Aboriginal communities on excisions of properties like Anningie and Napperby are today forced to depend heavily on the government for their economic base. Although they formerly worked in the station stock-camps, few are now employed. The introduction of award wages for Aborigines and more capital-intensive management techniques such as helicopter mustering have reduced demand for their skills. Most families therefore derive their cash incomes primarily from social security. Despite retaining their commitment to more traditional responsibilities for the land, the means for discharging such responsibilities are blocked. They, along with Anmatyerre visiting traditional country on properties where they no longer have permanent camps such as Coniston or Mt Denison, may find their movements heavily restricted. They are discouraged from semi-permanent or even brief overnight camps elsewhere. Thus, carrying out ceremonies such as initiation rites which involve lengthy preparation by the main adult participants and, for the initiates, days or weeks living in the bush close to the ceremonial area, is extremely difficult. As the actual locations for such meetings are specifically chosen to reflect individual and family relationships with land, this could mean that people are unable to fulfil their spiritual responsibilities properly. Hunting and foraging on their own country can also be restricted. Although non-Aboriginal pastoralists, under the terms of their leases, are supposed to allow such activities, they can, and often do, indirectly discourage Aborigines from hunting. Methods used include locking gates, such as those on the roads linking Mt Allan with Napperby and Mt Allan with Coniston, blocking up entrances between Aboriginal camps and adjacent country to all but walkers and generally intimidating people by stopping vehicles and requesting information about where people intend to go and how long they intend to stay. It is not uncommon for Anmatyerre foraging on these properties to hide whenever they see a station vehicle approaching and they will go to considerable lengths to avoid contact if at all possible. In general they do not feel free to use the land as they wish. Under these circumstances it would not be surprising if they had abandoned their efforts to maintain traditional activities. That they have not done so is a clear demonstration both of the strength of their cultural foundations and their capacity to adapt their behaviour so that this social stability can be maintained.

Differences in Anmatyerre access to their country because of variations in land tenure also affect the transfer of vital knowledge to future generations. If children and young people cannot undergo initiation or even visit their ancestral country they lack the knowledge to carry out the appropriate ceremonies or make proper use of resources. Resettlement of Anmatyerre following the alienation of the land for pastoralism has had a marked effect on the continuity of spiritual responsibility (Young 1987). Some individuals have been 'adopted' into other country because they have been permanently resident there, and have lost contact with their ancestral lands; others, primarily of part-European ancestry, have spent most of their lives in Alice Springs and only learnt about their heritage through their direct involvement in the land claims; and others still, although resident elsewhere, continually return to maintain their spiritual linkages.

CONCLUSION

Different cultural groups do indeed see and interpret landscape in different ways—physically, in the case of boundaries or in the use of contrasting environments; and culturally, in their constructs of the values of land and resources. From childhood we are encouraged to accept those interpretations emanating from our own culture, and those belonging to others may be largely invisible to us. This obviously detracts from the richness of our understanding of the world around us. More seriously it potentially leads to lack of recognition of other modes of land and life. This can have quite negative results, both for people and their environment in general and also for specific population groups. In the context discussed here, with the recent occupation of highly fragile environments by people who lack a detailed and long-term understanding of the consequences of their modes of land and resource use, failure to pay attention to land-use concepts practised by their hunter-gatherer predecessors has been detrimental to resource sustainability. Moreover, the hunter-gatherers, whose lives have been economically and politically dominated by the superimposed industrialised society, have been forced into accepting an unhappy compromise. Such problems may have been less severe if the land ownership concepts of hunter-gatherer and industrialised societies had been mutually recognised. Moreover, acceptance of hunter-gatherer land ownership concepts by industrialised societies can be of practical relevance.

Possible contributions of hunter-gatherer concepts of land use to resource sustainability have been mentioned both generally (World Commission on Environment and Development (WCED) 1987) and specifically (Zarsky 1990; Young 1995). Examples referred to in this chapter include Inuit seal and caribou harvesting practices in Canada, and Aboriginal perceptions of the importance of natural resource subsistence as an alternative to extensive cattle grazing in arid rangelands. Co-management agreements for wildlife use in the Nunavut region of northern Canada (Usher 1996) and the recognition of the value of multiple land use in Australia's national rangeland strategy (ANZECC/ARMCANZ 1996) demonstrate positive moves to incorporate aboriginal concepts of land and resource use into policies for sustainable development.

Deeper understanding of hunter-gatherer concepts has implications not only for remote hunter-gatherer communities but also for all tax-payers. Service provision for the sparse populations in remote areas is very costly, and hence services must be located in places most convenient for the clients. As the Anmatyerre case study shows, population consolidation, a major outcome of the clash between the two cultural groups, has recently been disrupted by renewed dispersal of the hunter-gatherers into small scattered settlements. This, as has been described in detail elsewhere (Australia 1987; Young and Doohan 1989), poses a challenge to government agencies responsible for service delivery. Schools and health clinics, located at places which bureaucratic policy-makers judged to be central, are no longer conveniently situated for their Aboriginal clients. As a consequence their facilities are under-used and some are in danger of becoming expensive government-financed 'white elephants'. Plans for service delivery could be made much more relevant if the cultural and economic reasons for the new Aboriginal settlement patterns were taken into account. These to a large extent reflect Aboriginal concepts of land use and ownership; people move to places which are central to them, often because of the coincidence of a number of spiritual threads which enable them to explain their world. They need services in these new settlements, but because the populations are so small, the costs of service provision can be prohibitive. Possible responses from government agencies could include an increased number of smaller locally-staffed schools, health clinics which combine central location with regular mobile services and retail stores which link smaller units to larger central outlets. This could be expensive in the short term. However, in the long term it is surely more efficient to provide people with appropriate services in the right locations and hence prevent unnecessary waste of resources. Ultimately, recognising that the cultural realities of people's contemporary worlds inform their practical day-to-day lives might help to provide better forms of support for their future development.

NOTES

1 The term 'Aboriginal' refers only to members of the indigenous population of Australia; the term 'aboriginal' refers to members of Australasian and North American indigenous populations.

2 Since the land claim settlement and establishment of the Aboriginal Lands Trust the area has been renamed Yalpirakinu, the Anmatyerre name for the homestead location of the original Mt Allan property (Rugendyke 1998). For reasons of consistency the name Mt Allan is used throughout this chapter.

REFERENCES

Altman, J. 1987, *Hunter Gatherers Today*, Institute of Aboriginal Studies, Canberra.

Australia 1987, *Return to Country: the Aboriginal Homelands Movement in Australia*, House of Representatives Standing Committee on Aboriginal Affairs, Final Report, AGPS, Canberra.

Australian and New Zealand Environment and Conservation Council (ANZECC) and Agriculture and Resource Management Council of Australia and New Zealand (ARMCANZ) 1996, *Australia's Draft National Strategy for Rangeland Management*, Department for Environment, Sport and Territories, Canberra.

Berger, T. 1977, *Northern Frontier, Northern Homeland: The Report of the Mackenzie Valley Pipeline Inquiry*, Minister of Supply and Services, Ottawa.

Brody, H. 1981, *Maps and Dreams*, Jill Norman and Hobhouse, London.

Chatwin, B. 1987, *The Songlines*, Cape, London.

Cosgrove, D.E. 1984, *Social Formation and Symbolic Landscape*, Croom Helm, London and Sydney.

Cribben, J. 1984, *The Killing Times*, Fontana/Collins, Sydney.

Davis, S. 1993, *Australia's Extant and Imputed Traditional Aboriginal Territories* (map), distributed by Melbourne University Press, Melbourne.

Davis, S. & Prescott, J.R.V. 1992, *Aboriginal Frontiers and Boundaries*, Melbourne University Press, Melbourne.

DIAND 1988, *Dene/Metis Comprehensive Land Claim: Agreement in Principle*, DIAND, Ottawa.

Duncan, J. & Duncan, N. 1988, '(Re)reading the landscape', *Environment and Planning D: Society and Space*, vol. 6, no. 2, pp. 117–26.

Edwards, W.H. ed. 1998, *Traditional Aboriginal Society*, 2nd edn, Macmillan, South Melbourne.

Freeman, M.M. ed. 1976, *Report, Inuit Land Use and Occupancy Project*, DIAND, Ottawa.

Jackson, P. 1989, *Maps of Meaning*, Unwin Hyman, London.

Keith, R.F. & Saunders, A. 1989, *A Question of Rights: Northern Wild-life Management and the Anti-Harvest Movement*, Canadian Arctic Resources Committee, Ottawa.

Lewis, P.F. 1979, 'Axioms for reading the landscape: Some guides to the American scene' in *The Interpretation of Ordinary Landscapes*, ed. D.W. Meinig, Oxford University Press, Oxford, pp. 11–32.

Ley, D. 1983, 'Cultural/humanistic geography', *Progress in Human Geography*, vol. 7, no. 2, pp. 267–75.

Meinig, D.W. ed. 1979, *The Interpretation of Ordinary Landscapes*, Oxford University Press, Oxford.

Peterson, N. 1975, 'Hunter-gatherer territoriality: the perspective from Australia', *American Anthropologist*, vol. 77, pp. 53–68.

Rugendyke, B. 1998, 'Community participation as empowerment? Planning for change in remote Aboriginal Australia', in *Perceptions of Marginality: Theoretical Issues and Regional Perceptions of Marginality in Geographical Space*, eds H. Jussila, W. Leimgruber & R. Marjoral, Ashgate Publishing Company, Brookfield, pp. 257–78.

Stanner,W.E.H. 1979, *White Man Got No Dreaming: Essays 1938–72*, Australian National University Press, Canberra.

Strehlow, T.G.H. 1970, 'Geography and Totemic Landscape in Central Australia: a functional study', in *Australian Aboriginal Anthropology*, ed. R.M. Berndt, University of Western Australia Press, Perth, pp. 92–140.

Sutton, P. 1995, *Country: Aboriginal Boundaries and Land Ownership in Australia*, Aboriginal History, Monograph 3, Canberra.

Usher, P. 1996, *Contemporary Aboriginal land, Resource, and Environment Regimes: Origins, Problems and Prospects*, Report for the Royal Commission on Aboriginal Peoples, Ottawa.

Usher, P. & Bankes, N. 1986, *Property, the Basis of Inuit Hunting Rights—A New Approach*, Inuit Committee on National Issues, Ottawa.

Watkins, M. 1977, 'From Underdevelopment to Development' in *Dene Nation: The Colony Within*, ed. M. Watkins, University of Toronto Press, Toronto.

Wonders, W.C. 1983, *Overlapping Land Use and Occupancy of Dene, Metis, Inuvialuit and Inuit in the Northwest Territories*, DIAND, Ottawa.

World Commission on Environment and Development (WECD) 1987, *Our Common Future*, Oxford University Press, Oxford.

Young, E.A. 1987, 'Resettlement and caring for country: the Anmatyerre experience', *Aboriginal History*, vol. 11, nos 1–2, pp. 156–70.

Young, E.A. 1995, *Third World in the First: Development and Indigenous Peoples*, Routledge, London/New York.

Young, E.A. & Doohan, K. 1989, *Mobility for Survival: A Process Analysis of Aboriginal Population Movement in Central Australia*, NARU, Darwin.

Zarsky, L. 1990, *Sustainable Development. Challenge for Australia*, Commission for the Future Occasional Paper No. 9, AGPS, Canberra.

Index

SUBJECT INDEX

PLACE INDEX